MALE PROSTITUTION

D1235124

Male Prostitution

Gay Sex Services in London

D.J. West
in association with
Buz deVilliers

Duckworth

First published in 1992 by
Gerald Duckworth & Co. Ltd.
The Old Piano Factory
48 Hoxton Square, London N1 6PB

A catalogue record for this book is available
from the British Library

ISBN 0 7156 2383 4

Photoset in North Wales by
Derek Doyle & Associates, Mold, Clwyd.
Printed in Great Britain by
Redwood Press Limited, Melksham

Contents

Preface

Donald West was the initiator of the project and the main author of this book. Buz de Villiers assisted throughout in planning the research, designing the interview questions, conducting many of the interviews, interpreting the information and formulating the conclusions. He had an editorial and consultative role in the writing of the text, but the views expressed are those of the main author and do not necessarily concur with his own.

Input and assistance came from many sources. Donald West was awarded a Leverhulme Emeritus Fellowship and given a grant to cover expenses of the research. The work was part of the research programme of the University of Cambridge Institute of Criminology where Donald West, as Emeritus Professor, was provided with office accommodation.

The Management Committee, Director and Staff of Streetwise Youth provided facilities for the research interviews, and Barbara Gibson, Ken Fortune, Mark Kjeldsen and Richie McMullen shared information and experience concerning Streetwise clients. Barbara Gibson furnished details about Thailand and Rev. R.R. Rhudy of San Francisco Night Mission gave information on that city. Richie McMullen and Tom Woodhouse, a former colleague, provided suggestions for the content of interviews. Anonymous helpers visited and reported on masseurs and massage parlours. Dr N.D. Thompson interviewed one street worker.

Introduction

The need for realism

Popular images of the male prostitute are confused and contradictory, poorly informed and often more concerned with moral condemnation than humane understanding. The aim of this research has been to record factual observations about the operation of the male sex industry in London in the hope that this will assist in the promotion of realistic social policies.

Prostitution is generally thought of as a woman's occupation, but the 'oldest profession' caters to all sexual demands and the desire of some men for sexual contact with their own kind has been known throughout recorded history. Male prostitution is probably as old as the female variety (Benjamin and Masters, 1964). It was certainly well known to the Greeks and actually licensed and taxed in Augustan Rome (Halpern, 1990; Boswell, 1988, pp. 112-13; 1980, p. 70), but social inquiry has been largely limited to women servicing men. The assumption that women, including lesbians, have no need or no wish to pay men for sexual services has become less certain since the advent of the 'toy boy' fashion, but young male prostitutes still seem to cater mostly to older males.

The somewhat contemptuous term 'rent boys' does not mean that they are actually children, any more than 'boyfriends' or 'girlfriends' or even 'girls' (when used in a sexual context) are necessarily juveniles. They become newsworthy when scandal breaks, for example when it was reported that nurses in Broadmoor secure hospital had taken bribes to secure rent boys for the benefit of their notorious patient, Ronald Kray, one-time leader of a violent criminal gang (*News of the World*, 11 Feb. 1990). A more common type of scandal occurs when an erstwhile paid sex partner in need of ready money, or as an act of spite or blackmail, informs the press that he has been involved with some prominent person. Sometimes would-be blackmailers are unsuccessful. Under the heading 'Rent boy's sugar daddy rip-off' the *News of the World* (10 Dec. 1989) reported the case of a man of twenty-one given an eighteen-month custodial sentence. He had been showered with money and gifts, but when his patron got into debt he threatened to expose him unless payments continued. The victim went to the police, who provided a concealed recorder which was used to tape the blackmail demands. In recent years rent boy scandals have involved White House officials and an American Congressman (*The Times*, 30 Jun. 1989), a former Member of Parliament who liked spanking (*Guardian*, 21 May 1987), an actor whose continued participation in a TV series was jeopardised by adverse press comment (*News of the World*, 22 Jan. 1989) and a detective working as bodyguard to the Queen (*Sunday Times*, 13 Feb. 1983).

Being taken to bed by a stranger, whether for payment or for the sake of shelter for the night or simply for sexual enjoyment, is not without risk. Rent boys get into the news occasionally when they become murder victims. A sad story that hit the headlines in 1989 concerned a fourteen-year-old boy prostitute, Jason Swift, who had agreed to go home with a group of men with the promise of £5 from each. He was given drugs, subjected to violent sex and smothered to death in the process, his body being found later dumped in a wood (*The Times*, 13 May 1989). He was an educationally retarded runaway who was said to have fled from bullying at home and at school on account of his effeminacy. His last days were spent begging on the streets and selling his body. Four men were sentenced to a total of 62 years' imprisonment for his manslaughter.

Jason's death was presumably unintended, but this was not so in the case of the victims of the serial murderer Dennis Nilsen (Masters, 1985). He frequented bars where he could pick up young men ready for drink and sex and wanting a bed for the night. Some of them never re-emerged, except as burnt remnants buried in the garden or bits of flesh blocking the drains – a complication which brought about Nilsen's eventual arrest. In Houston, Texas, the sadistic killer Dean Corll was credited with murdering at least 27 youths. He employed a teenager who procured boys for him with the promise of drugs, drink and exciting parties. Victims were stripped, tied to a torture board and finally killed. As with Nilsen's victims, many were runaways or marginal characters whose disappearance created little stir (Olsen, 1974). Of course, not only the rent boy is at risk. Murders of homosexuals by young men who claim they reacted with panic violence to unexpected sexual approaches are not uncommon; but sometimes this is just a cover for robbery with violence in the context of a prostitution transaction.

Dwelling upon these terrible but rare events gives a wrong impression of the humdrum reality of male prostitution. Moral panic is encouraged by media linkage of the sex trade with the AIDS epidemic. Evidence from clinics of a reduction in sexually transmitted infections among homosexual men shows that the dissemination of information about AIDS has encouraged more cautious habits among the gay population. Nevertheless, the activities of homosexual prostitutes are thought to carry a high risk of HIV infection (Thomas *et al.*, 1989). Since many clients are married or bisexual they could provide a channel for the more general transmission of infection, putting their own wives and future children at risk.

Except in third world countries (Campagna and Poffenberger, 1988), child prostitution is probably less frequent than some lurid press reports might suggest. One account of the Jason Swift murder case (*Daily Star*, 13 May 1989) speculated that he might have been killed because he knew too much about a 'ring' of paedophiles with international connections who systematically recruited young boys for sexual purposes, passing them on from one to the other. In the same year there was a report about 'Britain's biggest child sex ring' (*The Times*, 4 Feb. 1989). Four men, including a barrister and the manager of a football team, were sentenced for relations with boys recruited by bribery, deception and the use of drugs and laced drinks. The judge commented that the harm they had done or may have done to the boys 'hardly bears thinking about'. Presumably he had in mind the common belief, supposedly backed by research, that male homosexual seduction or exploitation in childhood produces numerous disturbances (Hunter, 1990), encourages precocious homosexuality (Van Wyk and Geist, 1984) and leads either to sexual offending in later years (Ryan *et al.*, 1987) or to entry into prostitution (Janus *et al.*, 1984).

Systematic research into male prostitution has so far been rather limited and assessments of the size of the trade and the extent of the risks associated with it remain speculative. Results have varied according to the methods of locating and questioning informants and the cultural backgrounds from which samples were drawn. Prostitutes found on street corners or seen in penal or clinical settings are not necessarily typical of the male sex industry at large. Some investigators suggest that rent boys gravitate to their trade through choice, being already homosexually orientated, inclined to promiscuity and attracted by the lure of the big city with its gay bars, clubs and easy picking-up places, without which 'scene' they might not otherwise think of selling their bodies or be able to find a market for them. Others maintain that a desperate want of money for the essentials of life is the driving force, sexual orientation being hardly relevant to the need to sell one's body to all and sundry. The latter view finds support in stories of innocent boys in dire need being reluctantly corrupted by predatory perverts. The rent boys themselves, however, are also sometimes depicted as dangerous amoral delinquents out to exploit and rob (Klemens, 1967).

The evil image of the male prostitute featured in medical literature before the advent of gay liberation is typified by a case report from the *Delaware State Medical Journal* (Freyhan, 1947). A nineteen-year-old delinquent and prostitute, who met his customers in the notorious Times Square area of New York, declared, 'I like easy money and I know how to get it.' He was diagnosed as 'a rather malignant type of psychopathic personality' for whom 'one may consider lobotomy as a somewhat desperate attempt to change present personality patterns'.

More recent literature is in marked contrast. Richie McMullen (1989; 1990a) in a two-volume autobiography constructed like a novel, depicts rent boys as individuals, varied in character but usually gay, as much in need of friendship and sexual love as other young people, but who happen to have chosen prostitution as a temporary method of surviving in impoverished social circumstances.

The scenario that has perhaps gained the most credence recently is that of the adolescent runaway from an unhappy, neglectful or abusive home who wanders into the city without money or shelter and is swiftly picked up by older homosexuals experienced in sexual exploitation of the young. Sometimes it is suggested that sexual exploitation begins at a tender age, either in the home or through membership of a child sex 'ring' serving the interests of a paedophile coterie from which, once enlisted, a sense of shame and fear of reprisals make it difficult to break free. An alternative stereotype is that of the delinquent youth who finds the prostitution game just one of a number of illegal money-making activities available, a change from housebreaking, shoplifting and mugging. He need not be homosexual, he may indeed have contempt for his clients and he may use the transaction as a prelude to extortion, blackmail or robbery.

Female prostitutes have always had a higher profile than rent boys, being more organised and concentrated in obvious 'red light' districts featuring call girls, brothels, touts and pimps for the 'working girls'. In some countries the women and the brothels operate under state licence, and even in Britain political pressure groups, notably the Women's Collective of Prostitutes, work on their behalf. Nothing comparable exists in a homosexual context, although, according to Kinsey (1948, p. 556) and more lately Janus (1981), in large American cities there are almost as many males as females among adolescent street prostitutes. Some French authorities once produced a guesstimate of around 13,000 boys under the age of eighteen working as prostitutes in France (Boulin *et al.*, 1977). In England, venues for male prostitution have been featured in the media and are easily discoverable by interested youths. For example, Lois Rogers writing in the *Evening Standard* (20 Sept. 1989) describes a 'booming rent boy trade' centered around Piccadilly Circus, watched by plainclothes police officers from the Juvenile Protection Unit. Punters, 'classically pudgy and middle-aged', stare into shop windows while furtively glancing back at the youths who are standing around ready to offer their sexual services at £40 a time. According to the police, most of the boys, who are in their early teens and can be seen clutching plastic bags containing towel and toothbrush, are runaways from children's homes or from 'fights between mum and dad'.

Female prostitution, although in principle not illegal in England, is hedged about with laws against street soliciting, living on immoral earnings or allowing premises to be used for immoral purposes. Much of the business has to be clandestine, with earnings undeclared, a lifestyle on the edge of the law, and involvement with male pimps who are often engaged simultaneously in other criminal activities, especially drug dealing. If their ambiguous legal situation helps to drive women prostitutes into a criminal milieu, one might expect the same to occur to an even greater extent in the case of males facing sterner legal penalties. Male importuning of other males, unlike female soliciting, is an imprisonable offence, and not only if it occurs on the street or if payment is involved. For those under twenty-one, any sexual act with another male is a crime for both participants and if anal penetration occurs the crime is susceptible to a maximum penalty of twenty years' imprisonment (Howard League, 1985). The severity of the law, however, about which there is widespread ignorance, probably has less effect than public attitudes, which are especially condemnatory of both client and prostitute when the transaction is homosexual. Rent boys who still care about parents or girlfriends or contacts in the straight world have reason to dread the effect of arrest and public exposure more than any sentence the courts are likely nowadays to impose. To avoid probing questions some deliberately cut themselves off from family and former friends, limiting their socialising to fellow members of the 'scene', that is other rent boys and punters (clients), thereby increasing their alienation. Many young male street prostitutes come from the same disorderly and deprived family backgrounds that characteristically generate young offenders, so it would not be surprising to find that they share the same antisocial characteristics, such as impulsive hedonism (drink, drugs, gambling and promiscuity) and cafeteria delinquency (theft, fraud, burglary and violence) (West and Farrington, 1977). The unfortunate characteristics thought to be typical of rent boys working the streets were effectively summed up long ago by Caukins and Coombs (1976): 'They appear to have poor judgment and to suffer from immaturity. Innumerable examples of family rejection and self-destructive behaviour were found. These findings are compatible with those of other researchers.'

A different image is that of the young, promiscuously inclined homosexual who finds occasional prostitution a congenial and profitable activity, one that brings him into contact with interesting people and luxurious surroundings and an exciting lifestyle which he could never afford on his own earnings from a conventional job. Involvement in delinquent acts would be for him counter-productive, alien to his image as a gay-identified, fun-loving young charmer. In the world of heterosexual prostitution the image of the harassed streetwalker contrasts with that of the highly paid model available only by prior appointment to affluent clients. Similar contrasts exist in the gay world where images of 'kept boys', 'stars' from pornographic films and sophisticated paid 'escorts' clash with images of homeless, destitute youths trailing the streets.

Only exceptionally has published research ventured beyond the full-time street prostitute. Allen (1980) noted with some surprise the presence among American male street workers of temporary or part-time

operatives from more secure baekgrounds, participating from choice
rather than necessity, whose occasional incursions into the profitable
game did not prevent them continuing to pursue conventional student
careers. British research, based at the Polytechnic of the South Bank
(Robinson, 1989) has drawn attention to the great variety of male sexual
services operating in London, but ignored by researchers fixated on the
image of the runaway adolescent who takes to the streets to escape from
an intolerable or abusive home. Advertisements in the gay press inserted
by male masseurs, models and escorts, listing the attractive features of
their appearance and physique, leave the reader who can follow the coded
messages and innuendoes in little doubt about the kind of sexual services
on offer. The existence of a sex industry catering to the requirements of
the homosexual minority affords what amounts to a business career for
the more enterprising male prostitute. Market forces determine the size
and profitability of the industry; the social and sexual talents of the
individual operatives in these pseudo-legitimate enterprises determine
their earning capacity. Successful participants in such businesses, who
have freely chosen their particular line of work and benefit from a
consistent and satisfied clientele, may have little in common with the sad
characters picked off the streets by police. The image of the male
prostitute as necessarily a problem person could derive from undue
concentration on those who have failed to establish themselves in the
profession.

The present research was undertaken in an effort to dispel myths and
confusions and to describe the male prostitution scene in London in more
objective terms and with fewer preconceptions than writers on the subject
have shown in the past.

Focus of the present research

Prostitution is a harsh word with heavily condemnatory overtones. It is
ill-defined and can be applied to a wide range of socio-sexual interactions
that fall short of the romantic ideal of mutual giving and receiving of
sexual pleasure divorced from all material considerations. Traditional
marriages have often been described as a form of prostitution, the woman
surrendering exclusive rights to her body in return for her marital status
and expectation of lifelong financial support. The kept woman or mistress
also receives reward for sexual favours, but with less security or legal
backing. The notorious 'casting couch' situations involving submission to
sexual requirements in return for a job or promotion, are virtually acts of
prostitution. The behaviour of the good-time girl who avoids personal
commitment while taking as much as possible from a multiplicity of
lovers is less likely to be thought of as prostitution. The promiscuous male
seducer concerned only with satisfying his own sexual desires is behaving
like the clients of prostitutes, although the resemblance is not often

noted. The hostess in a clip joint, conning customers into buying her drinks when she has no intention of fulfilling the sexual expectations she arouses, could be called a fraudulent prostitute. Less glaring exploitations of sexual attraction occur all the time in ordinary social intercourse. Sexual performance in return for a fee is but an extreme form of the more muted transactions of everyday life.

Social convention expects a heterosexual man to be living with a woman. Gay men, whether by choice or because of social disapproval, less often live together as couples and so have more opportunities and possibly greater need for sexual roaming. Cruising in pick-up areas and spending evenings in gay bars in the hope of finding an exciting new companion for the night are common features of gay lifestyles, especially in the big cities. Younger participants, who are prime targets for the sex hunter, receive treats, presents and sometimes money in return for companionship and sexual enjoyment. In an extensive survey of lifestyles in the San Francisco Bay area, Bell and Weinberg (1978, p. 86) found that a quarter of the white male homosexuals they interviewed, and a larger proportion of blacks, had been paid for sex at some time or other. Of course young men need not identify themselves as gay in order to make money out of sex. Sorensen (1973, p. 289, Table 106), analysing responses from a nationally representative sample of American adolescents in the age range fifteen to nineteen, found that 12 per cent of boys agreed with the proposition that 'It's just possible that sometime, if I really needed the money very badly, that I would have sex with a man who would pay me for it.' Older homosexuals recall nostalgically a time when servicemen were poorly paid and could be bought for a modest sum by visitors to their favourite drinking places in London.

Barrington (1981, p. 209) is one of the few writers who have tried to show the virtual impossibility of setting precise limits to gay sex trading in the UK because 'there are also young men who frequent pubs, night-clubs, discos and fashionable restaurants who are also "available" for homo-sex at a price.' His information comes from a self-selected sample (5,000 responses to 120,000 questionnaires distributed) but one large enough to include examples of a wide range of situations. One history contributed by a man of sixty (op. cit., p. 215) illustrates the ambiguous and shifting nature of client-customer interactions: 'I've been a whore too, not from necessity, but because money was forced on me. Some men don't feel happy after sex unless they can pay the guy . . . [Myself] I enjoy "rewarding" a guy, or even a friend, showing that I've appreciated what he gave me. . . .'

While recognising the existence of a vast grey area, research must focus on specific behaviours. For present purposes a prostitute or sex worker is defined as one who proffers personal sexual services to a variety of customers chosen primarily for what they are prepared to pay. How frequent or prolonged the behaviour has to be to justify the label

prostitute is as difficult to decide as how many thefts make a thief. The
operational definition adopted here excludes lucrative sexual
relationships with a single patron (the 'sugar daddy' or 'kept boy' set-up),
sexual adventures in which payment is unsolicited or a secondary
consideration, and those whose relationships are entered into with an eye
to personal advancement. Sexual behaviour that falls short of direct
contact with a client, such as striptease performances, nude modelling or
acting in pornographic videos, is not counted, although such activities
often do spill over into or come dangerously close to prostitution, as an
amusing short story by Dave Royle (1990) illustrates. Persons who
facilitate the prostitution of others, such as pimps, massage parlour
managers, brothel keepers and pornographic video producers, are
likewise excluded from consideration, as are those who provide sexually
explicit material or conversation via the telephone. Finally, the research
is restricted to male sex workers who cater to male clients; toy boys,
gigolos and escorts patronised by heterosexual women are not considered.
It might have been interesting to compare the hard core of regular sex
workers with some of those only marginally involved, but time,
opportunity and finance set limits to what was possible.

The study is intended to be descriptive and exploratory, but with some
attempt at evaluation of the relevance of factors that have been
supposedly linked to male prostitution, notably inadequate parenting or
lack of family support, financial hardship, homosexual orientation, sex
abuse in childhood, the attraction of the sex market and the element of
personal choice. Different factors seem to be important according to the
type of sex work under consideration, whether forced by necessity or a
chosen form of enterprise. Other matters of interest include the methods
of securing clients and obtaining payment, the sexual practices and
health risks involved, the links between employment in the sex trade and
involvement with crime and drug abuse, the sex workers' attitudes to
their job, their relations with clients, their experiences of the police and
the law and the effect of sex work on lifestyles at the time and later.

The research plan in outline

The first essential of any survey is to find samples of subjects who will
provide information. The idea of carrying out a survey of male
prostitution arose opportunistically when the author was asked to chair
the Management Committee of Streetwise Youth, a London-based charity
dedicated to befriending and counselling young men involved in
prostitutional activities. The organisation runs a drop-in Day Centre
where they can attend for advice and counselling, receive a free meal,
wash themselves and their clothes and obtain help in dealing with
welfare and legal authorities and in finding accommodation. Workers
employed by the agency were in direct contact with rent boys, both those

attending the Centre and others seen on the streets and elsewhere during 'outreach' work. With their co-operation it was possible to interview systematically, using a pre-designed schedule of topics and questions, a sample of 50 young men attending the Day Centre and to obtain a fair picture of their personal characterisitics, backgrounds, attitudes and current situation. In addition, seven of the 50 were re-interviewed and a further eleven attending the Day Centre were also interviewed, but in a more leisurely and less structured manner, in order to elicit further information on specific topics, particularly their interactions with police and their experiences with difficult or violent clients. All of these men were or had been soliciting on streets, stations or in gay bars. An additional sample of 25 men, currently or formerly active as street workers, was recruited largely from gay bars by the snowball system, making use of the help of one or two initial contacts, asking respondents for introductions to others and by paying one former rent boy to secure further introductions. This sample included some older men who were no longer active participants; their contributions afforded information about ways in which prostitution careers come to an end and what happens subsequently. Although this was an opportunistically selected group it served to show that street workers drawn from elsewhere, many of them of a different generation, shared in large measure the characteristics observed among the Streetwise Youth Day Centre sample.

With only occasional exceptions interviews were tape-recorded and the subjects' own words form the basis of this report. This makes for a discursive presentation, but helps convey the original flavour and emphasis of their accounts. When quoting their words each man is identified by a Case number of which the first digit indicates to which sample he belongs. The main sample of 50 systematic interviews with Day Centre attenders comprise cases 001 to 050, the additional interviews with others at the Centre are Cases 051 to 061 and the interviews with present or ex-street workers from elsewhere are Cases 201 to 229. This last group, in addition to the 25 London street workers, included four examples of street workers operating abroad. (The case-numbering system is summarised on p. xix.)

A third series of formal interviews was carried out with twelve men who were self-employed in the sex business under the guise of masseurs and the like, working from their own addresses. They proved to be interestingly different in background and motivation, most of them never having worked on the streets. They were rather more difficult to recruit for research purposes, a small interview fee being of no interest to individuals who were running a successful business. Initial contacts, setting in motion the snowball system, were made through personal introductions, sometimes via men who had made use of their services, or, in one or two cases, by answering advertisements. The schedule used for this sample was longer and more discursive than that used with the street workers. It was devised in collaboration with a colleague, Buz de Villiers, who conducted most of these interviews. Sixteen such self-employed workers (one of them already interviewed) were visited by volunteers, gay men who prefer to remain anonymous, who took the role of clients and reported on the service provided. These men are identified in the textual citations as Cases or Visits 101 to 127, the word 'Case' being reserved for those formally interviewed.

Formal interviews were also conducted with nine employees of agencies supplying sex workers under cover of massage parlours or in the guise of so-called escorts or masseurs prepared to visit clients. They were contacted in similar ways: two of them were clients of the Streetwise Day Centre who had not been included in the initial survey; a further seven agency workers were visited and described by volunteers acting as clients. These sixteen agency workers are identified in citations as Cases or Visits 501 to 516.

It did not prove possible to collect a sample of clients of male prostitutes, although three such were interviewed apart from the several members of the street worker samples who had themselves become clients. A few additional interviews were conducted with men who had experiences relevant to special topics, such as paedophilia. For convenience in citation quotations from these extra interviews are numbered from Case 301 onwards.

The picture obtained from structured interviews has been supplemented by discussion with a variety of informants in England and abroad, some of them professional welfare workers, others individuals with personal contacts in the sex industry. Particularly helpful have been the notes and observations of Mark Kjeldsen, leader of Streetwise Youth's outreach department, who has unique experience of direct communication with street workers on the ground while they are actually 'at work'. A solicitor who had dealt with prosecutions for male brothel-keeping supplied some documentation on that matter. Contacts in Thailand provided information enabling some comparisons to be made with their male sex industry. Finally, reviewing the results of other published surveys, many of them included in the list of references, has helped place the observations from these limited samples in a wider context.

For convenience of reporting the sex industry workers have been divided into two broadly distinguishable categories, similar to those used by Waldorf and Murphy (1990) in a survey in San Francisco. The first group, which we have called street workers, they identified as 'hustlers', who 'utilise face-to-face encounters with clients in public places such as cruising areas, arcades, theatres, bookstores featuring erotica and gay bars'. The second group, basically off-street workers, they refer to as 'call men', a term that includes 'erotic masseurs', and supposed 'models' and 'escorts'. In London a similar group exists whose services are advertised in gay magazines. We have subdivided them into workers for agencies and self-employed masseur/escorts advertising under personal names, although individuals sometimes alternate between the two systems. Part I of this book describes street workers, Part II the off-street advertisers.

Because of the link with Streetwise Youth the research began as a study of street workers, who were the easiest to contact. As the research went on and it became clear that limiting observations to young street workers is a source of bias in prostitution studies, efforts were made to contact men working more organised off-street services contactable through advertisements. They are not so much in the public eye and they display fewer overt social problems. Access to them is more difficult for researchers to secure and so our samples of off-street workers are smaller, but that does not mean they are in reality less numerous or less important to an understanding of the functioning of prostitutes in modern society.

Summary of reference numbers for interview citations

	Case/Visit no.	*Total seen*
Street Workers		
Main Sample of Streetwise Day Centre attenders	1 – 50	50
Additional Day Centre attenders	51 – 61	11
Second sample of current and former street workers		
(London and abroad)	201 – 229	29
Off-street workers		
Self-employed masseurs (interviewed or visited)	101 – 127	27
Agency workers (interviewed or visited)	501 – 516	16
Clients and miscellaneous informants	301 – 306	6
		139

Part I
Street Workers

1

Composition of the Main Sample

The 50 young men who were interviewed were all current, prospective or former clients of Streetwise Youth and were contacted at the agency's Day Centre in West London. Whoever was first available when either D.J. West or Buz de Villiers was at hand was asked if he would be willing to be interviewed and was offered a modest fee for his trouble. In preparation, a notice had been put up at the centre which read as follows:

> So that we can work properly and raise money to help people we must be able to show that we know about their needs and difficulties. For this reason we would like members to help in a research survey.
>
> Each of you will be asked to have a confidential interview with Dr Donald West and tell him as fully and truthfully as you can about your experiences. Donald is chairman of our management committee, so it will be a chance to tell him what you think about Streetwise.
>
> There is a small fee (£10) for giving your time to this.

The workers at the centre encouraged people to take part and only one request for an interview was met with a firm but polite refusal. The sample was therefore fairly representative of the young men in touch with the agency at the time, that is over a period of one year commencing in June 1988. A helping agency might be expected to attract those in difficulties of one sort and another, so this sample is not necessarily representative of street prostitutes in general, but, as described later, a sample drawn from elsewhere displayed much the same characteristics. All of the sample were or had been contacting clients in public places such as streets, stations and gay bars and could be fairly described as street workers.

The interviews were guided by a structured schedule of questions, some of them open-ended, some calling for categorical answers, which were put as systematically as was practical to every participant. A sample schedule is given in the Appendix. The forms were used as prompts and the interviewers could vary the wording or add questions for further clarification in the interest of ease of communication. This will be evident from the extracts quoted later. Open-ended questions were used to encourage interviewees to express themselves in their own way. The interviews were tape-recorded and transcribed later so that it was

3

unnecessary to interrupt the flow of information by making extensive notes on the spot. It was explained that this saved time and none of the interviewees objected.

The choice of topics had been decided after discussion with several experienced colleagues, study of previous published reports and scrutiny of questions used in a previous exercise with Streetwise Youth by Richie McMullen. Some interviews with former street prostitutes had already been carried out and observations from these also influenced what was included.

The interviews took place on a one-to-one basis in a private room, usually in the Streetwise office headquarters situated in a building near but separate from the busy, crowded Day Centre. They began with an assurance of strict confidentiality and a promise that identifying particulars would not be divulged to anyone other than the Streetwise staff. This was particularly important to one or two of the young men who had heard of newsworthy stories about rent boys being disseminated by the media in such a way that friends and relatives could recognise them.

The great majority cooperated well, being frank and confiding and volunteering details that might have been thought embarrassing or compromising. The information given could not be checked directly, but it was possible to look for inconsistencies. By accident, one man was seen by both interviewers, and seven others were re-interviewed later to get more information about specific topics. No serious discrepancies emerged between the information volunteered on different occasions. The interviewers got the impression that, except on certain topics – such as amounts earned from punters, where there may have been boastful exaggeration, or the extent of homosexual feelings, which may have been under-played – the information was reliable. After all, many of the participants had known and confided in the Streetwise staff over long periods. Buz de Villiers, who did almost half the interviews, was working as a volunteer at the Day Centre at the time and was seen by the young men as one of the staff who already 'knew' them. It could be argued that the offer of payment, by encouraging otherwise unmotivated participation, increased the likelihood of untruthful responses. Indeed one interviewee was reported to have remarked later: 'I was paid, so I just told lies.' If he really did so persistently that was probably exceptional. On most issues deception would have served no obvious purpose and might have risked annoying questions being asked should discrepancies be noticed between information disclosed on other occasions or at different stages during the interview. Survey research has to balance risk of bias from the refusal of a significant proportion to cooperate with risk of bias from the offer of inducements. In view of their often impecunious circumstances it was thought appropriate to offer all the same small sum for the service they were giving. Although many claimed to be making substantial, if erratic, profits from their activities, it was quickly spent and nearly all were eager to get their £10 fee. One of the Streetwise workers expressed doubts on the grounds that the money was encouraging a form of prostitution, but we thought it fair to offer a small fee.

The last man to be interviewed by D.J.W. had seemed forthcoming and quite happy to talk, and the taped record did not show otherwise, but he complained to the staff afterwards that he had been upset by the questions and suspected the researcher's motives. The staff, who it must be said were admirably protective of their clients, did not want D.J.W. to continue interviewing, but as the sample of 50 was by then complete this did not interfere seriously with the research plan. At this point, Buz de Villiers, having taken up other work, secured the help of a young American psychology graduate, John Friend, who re-interviewed seven of the original sample of 50 and carried out supplementary interviews with eleven other attenders at the Centre. These less structured interviews were intended to explore in greater detail matters of special interest, such as dealings with the police and experiences with difficult or violent clients. Except where otherwise stated, from now on the statistics and quotes concerning street workers refer to the main sample of 50.

The sample ranged in age from sixteen to twenty-five, with a majority of 27 aged eighteen to twenty, thirteen aged twenty-one to twenty-three and four aged twenty-four or five. The agency was intended to serve the under twenty-ones; the older participants were former clients still visiting the Centre. The majority were unexceptional in dress and physical appearance, their casual attire, mostly jeans and T shirts, being no different from what might be seen in any youth club. Their wardrobes were often very limited and a few had to be interviewed wearing dressing gowns while their only set of clothes was being washed in the Centre's machine. A minority sported specialised dress codes, some in skinhead style with visible tattoos, metal-studded leather accessories, heavy boots and other symbols of an aggressively macho stance. A contrasting group wore cosmetics and large earrings and flaunted effeminate mannerisms and camp expressions.

2

Early Backgrounds

As in previous surveys of street workers, questions about childhood yielded abundant evidence that many in the sample had suffered early social and emotional deprivation and some had been exposed to appalling conditions. Parental squabbling, desertions, drunkenness, emotional coldness or violence meant that few had received consistent and stable parenting during their formative years. In some cases their own difficult behaviour had alienated boys from parents or parent substitutes. Only a fifth of the sample had lived with both their natural parents up to the age of fifteen. A majority, 66 per cent, had spent at least part of their childhood in children's homes. As many as 40 out of the 50 interviewees had been childhood runaways and these included nine out of the ten who came from intact, two-parent homes. A majority, 56 per cent, rated their childhood as having been unhappy or very unhappy, and some of those who said they had been 'OK' reported details that sounded more than enough to have justified a rating of 'unhappy'. Since only a minority of boys from adverse backgrounds take to prostitution, this cannot be the only reason for these particular individuals having done so. Nevertheless, the finding is important in highlighting the unhappy antecedents of many male street prostitutes and demonstrating the challenge they present to helping agencies. The examples which follow are quoted in some detail to show the extent of family pathology revealed by these 50 young men.

Case 001 said he was very unhappy at home. He never got on with his father who had turned against him after his only sister's death in infancy. She had been left in a cupboard and suffocated. He was frequently beaten by his father who 'just came in drunk and just sort of started on me'. He loved his mother, but she was dominated by his father. When he was nine he was sent away to boarding school. He came home for a few months at the age of eleven, but ran away on account of his father's beatings.

> Q. You say you ran away from home?
> A. I just ran out of the house and never went back.
> Q. Yes, so who did you go to?
> A. I went to a hostel.
> Q. How did you know about a hostel?

A. It was there in the centre of the town and it said so. I knew about day centres and I just went in and it was a hostel and they kept me for a couple of days and then rang the police. The police took me home and my mother said they didn't want me. So I got put in a training school . . .

Q. And how old were you when you left this school?

A. Fifteen.

Q. And since leaving have you attended any sort of college?

A. When I left I went to college, but it only lasted three weeks.

Q. What sort of college was that?

A. I was doing domestic science.

Q. What was the trouble?

A. I couldn't handle it. I was actually paying them more than they were paying me.

Q. Where did you get the money to pay them?

A. From my parents. They gave me the money to keep me away.

Case 006 had run away from adoptive parents:

Well, as far as I know, just after I was born, I think I was one year old, I was put into a children's home and between then and seven years old I had no contact with my parents. I still haven't. Then I was adopted and my step-parents I have lived with until I was sixteen.

Q. So you don't know much about your natural parents?

A. I know a bit. I was given a letter by my social worker and it gave me a rough outline. They don't know where my parents are.

He went on to explain that his adoptive parents divorced when he was thirteen. Things seemed suddenly to have gone wrong and they had rows and actual fights 'which I had to spilt up a couple of times'.

Q. So what happened to you then?

A. Well, I was upset, but I helped my Mum through it.

Q. You stayed with your Mum?

A. Yep. I helped my Mum through it and when I was fifteen things started to get a bit bitter between me and my Mum and I left home and I moved across with my Dad, and then, when I turned sixteen, I moved down to London . . .

Q. Did you ever run away from home?

A. Yes, numerous times.

Q. How old were you the first time?

A. Fourteen.

Q. What made you run away?

A. Scared . . . of my Mum and her new husband. I had started smoking and I started pinching cigarettes from my Mum's husband. She found out and said, 'He will give you a right battering when he comes back.' So on the way back from school I hopped off the bus and hitch-hiked it back to Glasgow. The police picked me up . . .

Q. And did you run away again?

A. Yes. That was the day before I left my parents. I was fifteen.

Q. What happened?

A. I ran away and hid. The police were out looking for me. Most of the time I was only a little way off.

Q. Why had you run away this second time?

A. I came in late from my night out. I missed the bus and had to get a lift home, so I never got in till about twelve-ish. My Mum wasn't happy even though she was up. I went in and said sorry and she flipped her lid. So I flung the key from the back door and I ran away.

Q. And you left altogether after that?

A. Yes. In the morning I went back. My Mum said, 'Right, the next time you do that you are out.' I thought she said, 'Right, you're out,' so I left and didn't go back.

Case 014 was frank about his inadequate parenting:

Q. Were you brought up by your own parents?

A. Yes. Not all the way through though. I was only brought up for four years with my own parents and then I was put in a children's home.

Q. What happened? Why was that?

A. 'Cos my dad was an alcoholic and my mother was mental and my mother and dad had an argument and split up. Dad couldn't cope with the six of us and put us in a children's home . . .

Q. You say your mother and father didn't get on very well?

A. No, my mother was mentally disturbed, you see, and with my dad's alcohol problem, you know, it clashed together, it didn't work out.

Q. Did they have actual fights?

A. Yes.

Q. And what was your mother's mental problem, do you know?

A. No, I was too young to know . . .

Q. And your father, are you in touch with him?

A. When I was in the children's home I used to go and visit him every fortnight, but I remain in touch now and when I want can go and see him . . .

Q. What is his occupation?

A. He's on the dole. He used to work on the buses . . .

Q. And how do you get on with your father?

A. Well I like him in a way, but I don't like him in another way. He rejects somebody that's gay.

Q. Are you the only gay one in the family?

A. Yes.

Q. And he doesn't like you?

A. I'm the odd one out . . .

Q. And is your mother alive?

A. Well I don't know, I don't know where she is.

Some of the histories described a rapid transition from unhappy home life to premature independence achieved by crime.

Case 015 was one of those coming from a broken home whose own behaviour contributed to his disrupted upbringing.

Q. Were you brought up by your own parents?
A. I can't really say I was brought up because, like, when I was in school I was a right little twat and I got expelled at nine years old and from then on I went from boarding school to two approved schools and then I did detention centre, so I've been in institutions mostly.
Q. But until that time you were with your parents?
A. Well I was with me mum and me step-dad that I didn't like.

His parents had divorced when he was three and he did not know his own father until they met when he was seventeen.

Q. Were you often beaten when you were young?
A. My step-father was really heavy with me. I mean, I was really bad anyway.
Q. I see.
A. I was stealing money from the house and everything . . .
Q. So when you were at home with your mum and step-dad did you feel happy . . .?
A. I couldn't wait to get out of the house.
Q. And what was the reason for that?
A. Just like see, 'cos my step-father had his two daughters and if he had a go at me my mother would find reason to have a go at one of his daughters. It was like tit for tat all the time . . .
Q. Did you run away from home at all?
A. When there was a row I used to go to my grandmother's, which was when I was about eight, I think . . .
Q. What was the reason for running away?
A. I just couldn't stand it, couldn't stand the atmosphere in the house.

At first he attended a school for maladjusted children where he 'was the toughest there and used to have a gang, you see'. At the age of ten, stealing from home and rebelliousness at school led to a residential placement.

It was supposed to be a nice school, but it was all full of bloody crooks in there. My mother and father didn't know it was like that.
Q. And how long did you stay?
A. A year and a half, then I got expelled.
Q. And then what did you do?
A. I went to an assessment centre for three months and then at the assessment they decided it was best if I went to an approved school.
Q. What was it that had caused them to expel you?
A. I was running away all the time.

After some eighteen months at the approved school he was sent home to attend a comprehensive school but 'I was expelled after six weeks and sent back to a senior approved school.'
Case 016 was another delinquent recently out of prison where he had been sent for 'stabbing a geezer'.

Q. Were you brought up by your own parents?
A. No, My mum died and I didn't know who me dad was.
Q. Your mother and father never married?
A. Yes, they married, but I never knew. They divorced after I was born . . .
Q. And your mother, you stayed with her till she died, did you?
A. No, they put me in a children's home when I was three.
Q. And why was that?
A. My mum was a heroin addict.

His mother visited the home but when he was about seven she died of an overdose. 'She was always in hostels, never had a place of her own.'

Q. How old were you when you first ran away from the children's home?
A. Nine.
Q. And what was the reason for that?
A. Didn't like the place.
Q. What was wrong with it?
A. Everything, really. Didn't think much of anything.
Q. Yes, but can you tell me what was nasty about it?
A. The people who worked there. If you done anything wrong they used to beat you, beat you hard.
Q. And when did you first go out to foster-parents?
A. When I was eleven. I've been there on and off for five years.
Q. Do you mean you've been back to the kids' home?
A. Yea, I've been back to there once.
Q. And where else have you been when not with your foster-parents?
A. In prison and on the run.
Q. How old were you when you first ran away from your foster-parents?
A. Thirteen.
Q. And what happened to you then?
A. I went down to Piccadilly and that, but I never really got into the rent scene till I was fifteen, about.
Q. At thirteen, what did you do when you ran away?
A. I used to live with this – er – prostitute girl.
Q. How did you come to meet up?
A. In Soho. I lived with her for about a year.
Q. And then you got taken to prison you say?
A. Yea, they caught me when I was fourteen, put me in a secure unit.
Q. What did they catch you for?
A. Absconding from care.
Q. Now what sort of schools have you been to?
A. I've been to borstal, detention centre.
Q. And an ordinary school, as well?
A. Yes, comprehensive.

Case 017 had experienced two family breaks and obvious neglect. Up to the age of seven he was with his own parents but then they split up and he went to live with his mother and maternal grandmother. His mother then cohabited in succession with two men, neither of whom he liked, and at thirteen he was placed in a children's home on account of his bad behaviour.

Q. So let me ask about your own father. How old would he be?

A. I haven't a clue. I think he'd be about forty odd. I only know his name, that's all I know, but I can still see a vague picture of him . . . He used to beat us up, my sisters and me mum, so we went to live with me grandparents. We moved well away from him . . .

Q. Can you remember what your feeling was about him?

A. Hatred.

Q. Hatred?

A. Yeh . . .

Q. When you were living with your mum and stepdad did you get looked after all right in the way of regular food?

A. No.

Q. Why was that?

A. Because he used to take the food and what have you for drink.

Q. And did you get proper clothes, clean clothes?

A. No.

Q. Toys?

A. No.

Q. And were you often beaten?

A. All the time, whenever he came in the house.

Q. Did you run away?

A. I ran away from the children's home where they put me, five times I ran away.

Q. And did you run away from your parents before that?

A. Four times.

Q. What was the earliest age you ran away?

A. Nine.

Q. And that was from your mother, was it?

A. From both, her and the boyfriend. I didn't like the boyfriend. It was a different person she was with then. I didn't like him either.

Q. So you ran away quite often?

A. Yes, that's why they put me in a children's home.

Q. So the reason you ran away was that you didn't like your mum's boyfriends?

A. I didn't like the way they were treating me, not sending me to school, not cleaning me, not dressing me, not doing anything to help me, not feeding me properly and so on.

Q. So you got sent to a children's home?

A. Yeh. They took a care order out for me till I was eighteen.

Q. The Social Services did?

A. No, they did, they had me put in care. They said it was for me own good.

He subsequently absconded from the children's home and was on the run a long time without ever being caught.

Not all of those who had experienced interrupted schooling, residential placements and periods 'on the run' blamed these events on parental shortcomings.

Case 027, aged eighteen when seen, had stayed with his parents consistently apart from times when he had run away from schools, lived on the streets or been committed to detention centre or youth custody. He liked both parents and said they had looked after him well as regards food, clothes and toys. His behaviour in school, however, was disruptive and Social Services placed him in a residential school, but he kept running away. He was moved through five different schools in different parts of the country over a short space of time.

> Q. What was it about school you hated so much?
> A. People telling me what to do, couldn't do my own thing. I just wanted to go out, mix with girls like, and other people, but they wouldn't allow that . . . I loved London, I was born and bred in London. It was like taking away someone's best toy . . .
> Q. From what age were you running away?
> A. Thirteen . . .
> Q. And then what happened?
> A. I was on the run and I went to prison.
> Q. Can you tell me something about that, what happened that you went to prison?
> A. Lots of things, burglaries, robberies, conspiracy to defraud the clearing banks.
> Q. So how many times have you been to prison?
> A. Five times. The first time was three weeks detention centre, the second and third I got six months each, the next I got four months one day.
> [The fifth episode was a remand in custody.]
> Q. Where did you go, detention centre or prison?
> A. No, youth custody . . .
> Q. When you were at school how did you get on with lessons?
> A. Didn't do 'em.
> Q. You must have been below average?
> A. Yes, until I taught myself to read and write.

It would be tedious to continue citing examples at length, but to show the extent and range of disorder in the antecedents of these street workers here are brief summaries of each of the remaining 43 cases:

Case 003 was reared by his own parents, but in 'very unhappy' home circumstances. He got on badly with his father, who was harsh, punitive, nagging, never satisfied and beat him frequently, especially after drinking. His mother also drank heavily and there were rows between his parents over this. His father's work took him away from home a lot and 'then it was OK'. At fourteen he ran away from home to get away from his father, lied about his age and found work in a hotel.

Case 004 was brought up by his mother, his father having deserted when he was two. He felt unhappy as a child because his mother was very restrictive and he could not go out with friends. He ran away for brief periods and then, at fifteen, after his mother had moved to Ireland, ran away for good, came to England and surrendered to the social services who took him into care in a children's home.

Case 007 stayed with his mother after his parents split up when he was four. His mother used to beat him up for being a nuisance and the child protection authorities took him into care when he was six. At ten he went to live with his father who by then had another woman with him. He did not get on with her and there were 'loads of arguments'. He wanted to get away. Finally, at sixteen, he ran away taking some of his father's money.

Case 010 recalled a very unhappy early childhood, often beaten by drunken father, rows between parents constantly, no regular food, clothes or toys. When he was eight his mother left taking him with her, but she had no place to stay and he was taken into care. He was fostered at ten. He left his foster-parents at fifteen to come to London.

Case 011 was placed with foster-parents after his own parents split up when he was three. They used to beat him a lot. He returned to his mother and stepfather when he was ten, but was 'very unhappy'. He hated his mother who used to make him get his own food and wash his clothes and 'did things like trying to hit me with a crowbar'. She had a wild temper. 'I think she's got a mental problem.' He got no pocket money so was forced to steal. He was put into a children's home at thirteen. At fourteen he ran away and started living on the streets.

Case 012 lived with his parents till he was nine when his father killed his mother by strangling her in the course of one of their numerous quarrels and was sent to prison and died there a few years later. He was uncertain whether his childhood up to that point had been happy. He remembered his parents always arguing and fighting, and his father was unemployed and under psychiatric treatment. He used to get a slipper thrown into his face for silly little things like picking his nose. He hated his mother when she used to drag him to school where 'I was a little lad, you know, and I used to get picked on a lot'. After his mother's death he was put in a children's home and the following year he was fostered, but 'I got sent back to the kids' home after three months. They kept on beating me up and I stole some money.' He remained in that home until transferred after being the victim of a serious sexual assault. He left on reaching seventeen.

Case 013 was brought up, from the time his mother died when he was five, by his elderly father. His siblings were much older and already away from home. His father was demanding and punitive. As a child he was afraid of him and disliked having to do cleaning and cooking which left little time to himself. At fourteen, following numerous arguments with his father, he ran away briefly to London. He left permanently at sixteen and has not been in touch since because 'every time we see each other there are fights'.

Case 018 said his childhood was 'miserable'. He was put into a home at two when his father ran off and his mother was only eighteen. He was in several foster-homes at an early age but remembers little of them. At eleven he went to one foster-home for two years, but that ended because he was stealing off them. Since the age of eight he had been a frequent runaway.

Case 020, an only child, stayed with his mother when his father 'abandoned' them shortly after he was born. He acquired a stepfather when he was nine. He got on with him 'just about OK'. He ran away once at thirteen after being told off for stealing. He recalled his childhood as 'sometimes sad'. At fourteen he was placed in a residential home for the 'maladjusted'. Since leaving home he has not been on good terms with his mother.

Case 021 was taken into care when he was six months old. He believes it was because he was born illegitimate while his mother's husband was in prison. He was adopted as a baby. His adoptive father beat him badly and often and he 'hates' him. His adoptive mother went along with whatever his father did. He is out of touch with them now because of all the quarrels he had with them, a lot of them probably to do with his homosexuality, although they would not admit that.

Case 022 was sent to stay with his grandmother abroad when he was two so as to learn his father's native language. He returned to England at five but was put into a children's home at six by a court order on account of beatings by his father. He remained there till sixteen, 'hardly ever' visiting home. He has no contact with his father who is now with another woman.

Case 023 lived with both parents till he was thirteen when his father received a long prison sentence for incest with his sister. His mother, who was only sixteen when he was born, was 'a violent person who used to whack me very bad'. He ran away from home 'because she whacked so hard I couldn't bear it'. She left after his father was imprisoned and 'doesn't want to know her past family at all'. He was put into a children's home and from there he was sent to a secure unit on account of persistent absconding.

Case 024 lived with both parents initially, but when he was five his father deserted. He knows virtually nothing about his father. He stayed on with his mother until fourteen, then went to an aunt, but when he was thrown out of his school she asked him to leave. He did not try to get back with his mother.

Case 025 was brought up by mother and stepfather. He knew nothing of his natural father who had left when he was very small. His parents argued a lot about him because his stepfather 'doesn't like me at all'. He was often sent to stay with relatives and when he was thirteen was put in a boarding school. When he got into trouble with the police his stepfather chased him in the street and gave him a 'battering' with his fists. At sixteen, when in trouble for driving stolen cars, he was put into a hostel because his stepfather wouldn't have him at home. He has recently broken contact completely since being turned out by his stepfather because he was found in bed with a man.

Case 029 described an idyllic home life until he was twelve when his parents suddenly got divorced. He stayed with his mother, but his father, of whom he was very fond, tried several times to run away with him. His mother remarried quite soon and his stepfather turned out to be uncontrollably violent. There were quarrels with his mother even on the street. He was about fourteen 'and my stepfather started beating me up, he broke my leg, he beat me very severely, made me frightened. I was being sick all the time . . . He was beating me senseless basically, laying into me for no reason at all, beating my brothers and sister up, beating my mother up in front of us as well . . . As soon as I said anything he would automatically smack right to the face. He caned me, hit me with a metal buckle on a belt, really bashed shit out of me . . .' When he was sixteen he retaliated on one occasion, grabbed a baseball bat and started hitting his stepfather, permanently crippling one leg. Had his mother not struggled to restrain him he could have killed the man. Police were called, but he pleaded self-defence successfully. While his stepfather was in hospital he left home and started life on the streets.

Case 030 had no contact with his natural father. His parents divorced when he was seven and his mother had had three husbands since then. The first lasted till he was thirteen when she divorced him. This man had his own children and would have liked to be rid of him and his siblings. The stepfather 'used to try to rape my older sister, and used to try to beat my mother up all the time'. He was unhappy and a frequent runaway. At thirteen, when his mother was having an affair with another man, he was sent to live with his grandmother.

Case 032 had no contact with his natural father. His parents split up when he was only a month old. He was brought up by a stepfather who drank a lot and beat him and had fights with his mother when drunk. She too was alcoholic. He was very unhappy and used to run away for long periods, surviving by begging. He was expelled from school at fourteen 'for punching a teacher in the mouth' and put into a children's home.

Case 034 recalled his childhood home as 'very unhappy' on account of numerous violent rows between his parents and between himself and his older brother. He ran away several times. This went on for some years until at thirteen he was sent away to a children's home since when he has 'hardly ever' been in touch with his parents.

Case 035 knew nothing of his natural father. His mother married when he was two. He had never got on with his stepfather who used to shout and swear at him but treated his own daughter 'like gold', giving her money when she wanted it but refusing him. He ran away after a row at thirteen, but went back after some hours. At fourteen he was expelled from his school and spent the next two years at a residential school. At seventeen there was a final 'bust up' over a debt incurred through fruit machine gambling and he left home and stayed away for four years.

Case 036 never knew his natural father, but for as long as he could remember he was brought up as an only child by his mother and a maternal uncle. He had mixed feelings towards both, to his mother because she had a nervous disorder and took lots of tranquillisers and was to blame that he did not have a father, and to his uncle on account of some sexual molestation.

Case 037 was not the son of the man his mother married. When he was three his stepfather and his stepfather's parents took him over from his mother and looked after him until he was seven. After that he was in numerous children's homes, including two 'secure' homes, and spent periods of about a year each with two different sets of foster-parents. He has seen his mother a few times since he was sixteen, but 'She doesn't want to know me and I don't want to know her'.

Case 038 was adopted as a baby into a middle-class family and knew nothing of his natural parents. He described his childhood as 'very unhappy' on account of never getting on with his parents. He was a frequent runaway and was sent to many different schools, including a residential school, where he was discovered, at fourteen, in homosexual involvements with other boys. Thereafter his disputes with his parents centred on his homosexuality; they would not accept that this was other than a 'phase' and sent him to psychiatrists. At fifteen he was taken into care. Weekend visits to his parents decreased in frequency as he still could not get on with them.

Case 039 was out of touch with his natural father, his parents having divorced when he was six. He remembered his father as a 'right pig' who beat him a lot and punished the children by refusing to allow them to go to the toilet. He also 'hated' his stepfather who had a drink problem and would hit his mother after drinking. From seven he kept running away from home and at nine he was put into care at a residential school which he liked and was sorry to leave when he was sixteen.

Case 040 had only slight contact with his natural parents who divorced when he was nine while his father was in prison. He had been put into care at seven because his parents were 'on drugs' and he was spending most of the time with grandparents. He said he 'disliked' his father who also disliked him for being gay. He was fostered at ten and then returned to his father briefly, but it did not work out. Back at the children's home he was thirteen and being 'hassled' a lot about being gay, so he ran away. He remained in residential schools till sixteen when he left to go to work in hospital kitchens on a YTS scheme, but he was there only two months before being accused of stealing money and selling drugs and dismissed.

Case 041 was taken into care at five when his mother left to live with another man. After six months he was returned to his father who was an alcoholic. He was unhappy, felt deserted by his mother, hated his father's drinking and felt 'picked on' more than his siblings. He often ate at friends' houses because his father was out at the pub and not doing the cooking. He kept running away until taken into care again at eleven. At fifteen he was sent for six months to a psychiatric hospital because of uncontrollable rages. He sees his father rarely. They don't get on. His father doesn't accept that he is gay.

Case 042 was out of touch with both parents. They had separated when he was eleven, but he had been 'in and out of care' since the age of five and in various children's homes and hospitals under treatment for epilepsy. He never got on with his mother. He was 'troublesome' and always running away and his mother used to hit him with a broom and stiletto heels. She looked upon him as a 'let down'. When, at fifteen, he got into trouble for arson she had to have treatment for a near 'breakdown'.

Case 043 was brought up by mother and stepfather, his parents having been divorced just after he was born. He was in touch with his natural father but resentful of 'what he did to me when I was little'. During his mother's second marriage, from four to thirteen, when his stepfather died, he was 'a spoiled brat'. After that things changed, money was short, he started getting into trouble at school and after an outburst when someone said something against his stepfather he was sent to an adolescent psychiatric unit.

Case 045 was taken into care at eleven after persistently running away from home where he was 'very unhappy'. His father was a compulsive gambler and when he lost used to come home and take it out on him and his mother, hitting them both. His parents were now divorced and his mother had remarried. He hated his father and had no contact with him.

Case 047 was put temporarily into a children's home at three when his mother deserted him while his father was away working at sea. His father then got work on land and he went to live with him, but being partly looked after by friends of his father who were 'very strict'. From an early age he and his sister used to have to cook for themselves. At thirteen he and his sister ran away after his father came home drunk and 'had a go at us'. They were picked up and social services kept them for a few weeks. Then his father remarried, but he did not get on well with his stepmother. He ran away again at fifteen after his father had threatened him with a knife during a row and was taken into care for the last time.

Case 048 was put into the care of grandparents at four when his mother left home and remarried. His natural father had 'disappeared' from the home when he was two. When he was eight his mother returned with his stepfather and new half-siblings. He went to live with them but was unhappy. He 'hated' his stepfather who would 'slap me about' and so went back to the grandparents. At fourteen he was getting into trouble 'sniffing glue and stealing cars'. The court tried to get him back with his mother and stepfather, but they could not get on and he was put into a hostel.

Case 050 was brought up by his mother after his parents divorced when he was four. He still visits his father occasionally, but feels they don't know each other. His mother remarried when he was eight and he hated his stepfather to the extent of being glad when 'he got beaten up the other day'. He was unhappy at home, slit his wrists several times and at fourteen, on his stepfather's initiative, was put into care. He was in many different homes because he used to run away a lot and sniff glue. He was also expelled from school 'for being outrageous in the classroom'.

Not all of the products of 'broken homes' described unhappy, chaotic upbringings:

Case 026 was put into a children's home as a baby and taken out by elderly adoptive parents when he was about three. He knows nothing of his natural father but has since met his mother. When he was ten his adoptive father died and he stayed on with his adoptive mother until he was nineteen. He attended a residential school for slow learners until eighteen and then went to work there as a cleaner. He recalled his childhood as 'happy', said he liked his adoptive mother 'very much' and was well looked after as a child. At nineteen he left Ireland, his place of birth, because his job was so low paid, and came to London.

Case 002, referring to the years spent with foster-parents, described his childhood as 'very happy', although in fact he had been through some traumatic experiences. His father died when he was two. At six he went into care because his mother's intermittent cohabitee, who was a drunkard, was treating them badly. At seven he was sent to foster-parents, but the foster-father went off with another woman. His mother's cohabitee would 'sort of come and go ... Stopped me from getting home.' He remained with his foster-mother until he was sixteen.

Case 028 was brought up by his own parents up to the age of eight, when both died. He could remember little about them. After a short time in a children's home he was fostered with a couple with whom he was 'very happy'. He regards them as his father and mother and is still in touch with them. He used to wander from home in his early teens, but for 'adventure' rather than because of unhappiness. At twelve he was expelled for 'dodging school' and sent to a boarding school where [paradoxically?] 'it was great being away from home'.

The majority of the remaining cases, although ostensibly brought up by their own parents, reported varying degrees of family conflict:

Case 005 was difficult to assess because he was a persistent liar and had told different life stories on different occasions. He described a very happy childhood with his own parents, but he had also told a Streetwise worker that his parents had divorced, much to his surprise, when he was twelve, that this was after his younger sister had been sexually molested by his father, and that his mother had remarried soon after. He said that at fifteen he had stolen £400 from his father's [presumably stepfather's] brother who was sleeping in the same room at the time. Because of this and 'because I wasn't going to school, and when I did I was being disruptive' the social services put him in a home as he was 'getting too out of hand'.

Case 009 had mixed feelings towards his father. 'He seems to love me, but we always fight, but I don't like him, no.' Their relationship soured when at the early age of eleven he wrote his father a letter saying he was gay. At thirteen he ran away to the parents of a friend, 'mainly' to get away from his father.

Case 019 recalled being 'unhappy most of the time' as a child, with frequent beatings by his father. From nine to fourteen he was put into a residential school on account of persistent truancy. From fourteen onwards he kept 'coming and going' from his parents' home until leaving altogether at sixteen. He is no longer in touch with them.

Case 033 was brought up by his own parents but was 'not really happy' at home. His father was 'an alcoholic, so there's lots of arguments in the house' and 'we don't get on too well'. From thirteen onwards he ran away from home frequently. The first time he was brought back by police. After he left school he started staying away for longer periods because 'I don't get on too well' at home.

Case 046 complained of his father that 'we don't get on because we've nothing in common'. As a child he had been a 'wanderer' from home and since fifteen a persistent runaway. 'Most of the time I was chucked out because of being gay.' Recently, because he had contracted an HIV infection, both parents had told him to keep away.

Only four cases out of the 50 came near to the ideal norm of stable development under the care of both natural parents in families free from conspicuous social problems:

Case 008 described his childhood as neither happy nor unhappy, 'just OK'. He 'hated' his father who was a drunkard. Nevertheless, he was looked after well as a child and is still in touch with both parents. His reason for leaving home was inability to find work locally.

Case 044 reported a 'distant' relationship with his father but a 'very happy' childhood. He left home at sixteen because he had 'always been very independent' and because he didn't want to have to confront his parents with his bisexuality.

Case 049 was on good terms with both parents, but they were both business people and their work took them for long spells to different countries. He had travelled about with them and attended many schools in different places, but they were at present in South America and he had opted to stay in England and live on a student grant. He had had a happy childhood except at an earlier stage when having some trouble at school being called names on account of his homosexuality. There would be no problem about contacting his parents if he wanted to, but he 'hadn't phoned' recently.

Case 031 was the best example of someone who had had a well-regulated and secure upbringing by parents he was fond of. They were both in business and he still had prospects of joining in a family concern. He had not broken with them but was living very independently with a girlfriend with whom he had had a baby.

*

The impression left by this collection of personal histories is of an overwhelming prevalence of disruption and discord in their early years. Gross physical neglect was less frequent than emotional deprivation. The majority had sprung from working-class backgrounds where social problems are relatively frequent, but both in quantity and quality the incidence among this sample seemed abnormally high. In the absence of any comparison group drawn from the same social level, however, it would be technically possible to argue that rent boys' early experiences are really no worse than those of their peers who have not become prostitutes. A rough comparison is possible with a cohort of London boys from a working-class neighbourhood born a decade earlier and studied by the present author. That sample, fully representative of its neighbour-hood and generation, included a much smaller proportion separated from a natural parent (18.5 per cent against 80 per cent) and only a fraction of the proportion who had spent substantial periods in care (West, 1982).

How far these observations apply to agency workers and masseurs in the more up-market sectors of the male sex industry is a question to be considered later. The findings are, however, in line with those from previous surveys of male street prostitutes. Janus *et al.* (1984), reporting on young male street prostitutes in Boston, found that relationships with parents were mostly unhappy, beset by conflict, rejection or emotional disturbance. Only one in five had 'intact natural families' at the time of interview. Earls and David (1989), in another American research project made more systematic comparisons. They recruited 98 rent boys found hanging about 'downtown parks' and bus stops waiting to be accosted by punters. They obtained a control group of similarly aged youths wandering in the vicinity of a pin-ball arcade. Some of these had to be eliminated because, on questioning, it was found that they had been involved in prostitution. Compared with the non-prostitute group a significantly higher proportion of the rent boy sample (54 per cent against 32 per cent) had been placed in adoptive homes at least once, were not living with parents (92 per cent against 56 per cent) and had witnessed alcohol or drug problems in the parental home (70 per cent against 34 per cent). Similar findings emerged as a by product from a Canadian survey of *Street Youth and AIDS* (Radford *et al.*, 1989). A sample of 391 males and 321 females aged fifteen to twenty who were living on the streets in ten different Canadian towns were questioned. They were drawn from five targeted sources, homeless youths, young offenders, unemployed, drug abusers and prostitutes of both sexes (42 males and 57 females). Among all these groups chaotic or abusive home situations were far more prevalent than among control samples of schoolchildren and students, but prostitutes had much the poorest relationships with parents of all the street types. (op. cit., p. 25). The figures for the prostitute group were not divided according to sex at this point, but it is unlikely that the male prostitutes were any better off than the females in their relations with parents. Thoughts of suicide were expressed more often by male prostitutes than by males from any of the other groups. Poor relationships with parents, as well as missing or ineffectual parents (71 out of 89 cases), were also emphasised in the earlier survey of American hustlers by Allen (1980).

From their own frank descriptions of their rebellious attitudes and actions it seemed that many of our sample had contributed by their own behaviour to the rejections and estrangements they had experienced. As accounts of later developments will show, their unfortunate early histories were all too often a prelude to continuing social problems as young adults. As a group they were sadly ill-equipped to cope with the difficult situations in which they found themselves. In some cases the development of overt homosexual attitudes was a major factor in provoking further conflict with disapproving parents and unhelpful authorities.

3

Sexual Orientation

Sexual orientation is not easy to define since sexual behaviour, sexual feelings and social identity are not always congruent. For the purpose of this survey sexual orientation is defined by feelings, that is whether contact with the same or opposite sex more readily produces sexual arousal, or whether the two sexes are more or less equally arousing. It makes some sense to classify mature adults as homosexual, heterosexual or bisexual since most are aware of a fairly stable preference and identify themselves with one of these groups, many feeling that they have been well aware of their orientation since puberty. Among teenage males, however, especially those of unsettled habits, there are some whose attitudes are ambivalent, whose erotic responses are aroused in a multiplicity of situations and whose orientation remains uncertain. Affection and sex can occur between males in the absence of a basic homosexual orientation. Youths at the peak of sexual arousability can respond to stimulation from almost any quarter and may do so to show gratitude to partners who are far from ideally attractive. A firm sexual preference is not always established until adolescence or later (Coleman, 1989). Sexual practice ('reinforcement' in psychological terms) may exert some influence and an element of choice bolstered by social demands may enter into the adoption of a gay or straight persona. Nevertheless, a great many homosexuals are aware from a tender age of a strong and exclusive attraction to their own sex and find little satisfaction in attempts at heterosexual performance. The evidence of this survey supports the view that this hard core of so-called 'primary' homosexuals (estimated as up to 5 per cent of the male population) are much over-represented among male prostitutes, as are also young men whose sexuality is confused, catholic or changeable. Assertions made in some publications that male street workers are either all homosexuals or all heterosexuals are certainly fallacious.

Most older surveys suggest that male street workers are generally heterosexual (Butts, 1947; Coombs, 1974; Deischer et al., 1969; Reiss, 1961). Pieper (1979), basing himself on earlier reports, confidently asserted that 'Male prostitutes usually classify themselves and are classified by the researcher as heterosexual, the percentage of homosexuals never exceeds 10 to 20 with some additional bisexuals' (op. cit., p. 246). Jersild (1956, p. 59), drawing upon a sample of 300 youths (average age seventeen) known to the Danish morality police, used notes about girlfriends contained in prior records, as well as what the boys themselves had to say, to conclude that at the outset of their work as male prostitutes only 15 per cent were homosexual or bisexual. Ginsberg (1967), who studied male prostitutes in San Francisco by intermingling with them informally on their 'meat rack' in the Tenderloin area, challenged the idea that most were natural homosexuals. Responding with erection and ejaculation when stimulated by clients was no proof of homosexual preference. He agreed, however, that there might be some truth in the gay world adage 'Today's trade is tomorrow's competition'. He found a few older hustlers who said they had developed homosexual interests through long practice with clients.

Later research has reported more homosexuality (Deischer *et al.*, 1982). In one American survey (Urban and Rural Systems, 1982; Weisberg, 1985, p. xiii) 47 per cent of young male prostitutes identified themselves as gay, 29 per cent as bisexual, 16.5 per cent as heterosexual and the rest as transvestite or transsexual. In another sample of 98 young American male prostitutes (Allen, 1980) 28 rated themselves as bisexual and 52 as predominantly homosexual on the Kinsey scale. Most (63 of 98) had had their first sexual experience with another male. Boyer (1989) compared a sample of 47 male prostitutes, who could be seen hustling on street corners in downtown Seattle (average age 16.2 years) with a control group of 50 young delinquents who were not prostitutes. Sexual identity was the most prominent feature distinguishing these groups; 70 per cent of the prostitutes but only 4 per cent of the controls identified themselves as either homosexual or bisexual. In a survey sponsored by the Canadian Government 84 young male street prostitutes from eight cities were interviewed (a majority of 69 per cent being seventeen, eighteen or nineteen years old). Only 22.6 per cent claimed to be heterosexual, 31 per cent said they were homosexual and a further 31 per cent identified as bisexual. In addition, 7.2 per cent were classed as transsexuals or transvestites and 8.3 per cent were undecided (Canada, 1984, p. 969). In a later study of 50 male street prostitutes in Montreal (average age 21.58 years) most declared themselves homosexual or bisexual and only 30 per cent said they had a heterosexual preference. In a small but intensively studied sample of street prostitutes Visano (1987) classed a majority, eighteen of 33, as gay.

It may be that the stigma attached to a homosexual orientation and the need to maintain a macho image have decreased somewhat since the frequently cited survey of 'street hustlers' by the American sociologist Al Reiss (1961). He found that most had no conception of themselves as either prostitutes or homosexuals, although this was in contrast with what had earlier been reported of 'bar hustlers' (Ross, 1959). The young street workers were predominantly lower-class delinquents. They would seek out older homosexual males in well-known pick-up areas, such as bus stations, parks and toilets, and allow themselves to be fellated for a fee. The transaction had to be seen as a way of making easy money with little risk and with no sexual motive on the boy's part. Displays of affection by clients or requests for more intimate sexual contact were rebuffed with violence. The business was considered a temporary expedient, just one among a range of delinquent activities indulged in pending either graduation to more sophisticated forms of crime or the adoption of adult conformist behaviour. The boys had no intention of becoming long-term career prostitutes or becoming identified with the despised 'queers' whose money was all they wanted. In a later American survey, although heterosexuals were no longer claimed to dominate the scene, they were found likely to rob and assault rather than provide a sex service (Deischer *et al.*, 1982). Great hostility to clients is still expressed by some UK rent boys. One young man, working for an agency, is quoted as saying 'I see them as skin and bone who want to pay me money for touching them. There's nothing emotional about it: if they died in front of me I'd walk away quite happily' (Philpot, 1990).

It was noticed again in the Canadian survey of Visano (1987) that many young male street hustlers hesitated to become known as specialists in the male sex racket for fear of being suspected of being gay themselves. Newcomers to the street scene had to assume a homophobic stance in order to be accepted, but some of them, who perceived themselves as gay, had difficulty keeping up the pretence of disliking and not fraternising with clients and limiting their services to brief and minimal sexual contact. The more homosexually inclined tended to drift away from the street-corner groupings, to avoid joining in with generalised delinquent activity, to seek business in the vicinity of gay establishments, to present themselves to clients as gay and to form contacts in the gay world. In fact, perhaps because of the increased availability of supports for a gay lifestyle, less than half were classed as 'defiantly straight' (op. cit., p. 110).

Some earlier observers have always been sceptical of rent boys' claims to exclusive heterosexuality, being convinced that a substantial proportion are natural homosexuals who have taken to the trade partly for that reason. Benjamin and Masters (1964) cited evidence from the experiences of clients describing how purportedly straight rent boys get carried away during sex and begin to initiate activities they are supposed to dislike. They also mention the phenomenon of former prostitutes becoming clients themselves when they get older, commenting cynically that the restrictions boys insist upon for the sake of appearing straight, that is being fellated but not fellating the customer, are economically foolish. They often charge more, but logically should charge less, for passive acts that do not require them to ejaculate and put themselves temporarily out of action for further work. (Of course this comment was made before the advent of AIDS.)

The 'strictly business' attitude adopted by some rent boys to their clients is not a reliable guide to sexual orientation. They may distance themselves, profess reactions of distaste or boredom, or try to disguise real dislike with insincere expressions of friendliness, but none of this means they are necessarily averse to male sex. They may simply yearn for partners of their choice within their own age group. Some may want their clients to believe their compliance is forced. John Rechy (1977), the well-known author of gay novels, in an autobiographical 'documentary' about his adventures as a gay hustler, suggests that the macho stance may be put on for a variety of reasons. He explains (p. 67): 'On the street I disguise my feelings, I play distant, tough.' In reality he loves to be admired and to be paid for being desired is 'a terrific, terrible excitement'. By adopting 'that strict code, not to reciprocate in those encounters' he experiences a real feeling of sexual power (p. 153). According to Rechy (p. 155), hustlers are often expected, even required, by their clients to play the role of a straight man. They may even think of themselves, defensively, as being so, and they will act the part when in the company of other hustlers. Yet some of them will wander off to male cruising areas to satisfy their desires in unpaid contacts.

There are many reasons why rent boys should sometimes want to deny homosexuality. Stigma may have lessened, but it remains considerable, more especially among the working-class adolescent peer group where the intimidation of those thought effeminate is a very real threat. In confrontations with authority figures such as police, social workers, the staff of penal establishments and would-be therapists they may hope to be more sympathetically dealt with if they maintain the pose of reluctant victim of homosexual exploitation. Likewise, in interacting with clients, they may stand to gain by a show of reluctant submission to supposedly uncongenial sexual acts.

The researchers Davies and Simpson (1990), surveying the contemporary male prostitution scene in London, voice scepticism of the 'themes of seduction; of innocence betrayed and of economic necessity leading to a denial and subversion of a boy's natural sexuality'. In a subsequent report from the same research project (Robinson, 1989, p. 19) it was stated that about half of the street workers were prepared to identify themselves as gay and a further quarter as bisexual. The reluctance with which some claim to be forced into homosexual acts may sometimes be put on to gain the sympathy of an investigator. The real views of one rent boy are set out in Jeremy Sandford's study of prostitution (Cusack, 1975, pp. 171-9). When asked about the suggestion that entry into prostitution can be traced back to early deprivation he responded: 'I'd say they're talking a lot of crap.' He explained that his father was a successful businessman and that he himself had a resonably well-paid job, but he was selling sex because he wanted to make more money to set up an escort agency. He was highly sexed, enjoyed relations with both men and women, and said of his customers 'more fool them' for paying him for what he liked and would willingly do for nothing.

The questions put to the sample of 50 street workers were meant to determine which sex they found the more sexually arousing, rather than what social identity they had adopted or the form of their current sexual activity. They were asked about their earliest sexual feelings and whether they were towards boys, girls or both. Then they were asked what now 'turns you on' – 'females only; females mostly but sometimes males; both about the same; mostly males; or only males?' To this, 46 per cent said they were aroused mostly or only by females, 36 per cent only or mostly by males and 18 per cent more or less equally by either sex. The figure of 46 per cent of heterosexuals almost certainly overestimates the position since some, particularly those with a macho stance, were reluctant to admit to belonging to a stigmatised minority. When later in the interview a question was asked about sexual friendships, present and past, the replies helped to clarify earlier statements about sexual preference and provided further evidence of some resistance to acknowledging homosexuality.

Many respondents were emphatic about their sexual orientation:

Case 041

    Q. Who were you interested in the in those [school] days?
    A. That's the funny part about it. I've never been interested in girls.
    Q. And do you identify as gay?
    A. I never deny it.
    Q. You think of yourself as gay?
    A. I am gay.
    Q. And never women at all?
    A. I've never, ever been with a woman . . .
    Q. What about sex outside the rent scene?
    A. I am very active, if that's what you mean. I haven't got a favourite boyfriend . . .
    Q. And you've never been with women?
    A. Never once, never wanted to either.

Some were equally emphatic in an opposite sense:

Case 017

    Q. And what were your first sexual interests, mostly towards boys. girls or both?
    A. All with girls.
    Q. And nowadays . . .?
    A. 100 per cent girls.

Q. 100 per cent?
A. Yes . . .
Q. Now, apart from punters, do you have any sexual friendships with anybody at the moment?
A. Some girls, two, three girls.
Q. Do you have a particular one among them?
A. No, I fuck all three of them.

The more assertively heterosexual informants sometimes expressed considerable disgust about their sexual activities with clients:

Case 043 recalled feelings for girls since infancy. He remembered being caught with a small girl in a Wendy House trying to imitate his mother and stepfather whom he had seen having sex.

Q. When you were younger was it mainly towards girls or boys or –?
A. Girls.
Q. Only girls?
A. Yeh.
Q. And now?
A. Still women.
Q. Only women?
A. . . . I've had sex with guys [punters] so I can't say I'm dead straight.
Q. Do you ever find you are attracted to guys when you are having sex with them?
A. No, because with them I was always thinking of women.

He was asked about his first experience of selling sex:

There were parts of it made me feel like throwing up. I mean the first time I ever saw two guys kissing I literally threw up you know . . . [but] . . . well yes, I cashed in on it . . . it was easy money, I was getting more than when I was working.

Case 015 said he was turned on

Always by girls, not by men at all . . . At first it's really revolting, and then it's sort of like – you never get to enjoy it – but then it doesn't bother you so much . . . [The first time] I was closing my eyes and I was thinking of the nice times I had had with a girl. I'm quite good with my brain that way, I can put myself somewhere else.

Except for the homosexuals, few expressed positive feelings about the sex they had with punters, but there were some exceptions among the bisexuals:

Case 011

Q. Have you any more thoughts on the rent scene?
A. You see it's quite fun. You get different people you know and different ways of sex. So when you go back to your partner you can experiment and really enjoy your sex life a lot more . . .
Q. So it opens up sex with your boyfriend?
A. And girlfriends. You learn different little things. Sex is a very important part of my life.

Case 036

I'm very promiscuous and experimental, so it's nice to see other angles of things and sides, I think it can broaden your horizons, I think it's good in that respect.

Men who declared themselves completely heterosexual generally described a relatively restricted repertoire of sex acts they were willing to do with punters:

Case 048 said he had always fancied only females since he was eleven. With punters he would have mutual masturbation and allow men to suck him but he would not have anal contact. 'If I don't want to do something I just say no.' He had once had a penile infection, but not from a man. He had a girlfriend of similar age who knew he went to gay bars. He had told her he was meeting some friends who were gay, but not that he went with punters. Only once had he had contact with a man without payment and that was with a fellow rent boy.

Q. And did you fancy him?
A. No, he fancied me.
Q. He fancied you?
A. I was a bit stoned.
Q. So you just did it?
A. I just let him carry on. It was not really – I did not have sex with him or anything – I just sort of like – he sucked me off really.

Case 027 was even more negative. He said he went with clients only to avoid asking his girlfriend for money. Re-interviewed after release from imprisonment for robbery, his girlfriend had left him and he was still selling sex to support a heroin habit.

The only contact [with punters] I really have is with my hands really.

Q. So that's wanking. Do you allow someone to suck you?

A. Umm. I have on a couple of occasions.

Q. So you would allow it?

A. Yes.

Q. But you are not too happy with it?

A. No, not too happy.

Q. OK, and you definitely don't suck them?

A. No.

Q. And fucking, you don't either way?

A. I don't either way. Definitely out. 'Cos as far as I am concerned that is one of the dirtiest parts of your body, you understand. It just doesn't appeal to me at all . . . I would never even think of it, he could offer me £1,000 and I wouldn't do it.

Q. Have you ever been asked to be tied up or to tie someone up, spank them or – ?

A. I've been asked to cane somebody.

Q. Were you happy with it?

A. Oh I loved it. You should have seen the state of his backside afterwards . . .

Q. Do you use condoms with punters?

A. Yes, sometimes I do.

Q. OK. What situations?

A. Car situations basically, when we are in a car, 'cos they don't want it to come all over their seats and that.

Q. So you're not doing it for health reasons, you are doing it to keep clean?

A. Oh I'm doing it for health reasons as well. When the guy's coming he's nowhere near me, you understand. I tell him to turn around so it doesn't come near me because I don't want to catch AIDS.

Q. What happens if the guy doesn't want to use a condom?

A. Then he just has to make sure he's not facing me.

In his further answers he indicated that some rules could be bent. His usual charge is £25, but 'if he sucks me it's £45. And I do actually get it as well, every time.' He always carried a knife with him, which he used to threaten any who didn't pay up, remarking: 'When they are over sixty it is much easier to get money off them.' 'You do what you do and that's it, finished, you just do your business and walk off. I refuse to have a friendship with a punter.'

He had lived in fear of exposure:

I mean it's a nightmare. Like when I was at home, something came on telly, like say something about gays. I'd sit there and I'd think, 'I bet they're thinking about me' – you know, my parents, they know little bits. And my brother and sister, I bet you they think I'm horrible and a poofter and everything, and you can't sleep at nights and I wonder what everyone's thinking about me. It just does me in, it does, it just does me head in.

It has been suggested (Deischer *et al.*, 1982) that heterosexually oriented male prostitutes are uncomfortable in homosexual situations, less likely to follow through with a sexual transaction and more likely to assault or rob customers. None of the sample admitted to this, but it was plain that in restricting the sexual contacts they would permit some strongly heterosexually identified men were distancing themselves from their clients and feeling contempt for their clients' sexual needs.

There were instances in which insistence on virtually exclusive heterosexuality appeared doubtful in the light of other information:

Case 032. This exaggeratedly macho skinhead said that his earliest sexual interests had been in girls and that these days his attraction was 'mostly' towards girls. He had no male sexual friendships and he had had a girlfriend for the past eighteen months with whom he was having sex. With punters he refused anal sex having just 'mainly masturbation', but sometimes allowing himself to be sucked but not doing that to them. He had also tied up and whipped some punters which 'I enjoyed in a way 'cos I thought I can give someone else what people have given to me'. He was mainly concerned about AIDS, but getting it from women, because with men he did nothing to get infected. In answer to questions about trouble with the police, however, he mentioned that about six months ago he had been convicted for indecency with a man much older than himself, someone he counted as a friend with whom he used to stay from time to time. On one occasion they had 'played about' and shortly afterwards this man had got into trouble for 'raping a young lad' and his relationship with the man had become known. Being under age he was found guilty of gross indecency and 'was convicted, but got no sentence'. Apart from this, he also described a sugar daddy, a gay man who was 'mainly a good friend' with whom he did not have sex but from whom he could get 'whatever I want – like I had a big fine to pay. If I hadn't got the money off him I'd have got sent down.'

Many of those who expressed a clear preference for women were not averse to a male relationship when it suited them:

Case 004. This man, whose earliest sexual interests were towards girls and who said he was now turned on mostly by females, described a sugar-daddy-type relationship lasting two years with a man of forty-five. He visited weekly and 'he used to turn me on sexwise. We used to watch a blue film.' He got money and clothes in return, but now the man had left for Holland.

> Q. Would he want you to go and live with him?
> A. Well, he'd want it I think.
> Q. So is that something you are wondering if you will do?
> A. Yea, but I don't want to go and live in Holland.

Questions were asked about the age when the boys first began to take a sexual interest in anybody and whether their earliest feelings were directed towards males or females or both. Some found this difficult to remember and some needed to have the difference between sexual practices and subjective feelings explained. For example, *Case 002*, aged twenty-one, said he was sixteen when he first felt sexually attracted to anyone, before that 'I never done nothing with anybody'. Pressed further he still insisted his sexual awakening occurred at sixteen when he had contact with a man of thirty-five to forty. He was at the time on a visit to London with a friend who showed him the gay scene and arranged for him to meet and stay the night with this man who fellated him but did not require him to reciprocate.

> Q. And how did you feel about it then? Did you enjoy it?
> A. Yes, it was good. That was the first time I ever came.
> Q. So you enjoyed it a lot?
> A. Yes, a lot.

Asked about his present feelings he said he was turned on by both sexes, but at the moment had no regular sexual partner.

In order to investigate changes in sexual orientation statements about earliest sexual interests were set against present feelings in the following table:

	Currently attracted by		
Initially *attracted by*	Mostly or only males	Males and females about the same	Mostly or only females
Boys	13	3	0
Both sexes	3	2	3
Girls	2	4	20
	18	9	23

It can be seen at a glance that initial and current sexual interests remained the same in the great majority of cases. Of the fifteen who acknowledged some shift, nine had moved in a homosexual and six in a heterosexual direction. Of the eighteen who said they were currently homosexually oriented only two had been initially attracted to girls only, but neither mentioned prostitution as a reason for the change.

For example, *Case 001*, whose earliest fancies, from ten onwards, had been towards girls, said firmly 'I'm a gay man' although 'sometimes' turned on by females. He was a particularly macho type often to be seen in leather gear with heavy boots and ostentatiously dangling chains.

Case 023, whose earliest interests had been 'only girls', said: 'Occasionally I might see a woman walk down the street and I get an erection, but that's not very often, so I should class myself as gay.' He had

had sexual affairs with other men unconnected with the rent scene, but never with a female.

There were, however, one or two men who voiced a doubt as to whether their prostitution activities might be affecting their heterosexual orientation. For example, *Case 003*, who said he had lost his virginity with a girl when he was thirteen. He was still turned on '99 per cent by females, but sometimes males'. During a later discussion about wanting to give up prostitution he reverted to the topic of sexual preference. 'It's degrading, isn't it. Like I say, before I started doing it I wouldn't have even looked twice at a man you know. But now I've been doing this I suppose, in a way, I'm turning – well I won't say gay – but bisexual, because I do look at men now and think.'

*

The statistics of sexual orientation derived from these interviews must be regarded with some reserve. They were based on questions about arousability, whether maximal with males or females or about the same with either sex. Social identification with a gay self-image, or attraction to feminine roles, were not considered. Bias in responses was almost certainly in the direction of denial of homosexual inclinations, especially by those presenting a macho front and expressing anti-gay sentiments. It was clear enough, however, that the street boy sample was heterogeneous, with substantial representation of individuals broadly categorisable as having homosexual, bisexual and heterosexual arousal patterns respectively. There was little evidence that prostitution practice was producing great changes in these patterns. It was noticeable that declared heterosexual orientation was generally linked with more negative attitudes towards prostitution and more restrictive sexual interchanges with clients.

4

Sex Abuse in Childhood

The belief that sex abuse in childhood is a cause of male prostitution has become almost conventional wisdom. The journalist Gay Search (1988, p. 31) confidently asserts that 'almost all male prostitutes were sexually abused as children'. A particularly high prevalence of histories of sexual abuse in childhood has been reported in studies of female prostitutes (James and Myerding, 1978; Silbert and Pines, 1981) and now the same is being said to hold true for male prostitutes (Justice and Justice, 1979, p. 197; McMullen, 1987). Bolton *et al.* (1989) regard prostitution as simply a continuation of earlier abusive sex. In a group of young male prostitutes contacted through The Bridge, a Boston agency that helps youths who are runaways or otherwise in crisis, 24 out of 28 questioned said that, before becoming involved in prostitution, they had had one or more earlier experiences of being forced to serve another person's sexual demands (Janus *et al.*, 1984, p. 135) and eleven had been sexually involved with a family member. Of three examples quoted, one had been forced at the age of ten to perform oral sex on his child minder, another had been forced into oral and anal sex by his father when he was twelve and the third had suffered forced anal penetration by a stranger when he was only six.

Asked whether, as boys under fourteen, they had ever been involved in sex acts against their will, seventeen of the 50 young men in the Streetwise sample answered affirmatively. Only one of the incidents concerned molestation by a woman. The question was phrased deliberately to exclude consensual sex acts between peers or contacts with older persons that the boys may have purposely sought out.

In a national sample from the UK, surveyed by the MORI organisation, 8 per cent of men reported having been exposed to sexual abuse in childhood (Baker and Duncan, 1985). The definition of abuse used by MORI was 'A child (anyone under sixteen years) is sexually abused when another person, who is sexually mature, involves the child in any activity which the other person expects to lead to their sexual arousal. This might involve intercourse, touching, exposure of the sexual organs, showing pornographic materials or talking about sexual things in an erotic way.'

Since our definition was more restrictive, asking only about incidents before the fourteenth birthday, and since all the incidents described were of definite physical molestation, often recalled as decidedly traumatic, the prevalence rate of 34 per cent in the Streetwise sample, over four times that in the MORI survey, was clearly a significant finding.

In reported incidents of sex abuse of boys the perpetrators are nearly always men. In a recent small-scale survey of community samples in London and Cambridge (West and Woodhouse, 1990), about one in five men recalled a sex encounter with an adult male when they were still under sixteen. This larger figure does not, however, provide a true comparison, since it included many brief and trivial incidents and approaches that were rejected without any physical contact taking place, as well as some instances in which boys older than fourteen had been willing participants. The prevalence of incidents resembling the situations described by the Streetwise youths was actually less than the 8 per cent reported by MORI.

The belief that the unhappy experience of having been exploited sexually for the pleasure of others when they were children should lead men to choose similar sex work as an occupation seems on the face of it implausible. Nevertheless, the many accounts of child sex abuse reported by the Streetwise sample call for some explanation. There was no obvious motive for fabrication, the details given bore the ring of truth and similar findings have emerged from other studies.

The Streetwise sample included many homosexuals, and it has been found that homosexuals recall sexual encounters with older males when they were children more often than do heterosexuals (Bell *et al.*, 1981; West and Woodhouse, 1990). It has been suggested that a homosexual orientation provides a reason to dwell upon rather than to try to suppress memories of boyhood encounters with older homosexuals. It has also been suggested that boys who are developing homosexually are receptive to sex approaches from men, their demeanour may attract would-be molesters and their early experiences may reinforce a homosexual orientation.

Whatever the reason for homosexuals recalling such incidents more often than heterosexuals, there was no evidence that this was the reason for the prevalence of abuse histories in the present sample. Early sexual abuse was reported no more frequently by those whose sexual interests as boys had been directed towards other males (3 of 15) or by those who said that they were currently aroused solely or predominantly by other males (6 of 18) than by those self-rated as heterosexual or bisexual (8 of 27). We had been careful, however, to ask about unwanted or forced involvements. These are less likely to be related to a victim's own inclinations than are homosexual encounters entered into willingly and not regarded by the subject as unwanted. By including all early homosexual experience under the all-embracing heading of 'abuse' theorists have wrongly assumed a proven link between homosexual assault in childhood and adult homosexuality.

None of the 50 interviewed men connected early molestation

experience with either becoming homosexual or becoming involved in prostitution. In the following example the victim's pre-existing homosexuality may have been a factor in bringing about the incident, but it was perceived by him as highly aversive and hardly a reason for wanting to be a prostitute.

Case 021. Estranged from his adoptive parents, this man had never been interested in the opposite sex and had been in trouble as a schoolboy for sexual behaviour with other boys. He didn't like games, preferred girls' company and suffered sexual bullying.

I was taken behind the bike sheds, five or six boys got on top of me.
Q. What did they do to you?
A. They played with me and touched me and asked me to do things to them.
Q. And were you upset by that?
A. Very upset.
Q. Did it happen just once?
A. No, it happened on a few occasions.
Q. I see. And was that because they thought you a sissy boy?
A. Yes.
Q. And you disliked it very much?
A. Yes.

It can be argued that the aversive aspects of child sex abuse are counteracted by the discovery that sex can be used to make money. Gay Search (1988, p. 51) comments on the fact that children are often given presents after cooperating with an abuser and writes: 'It is easy to see how being rewarded for sexual favours can lead ... very naturally to prostitution.' A similar opinion, backed by some statistics, had been reached earlier by Coombs (1974), who interviewed 41 male prostitutes, average age nineteen, and contrasted them with a comparison group of similar age and class. Proportionately over four times as many (64 per cent) of the prostitutes had engaged in homosexual behaviour at an early age, and usually they had received rewards for so doing. One of them, for example, had been 'sold' by his father when he was ten to an adult homosexual who gave him clothes and presents. Coombs concluded that learning at an early age how to use sex to manipulate others for gain was a significant factor in opening up the prospect of more systematic prostitution later on.

Later surveys have taken up the same theme. Allen (1980) studied 98 young American male prostitutes, 63 of whom had had their first sexual experience with a male, their average age at the time being 12.9 years. Of these 63, 35 had been seduced rather than either initiating the sexual acts or participating by mutual agreement, and 21 of this 35 had received money or favours for their collaboration. Since most of this sample (80 of 98) were self-rated homosexual or bisexual one may question the concept of 'seduction' and query how importantly the money featured. Weisberg (1985) noted more dramatically that 9 per cent of a sample of 79 young male prostitutes had been paid for sex at eleven or earlier and a majority of 70 per cent by fifteen. Her sample was, however, hardly representative, being unusually young (mean age 16.96) and recruited via social agencies, which may also account for the startling statistic that 29 per cent were said to have been sexually abused by a member of the family.

In the present sample, only one of the seventeen men who reported boyhood molestations described circumstances that could be construed as training in how to secure material rewards for sexual favours. He recalled two episodes of bribery by different paedophiles:

Case 011

> I didn't know what it was all about, but in the toy shop where I used to live when I was with my foster-parents – about seven or eight years old – he showed me these dirty books and told me what to do and all that. So I had this fantasy about doing it from a very early age.
>
> Q. Doing it with girls?
> A. Yea. And he used to be gay and he used to try it on all the time and one time he actually came on too strong . . . He used to take me upstairs and show me dirty magazines and things.
> Q. And what happened then?
> A. He'd just play around with me like.
> Q. He'd play with your penis?
> A. Yes, and he actually went out to screw me once, but he didn't, because I wouldn't let him. I started crying and all that.
> Q. So what did you feel about it at the time?
> A. Well I couldn't tell anybody about it because me foster-parents would have just kicked the shit out of me.
> Q. But you went back to the shop a number of times?
> A. Yes, but I was very scared. But then again, I wanted things off him, because he used to give me things my parents wouldn't.
> Q. So he sort of bribed you?
> A. Yes, sort of.
> Q. And was there something else that happened to you when you were under fourteen?
> A. Yes. The headmaster.
> Q. That was at boarding school? What happened?
> A. Well he kept trying things on and giving me money and all that. Sort of bribed me for doing things.
> Q. How old were you when he started?
> A. It was a few months after I went to that school – thirteen.
> Q. Tell me about this headmaster, how old was he?
> A. Quite old. His name was Mr. W —.
> Q. Fifty?
> A. About that age.
> Q. How did it begin? What happened?
> A. Well all the other boys, lots of the other boys, used to do it with him. He's up for charges now. He used to give us money to go out and have a good

time and things like that. A lot of money, like, for then you know.

Q. He gave you money to do what?

A. Well usually he just used to touch your leg and things like that, and sort of rub you around. And it got a bit heavier and a bit heavier.

Q. When you say a bit heavier, what was it he wanted to do?

A. Wanted to do everything.

Q. To fuck you and you to fuck him?

A. Yes. Things like that.

Q. And other things?

A. Blow jobs.

Q. And did you do all those things sometimes?

A. No.

Q. So what did you do with him?

A. Nothing, I just took what I could, do you know what I mean? Being young, I just wanted to have things to enjoy myself.

Q. So what did you let him do?

A. Just feel me, and a couple of times he would get it out.

Q. He took his out and you would have to play with him?

A. Yes.

Q. And how did this come to an end?

A. He came on too strong once and I told somebody and they got the police.

Q. And what happened then?

A. Well, I spent a whole day in the police station and wrote out a statement. But nothing came of it because I ran away too soon after that.

Q. You ran away before anything could be done?

A. Yes.

The hypothesis that boys learn through early abuse the power of their sexuality for material exploitation received little support from this study. The notion that child sex abuse can be held responsible for prostitution is not helped by recent claims that it may also lead to many other undesirable developments. Reports of an unusually high incidence of early sexual abuse come from inquiries among many different deviant groups, including, in addition to prostitutes, psychotics, sex offenders, addicts, neurotics, delinquents, anorexics and multiple personalities (Wyatt and Powell, 1989). It is well established that inadequacies and peculiarities of upbringing are characteristic of all these groups. The recognised precursors of adult deviancy, namely pathology in parents, disorderly environment and poor standards of care and supervision, also allow unusual opportunity for child sexual abuse. The statistical connection between sex abuse and many different types of problem could be indirect. Sex abuse is often only one among many features of a disordered upbringing. It may be the totality of adverse influences, not the sexual incidents in themselves, that encourage deviance.

Some of the histories from the Streetwise sample revealed how unhappy or disorderly home backgrounds or inadequate parental care or control could contribute more or less directly to the circumstances which enabled sexual abuse to occur. In the following example the boy had run away from an unhappy home and was sleeping in an outdoor hiding place when an intruder broke in and sexually assaulted him.

Case 038. Aged twenty, this man recalled a 'very unhappy' childhood with adoptive parents, with whom he came to have many arguments relating to his homosexuality. He had 'got addicted' to sex in bed with other boys in his boarding school dormitory and been discovered and segregated. On several occasions he ran away from home and one time, at the age of twelve:

I was on the run and I was walking through the church fields. It was almost near to where I was living and some holidays we used to have things like dens there. We used to build dens out of planks of wood and branches and leaves and then we'd put a Tarzan swing up. In the summer holidays, all the people from the road, all the kids, used to gather round there. I'd walked out and went off on me own and I'd stayed in this den about three nights on me own. And then I just woke up and this old fella was in with me. So obviously he must have, he must have probably used it before I was there. He must have been using it like, it was a pick-up place and take 'em back there kind of thing. So it just happened there. I was screaming and crying and he just, he come and tied me mouth up. I think he didn't handcuff me or anything. I couldn't defend myself because I was so young.

Q. How old would he be?

A. He was about forty-seven I'd say, something like that.

Q. Obviously a lot stronger than you?

A. Yea.

Q. And was it at night?

A. Yea. I was asleep. I'd been to sleep and he woke me up.

Q. And he what, he just attacked you?

A. He just attacked me straight away. There was no violence, he just – I mean – it was a struggle, because I kept stumbling around. I wanted to get away from him. But it wasn't, he didn't pull a knife or anything, or a gun or anything like that. I was struggling violently, that kind of thing.

Q. He gagged your mouth. Did he stop you screaming?

A. Yea.

Q. Did you carry on screaming?

A. Yea, well I did, but nobody could hear me, kind of, I mean you could hear it, but not enough to bring any attention from where we were.

Q. And what did he do, presumably anal penetration?

A. No, he didn't, he put it down me throat. And then he – I had it down me throat, I had it all round me mouth and all round me face. And then he got me to give him one and that was it. That was all I can remember. It was years ago.

Q. Was it a horrible experience?

A. Yea. 'Cos I stayed. I didn't stay there again, but I found somewhere else and I stayed away for about another five days and went home . . . He left me and walked off and I walked off as well, but not with him. I stayed there until a bit later on and walked off later on and then went back to one of the other ones by the river. It was a better one because it was in a tree.

When he returned home his mother questioned him closely and he told her what had happened. 'She called Dad in and told him what had been going on and they both seemed to have got really worked up', but they did not report the matter.

A second example illustrates a similar train of events, unhappiness at home, running away, exposure to risk of abuse:

Case 045. This twenty-year-old bisexual, who had had a very unhappy childhood, recalled an assault which occurred some time before he became a rent boy.

I'd run away from home. It was almost the third time I'd ever run away from home. It was in King's Cross. I decided to walk up to Euston. Actually I didn't know London that well. So I asked somebody the way, who literally walked me up there. He asked me why I wanted to go to Euston. I told him that I was on the run away from home.

Q. How old were you then?

A. Twelve and a half or thirteen. [Possibly younger according to other statements – D.J.W.] Well this guy walked me up to Euston Station and when we got there he offered me a cup of tea and something to eat, which I gladly accepted. He told me that he was living in a bed and breakfast in King's Cross and would I like a bed for the night, which I did take. While I was asleep he tried something that was definitely against my wishes. And the following day I was arrested in King's Cross, through being on the run, you know. Seeing a young person walking around there, because it was known in them days. The police picked me up. I was tested by a doctor. Stuck on a glove. [He said] I had been interfered with. Obviously I told the police I'd been interfered with and this guy was brought to justice. He was given four years imprisonment.

Q. Were you involved in the trial?

A. No they kept me well away from that.

Q. When it actually happened, when you woke up, he was trying it on?

A. He wasn't trying it, he was forcing it.

Q. And he actually succeeded?

A. Yes.

Q. Was that a traumatic experience for you?

A. It was very frightening. When you are asleep and you are all of a sudden woken up by pain. This guy sort of being fierce with you, threatening to beat you up and all this and that, you're sort of frozen and just trying . . .

Q. Did it go on for a long time?

A. From what I can remember, yes it did.

Q. And what happened afterwards?

A. Well that morning, well it wasn't that morning actually, it was the early hours of that morning, when I thought he was asleep, I quickly grabbed my clothes and ran out into the hallway, got dressed and legged it down the street. And come 6 or 7 in the morning I was arrested. Because there were cameras around King's Cross. They picked me up, a little time before I think. And the police said I'd been hanging round a couple of hours, why? And I was arrested and taken to the police station off Gray's Inn Road. And about 11 o'clock my father come. The doctor had already seen me. And the police had spoken to my father and he started hitting me inside the police station. It took three police officers to hold him back. And that was the time, exactly the same night when I told them if they sent me back home I would run away. So my father was removed from the police station and I never did go back.

Q. How did they treat you, the police?

A. They were nice to me. They were concerned with my safety, because I was so young. Well the guy was brought to justice, because a couple of years later I was in King's Cross and I saw this guy. He was with a female and they were both very drunk. This female approached me and said, 'You sent my husband to prison', and started lashing out at me. And I legged it, I wasn't going to stay around. So that's how I found out. And then through some more information I found out the guy [had been] in prison . . .

Q. Did anything else like that happen to you when you were under fourteen?

A. No.

Unsatisfactory home circumstances often lead to placement in children's homes where there is a risk of sexual molestation either by fellow inmates – among whom there is usually a fair proportion of maladjusted or delinquent children – or by members of the staff. Work in these places inevitably attracts people with a sexual interest in the young and sex scandals are endemic. Incidents are apt to continue for a long time and involve many boys before complaints are made and taken seriously (Finkelhor *et al.*, 1989; Smith, 1987). A major scandal broke out recently in Canada when men who had once been pupils of a Catholic orphanage in Newfoundland began revealing that they had been frequently sexually assaulted as well as regularly beaten by teachers. Similar revelations soon emerged relating to other schools and dozens of priests were charged with sexual crimes committed years before (Taylor, 1989).

In four examples from the Streetwise sample abuse occurred after boys had been placed in children's homes on account of family problems.

Case 037. This informant, aged nineteen, recalled being attacked when he was thirteen by a youth of eighteen when both of them were resident in children's homes. His sexual interests at the time were 'half and half' towards boys and girls, and before the frightening and painful attack he had counted the offender as a friend. Although the attack did not occur within the confines of the children's home it was related to the circumstance of being in care:

Q. Tell me something about the rape.

A. Not really much to say. It's not the sort of thing I talk about.

Q. OK. You were thirteen?

A. Yea.

Q. And were you at school?

A. No, I was in a children's home, had just run away from the children's home . . . I was on my way back to it. It was freezing that night, so I was on my way back. I know the person who done it to me.

Q. You do?

A. Umm. One of the best mates I had, someone who'd fancied me since I was twelve . . .

Q. And you knew him?

A. Oh, Yea.

Q. Very well?

A. Yea.

Q. Did you know that he was interested in you?

A. Not really, just a bit, only what somebody told me.

Q. So what happened . . .?

A. At night, I thought I was gonna die when he jumped on me.

Q. Where did it happen, inside or were you outside or – ?

A. Outside. I nearly screamed my poor little lungs off.

Q. You did? It didn't help did it?

A. No, give me a sore throat. I lost my voice five minutes after I started screaming.

Q. And you say he was a good friend?

A. Yea.

Q. And did he stay your friend after that?

A. No. He moved on, moved to another country. He thought I'd grassed on him.

Q. He was in the children's home as well?

A. No. He was in another children's home. He thought I'd grassed on him and he went to another country.

Q. Were you badly hurt?

A. No, not really. I never told anyone.

Q. You didn't go to see anyone?

A. You're joking. I ain't gonna grass on him! Most people could grass on their own mother for rape, but I couldn't. I could on my own mother, but not on my mates.

Case 041. This twenty-year-old man had never developed the least interest in the opposite sex. He spent much of his childhood, following parental divorce, in children's homes and recalled an abusive incident when he was about twelve. He had felt some pleasurable sensation from the sexual manipulation, but it was nevertheless unwelcome and anxiety provoking.

Q. And have you ever been sexually interfered with in any way?

A. Do I have to answer it?

Q. I'd like you to if you can.

A. I'm not going to go into explicit detail, but yes, once.

Q. Can you give me some idea?

A. Well when I went back into care, the second time I went into care, I was staying in a short-term place, which had people coming in and out all the time, workers I mean. One of them, one night, touched me, didn't do anything fierce, but he fondled me.

Q. Did you like it or dislike it?

A. I didn't admit to liking it, but the funny thing was I felt good. I know it sounds crazy, 'cos I didn't want it to happen, but I can't deny it and say I felt bad, because I didn't. He doesn't know that and he never will know that.

Q. Did anything happen about that?

A. No. I told my social worker, but nothing ever came of it.

Q. If you liked it, why do you find it difficult to talk about it?

A. I don't know. It's something that I didn't want to remember. I didn't like the way it happened, but I can't say I felt bad, 'cos I didn't.

Q. You mean you liked it at the time?

A. Yea. Maybe that sounds sick, but I liked it. I didn't like him, but what he did to me was enjoyable.

Q. Did it affect you at all?

A. I dunno.

Q. Was it just purely sex you liked?

A. Yea. Plus that I'd never felt anything like it before.

Q. You hadn't had sex with anyone at that stage?

A. I was only a lad . . .

Q. Were you made to feel guilty . . .?

A. No, not guilty. I was scared, but I never felt guilty because I never did anything . . . I didn't know anything about sex then. I don't even think that I realised I was gay then. Maybe I did, maybe I didn't, I don't know. But it just shouldn't have happened.

Case 022. This man from a disrupted and unhappy family said he had always felt happier when away at children's homes or in boarding schools where most of his childhood had been spent, and had spent most of his childhood. He was sexually interested only in males. The incident happened when he was twelve:

I got raped by six prefects.

Q. How did that come about? What happened? What were the circumstances?

A. I just got raped.

Q. Was that at night or during the day?

A. During the evening.

Q. How did it start? How did you come in contact with these people?

A. They had their own dormitory, the prefects, and I was in one of the dormitories where the prefects are.

Q. You were in the dormitory where the prefects were?

A. Yes, 'cos they asked me if I wanted a game of cards or something like that.

Q. I see. So they invited you in.

A. Yea.

Q. And then they pounced on you?

A. Yea.

Q. And when you say they raped you, what do you mean, had anal intercourse?

A. Yes.

Q. They fucked you?

A. Yes.

Q. More than once?

A. All six.

Q. And what did you feel about that?

A. I felt bad.

Q. Yes. And did they injure you, hurt you in any way?

A. Yes, but I didn't say nothing.

Q. How did they hurt you, what happened?

A. They just pinned me down and just raped me.

Q. Yes.

A. Gagged me.

Q. So you couldn't cry out?

A. Emm.

Q. And did it cause bleeding?

A. Yea.

Q. And how long did the pain last after that?

A. It lasted a few days.

Q. But you didn't tell anybody about it?

A. No.

Q. Why didn't you tell anybody?

A. Because I was scared that they would beat me up.

Q. You were scared of the prefects?

A. Yes.

Only a minority of children's sexual encounters with adults are reported by them to parents or to police. Even violent incidents may remain concealed, as in the next example, also in a children's home.

Case 012. This boy was brutally attacked by a worker from the home where he was an inmate, but it came to light only when he became unwittingly involved in police inquiries.

Q. There was a scandal at this home? What was that?

A. Well there was me and this other kid and there was a voluntary worker there. He'd actually been with the vicar. He worked at this church, voluntary work. And the vicar knew, like, that he was a child molester, but he'd become a born-again Christian or something and wouldn't do it again. He recommended him for the work at the kids' home. The guy messed about with me and this other kid.

Q. And how old were you then?

A. Twelve.

Q. What did he do?

A. He screwed me and I had to have stitches. I don't know what he did to the other kid, he could have done something else.

Q. How did this come about? Was he friendly with you for some time before?

A. Yes. He used to take us out fishing and stuff like that.

Q. And when he took you fishing, did he play with you?

A. No. He didn't do anything then.

Q. So how did it come about?

A. One day he asked the staff if he could take me and this other kid out to his flat for dinner you know. The staff said 'Yes, OK'. And he got us drunk. I only got two cans and I was scalped, you know. That's when he done it.

Q. You were drunk?

A. Yea. He got this other kid to stand there with a polaroid and that. That's how he got caught.

Q. So he must have hurt you if you had to have stitches?

A. Yes.

Q. So when that happened, and he hurt you, what did you do?

A. Well I didn't say nothing, you know, at the time. But in a couple of days' time they searched his house for something else and they found out then.

Q. Why did the police go round?

A. He'd been messing around with other members of staff's kids as well.

Q. So somebody complained, not you, and the police went round?

A. Yea. They found photographs and the coppers came to see me. I was taken up to the hospital.

Q. And you had to have stitches. This must have been very painful?

A. It was.

Q. You were in pain before you went to the police station?

A. Yea, a lot.

Q. But in spite of that you didn't tell anybody. Why not?

A. I don't know. Was feeling ashamed you know.

The next six examples are of incidents involving family members or family friends. It is well known that sexual abuse can occur in families that seem orderly and respectable, but is probably more prevalent where there are evident deficiencies in parental care and supervision, as in several of these six cases.

Case 036. This boy's mother, a single parent, put him to sleep with a living-in bachelor uncle, now deceased, who took the advantage of him. When interviewed at the age of twenty-three he said of his sexuality: 'I'm more for women, but I can get turned on by guys in certain ways.' His childhood situation, and the confused, inhibited account of the indecencies, are typical of the sort of intra-familial sex abuse incidents that preoccupy social workers:

I mean I loved him and he brought me up . . . but I think he also interfered with me, so that's why I've got that extreme feeling with him. You know, I don't hate, well I part hate him and I part love him you know . . . I remember I used to sleep with him, he would like take me to bed and sort of play funny games say. I mean, now I've spoken to people about that later and they said, 'You've been interfered with.' I knew he was, he was a bit over-affectionate with me you know like, he'd smother me when he saw me, but I think now looking back on it that's love mixed up with sexual attraction. That's how I would see it. I never knew him to have a woman friend or what not, he seemed very much a loner. So it's very hard to surmise what the scene was.

Q. How old were you when that started?

A. Oh, about – er – I don't know, eight, nine, ten perhaps.

Q. OK. And how long did it go on for?

A. Oh, a couple of years I think, yea, something like that.

Q. It definitely stopped?

A. Yea, I think it – well he had ways of mucking about you know, but after [age] twelve it sort of stopped. He'd give me the odd cuddle and the odd kiss now and again, you know what I mean, in an over-affectionate manner.

Q. Your mother never knew anything about this?

A. I think my mother did know about it . . .

Q. Did you like it, dislike it?

A. Oh, I disliked it, I disliked it.

Q. Always?

A. Umm. I think I might have liked it sometimes, 'cos it was a form of affection . . .

Q. So it was mainly playing about?

A. Yea, touching.

Q. Anything as close as sucking?

A. I don't know, that might have happened. I don't think I done it, but he might have done it to me, I'm not sure.

This man was at pains to explain 'I want to be objective, I don't want to sort of say "Oh I was interfered with, that's why I'm fucked up now" and have something to blame it on. I realise whatever state I'm in now is partly my own fault . . .'

Case 003. This was the only example reported of abuse by a female. He had grown up in a rough neighbourhood and in an unhappy home where both parents were drunkards. At twenty-one he counted himself as heterosexual, although he was also enjoying sex with a young man his own age:

Q. When you were young, say under fourteen, did anyone ever involve you in sex that you didn't want, someting against your wishes?

A. Well – er – [pause] in a way. But I suppose in a way I was willing, see what I mean. It was a woman. It was a friend of my Aunty's. It was when I was thirteen. And she just came on, you know what I mean. At first I tried to pull away and all that, so she did it against my will at first, but then afterwards I just –

Q. What did she actually do?

A. She started feeling me and touching me and putting my hand down her. At first it wasn't in my mind, I hadn't done anything like that before.

A. Did she make you come, or didn't it get that far?

Q. Well yes, because we started making love you see, that was when I was beginning to – I enjoyed it in a way, but at first I didn't want to.

Q. Are you talking about just one incident, or did she –?

A. Three or four times she did it.

Q. And eventually she got you to have intercourse?

A. Yes.

Q. How old would she have been?

A. She was thirty-one.

Case 047. Deserted by his mother during his infancy he was left with a lone father who had a 'drink problem'. Originally attracted to girls, he said he was now turned on by males and females 'about the same'. When aged about eleven, his father having gone out for the evening with his future stepmother, he was left with a male baby sitter who molested him:

Q. Was it someone you knew?
A. Yeah, he was a good friend of me dad's. My dad said would he mind watching me. Well it was me more than anything, 'cos my sister had gone out, I think with some friends, and she was staying round her friend's. I was on the settee watching the telly, if I remember rightly, and he come over and put his arm around me and that and tried touching me up. I just ran out of the house and went over to a friend's place and I stayed there about an hour and a half and took me friend back to our house with us. Dad was a bit upset. He wanted to know why I said a friend could stay. I just said that I asked Gary, who was looking after us, and that and he said it was OK. So I never really told. Me dad still don't know.

Case 019. He had been placed in a residential school from nine to fourteen on account of truancy and running away from a home where he was often beaten. He declared himself basically heterosexual with only occasional interest in males. He was twelve and at home for holidays at the time.

Q. Tell me about it, what happened?
A. Just that I was in bed and a friend of my father's was staying in the house.
Q. And what happened?
A. He just started feeling me up and everything, so –
Q. He came into the room?
A. He was staying in their room. I woke up and he was in my bed.
Q. And what happened then?
A. I just got out of bed and walked off.
Q. Did you tell anybody about it?
A. No.
Q. Why not?
A. Didn't want to.
Q. Why?
A. I don't know.
Q. Were you ashamed of what happened or something?
A. Yes.
Q. Anyway, you didn't like it?
A. I didn't like it, no.

Case 051. This man, flamboyantly 'camp' in manner and speech, who had been noticeably effeminate as a boy, gave dramatic descriptions of his experiences. His parents divorced when he was seven and his mother had had two more husbands since, one of whom was said to have tried to rape his sister. He related two incidents, the second one at his parental home.

Q. Tell me about it.
A. When I was eleven I was raped, when I was thirteen I was raped, when

I was fifteen I was raped. I came to London and I've been raped two and a half times in London.

Q. Tell me about when you were eleven.

A. There was a geezer that my mother knew. I did not want to go to school and I met him down the shops. I was like trailing down the shops so I did not have to go to school. So he goes to me, 'Come back.' I thought, 'Why not? My mother knows him, he's all right, a sweet geezer.' I was stupid as well and I went back. He just sat there and he was talking to me. He was going on, 'Do you know I'm homosexual?' And I was going, 'What's that?' 'It's that I like men.' And I was going on, 'That's nice,' and really stupid things like that. And he just started going on, 'I like boys as well.' And I was sitting there thinking, 'Really, that is nice for him.' And I was not thinking anything about it, do you know what I mean, even when it was happening. I was not thinking anything. I was still thinking, 'I wonder what he is doing.' You know, to me that was just like somebody playing around.

Q. Sure, you were very young. What did he actually do to you?

A. He had sex with me. He tied me up to the table and had sex with me.

Q. Was it a horrible experience?

A. To an extent, yes, when I realised what was actually happening. Because what really degraded me was the fact that he had done it and he let me go. He said, 'Go on, get to school.' That was the worst part, he just told me to get to school after what had happened. And that was the very first time it had happened to me.

Q. Did you ever tell anyone?

A. I told my brother. The guy does not exist any more, not in England. My brother got a couple of his mates and went around there and bashed him up badly.

Q. How long after?

A. A year or so later I told him. We were both drunk and I was depressed and we were being buddy buddy and I told him who it was. He hated him anyway, it gave him an excuse to hit him, and that was it.

Q. And when you were thirteen –?

A. When I was thirteen some blokes stayed in my mother's house. They were friends of my brother and they were supposed to be straight. As far as I knew they were straight. I was not supposed to come back for another two days, because I was on holiday, but I came back two days early. Well I usually trot around – if I am in my house I could not give a fuck – I mean I walk round without anything on. I was walking around with a short dressing gown that came up to there [upper thigh]. My mother has got some photos of me, loads and loads of photos, and they were looking through the albums. They had gone through the private album and there was pictures of me, like nude, with women's clothes and make up, all sorts of things, and they were saying I looked good as a woman. And I was thinking, 'That is nice.' Downstairs they were talking to me and they started, 'It would be nice to be gay.' I thought, 'I'm off to bed.' So I goes upstairs and they had gone upstairs. I did not think anything of it, I just thought, 'I want to go to sleep.' And they came in, two of them, one held me down and the other had sex with me. But I was still too stupid to think about it, you know what I mean, but they did actually regret it later on, what they had done. It was just because I looked like a woman, because they were actually straight, two of them were married and the other was going out with a friend of my sister's.

Q. And they were what, in their twenties?

A. They would be about nineteen, twenty and twenty-two.
Q. Did you see a lot of them after?
A. Yes, I still see them. I mean I did not hold it against them because, actually – not being egotistical – that happens a lot. Well not a lot, but a lot of blokes would like to attack me, but don't dare. It's because of what I look like. I look like a slag basically.

Case 052. This seventeen-year-old skinhead, who insisted he was predominantly heterosexual, remembered an incident at twelve years of age with a man of about forty-two who was known to the family. 'He used to take me places, Bradford, sometimes down to London.'

Q. So he was a friend?
A. Yes, till he assaulted me . . . making me play about with him.
Q. Making you? How did he make you?
A. Threatened.
Q. With what?
A. That he'd harm me.
Q. What did he want you to do?
A. Just play about with him.
Q. He made you masturbate him?
A. Yea.
Q. And did he wank you too?
A. Yea.
Q. And did you come at that time?
A. No, I didn't want to know anything about it.
Q. You weren't interested at all?
A. No.

The last three examples are of boys whose experiences arose from casual encounters with outsiders. All three were in unhappy home conditions which may have meant that they spent long, unsupervised periods wandering about, a factor identified by West and Woodhouse (1990, p. 89) as being associated with increased risk of sexual encounters with adults.

Case 023. Originally attracted to girls, he said he was now mostly turned on by males. The incident happened at age thirteen, roughly the time his parental home broke up when his father was imprisoned for incest with his sister.

I was raped in the park. I went to the toilet and I was having a piss and one guy, he started playing around with me. And I said, 'Don't do that.'
Q. Go on, what happened?
A. He virtually – do you want me to go right into detail – he started playing with me and then he virtually forced me over the toilet.
Q. Did he have anal intercourse, fuck you?
A. Yes.
Q. And did that hurt you at the time?
A. Yes.

Q. And what happened then?

A. I reported it to the police after ... The police found out that he had a criminal record and was messing about ... I didn't have to go to court, the police were watching his moves ...

Q. They identified him from your description?

A. Yes.

Q. Were you badly hurt?

A. Not badly.

Q. Did you have to go to a doctor?

A. Yes.

Case 001. This tough, rebellious skinhead from Belfast, with a long criminal record, had spent much of his boyhood in residential establishments, his parents having declared him 'beyond control'. He classed himself as 'a gay man' who was also interested in females.

I must have been, I think, about eight.

Q. What happened?

A. I was in a park and some man just, like, dragged me in the toilet and started playing with himself and started playing around with me.

Q. You mean rubbing your genitals?

A. Yes.

Q. And what happened?

A. I ran.

Q. You ran away?

A. I surely ran away.

Q. What did you feel about it then?

A. Disgust.

Q. Did you tell anyone?

A. No.

Q. Why didn't you?

A. Too scared, especially of my parents – couldn't. They would have thought I was lying or something.

Case 010. This chronic drunkard, who lived largely by begging, gave a confused account. He had been in care from an early age following his parents' separation. He described an incident in a bus when he was eight and a man sitting next to him was leaning over with an arm round him. He 'got my pants down' and was 'playing with me' when 'my mother', who was on the bus, came around with some tea. She saw what was happening and told the driver. The police were called but the man had gone by the time they arrived.

*

In an effort to produce as complete a picture as possible extracts have been included from every case in which child molestation was reported. They provide no evidence for the notion that many men take to prostitution as a result of early homosexual molestation. The young men themselves did not suggest such a connection. Many were homosexuals and homosexually disposed boys may attract or seek out sexual experiences with men, but the disagreeable, coercive or violent incidents described in answer to the question about 'unwanted' sexual contacts seemed to bear little relation to the nature of their own sexuality. If there is any connection with sexual orientation it is that young men who consider themselves heterosexual may be more prone to label any early homosexual encounters with adults as having been abusive (West and Woodhouse, 1990, p. 120). In his Canadian study of young male street prostitutes Visano (1987, p. 151) noted that boys defining themselves as heterosexuals reported more early sexual encounters of a painful or violent character. The theory that boys bribed to provide sex learn from it the tricks of the prostitution trade likewise gained no support from these histories. Rewarding children for sex was exceptional.

Early homosexual incidents, usually with peers, where boys were willing participants, were not systematically explored. It was obvious, however, that the homosexually identified men recalled more of these experiences and that prior homosexual inclinations had facilitated entry into prostitution by those disposed to take such a step. As Visano (1987, p. 150) noted, 'A boy with a previously active sex life does not necessarily slide into this career', but prior sexual experience may 'offer a better appreciation of what to expect in delivering sex to clients' and for some 'prostitution facilitates a resolution of identity crisis'. However, so long as all early sexual experience is not equated with 'abuse', these observations cannot be used in support of the simplistic view that sexual abuse of young boys is in itself a cause of entry into prostitution.

The most likely explanation of the high incidence of unwanted child sexual molestation is that it is a secondary feature of the sort of backgrounds from which most street workers come. The only evidence located in other surveys to suggest that street prostitutes suffer a higher incidence of sex abuse than others from similar backgrounds who are not prostitutes comes from Janus *et al.* (1984, p. 143). They assert that what distinguished male prostitutes 'from male street youths not involved in prostitution was the incidence of coercive sexual activity at an early age'. In the absence of precise figures, or a controlled comparison to show that the backgrounds of the two categories of street youths really were similar, the basis for such a bold assertion seems very flimsy. A later publication from these researchers concerning adolescent runaways (Janus *et al.*, 1987) throws no further light on the matter.

As was extensively documented in Chapter 2, a majority of the Streetwise sample had experienced childhood adversity, neglect or emotionally conflicting relationships with parent figures, backgrounds that account for a high incidence of child sexual abuse. In a number of instances exposure to sexual molestation was clearly a secondary consequence of such circumstances. By provoking running away, by placements away from home and by inadequate supervision boys were put into situations of risk. The isolated and aversive sexual incidents from the distant past that had mostly occurred in the context of multiple deprivation seemed less important landmarks on the road to prostitution than more immediate factors, such as lack of family support, lack of work training, and lack of accommodation. Rather than operating as a prime cause of taking to prostitution, as some commentators suggest, abusive sexual experiences in boyhood are more likely merely symptoms of the more generalised social malaise that helps to propel some young men into street prostitution.

5
The Drift into Homelessness

Progress up the conventional ladder, beginning with scholastic achievement, progressing through work training and employment and leading to financial independence and the acquisition of secure living space was little in evidence among the street-worker sample. In most cases a dropping out process began at school and ended in homelessness. For most of the clients of Streetwise Youth, finding accommodation was their most pressing need and the one for which they most often sought the organisation's help.

Under English law attendance at school is compulsory up to the age of sixteen, after which young people are expected to be either in continuing education – for which grants are available to those with the necessary qualifications to obtain a place – or else to attend a 'career office' and register as being available for work or for a place on a youth training scheme. Needless to say, worthwhile jobs are unlikely to be on offer to those without scholastic attainments and jobs of any kind are less readily available in areas of high unemployment.

Since September 1988, when new legislation came into force, able-bodied young persons under the age of eighteen have been denied the right to state subsistence – now called 'income support'. This is because a place on a youth training scheme, which provides a small living allowance, is supposed to be guaranteed to everyone. In practice, according to Shelter, a charity concerned with the homeless, many teenagers are unable to get onto a scheme but still cannot get any welfare support (*Observer*, 26 March 1989). Exceptions are made to allow support to be given temporarily, for about three months, to those waiting for a job or training placement who are unable to stay in the parental home. To qualify they have to show that they have no living parent or acting parent, that they have recently been in care, or that in their own home they are at risk of physical or sexual abuse.

One can easily see how young people from the sort of backgrounds prevalent among the street-worker sample fall outside the rigid rules of state welfare and become homeless. Voluntary absence from unhappy home circumstances does not entitle the young person to state support. Even if he is demonstrably without a viable parental home the support he

52

receives falls short of what is generally necessary to secure accommodation, especially in London. The standard weekly allowance on 'income support' or on youth training is less than what a single, brief sexual encounter with a punter on the street will produce. Even if he qualifies for it he cannot make a claim for income support if he lacks proof of identity in the shape of a birth certificate or medical card. Even if he can get this documentation out of the home he has left he has no address to which it can be sent. Since income support, if he gets it, is payable in arrears, he is in no position to put down the advance demanded by those who let rooms or provide bed-and-breakfast accommodation. There is now a discretionary Crisis Loan system which one might think could be used to get young people off the street, but if they have no official source of income from which to make repayments they are likely to be refused. According to one survey, young, single homeless are considered 'low priority' for help from the social fund. 'Many local authority offices also appear to consider any rent-in-advance as a low priority item' (National Association of Citizens Advice Bureaux, 1990, p. 20). If he has no fixed address, employers, whether in youth training schemes or otherwise, are unlikely to accept him. Thus, as regards securing work and accommodation, it is easy for the unattached, unsupported adolescent to find himself in a 'Catch 22' situation.

Apart from the statutory limitations on benifits for rootless, young, single men, the process of making a claim is stressful, with the likelihood of endless waiting and referrals back and forth from one office to another without result. Brendan O'Mahony (1988, p. 33) of Barnardos comments that 'these offices are often described as violent places where the young homeless are treated as little better than common criminals asking for that which they are not entitled to'. There are innumerable complaints of inconsistency, rudeness and obstruction and applicants are told repeatedly to leave London and 'go home'. No local authority wants to be landed with the cost of supporting unwanted indigents from other areas. In any event, young, unemployed, single males have very low priority for housing in comparison with groups for which local authorities have some statutory obligation to provide shelter. It is always the least educated, least fluent, least prepossessing (in other words those from the kind of disadvantaged backgrounds prevalent in the Streetwise sample) who are least able to cope with the bureaucracy, who fall foul of the system and turn to activities like begging, theft and prostitution as seemingly their only options.

A recent worrying increase in the number of young homeless persons found begging in London and prosecuted under the Vagrancy Act 1824 has been commented on by the National Association of Probation Officers (*Guardian*, 3 Jan. 1990). The prostitution option is always present. A survey of the clients of Centre Point, a voluntary organisation that provides temporary accommodation for young homeless in London, found that 'one in three had been approached to become involved in prostitution since they came to central London' (Randall, 1989, p. 4; Hardwick, 1990).

In keeping with the unhappy and disrupted upbringings reported by so many among the streetboy sample, poor performance in school and an unsatisfactory work record subsequently was the general rule. A few had attended special schools on account of learning difficulties and a small minority, perhaps 8 per cent, gave dull or confused responses to questions during interviews and may have been of low intelligence. Otherwise all were fluent and some gave impresssively vivid accounts of their experiences and feelings. Intellectual impairment was not the explanation for their lack of success.

A majority, 70 per cent, had left school with no examination qualifications whatsoever. Truanting was described by 66 per cent, 36 per cent admitting to persistent truancy. Asked whether they thought they had been above, below or about average at school lessons, 42 per cent rated themselves 'below'. Lack of motivation and disciplinary confrontations seemed to have been the main reasons for these trends.

After leaving school some found placements on youth training schemes, but often gave them up after relatively short periods. A minority undertook college or apprentice training in things like catering or hairdressing, but few completed the training or were making use of it currently. At the time they were interviewed, 84 per cent were without any employment other than prostitution and 34 per cent had never had a full-time job. Asked at interview where they were living, it emerged that few had a stable place of residence. Some had spent the night before out of doors, relieved in some cases by periods spent in late night cafés or on the underground trains. Many were in unauthorised squats or imposing on friends as non-paying guests. Some were in hostels that provided only temporary accommodation. Hostels were often intensely disliked and regarded as a last resort. A worker had noted on the file of *Case 037*, for example: 'He's living from place to place, punter to punter, but would rather do that than seek hostel accommodation.' Restrictions on their liberty imposed by hostel regulations were a common reason for this dislike. Another reason was anxiety about propinquity with peers, especially where rooms are shared, since any revelation of their rent-boy status would arouse prevalent anti-gay feelings. Some were in short-lived cohabitations with boyfriends or girlfriends. Homelessness, with its consequential difficulties in keeping clean, changing clothes and paying for meals out of doors meant that the Day Centre's washing facilities and free meals were important to many in the sample. Because the living arrangements described were so precarious and changeable it was difficult to put an exact figure on the proportion who might be described as 'homeless', but some 90 per cent had a housing problem of one kind or another.

The following examples illustrate the drift from disaffected schoolboy to homeless street worker that was typical of a substantial proportion of the sample:

Case 004 left school in Ireland at fourteen and a half with no qualifications. Left for London at fifteen 'to get away and see the world, see what I was missing'. Spent six months in care. No further training. Has had several unskilled jobs, portering, washing up, etc., but was now twenty-one, unemployed and homeless.

Q. What was the last job you had?
A. A porter.
Q. That was for how long?
A. That was about four months, one of the longest.
Q. Have you walked out of jobs a lot?
A. Well I walked out of that one because they wanted me to do too many hours. I usually leave the job.
Q. Why?
A. Because I always turn around and get fed up with the work, 'cos it's like washing up and that . . .
Q. Do you have a regular place to stay?
A. No, I don't live anywhere.
Q. So where did you spend last night?
A. At a friend's.
Q. Was that a punter?
A. Well it was just a friend, like.
Q. Have you had anywhere regular to stay during the last six months?
A. No. I ain't, 'cos I like went home with a punter for a month, I was staying there.

Case 018. This eighteen-year-old 'punk' had attended 'a school for people with deprived education, people who had missed education'. He 'wasn't too good' at lessons and did not pass any exams. He left at fifteen and said he had been on the run from care authorities and living on the streets ever since. He had never had a job. The night before the interview he spent 'in a sort of squat' and before that 'just staying where I could'.

Case 006. He left school at sixteen after failing all his O' level exams and has had no further training. He has had 'numerous' jobs, mostly temporary casual work for a few days at a time. The longest job he had was as a barman for four months. He had stayed in his last job six weeks.

Q. When was that?
A. Four weeks ago.
Q. And how did it come to an end?
A. Because I was in it with my boyfriend and we had an argument and I walked out.

He had been staying recently with various friends, but was hoping to move into a flat owned by someone who would be away a large part of the time. A note in the Streetwise files a few days later recorded that his 'housing plans seem to have fallen through. Realised today that he is homeless and penniless and without an identity [document] which he needs to sign on. Needs money for this, £5.50 for a Scottish birth certificate.'

Case 030

Q. Did you run away from school?

A. Yea, I was never there . . . On my sixteenth birthday I left school. I got on YTS . . .

Q. How long were you on YTS?

A. The first one was a week, the second one was two days, the third was three hours [laughs].

He explained that he had had many jobs as barman, waiter etc., but they usually lasted no more than a week or two. His flamboyantly camp behaviour on occasion may have been responsible. He had no place of his own but was being temporarily accommodated by a girlfriend.

Case 033

Q. How did you get on with [school] lessons?

A. Umm. Not too well . . .

Q. And you started playing truant . . .?

A. In the last year.

Q. Did you do that a lot?

A. Yeh.

Q. Did you pass any exams?

A. No.

Q. Have you been on a YTS scheme?

A. No.

Q. Have you ever been in work ?

A. Done messenger work, that's only temporary, warehouse work, but I don't like it all that much.

Q. And are you in full-time or part-time work at the moment?

A. No, I'm unemployed . . .

Q. Have you a regular place to stay at the moment?

A. Um, I stay all over the place.

Q. So where, for example, did you stay last night?

A. Centre Point [hostel].

Q. How long have you been there?

A. It was me first night there.

Q. How long can you stay there?

A. They said two weeks, and after that I have to move.

Q. And where were you staying before?

A. I usually stay with me parents, but we don't get on too well.

Q. So you have been staying in a lot of different places in the last six months?

A. About ten different places I'd say.

Case 044

>   Q. Did you like school?
>   A. No.
>   Q. Why was that?
>   A. I was a bit of a rebel, the discipline and everything. If someone told me
>   to do something then I just wouldn't want to know.
>   Q. How did you get on with lessons . . . ?
>   A. I could do them, but I didn't do them.
>   Q. I see. Did you pass any exams?
>   A. I didn't turn up for them.

On leaving school at sixteen he tried working as a waiter on a YTS scheme, but after two months left that to go into college. He was there for two months but was soon bored. He had left home and that made it awkward to continue attending. He had had a number of jobs in waiting and bar work, but 'I walked out of most of my jobs' and the longest time he has ever kept a job was about three months. He was at present unemployed and homeless and prior to being interviewed he had been out on the streets all night unsuccessfully looking for a punter.

Case 047

>   Q. Did you like school?
>   A. No, not really. I just thought it was a waste of time, 'cos, like, when I
>   was younger I was always one minute at one school, the next minute I was
>   at another school. Through going in and out of children's homes and that
>   sort of thing my school life was always getting interrupted really.

Nevertheless, he did 'not too badly' at lessons, but he 'walked out' when he was fifteen without taking any exams. He got a job as a kitchen porter, but gave it up after three months to go to stay temporarily with his mother. He has had only two jobs since, one for two months and the other for two weeks, from both of which he was dismissed. For the past three years he has had no job. He was staying in a bed-and-breakfast hotel, paid by state income support.

In the cases just cited keeping a job was as much a problem, if not a worse problem, than finding one. This was also evident in the cases of young men who had had the opportunity of work training but were not benefiting from it:

Case 014

>   Q. How old were you when you left school?
>   A. Sixteen.
>   Q. Since leaving school have you attended any sort of night school or done
>   any special courses?
>   A. I have done catering courses at X College.
>   Q. And did you get some sort of certificate from that?

A. I got City and Guilds.

Q. Was that a residential course?

A. Yes.

Q. And what age were you then?

A. Seventeen.

Q. So you finished when you were seventeen?

A. Well I only done one year, it was a two-year course, but I only done one year.

Q. Why was that?

A. Because I moved out to London.

In fact he moved to London and joined the rent scene, since when he has had only short-term jobs. Now, at eighteen, he is unemployed and staying in bed-and-breakfast accommodation paid by social security. Before that he was 'sleeping rough on the street'.

Case 041 left school at sixteen. Now twenty, he was without a place to live and staying 'on and off' in a friend's one-bedroom flat. He had trained in catering at a college and then worked in a catering job at a London club. 'Then I gave up catering and just started doing bar work. I've had a couple of bar jobs, but that's about all . . .'

Q. Why did you leave?

A. I wanted to get out of catering.

Q. Did you walk out or give in your notice?

A. No, in the end I got the sack, because I wasn't interested any more my work just collapsed.

Q. And the bar jobs, why did you leave those?

A. Well the Lion I got sacked from because I took a day off and didn't phone in. The other one I left. That was when they hadn't paid me, so I didn't go back.

Now he had no job and was dependent on prostitution. 'I'm homeless, ain't I. I lost my job and it's the only way I know of making it.'

Most of the cases cited might be regarded as unhappy social failures. The most striking exception was one mentioned earlier as having come from an unusually supportive background:

Case 031. This man, who came from an apparently contented and secure family background, was unusual also in having a substantial commitment to legitimate work and fairly stable living circumstances. He was less dependent than most upon the rent business. He had rarely been unemployed, never been dismissed, and was currently and for the last three years doing part-time evening work for an agency that supplied security services at functions. He also did occasional driving jobs during the day. He was not 'signing on' for any welfare benefits. He had been cohabiting for two and a half years, but did not much like the fact that the council flat where they were living with their baby was in the woman's name. He would like it better if the situation were 'reversed and it was mine'. But, 'I don't want to ask my father for money. I'd probably get it, but I wouldn't want to have to ask.' He was not dependent on money from punters. He had a 'sugar daddy' who lent him money when he needed it. But, 'If my money's a bit low during the day I'll say "Yeh, all right then, let's have a go", but I don't go out of my way looking for a punter these days.' He meets people in bars, never on the streets. 'I wouldn't like to get myself nicked for importuning or anything.'

Notwithstanding the occasional exception, most of the sample were in chronic and continuing social difficulties for which their engagement in prostitution had provided no satisfactory solution. It seemed that in many cases temperamental instability had prevented them from making use of such opportunities as came their way. One indication of this was the observation that when hostel accommodation was secured for the homeless many of them left or were told to go after the first few days. The case of 'Harry', taken more or less at random from the Streetwise files, was fairly typical. Having been found a hostel he was kicked out of it within a week and a half and was sleeping at night in a British Rail carriage. He soon found a 'sugar daddy', however, and returned to the Day Centre with all new clothes. The Annual Report of the organisation (Streetwise Youth, 1990) in fact refers to their clients' frequent and recurrent failure to maintain the places found for them through their inability to conform to the rules and expectations of the hostels.

A tendency to leave their jobs impulsively was another factor in preventing some of these young men from achieving a more settled life style:

Case 022. This man had had a substantial period away from the rent scene working in a provincial town. Becoming bored, he obtained a job in London, but soon 'walked out' because he 'didn't get on with the manageress'.

Q. And having walked out you then went back on the game?
A. Well I didn't go straight away, but I did after, because I had nowhere to live. I got chucked out of my place because I had no income to pay the rent.
Q. And went back on the game?
A. I had to do it to survive, because social security wouldn't help me because I was on the street, no fixed abode, so they didn't give me any emergency money or anything. They just pushed me around here, there and everywhere. I didn't have no help.
Q. So you've been dependent on punters for the past year?
A. Well the last six months.
Q. And now you have this importuning charge. Do you have a solicitor?
A. Yes.

*

The very real difficulties in the way of finding jobs and accommodation do not fully account for the street workers' continuing problems. Two contrasting letters in the *Independent* (16 Jan. 1990) highlighted a paradox. The first (from D. Devore) compared favourably the wages on offer for cleaners, cashiers, waiters, kitchen porters and bar staff with the advertised costs of cheap accommodation. Considering that some of these jobs provided free meals, the writer concluded that 'one should look for reasons other than lack of work or affordable accommodation to explain why people sleep on the streets'. The second letter (from M. O'Donovan) calculated a take-home pay of £78 for a 40-hour week at a restaurant job, which he did not consider 'a living wage'. In practice, what may appear just about adequate for some may not be enough for others. The ability to survive on very low wages requires skills – home cooking and budgeting for example – which many in the sample did not possess. Finding jobs, even at the lowest level, is more difficult for those with no experience and no qualifications and still more so for those 'on the run'. But, as their own accounts show, keeping jobs and accommodation was as big a problem for these young men as was finding them in the first place.

The factors that so far stand out as influencing these men's precarious lifestyles and their choice of street prostitution as a means of supporting themselves include absence of family backing, homelessness, temperamental difficulties, lack of training, employment options limited to boring and low-paid work and the presence of the rent scene as a deceptively easy option, especially for those of homosexual or bisexual orientation.

6

Entry into Prostitution

Questioning the young men about how and when they first began to trade in sex revealed much about their varied circumstances and declared motives and showed the limited applicability and over-simple nature of many popular notions about male street workers. The idea that they were forced by desperate need and had no other choice was one supported by many of their accounts. A majority (80 per cent) said that they had first resorted to prostitution when they were either very short or, more often, desperately short of money, sometimes to the extent of having no access otherwise to food or shelter. The following are typical examples in which lack of money was said to have prompted the decision to begin prostitution, although it is apparent that other influences, such as knowledge, opportunity and inclination, must also have played a part.

Case 042

I got picked up and I went back. He actually offered me money. At the time I hadn't done anything like that before. I didn't know what he was after. I took the money because I was homeless, and I went with him.

Q. You were still eighteen then?
A. Coming up to nineteen.
Q. And this was the first time you got money for sex, was it?
A. Yes.
Q. How did he come to pick you up?
A. It was in the daytime. I was standing up the back of the station as we come up the steps talking.
Q. How old was he, roughly?
A. In his thirties.
Q. And what sort of sex happened? You didn't fuck him or he fuck you?
A. Oh, yea. He fucked me.
Q. He did. And how did you feel about that, that first time? Did you enjoy it, or indifferent, or dislike it, how was it?
A. I didn't really enjoy it, no.
Q. So you were indifferent?
A. Yes, I just needed the money.
Q. Did you come yourself, did it excite you, make you come?
A. Yea.
Q. So how did you first learn about getting money for sex?

A. I met other people that were on the game. I used to sort of slag them off till I realised how much they were getting.

Q. So you decided it was a good way of making money?

A. Yes, especially because I was homeless.

Q. So the reason for doing it was that you were really short of money?

A. Yea, well, I wasn't getting the DHSS because I was staying at Centre Point [hostel] . . ..

Q. That first time you got money for sex, were you on the run from anything?

A. No, I wasn't . . ..

Q. Why had you come to London, what was the reason?

A. I was made redundant from my job. I didn't get on with my mother. I was more or less told that if I didn't find work I'd got to leave.

Q. And so you came to London looking for work, did you?

A. It was the obvious place to come.

Case 007

Q. How old were you the first time you got money for sex?

A. I was seventeen, seventeen and a half. When I left home I tried to stick it out, not doing anything like prostitution. Because I'd heard about it you know, the meat rack and all this lot. I knew someone who was a prostitute . . . He told me about it. But I met a person on a train, you know, on a tube station, who said, 'Do you want to come back with me and I'll give you 35 quid for an easy time?' So I couldn't refuse it you know.

Case 050

Q. What age were you when you first went on the game?

A. About eighteen.

Q. Can you tell me about the first time, can you remember?

A. Well it was in Brighton. Me and my friend used to go down under the pier, like it's easy to pick up trade [i.e. sex] down there. After the pubs close all goes down there for a piddle, so we goes down there and some bloke was really pestering me. I told him, 'Fuck off, you can't afford it', or something, and he goes 'How much?' I didn't realise there were rent boys down there. I thought, 'Wait a minute, if I am going to get some money I will do it.' So when he says, 'How much?' I said £25 and then I gave him a blow job in his car. And he said to me that he had a £50 note and 'If you give me your telephone number I'll give you it all'. I ran back to my friend and I told him I could not believe it. He said, 'You want to go up to London if you want to do that.' I said, 'Oh!'

Q. How much later was it that you came to London?

A. About a week, packed my bags and went.

Q. Did you know about the rent scene?

A. No, I didn't. I knew about rent boys and all that lot, but I always thought it was like dirty skinheads and things like that.

Q. And so it was just really by chance that it happened?

A. Yes.

Q. You were not desperate for money or anything?

A. At the time I had just lost my job and I didn't really have any money, and I weren't signing on, so I come up to London with no money and just started doing it . . .

Q. That first time in Brighton, what happened, you just gave him a blow job?

A. Yea.

Q. Did he give you one?

A. No.

Q. Did you enjoy it?

A. In a way I did, because he weren't bad looking. But he was a bit snobby, and I don't like snobby blokes.

Q. How old would he have been?

A. About thirty.

Q. So you came up to London and how did you find out about –?

A. I didn't know. No one mentioned the Dilly, they just said London. I knew that prostitutes was in King's Cross because of something in the paper, so I came up to King's Cross and I was just sitting there on my suitcase watching all these prostitutes at work.

Q. Was this women or men?

A. Women. And I just went up to one of them and asked 'Do you know of anyone who could use me?' They said you want to go down the Dilly. By the time I walked down to Piccadilly Circus it was quite late and there was no one about apart from one boy walking around. So I was watching him and started talking to him and then I went back to his house and stayed there for a while. Then we started working together and we started meeting poeple and the rest is history . . ..

Q. OK. Just to make it clear, that first time, were you on the run then from police or social security?

A. I was not actually on the run, but there was a court case going on that I should have attended, but I didn't really bother about it.

Coming to London for work, but not finding it, and being without money was a common prelude to accepting a proposal to provide paid sex, as in the following examples:

Case 008

Q. How long have you been on the rent scene?

A. Three weeks after I came down to London. [At sixteen.]

Q. And why did you come to London?

A. To look for a job. I couldn't get a place to sleep 'cos I didn't have enough money. Couldn't get a job, so couldn't get enough money for a place to stay, vicious circle.

Q. So what happened, how did you end up on the rent scene?

A. One day, it was summer, I was in Leicester Square and this bloke just walked up to me and goes, 'Do you fancy earning yourself fifteen quid?' So I thought, 'Sod it, why not!' 'What have I got to do?' And he told me. I was a bit disgusted, but I thought, 'Money is money, isn't it'.

Q. So what did he want?

A. Just a quick hand job . . .

Q. Had you known what was going on before?

A. Yeh, I knew what was going on, but I never thought it would happen to me. The money felt good at the end of it.

Case 026. At nineteen he left a job in Ireland and came to London. Being gay and having found no work or accommodation he managed 'by sleeping with people, just meeting people in pubs and clubs', not for money 'just purely staying the night with somebody'. Then, when he was in a hamburger bar at Piccadilly, he got talking to a young man who turned out to be a rent boy and who told him about the scene.

Q. And what made you try it out?
A. 'Cos I needed the money, I didn't have anywhere to live . . .
Q. And you met somebody in Piccadilly, or did they come up to you?
A. They came up to me.
Q. And what sort of sex happened that first time?
A. Just ordinary sex.
Q. Do you mean that he fucked you or you fucked him?
A. No, there was none of that.
Q. Sucking?
A. Yes.
Q. He sucked you and you him?
A. Yes.
Q. How old a man was he, that first time?
A. I'd say he was about forty-four.
Q. And did you come yourself with him?
A. Yes.
Q. And did you enjoy it a lot?
A. Yes . . .
Q. Now, after that, did you carry on being a rent boy?
A. I carried on. [In fact he was arrested twice for importuning.]

These examples have been cited at some length because they show that having no money is in itself a reflection of other circumstances, notably lack of family support, a factor considered in the previous chapter. Contrary to a common belief, the likely time for introduction to prostitution is not during schooldays, as a result of encounters with an adult paedophile, but in later years when youths are expected to start providing for themselves. The first remembered prostitution transaction most often took place after leaving school and/or home when youths were trying to make their way independently without work training, family support or a proper place to live. Most were aged fifteen to eighteen at the time (28 per cent were fifteen or sixteen; 50 per cent were seventeen or eighteen), a few were younger (12 per cent) or older (10 per cent). The youngest was eleven. Most (70 per cent) came from out of London and most (74 per cent) of those who did first prostituted themselves shortly after arriving in the metropolis.

That the most likely time for entry into the business is the late teens has been noted in other studies. Lowman (1989), reporting on a sample of male street prostitutes in Vancouver, found that the average age when they first 'turned a trick' was fifteen and a half. Judith Ennew (1986, p. 81) remarks that 'a distinction must be drawn between pre-pubertal child prostitutes and post-pubertal minors who are involved in prostitution'. There is a strong preference for young adults and adolescents among the clients of both male and female prostitutes, but the market for children is limited to those with a minority preference. Moreover, many paedophiles prefer longer-term relationships with children they know to brief encounters for money (op. cit., p. 83). Possible connections between paedophilia and prostitution excite much public interest and the topic will be mentioned again later (see p. 278), but there was little evidence of it in the present sample.

The belief that rent boys are mostly heterosexuals, forced by necessity to participate in sexual acts to which they would never otherwise agree, received no support from this sample, where men claiming to be completely heterosexual were in a minority. On the other hand, although many of the young men enjoyed homosexual activity, and some liked casual encounters, that did not mean they would relish meetings under ambiguous and sometimes dangerous circumstances with persons not of their own choosing whose desires they must satisfy regardless of their own feelings. The age difference between rent boy and punter, usually 20 years or more, can hardly be much to the liking of the younger participant. In this survey the respondents, particularly those who identified as heterosexual, usually described their reaction to the sexual experience in their first prostitution engagement as having been one of indifference or positive disgust. On the other hand there were some who had entered into the arrangement out of interest or curiosity and found it enjoyable. Some had not taken the plunge until encouraged by unexpected propositioning, others had taken the initiative in finding a punter. Many already knew about the rent scene, having heard of it through the media or having been told about it or introduced to it by friends. Motivation was often mixed and reactions varied greatly, as the following examples illustrate:

Case 029. This man, who identified himself as exclusively heterosexual, was somewhat ashamed of allowing easy money to overcome his sexual distaste.

Q. Can you tell me about that first time [at eighteen] how it came about?
A. Basically, I was walking around Victoria Station depressed, no money. A guy came up to me and said, 'Do you want to earn some money?' I says, 'How?' He says, 'Well all I want you to do is wank me off, I'll wank you off', and he offered me £40. So I says, 'Yeh, fair enough!' Went into his car, drove off somewhere, done our things, he give me the £40 and I was happy.

Q. So you just wanked one another?

A. Yea.

Q. Did you come?

A. Yea.

Q. And how did you feel about it?

A. I didn't really feel nothing at all.

Q. You didn't dislike it?

A. Umm. I didn't like the idea of him grabbing hold of my cock. I felt dirty, understand, but the money counteracted feeling dirty, understand what I mean.

Q. Yes. Would you say you felt dirty enough actually to hate it or you just didn't like it?

A. I just didn't like it really, basically ... I was just genuinely walking about ... I wasn't actually looking for it, I knew that these sort of things went on, but I didn't know about Victoria.

Q. So you were just propositioned?

A. Propositioned, yeh, out of the blue.

Q. You say you did it for money?

A. I was skint, I had about £1 in my pocket ... I had a place to stay but no money ... And basically the money I've earned off doing this I can honestly say has bought me a lot of things that I never thought I could have, like a TV, a video, a stereo system, a brand new carpet. It's bought me things I never would have had, but I still feel like that I shouldn't have done it, and I feel that I shouldn't still do it, but I do.

Case 031. This was another heterosexual. He was in steady cohabitation with a girlfriend and said he 'only once went to bed with a bloke for pleasure'. He too recalled scruples about sex with punters, but he had been rather easily persuaded to cooperate with older men who were good to him. He was seventeen at the time and had just come to London with £35 in his pocket.

Q. You didn't know London?

A. No. I thought I'll make my way to the West End. Anyway. I'm walking up and down Shaftesbury Avenue with this bag over my shoulder and I bumped into this bloke I knew from Scotland. Unbeknown to me at the time he was doing rent anyway. He said, 'Do you wanna go for a drink? Come for a drink.' He was only eighteen. I said, 'Yeh' and he took me into this pub. Now I know it's a well known gay rent pub, but I didn't know at the time. I was naive, I had just walked off the bus. I walked in and straight away every head turned – new face, sort of thing. I thought, 'What's happening?' We were in there having a couple of drinks and this bloke down the end of the bar, who I know now, he's a friend now, he sent a drink over. So I said to my mate, 'Why is this bloke doing that? He don't know me from Adam and he's buying me drinks.' My mate says, 'Come and sit down' and he filled me in on all the details.

Q. He told you about the rent scene?

A. Yea, and straight away I went to get out, started to walk out. The bloke stopped me and says, 'What's up, what's wrong?' I says, 'Look, don't get me wrong, but I don't think I should be in here.' He says, 'Why not? Have a drink and tell me all about it.' So I sat down and had a drink with him and he took me for a meal and we had a chat and he was my first sugar daddy – sweet.

Q. Where did it happen with him, the first time?

A. It didn't. You see he was nice, he didn't take a liberty or anything. It was like a week before he bothered, 'cos I didn't know what was going on or anything. He never, like, put any pressure on me. He put me up at his house, let me stay there and everything, so the first day I came down I had money in my pocket and everything.

Q. And was he the first guy you had sex with?

A. Yeh, after about a week.

Q. And what sort of sex that first time?

A. Not anal, I wasn't into that, but he didn't even want to do that, all he wanted to do was to give me a blow job and he just wanted me to give him a wank . . .

Q. Did you come?

A. Yeh.

Q. How did you feel about it at the time?

A. Weird, like it was the first time I'd been to bed with a bloke . . . He was a kind, sincere, genuine bloke . . . [but] it just felt like, improper, if you like, it didn't feel right, but it was too late then 'cos I'd already done the job.

The next examples are of men whose initial entry into prostitution was out of curiosity or opportunism rather than necessity:

Case 036

The first time I met someone in Leicester Square I think I must have been about sixteen . . . I was just sitting around and someone got talking to me. You know, it's a sort of a haunt there, it's got a slight reputation, but very thin on the ground, like. There's a toilet there and you get hold of people floating about and they're looking for someone perhaps a bit hard up who ain't eating or what not. And they just come up, you know. I remember this French guy just started speaking and invited me back to his hotel. It seemed a bit of an adventure and I went along . . . It was quite funny. I really didn't want to do anything and he gave me six quid.

Q. Did you know what he was inviting you back for? Did you know it was for sex?

A. I had the impression it was something like that, but – er – it was a bit alien to me then.

Q. Did you know about the rent scene at that stage?

A. No, I didn't . . .

Q. Can you remember what sort of sex you had that first time?

A. I think I masturbated him and he wanted me to suck him, but I said no. I'm not into that you know.

Q. Can you remember whether you came yourself?

A. I might have done, I'm not sure.

Q. How did you feel about it that first time?

A. I felt, well this isn't a bad way to earn money, but I'm not really into this with guys, you know, that's how I felt about it.

Q. So you were what, indifferent?

A. Not really liking that sort of thing, thinking, 'Well I got a few bob for that.'

Q. How old would he have been?

A. About thirty odd, thirty to forty . . .

Q. That first time, why did you go along with it if you weren't particularly liking it?

A. I think just to see what it was. And partly company. If you're sitting down bored by yourself and someone says, 'Do you want to come for a coffee?' it's company, do you know what I mean. And you might think, 'This person's took an interest in me, so I might get something out of it' – Do you see the sort of mentality? I just thought, 'Oh, I'll go with the flow', like.

Q. And you say you weren't desperate for money or anything?

A. No, I don't think so.

Q. Did it seem like an easy six quid?

A. Well then I just weren't even thinking of money, or I weren't materially orchestrated in any way. I just thought, 'Ah well, this is whatever.'

Q. And you weren't on the run, you were living at home?

A. Yes, I was living at home.

Case 028 was seventeen and staying in a hotel in London on holiday when he wandered into Piccadilly knowing nothing of the rent scene. A man of about thirty-five came up to him and made him an offer of £30, which he accepted.

Q. What sort of sex did you have?

A. Just had to wank him off.

Q. Did he wank you?

A. Yeh.

Q. Did you come yourself at that time?

A. No.

Q. Did you enjoy it?

A. It was OK.

Q. Just OK?

A. Yeh.

Q. You wouldn't say you enjoyed it?

A. I really didn't know about it then, didn't know much about it.

Q. So it was just OK?

A. Yeh.

Q. What was your reason for doing it?

A. Well I was bored stiff, a quick £30 seemed all right.

Q. Nobody had told you about it?

A. No.

Q. You weren't on the run, in trouble with the police or anything?

A. No.

Q. Your parents knew where you were?

A. Oh, yeh.

More typically, the next two examples are of entry under pressure of need and an initial experience recalled as providing no pleasure.

Case 001

Q. How old were you the first time that you got money for sex?
A. I would say seventeen.
Q. And how old was the person who paid you?
A. About forty-five.
Q. And what sort of sex happened then?
A. I just had to rub him off.
Q. Just wanking and nothing more?
A. No.
Q. And how did you feel about it then, enjoy it or indifferent?
A. I didn't enjoy it, but it was money.
Q. So you were indifferent?
A. Yeh.
Q. Did you ejaculate that time with him?
A. No.
Q. He did, you didn't?
A. Yes.
Q. How did you first get to know about taking money for sex?
A. When I first got to London, and I was seventeen, I just stayed at a night shelter and a few people there were doing it.
Q. Why did you come to London?
A. To get away from Belfast . . .
Q. And that first time, when you were seventeen, where did it happen?
A. Piccadilly.
Q. And what was the reason for doing it?
A. I just needed money.
Q. And you had no other source of money?
A. No.
Q. So you were really desperate?
A. Yes.

Case 004

Q. When was it that you started taking money for sex?
A. It was when I come back here and I was sixteen.
Q. And where did you go?
A. Well I went up the West End, to Piccadilly Circus.
Q. How did you know where to go?
A. Well I read it in the papers, about Piccadilly Circus.
Q. And had you also heard talk about it by your friends?
A. No. When I went up there I was sleeping around and then you get people who come up and talk to you.
Q. But it was from reading about it that you first discovered –?
A. Yea, right. Then there was all this trouble about Playland a few years before then. [Publicity about an amusement arcade where men picked up boys – D.J.W.]
Q. How old would the person be that picked you up that first time?
A. About fifty.
Q. And what sort of sex did you have with him?
A. Just masturbating, down the car park.

Q. And sucking?

A. No, because he was too worried, that fellow.

Q. And did you enjoy it at the time?

A. No, I just wanted the money you know.

Q. Did you dislike it, were you indifferent, or what ?

A. Well I disliked it, but then I thought you've got to do something you don't like.

Q. Did you ejaculate – come?

A. I didn't, he did.

Q. Why did you do it?

A. Well I had no money, I thought it's the only way, the quickest way of getting money.

Q. And at that time were you on the run from the children's home?

A. Yes.

Case 006. On the first occasion he accepted money for sex he was seventeen, unemployed, living on welfare payments, but not so desperate that he would have agreed to go with a really old man.

Q. What was your reason for taking money that first time?

A. Desperation. I was in the West End and at the time I was living in Finsbury Park [some 4 miles distant] and had no money to get home . . . I had money in the first place to start off with, but I had been down the West End all day. I knew of a gay club. It was closed, but there's always somebody there, but when I went up there was only this guy there. I thought there'd be his boyfriend there, or the manager or someone, there usually is . . . We had a couple of drinks and I first asked him for a loan of £2, which I would have paid him back, and he refused; he said, 'I don't lend money to people', and then he put his offer towards me . . .

Q. And how old was the person who paid you?

A. I'd say about forty odd. I mean I never knew him, I'd seen him at parties.

Q. And what sort of sex did you have that first time?

A. It was just oral sex, as it always was.

Q. Always?

A. Yes, I wouldn't involve myself in any intercourse.

Q. And how did you feel about it, did you enjoy it at the time or indifferent or disliked it or what?

A. Well I mean the reason I didn't make much money in prostitution was I was fairly fussy. I had to like the person a lot to go with them, I just wouldn't go with any old punter like some of them did . . .

Q. So that was how you got introduced to it?

A. Yea, he introduced me to his friends and so on.

Q. So you started by being introduced to people?

A. Yep, and then I got others, taken to the clubs.

The next two examples are exceptional in that prostitution began early, well before school-leaving age. The boys had taken some initiative themselves rather than having been seduced by predatory paedophiles. These cases may seem to contradict the contention in Chapter 4 that boys do not learn through sexual 'abuse' how to get money for sex, but they were not classed as abuse because the incidents were neither unwanted nor coercive. It is a sad consequence of society's disavowal of childhood sexuality (especially childhood homosexuality) that some boys whose homosexual feelings develop early find physical release and emotional understanding obtainable only from strangers contacted in public lavatories. They are too young to go to gay bars, are still under surveillance by parents and may fear their peers getting to know they are gay. If they continue with the habit they are likely to be offered money and so the transition from pleasure seeking to money seeking may be facilitated.

Case 049

Q. Have you ever been involved in sex activities against your wishes?

A. Emm. You see, it's quite weird. When I was eleven, the first time I ever had sex with a man was in a toilet. And after it happened – you think to yourself – and I told my sister. And the police were involved and stuff. But they never caught the guy, thank God, 'cos it was me. I was willing, but I told him I wasn't, because it just shook me up, sort of. Once I'd spitted it out I regretted it.

Q. What happened, did he take you in there –?

A. He did come into my cubicle, and it was masturbation.

Q. And what, you felt bad about it?

A. Yes.

Q. So you felt confused?

A. Well it was the first time that I'd done what I just done, it was terrible . . .

Q. Thinking back now would you think of that as sex against your wishes?

A. No, because it was me that invited him in. 'Cos I was eleven. Maybe it was wrong on his part, I don't know. But no . . .

Q. Can you remember the very first time you got money for sex?

A. I was thirteen. What it was, I had these two men asked me every week, one Tuesday and one on Thursday. And they used to pay me sort of thing. I was quite greedy actually, because I used to work for my father at weekends. So it was quite good.

Q. How did you meet these men?

A. Toilets.

Q. Can you remember the first time you met them, can you try to describe it for me?

A. Well, in Wales, where I was, when you go into the toilets you stand around and everything. And I don't know, something just made me ask for money. And it just started like that. They just said, 'Come with me.'

Q. What, they expressed sexual interest in you and you asked for money?

A. Well the thing is, you see, the first time we did it in the toilets, just masturbation sort of thing again, and they paid me and everything and that was it.

Q. And you met them individually in the toilets?

A. Yes.

Q. And you say you kept seeing them, was that in the toilets?

A. No, in their cars.

Q. Can you remember whether you came that first time you got money?

A. I probably did.

Q. Do you remember whether you enjoyed it or not?

A. The feeling I always enjoyed. But no, it was boring, just wanted to get it over with.

Q. Did you hate it or dislike it?

A. No. Not so much in Wales because there was no other form of relief, there was nowhere you could go, so it was sort of mutual.

Q. And how old were these two men?

A. One was about thirty-seven and the other about forty-eight.

Q. And what sort of sex would you usually have in their cars?

A. I'd just get naked and they'd masturbate and cuddle sort of thing.

Q. And did you enjoy that?

A. No, I didn't really. The first time you think, 'Oh, what the heck!' It just became routine and everything. I just did it for the money. It was sort of 'Hurry up' sort of thing.

Case 034

Q. When it comes to getting money for sex, how old were you the first time?

A. About eleven.

Q. So you started before you left home?

A. Yeh.

Q. How did that come about?

A. Well there was this bloke offered me [£20]. He was in the bus station and said, you know, '20 minutes or so at the top of the stairs.' And I thought, I really thought about it and I thought, 'No.' I went up to him and said, 'No thanks.' All I thought, you know, was the money is hot and my dad's gonna say where the hell did you get [£20] from, so I just said, 'No.' I would have loved it, but no.

Q. So you didn't actually do anything . . . When was the next time?

A. About three or four days later, about £10.

Q. What, again at the bus station?

A. Yes, it's a pretty busy place. I did it then.

Q. What happened, did somebody come up to you?

A. I was hanging around, you know, looking, sort of thing. I went and stood in this corner – well nearer the corner – and this coloured geezer came up and he offered. So I thought, 'Oh well, £10. Dad won't ask me where I got £10 from. I've only got to say I've been washing cars.' You know, I did that quite a lot.

Q. So he offered you £10?

A. Yes.

Q. And what sort of sex did you have?

A. Well it was just kissing mainly, and touching up and that, didn't do anything.

Q. Where did you go?

A. Back of the bus station.

Q. Did you have to wank him or anything?

A. Yes.

Q. Did you come?

A. No, I didn't.

Q. Did he?

A. Can't remember, probably did.

Q. How old would he be?

A. This bloke was sixty-five

Q. How did you know he was exactly sixty-five?

A. Well I said to him, 'You look around forty' and he goes on, 'Have a guess . . .'

Q. How did you know about that place at the bus station, was it a place where other people hang out?

A. Yes, quite a few people, but I don't know about it now . . .

Q. Did you know about it that first time?

A. [shrugs assent].

Q. Or was it just by accident that you were standing there?

A. The thing was an accident, sort of thing, but apart from that I knew it was a good place to stand . . .

Q. Were you actually looking for someone?

A. Of me own age sort of thing, you know, at the time, but £10 in me face and . . .

Q. Did he just come up to you or –?

A. Well we sort of stood there five or ten minutes staring at each other.

Q. So he knew and you knew what you were about?

A. I think I didn't know at the beginning, but now, over the years, I've got to know. He definitely knew, because of his age. It went on from there.

Q. Why do you think you did it that first time?

A. I was going to do it for the pleasure, but he said here's £10 and I just took it, no arguments.

Q. So you got the money and the pleasure?

A. Yeh.

Q. Did you do that quite often then?

A. Occasionally, yes, because me dad was wondering where I was getting to and I had to be back at a certain time you know. I couldn't make it back in time 'cos the bus would be late or something. I had to stop going over there and try to find somewhere else.

Sometime later his parents discovered the bank account book where he had put away his earnings and in his pockets a letter from a man arranging a meeting. He admitted he had been 'on the game'. After that he was sent to a residential 'special school'.

There were several examples of schoolboy runaways from institutions or unhappy homes resorting to prostitution as the most obvious way to get money to live. These cases came nearest to the popular idea of the juvenile runaway being picked up at the station on arrival and immediately introduced to the ways of homosexual prostitution. The boys themselves, however, were as likely to be knowing and intending that course as to be innocents taken by surprise.

Case 027

Q. What was it you hated about school?

A. People telling me what to do . . .

Q. When you used to run away from school, how did you spend your time, what did you do?

A. Because I had no money I used to go out on the gay scene.

Q. From what age?

A. Thirteen . . .

Q. Right, tell me a bit about being on the game. You say you ran away from school when you were what – thirteen?

A. Yeh.

Q. OK. And you –?

A. Met up with a bloke in Victoria.

Q. Did you know anything about the rent scene at that stage?

A. No, I was hungry.

Q. How come you were at Victoria?

A. 'Cos just like, I just come to the West End and that's where I ended up. And I was just walking around and a bloke come up to me and says do I want to earn £30. I said, 'How?' He said, 'Just give me a hand job.' I said, 'No,' but I knew what he meant. I see him a day later and I said, 'Is that still on?' He said, 'Yeh.' I had to eat.

Q. So what did you do?

A. Just wanked him.

Q. Did he wank you?

A. No. Well he touched me and everything.

Q. Where did you go?

A. To his house.

Q. You say he just touched you, did you come?

A. No.

Q. How did you feel about it?

A. Dirty, very dirty.

Q. You didn't like it?

A. No.

Q. Would you actually say you hated it?

A. At the time, yes, 'cos it was my first time.

Case 003. At fourteen he had come to London and was 'hanging about the station'.

Q. And what exactly happened?

A. There was this man, he just came up and said, 'Are you staying anywhere?' And I said, 'No.' I was naive and all that. And he said, 'I've got a place you can stay at.' I didn't ask for any money at the time because I didn't know anything about it, but in the morning he said, 'Here's a few quid for you.'

Q. So you just stayed the one night with him?

A. Yes. I went back and saw him a few times, because I thought as I got money from him and I needed money to eat and stuff like that.

Q. So that first time you came down [i.e. ran away] to London, did you live entirely on money you got from sex?

A. Yes, at first, yes.

Q. When you'd been with this man, did you then start picking up others?

A. It's a long story. But to cut it short, this man, he knew people who would pay me.

Q. He introduced you to others?

A. Yes. It wasn't like a pimp, because he didn't want pay, just out of interest. And I thought it was great at the time because I was earning all this money. But it was – I was pretty disgusted . . .

Q. At that time, when you were fourteen, what did you think about sex with men, did you enjoy it or dislike it?

A. I hated it.

Q. Yes, but you used to come, did you, when you wanked with these men?

A. Sometimes. You see most of them had videos on, like with women, because they knew I liked women.

Q. So that excited you?

A. Yes.

Q. So the reason you took money was simply that you hadn't any money to eat?

A. Yes.

Q. At that time, when you were fourteen, did you have a regular place to stay?

A. No. You see, although they gave me money they always used to let me stay at their place as well.

Q. So did you find you had somewhere to go every night?

A. Yes, because this first one I met introduced me to I think about nine, ten people and there was always one available one night of the week.

Q. Why did it come to an end?

A. I went back home because I felt as though, I don't know, I know I was young, but I felt as though I was going mad. I was angry with myself all the time.

Q. You felt it was the wrong thing to do?

A. I felt I wanted to be normal, I mean normal in inverted commas, you know what I mean [i.e. heterosexual].

Q. You met this man while you were hanging around the station. Why were you hanging around?

A. 'Cos I didn't know where to go.

Q. You'd just arrived?

A. Yes. I didn't know anybody, didn't know where to go or nothing, so I just sat there. I had just enough for a cup of coffee.

Q. What would you have done if this man hadn't come along?

A. I don't know. I'll never know.

Exploitation by older men of the dependent situation of young runaways is generally to be deplored, yet for the boys involved, as in the following example, the punter can appear as a much needed, caring adult rescuer. Such was the situation in the following case, but the boy's initial friendship with an older man did not prevent him from later becoming active as a West End street worker:

Case 045. Having run away from care at fourteen and come to London he went to Piccadilly, having been told by a man on a tube train that that was where it was lively at night. He had heard about young boys being picked up by old men.

I was sitting underneath Piccadilly Eros and a guy came up and told me what went on around the West End, offered me £20 . . .

Q. So when this guy offered you £20, were you surprised?

A. When he approached me, no, I wasn't surprised at all. When he offered me £20 I was a bit surprised, because I had never seen £20 before . . .

Q. Did you spend the night there, at his place?

A. Yes, and I've been staying there for five years.

Q. So once you had stayed there you just kept on staying did you?

A. Yea.

Q. And did he give you more money?

A. Yea. The sex part of it cut out quite a lot. We ended up very good friends. And he just looked after me, bought me anything I wanted. What I now know to be called a sugar daddy. He sort of treated me like he was my sugar daddy.

Q. What sort of sex happened that first time, can you remember?

A. Just playing around [masturbation and passive fellatio] . . .

Q. Just generally playing around, but not fucking?

A. No. He was pretty smart. He would have loved to have done it, but he knew I was on the run from home, because I told him. And he thought – he even said so – that if I got picked up the police may check me. And if they find out that somebody has done that they're going to ask me so many questions that I may burst out in tears and say. So for that reason he was pretty smart about it.

Q. And that first night you had sex with him did you come?

A. Yes.

Q. Did you enjoy it?

A. Em, yes.

Q. A lot?

A. Yes.

Q. So obviously, you liked him and enjoyed being with him?

A. Yes. He was very clever.

Q. Had you had sex with a man before?

A. No.

Q. Or with a boy?

A. Er, yes.

Q. You had. When he was talking to you and he offered you money, what was the main reason you went with him?

A. For his friendship, I got to like him quite a lot as a friend.

Q. So you thought he might look after you?

A. Yea.

Q. And what about the money?

A. That helped.

Q. But that wasn't the main reason?

A. No.

Q. You must have been pretty short of money?

A. Yea. It was somewhere where I could go when I ran away, if I felt like running again, which I did do. I ran away a lot.

It is generally assumed that male prostitutes don't have pimps, but this is not invariable. There was one case in the sample where a boy's first contacts were made for him by a pimp on a commission basis.

Case 009. At the age of eighteen he came to London because he had heard about the nightlife and gay clubs there. He had no money and was hanging about Victoria Station on his first day where he met a friendly man in his sixties who asked if he would like to make some money. He was told all about the rent scene and he agreed to a meeting fixed by telephone with a punter who came to a nearby café. He handed over a share of the takings to the man the next day. The arrangement ceased as he learned to find his own clients.

One of the eleven Streetwise Day Centre attenders not in the sample who were interviewed subsequently had also had a pimp for a time. *Case 054* was fifteen when he ran away from home, but 'by that time I basically knew what I wanted to do, so I headed down to the West End and very, very quickly I met someone. He was an older guy, what you would call an aged rent boy, and he sort of showed me where I could make money. And he sort of took care of me. I suppose now I'd say he was a pimp, 'cos I used to give him all my money to mind, money that I'd earned, and he used to give [me back some].' That went on for about six months. 'He was like my best friend, till eventually – he kept making trips to the bank to deposit money – and it one day just clicked. He was making money and I wasn't really making much.'

Pimping relationships tend to occur before the rent boy has learned to fend for himself. For instance, in March 1991 a man of forty-three was imprisoned for 'living off immoral earnings' of rent boys. He had collected some of them from Victoria Station, but his movements had been recorded on police video. He claimed that he was merely giving the homeless a place to stay (*Guardian* 25 March 1991).

One example of an exploitative pimp relationship was reported to the researchers by the Streetwise Youth outreach workers. An Asian man of twenty-five had left his strict Muslim parents to take up an offer of accommodation from a man who owned a flat. The arrangement had developed into a pimping situation, the landlord introducing two or three punters for him to service each week. He was bisexual and did not mind the sexual aspect, but he had to turn over £5 or £10 for each session in lieu of rent. The landlord would not let him sign on to get his rent paid by social security. Under threat of otherwise being turned out, he felt it preferable to comply rather than return to the parental home.

*

The men's descriptions of initiation into prostitution were very varied and often out of line with popular assumptions. Many of the sample had begun when they were mature and already sexually experienced and knew what to expect. None had been forced into sex acts against their will. Mutual masturbation and oral sex were the most common requirements. Those with prior homosexual interest or experience were much less likely to express active disgust, but even those who said they were heterosexual sometimes described indifference rather than strong revulsion towards collaboration with punters. Their first customers were not all 'dirty old men'. Of the 46 who hazarded an estimate four put the punter's age in the twenties, fifteen in the thirties, eighteen in the forties and only nine in the fifties or sixties.

Most mentioned urgent need of money as their prime motive for entry into prostitution. A majority had been in fact under varying degrees of pressure at the time, sometimes partly self-induced by running away from home or from institutions or from impending delinquency convictions. Many had migrated from the provinces and begun prostitution on arrival, or very soon after, when they found it difficult to support themselves otherwise. Discovery that more money could be made more swiftly this way than by any other means open to them encouraged continuance. A combination of economic need, absence of family support and the availability of the city sex market influenced the first step, but of course there were other factors determining these men's choice of prostitution in preference to the more common practices of the needy, namely begging and thieving.

Boyer (1989) has argued that the culture of gay bars and meeting places, often referred to as a sexual market place (Read, 1980), by its emphasis on casual encounters and sexual conquest, holds out to young gays the expectation of patronage by older males and presents prostitution as a more or less normal aspect of the gay scene. Weisberg (1985, p. 56) also noted that after want of money, mentioned by 87 per cent, the most frequently mentioned reasons given for engaging in male prostitution were sex (27 per cent) and fun/adventure (19 per cent). We found that joining up with the rent boy crowd was an easy step for youths who identified as gay and were aware that London was the place for gay rent bars and pick-up spots. In some cases, also, earlier experiences in public toilets and the like had shown boys that older men were willing to pay them.

Many had entered into their first prostitution transaction purposely and knowingly, some of them having been actively seeking a punter, but there were a few who had merely responded to spontaneous propositioning, perhaps without being fully aware what to expect or without anticipating payment. Absence of the restraining influence of a stable home background was a factor common both among those who had taken the first step out of curiosity, opportunism or in search of thrills and among those who had acted more from necessity. One or two of the younger boys had let the first man they met secure others for them, but in most cases, following a first contact, boys soon found further customers without needing any intermediary. Dependency on bullying pimps, said to be a feature of female prostitution, was not in evidence. Notwithstanding their varied reactions on the first occasion, none had been deterred from repeating the experience, but this does not mean that a single act of prostitution necessarily leads to a career in the trade. Boys put off after a first trial would have had no occasion to visit Streetwise Youth or to be included in the sample.

Finally, this was a sample largely made up of men who had taken to the streets and had no permanent place to live. As will be seen later, their motives for starting and continuing as street workers were very different from those of men entering the advertised sex industry and operating from their own secure premises or under the umbrella of a business agency.

7

Transacting the Business

The interviews included questions about how contacts were made with clients, what activities took place, how much money was received and how the amounts were decided, what sexual practices took place and what relationships were formed. As some said they were quitting the rent scene questions were directed to 'when you were most active'.

Contacting clients

The most common venues for finding clients were some streets around Piccadilly, the main railway stations and certain West End gay bars and clubs. Police surveillance of particular venues, such as Piccadilly Circus itself, causes shifts of the favoured sites, usually to locations nearby. Allowing a bar to be used for soliciting can lead to loss of licence and closure, so it is understandable that managers often discourage or refuse to serve customers thought to be on the game. Some gay customers dislike or disapprove of bars frequented by rent boys, which is understandable if their purpose is to meet someone on equal terms, not someone liable to demand money. The rent business tends to be concentrated in a few relatively tolerant venues that have an established reputation among both punters and rent boys. Four or five of these were mentioned repeatedly as favourite spots for the sex trade. A few of these establishments had been well known for years, others tend to come and go. In fact one popular bar nearby was closed by police intervention during the period of interviewing. The rent custom simply drifts to another bar when this happens. The generality of crowded gay bars and clubs are not altogether devoid of young men wanting to be paid for sex, but the regular 'professionals' do not normally use them. Even in their specialised venues the rent boys are not quite as conspicuous as some lurid descriptions in the tabloid press might suggest, as they dress and behave in much the same way as other gays.

The sample were of an age to gain easy entry to bars and clubs, but in earlier years many had had no option but to seek their clients in public places, such as certain streets and cafés around the Piccadilly area with an established reputation as renting areas. Those first arriving in London and still ignorant of where else to go often begin by street soliciting. Most of the interviewees, 43 out of 50, when questioned about their ways of making contact with punters, mentioned streets and other public areas, thereby confirming that the sample consisted almost entirely of those who were or had been street workers. Only three, however, said they had never obtained punters in any other way. Contacts in pubs and/or clubs were mentioned by 40 respondents. Being introduced to new clients by existing punters or by fellow rent boys was a common experience, mentioned by 32 respondents. Only ten admitted that they sometimes made use of men's public toilets, a traditional place for casual gay contacts (Humphreys, 1970). For most this was not a preferred method and tended to be seen as a last resort. One man (*Case 036*) said he avoided toilets because things could happen there without cash being handed over. Another (*Case 045*) commented, 'I used to use Victoria Station toilets . . . Obviously I know punters do go down there a hell of a lot, and stay in there and look, and stuff like that. But once they changed it to 10 pence to get in, it's gone very, very quiet.' Toilets have become too well known to the authorities as possible places for sexual misconduct. Many have been removed or reconstructed to discourage misuse and others are under periodic police surveillance, leading to many prosecutions for importuning or indecency (Walmsley, 1978). One man described how he had started off using toilets:

Case 039

Well I [would be] in a cottage and I passed notes – underneath this gap in the toilet – telling that I am nineteen and I have to make money to get back to G————, that being my excuse for why I was on the rent. And then they ask how much and what do you do and that. At that time I'd take £20 for anything. And I took them down to a warehouse which is near a station. Mainly they wanted to be sucked off and wanked.

A few men, seven out of the 50, had at some time worked for an escort or massage agency, but generally only for a short period. Agencies are generally more particular about the age of their employees than pubs are about the age of customers. One of the interviewees (*Case 049*), who was seventeen, had thought about applying, but 'You have to be twenty. Quite a lot of escort agencies are very particular, you know. If you haven't got the right ID they won't take you on.' None had ever inserted adverts for their services in the press.

From descriptions of the verbal ploys used to establish contact with punters it appeared that there was of an initial practice of 'hanging about' known pick-up places waiting to attract the attention of would-be clients (a method fraught with danger of arrest) and the subsequent development of more discreet arrangements via introductions or 'chatting up' prospective punters in gay bars. The following are typical descriptions:

Case 039

Q. Tell me how you make contact with punters, what sort of places?

A. Well I go to Victoria Station, stand over by the mirror . . . People walk past you and you keep looking. And you see if they walk past about three times and then I would walk out of the station and see if they'd follow me. And to start I'd say to them outside the station: 'Excuse me, have you got the time?' And I'd start asking if they are looking for anyone and that. If they say, 'Yes', you tell them you're rent. And they say, 'How much?' And they ask if you have a place. I usually take them down to the car park, do it there. And there's Piccadilly. Just follow each other round Piccadilly. Just ask if they're looking for business. Or there's the ———— Pub, where you start speaking to the punters. It's the same in the ———— Club.

Case 027

Q. Is there a specific place that you go?
A. Yes, by [a shop] in Victoria.
Q. Are the punters there ones that you've usually worked before?
A. Yes, some of them, but there's a lot of new ones.
Q. How do you go about finding a punter, picking out a punter . . .?
A. Say I go to Victoria, just stand by ————, a store right in the middle of the station. The punters stand all round the outside and I see them. They look at you, nod their head, shake their head to [indicate] to go over to the door. They walk out and you just follow them. When you go outside you arrange the price, what they want to do, and then you go back with them, get in their car, taxi or bus or tube . . .
Q. How often, would you say generally, that the police [are watching]?
A. Every time that I go down there.
Q. Every time, so they know who you are basically?
A. Yes.
Q. So do they watch you with an eagle eye?
A. Yes, yes, they've always got the cameras on, yes.
Q. And so how do you work in that situation?
A. You just have to try and ignore them. And when you see a punter they know not to come over to you. You just give them the eye and they walk out and you just follow.

Case 028

Q. Can you describe to me how you pick up people?
A. Just sitting on me own and someone just comes and chat to me and says, 'Do you want a bit of money?'
Q. What sort of places would you go?
A. Piccadilly, train stations, that's it.
Q. What about pubs?
A. Didn't go in pubs much, no. [He had only just reached eighteen when interviewed.]

Q. What about toilets?

A. I went down toilets at Victoria train station . . .

Q. Then you say you have some regulars, can you describe how that happened?

A. One lad says, 'I'll put you in touch with a good mate of mine.' He likes you and [so] puts you in touch with another. And you keep ringing them up and ringing them up. They say, 'Come round.'

Q. Has there ever been a time when you've only used your regulars and haven't had to hang around on the streets?

A. No.

Because of police surveillance of the public places that are well known for male soliciting the rent boys have to remain as unobtrusive as possible. Unlike female prostitutes they do not generally dress in any very distinctive manner and most casual passers by would be unlikely to be aware of what is happening. One consequence is that they may have to spend literally hours standing or walking around before making their first contact. In gay bars striking up conversations with prospective customers was generally easier and safer:

Case 002

Q. Can you tell me how you go about getting a punter?

A. In a pub it is usually like sit down and you will get people staring at you and you just either smile back and if they smile at you then you know you are one step up the ladder. Then you gradually work around and start talking to them, usually just talk about all different things. Then they start asking you about what you like doing in bed and you tell them and if they like it then they go with you.

One advantage of operating in bars rather than on the street was the chance to be more selective in the choice of clients:

Case 043

Q. How would you typically make contact with punters?

A. With me, what I did – I met quite a few of them and everything – I would select certain ones that I would not mind going with, and all that kind of thing. Ones that didn't make me feel too sick, you know. And I just kept with them. I know them, they know me, and that's it.

Q. Regulars, sort of thing?

A. Yes.

One man (*Case 041*) specifically mentioned the relative safety of the bars. 'I've never picked anyone up from the streets, I wouldn't. I like people to see who I'm going with – in case anything happens.'

Picking up in places other than in the limited number of recognised rent bars, especially in the more expensive hotel bars where better-paying customers might be found, presented difficulties for most street workers. Without money for smart suits or the facilities for maintaining a spruce appearance they would quite likely be turned away.

In spite of much police activity there, one or another section of Piccadilly has remained over decades a favourite place for male street workers. Their methods of avoiding arrest are considered later when interactions with police are described (see p. 287), but they were not particularly successful judged by the number who reported having been arrested or convicted for importuning (see p. 124). Apart from long tradition, the busy Piccadilly area attracts many tourists, both British and foreign. It is also a place where young people coming to the capital for the first time are apt to gravitate. It therefore provides the rent boys both with a source of potential custom and the possibility of melting into the crowd when necessary.   It may seem strange that so many choose to work literally on the streets in spite of the risk of arrest, the vagaries of the weather, and the need for swift commitment to strangers with minimal prior scrutiny. Youths out too late to get back into a hostel depend on finding a client for a bed and the temptation must be great to accept any offer, however small the reward or whatever the sexual demands. Queer-bashing by drunken revellers turned out from the bars after closing time is another danger. One man (*Case 061*) remarked that it was not only the police that rent boys on railway stations have to fear. There are young small-time gangster types who follow rent boys and punters in order to beat up the punter and take his money or who threaten the rent boys to make them get information about punters for them. Nevertheless, the streets cost nothing, are available all hours, and impose no age bar or restrictive code of dress or behaviour. To the homeless and penniless, lacking the facilities to keep up a decent appearance, the streets offer chances they can get nowhere else.

Fees

Questions were asked about fixing charges. Responses varied, reflecting individual negotiating skills and experience in the business. Sexual orientation, sociability in gay settings, sexual versatility, assertiveness and feelings towards clients all influenced the manner and effectiveness with which street workers secured their payments. Occasional difficulties with customers who tried to evade payment are considered later (see p. 102).

Substantial cash payments from punters were reported by many, the median range of earnings being £150 to £250 per week, seven putting the figure at £400 a week or more and only a minority of fourteen getting less than £150 a week. These sums equated with about six sessions a week at the generally recognised charge of £30-40 for a limited session involving only masturbation or perhaps fellatio. Much larger sums were sometimes proffered and affluent-looking clients might be asked for more. Anal intercourse, if agreed to at all, would cost perhaps double, and for more specialised activity – bondage, caning etc. – still more money would be asked. These amounts seem large, but there was great variability depending on circumstance. When desperate for money some men would take much less than their normal fee, others refused to lose face. Extras could be demanded for a requirement to stay the night, but not by those begging for accommodation. Fees were usually negotiated with the punter before setting off for a session and the money was usually expected to be given, or at least shown, before sex took place.

Inexperience was a factor in several instances where reported earnings were under £100 a week. *Case 025* had only just arrived from a provincial town where he had been used to charging men he found in streets or toilets only £5 or £10. He hadn't been using pubs because 'they' (i.e. the kind of punters he met) 'haven't got money to go to drink'. Similarly, *Case 019*, fresh from Ireland only two weeks previously, had been told he could find punters by just hanging about the streets in Earls Court. He had been doing just that, but finding only one or two a week and taking what they offered, which was only £15 or £20. In contrast, *Case 040*, who had been in London six months, said, laughing derisively, that in his own town he had been getting £15 a time, but in London £50 was typical and £35 to £40 the lowest he would go. Another of the experienced street workers, *Case 029*, regularly frequented the best known railway station venues, picking up four punters a day, sometimes more, charging £25 for masturbation and more for oral sex, and letting men 'walk off' if they did not agree to his prices. He estimated he was getting £700 a week during his most active periods. Other men were less confident of their position and less able to negotiate the sums they knew they should in theory be able to obtain.

Familiarity with the gay scene meant awareness of the services expected and the going rates for them. *Case 037* met his punters in two very well known haunts of rent boys – one a gay bar, the other a gay club. He would chat with prospective clients before going off with them, outline his prices according to what sex acts were wanted and negotiate accordingly. 'Some weirdos go in there just to have a cuddle for 50 quid', but others are so 'stingy' it feels 'like taking charity from a baby'. He put his earnings at £400 a week on average. Sometimes, however, it could be 'dead', no clients around, but he didn't mind that because 'it can be relaxing knowing I don't have to do a dirty old punter'. *Case 021*, who earned £400 to £500 a week, charged a basic £30 with extra for specialised sexual routines, in which he was versatile and compliant.

The amounts obtained during the most active phases of prostitution may seem substantial, but being unpredictably fluctuating they still left youths living from hand to mouth. Apart from an obvious lack of competence in budgeting and handling money and an 'easy-come-easy-go' attitude, the living circumstances of most of the men discouraged economy. Lack of a proper home base, long hours spent out of doors and in bars and clubs, and heavy consumption of alcohol and sometimes other drugs, quickly ate up earnings and made their eagerness to obtain a £10 interview fee understandable. Occasionally boastful exaggeration was suspected. Richie McMullen (1988, p. 38) has suggested that boys attending the Day Centre are 'likely to overstate the material gains', but in view of the consistency of the reports both from the Day Centre sample and from other sources this was probably a minor factor in the mismatch between claimed earnings and impecunious circumstances that has been noted in previous surveys of street workers (Deischer *et al.*, 1969).

Sexual practices

Questioning what sexual acts took place with clients might have been expected to be particularly sensitive, but in practice the men talked about this quite freely. If there was reserve it was not about the physical details, but about admission to having submitted to anal penetration, which some equated with weakness or effeminacy and some considered risky and unwise even with a condom. Submission to bondage and corporal punishment games, which implied trusting the punter, was reported by a minority. There was tension between personal reluctance, from fear, distrust or dislike, and temptation from the much larger sums some punters were prepared to pay for these things. There was more scope for negotiation when these extras were wanted. Clients generally respected the limits set. They might try to press for more, but coercive physical violence was unusual, although a number of bad experiences were related (see p. 103). It was often difficult to assess how far declared rules about what sex acts they would or would not agree to were followed in practice. Sometimes, on further questioning, exceptions were reported that had not been mentioned initially. It was unclear whether men really knew or could confidently recall what they had done during sessions at which, or before which, there had been heavy drinking or drug-taking.

They all reported masturbatory activity and allowing punters to fellate them, and many declared this was all they would do. There was a link between declared sexual identity and what practices occurred, the heterosexuals being less willing to accommodate additional requirements, except for administering beatings. Some of the more assertively heterosexual were as evasive as possible with clients, keeping their sexual services to an absolute minimum. Of the 23 self-rated heterosexuals only four (17 per cent) compared with half of the eighteen homosexuals and a third of the nine bisexuals said they had been anally penetrated by a punter. Save for one bisexual, all of the eight men who maintained that with punters they had never performed anal intercourse themselves or had it done to them were self-declared heterosexuals. All these eight expressed aggressively macho attitudes and seven of them were among the group of 29 whose services had included tying up and/or beating clients. Naturally, none of them were among the fourteen who had let themselves be tied up and/or beaten. (There were ten who had taken both the assertive and submissive roles in sado-masochistic eroticism.)

Case 035. This heterosexual was a typical example of someone reluctant to have close sexual involvement with clients.

Q. What sort of sex things do you do with punters?
A. Er, well.
Q. Wanking?
A. Yeh.
Q. Sucking?
A. Them to suck me, yeh, if they want to.
Q. Do you suck them?
A. No.
Q. Fucking?
A. No.
Q. No, neither way.
A. Neither way, never.
Q. Tying up or spanking?
A. Never been asked.
Q. Leather, rubber, dressing up, anything like that?
A. Never come across it.
Q. Any kinky things like pissing . . .?
A. Oh, no way, oh no no. I heard of somebody in B——— who invited people back to his flat, give you a couple of pints of canned beer you know, make you piss in [his mouth]. It were disgusting!

Some of the openly gay men were still choosey about what sex acts they would agree to, more particularly perhaps those who were not so heavily dependent on prostitution earnings. One man had discontinued his rent activity after only a few months, having begun it as much for pleasure as for need:

Case 038

Q. Why do you think you actually did it that first time?
A. I was invited to go out to Blackpool for the weekend and I didn't have any money . . . I did fancy him, yeh, but I still needed the money . . .
Q. And what sort of sex did you have with punters?
A. It was just wanking and sucking . . .
Q. Did you fuck at all?
A. No.
Q. Never?
A. No.
Q. Did you do anything else like tying up?
A. No.

Q. Spanking?
A. No.
Q. Dressing up?
A. Yeh, but not for a punter. I did it for a living, like, on the stage, but I wouldn't do it for a punter. I mean I never got the chance, but I wouldn't have done it . . . There was three of us and and we used to do like just a general drag show . . .
Q. Was it fun?
A. Yeh, it was good, I enjoyed it.
Q. Did you earn good money?
A. Yeh. A weekend on the rent would be like a night on the stage, kind of thing, yeh.

Generally, gay men were more versatile in sex exchanges with punters, but drawing the line at what they personally considered too outlandish:

Case 037

Q. What sort of sex acts do you have with punters?
A. Any sex act they want, but I don't get fucked, I used to but I don't now . . .
Q. What about tying up and spanking, have you ever?
A. Oh no, I haven't, I'm not into that rubbish . . . I was asked to do it to someone last night . . . just to tie him up and whip him till his arse bleeds . . . I refused, that's for people who are sex mad . . .
Q. Anything more kinky?
A. Only spit on someone's dick. I turned round and told him to fuck off . . . It's so revolting.

This man also mentioned that he had gone through a period when he couldn't stand the sight or smell of semen and would look away when clients ejaculated. In spite of his declared squeamishness he reported that he had had gonorrhoea 'in my throat, me anus and my cock'.

Availability of practices not so easy to obtain with unpaid partners is said to be one of the reasons for going with prostitutes. Asked what 'kinky' sex they had had with punters the most common response was to describe sado-masochistic acts. Willingness to tie up and spank others was more prevalent than willingness to have it done to them.

Case 007

Q. Did you have to go in for any kind of kinky sex?
A. Not half!
Q. What sort of things?
A. Chain 'em up and whip them.
Q. And did they ever do that to you?
A. No way! They would have to give me bloody £500 upwards! I used to chain them up and put a fist up their arse as well – all this stuff you know.

Q. And water sports as they call it?
A. Yes, water sports as well. Thank God they didn't do it on me.

Case 011

Q. Have you had to do some kinky types of sex?
A. Emm.
Q. What's that been?
A. Caning people, tying them up. There was one had about a twelve-inch dildo, it was about three inches wide, and you have to put it inside of him – things like that.
Q. And what about you being tied up?
A. Yea, I've had that as well.
Q. Spanked?
A. Yea, and things shoved up me and weights tied to me balls and things like that.
Q. Dressing up?
A. Yes, mainly punk gear and leather and all that. [He was in fact a skinhead youth.]

The sado-masochistic rituals were usually playful, with no real harm to the participants, although one or two reported more than sexual enjoyment in making their clients squirm:

Case 029

A. I've been asked to cane somebody.
Q. Were you happy with it?
A. Oh, I loved it. You should have seen the state of his backside afterwards.

Only one man suggested actually drawing blood:

Case 030

Q. What other things would you do in terms of kinky sex?
A. Slicing someone.
Q. Sorry?
A. Slicing – knives, razors.
Q. So you actually cut their skin?
A. Yes. Using my nails, because a lot of people like to be scratched or massaged or something. They like massage with your nails.
Q. Really hard, so it hurts?
A. Yes.

Odd rituals of a charade-like character were described by some:

Case 045

A. There was one guy that I went with wanted me to hide his clothes in a car park near Spitalfield Market, and he'd have to go and find them. Obviously he gave me the money first and then I hid his clothes . . .

Q. Did you hide all his clothes?

A. Yes, stripped him off completely.

Q. Where did he undress?

A. In the middle of the car park. It was 3 o'clock in the morning and there was hardly anyone around.

Q. And then he rushed round looking for them. Did you hang around?

A. No. You'd ruin it for him if you hung around. You had to be very honest and go leave him to do it himself.

Case 031

. . . He used to like me pretending I was a prison warden and he was the inmate. And he used to eat things like Fairy Liquid sandwiches. And mustard sandwiches. Oh he was really a freak, out and out freak, nice guy though.

This example called to mind a masseur's advert in *Gay Times* stating he was an 'ex prison officer'.

Case 012

Q. What sort of kinky things?

A. There was one bloke, he had this peacock's feather. He used to stick it up your arse and you'd grip it between your cheeks and stand there in the middle of the room with nothing on. And if you didn't laugh you got more money.

Some routines involved the rent boy dressing to fit the fantasy:

Case 047

Yes. This bloke one day said, 'Put all your football gear on and I'll give your botty a spanking' kind of thing.

Case 041

Dressing up is kinky to me, but that's as far as it goes. Mainly it's women's clothes. When I dressed up all I had on was a pair of tights and a pair of high heeled shoes and a suspender. That's what he wanted.

Two men had encountered a foot fetishist. *Case 050*: 'He just sat there and had a wank and sniffed me foot.' *Case 049*: 'He wanted to lick my feet, he masturbated while licking my feet. And he wanted them the dirtier the better . . . He had an orgasm. He didn't want to touch me at all.'

Tate (1990, p. 193) quotes a rent boy's account of performing with a mate while the client takes pictures. The research interviews did not include questions about photography and it was not mentioned spontaneously, save for a comment about how embarrassing it would be to be filmed unawares and appear in a porn magazine. There were other circumstances, however, where physical contact with the punter was not required:

Case 042

Yes. I had this black bloke and he used to meet me quite regularly. I was homeless at the time. And he would just want me to take my trousers down and masturbate. He would just watch and wank himself.

Several men mentioned the same punter who got them to sit on a commode and defaecate while he lay with his face underneath:

Case 027

He just lies down underneath it . . . He loves it.
  Q. Do you mind doing it?
  A. No, I don't mind. He doesn't touch me at all, I just think of the money and that's it.

A few, such as *Case 024*, mentioned 'having sex with someone, or having a sexual activity while the punter just watches'. In two examples the punter wanted to watch heterosexual intercourse:

Case 036

It weren't an actual threesome, what it was like – I met this Arab guy. He come up to me, he made me laugh actually, and said, 'Can you make sexy with a girl?' I said, 'Yeh,' 'cos I suppose there's some people who can't, you know. So I said, 'All right.' I went to his joint and he'd got this old peace pipe – you know what they're like, they're laid back and that. And he gave me a can of lager and he rung up this woman. It must have been a regular bird he was seeing, you know. I saw her and that, and we mucked about and he said, like, 'Touch her breasts,' which I did. And she said to me, 'You don't get brewer's droop do you?' I said, 'No,' 'cos I was having a drink. And we done it like. I was quite into it actually, because I found her attractive. Then she just whispered in my ear, 'Well, you're working like me love.' Then I come and he jumped on top.

Case 048

I've had sex with girls while punters were watching.
  Q. Tell me about that.
  A. Sex with this coloured girl while her boyfriend, I think he was, was watching.

Q. Was she paid, or just you?

A. Just me, I think it was just me, 'cos he knew her very well and that, but I don't know if he paid her or not.

One man claimed to have had a female client:

Case 007

Q. A female who paid you?

A. Yes, she gave me the most of them all.

Q. How much?

A. £250.

Q. Really, that's almost unbelievable.

A. I know, but I was on Piccadilly and she comes along and she says, 'I'm very lonely and I need sex and I'll pay you a lot of money if you give me a good night.'

Q. Where did you go?

A. Her house, it was posh. She was only twenty-eight. She had a very funny fella who works in . . .

Q. And you had intercourse with her?

A. Yes, with a condom, I don't trust no one.

One or two men were transvestites. One described working as a pretended woman prostitute:

Case 049

I have done prostitution as a woman as well. That sounds really funny. I didn't so much do prostituion, I did clipping. I did do a few punters as well, because I looked so realistic they didn't know. I got [a woman friend] to do the talking for me and say I was foreign . . . It's quite funny actually. I fooled so many people, it's unreal. That's quite scary, because you can get into a lot of trouble if they find out.

Q. Tell me a bit about the clipping.

A. That's the girls' territory. It's all done so . . .

He then went on to describe the practice of 'clipping' whereby a man is persuaded to give money in advance for sex, then for getting the key to a room and perhaps for a substantial deposit as 'protection money'. The prostitute then makes an escape without providing the promised pleasures.

Those heavily committed to the rent trade over a long period are generally led sooner or later, by persuasion rather than brute force, into scenes they find disgusting. The following description from a Day Centre member not in the main sample but interviewed later illustrates this rather well.

Case 059. Reared in a children's home where he had experienced sexual molestation, he followed an elder brother into the rent business thinking it 'easy money'. He was still in it after five years because he needed the money for his heroin habit. Some rent experiences he enjoyed. One man who wanted companionship and someone to sleep with, but no sex, had taken him away for a weekend staying at one of the best hotels. 'I thought that was brilliant.' The previous night he had been bought cigarettes and food and plied with drink and drugs and given £20 by a client who wanted only to get drunk and stoned and play (and of course lose) a game of strip Monopoly.

On the other hand he had had to participate in some scenes he felt weird and unpleasant. The last one was with a punter he met one morning in a leather bar where 'a lot of the blokes are really heavy'. An Irishman came up to him, bought him a drink, asked him if he was a rent boy and agreed to give £40 for coming back to his hotel and using a dildo on him. 'When he showed me the size of it, it made me feel a bit sick, I was heaving. It was right in front of my face . . . It went on for about 45 minutes – I don't know how he took it for that long – it was horrible.' Another client that he and a fellow rent boy had serviced loads of times 'sits under there sniffing poppers while you have a shit . . . He eats it and that, it's really sick . . . I've been there and done it and the smell – and that's my own shit – makes me feel sick. But it's money again.' Another, who pays £45, 'I do every week, he's into spanking . . . You have to put on these little shorts – There's always two [of us] . . . We have to call him Sir and say like, "I've been caught smoking." He makes you do these press-ups, they're the worst, the [punishment] exercises . . . [Then] it's his hand on the bare arse, six on each side, then a leather strap, then a tennis shoe, then he's got a small cricket bat thing – that's six on each with them, and then he's got a bamboo cane and it's six with them . . . He don't hit hard . . . John did the wrong thing when he went up there, like he tensed up and everything and that makes it worse. I said, when we were walking there, "When he's doing it just relax" . . . I've been up there that often I know exactly what to do.'

The unconventional requirements of some clients, which are alien to any sexual interest the rent boy might have, highlight an aspect of many of the transactions, namely their one-sidedness. The client has the power of money to command the cooperation required for his own enjoyment, but the notion he may have that his rent boy partner is getting any pleasure for himself, or getting any pleasure out of trying to please, is often nothing but a sad illusion.

Continuing relationships

Many sex workers distance themselves emotionally from their customers, using a forced insincerity to mask their boredom, hostility or digust. These reactions do not necessarily stem from dislike of homosexual contact as such, but from the obligation to meet the demands of a an older or unattractive partner chosen for reasons of commercial rather than sexual interest. In the vast majority of instances no continuing relationship develops, but sometimes, even if the paying partner is the only one to derive sexual pleasure, a bond of affection may develop. Robin Lloyd (1976, p. 82) records how boys under pressure to act as witnesses against prosecuted men will sometimes refuse because they have come to regard their patrons as friends with whom they continue to associate as much for the care, attention and affection they receive as for the hard cash.

Clients, initially merely lustful, do not always remain emotionally detached. Gita Sereny (1984, p. 221) considers this a danger to boys. Unlike most of the clients of female prostitutes, men who go with boys want to form a relationship. Most runaway boys, she believes, find themselves at some time or other offered more than casual sex. She gives examples of boys drawn into male love affairs in this way.

Sexual orientation apart, there are many impediments to the development of intimacy between client and rent boy, such as discrepancy in age, physical attractiveness, education, wealth, experience and social position and attitude, all of which imbalances make for fear of exploitation by either side. This theme is explored in an historic German novel by John Henry MacKay (1985) who wrote from personal experience as a lover of youths. The story tells of a homosexual in his twenties who meets and falls in love with a gay teenager who had recently arrived in Berlin and been assimilated into the local street hustling scene. The boy regards him at first as just another client and a particularly stupid one for donating money without demanding sex. In time they develop a mutually enjoyable sex relationship, but the boy won't share his private life with a client and persists with his street companions and assignations with rich punters. Gradually, however, he begins to understand the older man's strength of feeling and the advantage of having a stable place of refuge. Arrested and imprisoned, his hedonistic lifestyle at an end, he at last appreciates and reciprocates in a love relationship.

A few of the men in the sample described what sounded close to real love affairs with clients. This was exceptional, but those who had been on the game for some time had often built up a collection of telephone numbers of punters interested in repeat performances and some had established a regular relationship with special patrons that meant they were less dependent on a continual search for fresh custom. *Case 003* explained that he had reached the position where he now had just two regular customers he needed to service only once a month – 'People I've known for years. And they're like people who pay me a lot of money.'

Others had acquired so-called 'sugar daddys', mostly punters who had become fond of them and were prepared to provide continued financial or moral support on a friendly basis without always requiring sexual services in return. The distinction between this and an 'older lover', which a few claimed to have, was not always clear and was probably dependent on whether the younger partner felt any reciprocal sexual interest.

Case 004 had had 'a sort of sugar daddy' whom he had been visiting over a period of two years:

> Q. And what did he used to do for you?
> A. Well he used to turn me on. Sexwise we used to watch a blue film.
> Q. And what did he used to do for you in return?
> A. Well, give me money, buy me clothes, things like that.
> Q. So you got quite a bit of money from him?
> A. Yes, he used to give me £50, £100.
> Q. And you'd see him every week?
> A. Yea, every week . . . but he went to Holland . . .
> Q. Would he want you to go and live with him do you think?
> A. Well he'd want it, I think, but I don't want to go and live in Holland.

He went on to explain that he much preferred girls. He had told a Streetwise worker that he had three children by two prostitutes.

The rent boys' usual conception of a sugar daddy was a regular patron whose contributions did not depend on always having sexual satisfaction.

Case 030

> Q. Have you ever had a sugar daddy?
> A. Yea, I got one now.
> Q. What makes you classify him as that?
> A. 'Cos I get what I want out of him.
> Q. And how long have you known him?
> A. About two years.
> Q. And how old is he?
> A. About forty-five.
> Q. And do you have sex with him?
> A. Occasionally . . .
> Q. And does he take an interest in your welfare?
> A. Yes, a nice man. I mean, it's not like these blokes that when they see you they only like you for your body and that. But this bloke, I mean, he doesn't bother if I don't go to bed with him for months . . . He helps me out a lot if I ain't got money or nothing at the end of the month.
> Q. He will give you something?
> A. Yea, so long as I don't go over the top.

He went on to explain that his ambition was to set up his own small business, settle down with a girl, get married and have kids. He intended to ask his sugar daddy to help with the money for this, but so far had not got around to putting the question.

Relations with sugar daddys who became possessive or jealous and tried to restrict the younger men's liberty to 'do their own thing' were short lived. One man had had a patron who, though initially possessive, ended by becoming a supportive friend without making further sexual demands:

Case 031

Q. What was he giving you other than accommodation? Food, money?
A. Food. Like he took me out shopping, bought me all clothes, really nice clothes. I always had money in my pocket if I wanted to go out drinking.
Q. He gave you money as well?
A. Yeh. Bought me a nice gold watch, gold chain.
Q. How long did you know him for?
A. I still know him, like I still go out to dinner with him every now and then. There's no sex any more. Past that stage.
Q. How long did the sex last?
A. About three months, four months.
Q. And you stayed with him all that time?
A. Yes.
Q. Did you go with other punters at the same time?
A. Yeh.
Q. Did he know about it?
A. Yeh, well, he said he didn't mind 'cos he wanted me, like. 'Cos I was a new face and, like, he collared me as soon as I walked into the pub. He wanted me all to himself sort of thing. That's what I think, anyway. Like, if he walked into the Lion or whatever and found out that I was in yesterday and walked out with John or Tom or Fred or whatever, he'd give me a hard time about it. Blah, blah, blah – 'If you want money all you've got to do is to come and ask me.' Fair enough, but like you go into a pub and he's maybe given you £40 or £50 and all of a sudden somebody [else] is waving £100 under your face you go, obviously, you know what I mean. He got the huff about it, but there was not a lot he could do about it.
Q. Did that have anything to do with you leaving him?
A. No. He got somebody else, like another new face came about. So I just said, 'Fair enough, but don't just blow me out.' He says, 'No, I wouldn't do that.' And he's still there. If I'm stuck and I need cash quickly for any reason I know I can phone him up . . . He has talked to my mother on the phone and everything. She doesn't know the score. He's my boss as far as she's concerned. He got a message saying my grandmother had been taken into hospital . . . He handed me £200 to get up there in a hurry – just decent. I give it him back. My father give it me straight away because I told him my boss had given me the money, but it was decent of him to do it anyway. That was two years after I'd left him sort of thing. So I know he's all right, if I ever need him at any time. I've never done him a wrong. I've never robbed a punter, never ripped a punter off. If I keep in with a punter and I get on with them all right, I know that I can go back to them and say, 'Here, look, I need a favour.' I've taken little liberties, I don't deny that, but I've never like blatantly robbed a punter, never hurt any of them or anything.

Some men were wise to the danger that a sugar-daddy relationship may end as the rent boy gets older and less attractive to his patron:

Case 039

> Q. Tell me about your sugar daddy.
> A. Oh C————. I just go back to his place once a week, suck him off for about 15 minutes and he gives me £100.
> Q. And that's it, you don't spend the night with him?
> A. No.
> Q. Does he give you anything else?
> A. If I wanted it, but I don't . . .
> Q. Is he a bit like a friend at all, in any way?
> A. He's a bit like a father, he'll look after me.
> Q. Do you trust him?
> A. Yes, but I know when I get around twenty-three or twenty-four he won't want to know me.
> Q. So you know that he's interested in you for sex?
> A. For sex and for the age and the looks. When I get older he's going to find someone else . . . He's not going to hurt me when he finishes. Most people get attached to their sugar daddy. If I was somewhere else I would, but London's such a bitchy scene anyway . . .
> Q. How much do you like him?
> A. Quite a bit. I look at him a bit, believe it or not, like a father.

The next two examples show that the boundary between commercial and non-commercial relationships is sometimes unclear. One described a proposal from a man he did not regard as a punter that he should become a 'kept boy', the other hesitated to class his older friend as a sugar daddy because he actually enjoyed the sex they had.

Case 014 had been friendly with a forty-eight-year-old man for five months. They had met 'just on a pick-up basis', not for money. This man was going to California:

> He wants me to move over with him for a four month trial . . . But I've had sex with him just once, that would be about three or four days ago, in that five-month period.
> Q. So it's not a very sexual relationship then?
> A. No, but he said that if I was to move over with him he would want sex about three or four times a week.

Case 038

> Q. He wasn't like a sugar daddy?
> A. No. I mean no, not exactly. I mean a sugar daddy, you just use them for the money, there's no affection in it at all I don't think . . . [It was] not like a punter, 'cos I fancied him, but still he gave me money . . . I mean I moved in with him and then we used to go out at weekends, just go to clubs. I mean he had found what he wanted and that was it . . . If I asked him for money he gave it me.

*

Reciprocal needs, on the one side for stability and security and on the other for both companionship and sex, make for the conversion of some purely commercial arrangements into continuing relationships. This seems always to have been a feature of male prostitution and it mirrors what happens in the male gay scene generally. Clients who have chosen a rent boy as a young holiday companion differ from many other gays only in the formality of the payments involved. Likewise, the expectation that a relationship will break up when sex interest dwindles and fresh faces appear is not unusual in gay circles where heterosexual mores, based on family tradition and parental responsibility, do not apply.

you as the sort of person who is indifferent about how others look at him.
Indeed, there was a sort of over-compensated revelation throughout the film,
as if the opportunity for display was simply too good to miss. He was seen
in his bath in an early scene, reading the morning mail (mournful postcards
from love-lorn clients, that sort of thing), a scene which certainly added
to the general sense that he was concealing nothing but didn't actually
amplify his argument - even male prostitutes proud of the name are
presumably entitled to wash themselves in private.

Later, he made even more of an exhibition of himself, performing arabesques
in a swimming pool, his naked body weaving through the water like an
Attenborough seal. Even when clothed he was sometimes placed in the centre
of the frame, like a precious object, as when he lay on the immaculate grey
floor of the Saatchi Gallery, a studied contrast to the mannered obesity of
the paintings on the walls. Bratherton walked and posed with the careful
tension of those who know they are being watched, a bearing that you felt he
was well able to maintain in the absence of television cameras.

He is too bright not to have thought of this himself, confessing to the
'danger of getting your own sense of self-worth from other people's valuing
of you'. The idea that the client's desire is a deep pool in which you can
gaze lovingly at yourself would obviously not be entirely new to him. But I
wonder if, in his calculated self-exposure, he was aware quite how revealing
the film would be. More often than not it looked like an advert for a body,
rather than a defence of a lifestyle. Future clients will have the
satisfaction of employing the services of John Bratherton, 'as seen on
television'.

The Independent
Arts Page 16

By TOM SUTCLIFFE

'TRICK OR TREAT', an Open Space (BBC 2) documentary about male prostitution, opened with a conventional silhouette, television's standard shadow- play of shame. But after a few seconds of sombre confession ('I've been involved in the profession for more than seven years or so now") the lights came up and you could stare John Bratherton in the face.

In a jokey way this was presented as a gesture of sacrificial candour, even bravery, and for most of the film you were inclined to take it as such. Certainly Bratherton made a reasoned, unsensational argument that his own life story - from Cambridge philosophy graduate to male prostitute - wasn't a matter of some appalling slippage into the lower depths. He had weighed up the need to earn a living against the desire for personal control and this is where the scale had finally poised itself - a job ("profession' is surely a bit much, unless someone has recently founded the Institute of Chartered Sex Workers) that didn't appear to offer immense material rewards but that allowed him to travel and, by his own account, broadened his mental horizons considerably. A case of join the rent-boys and see the world.

By the end, though, you began to wonder whether something else was involved here - not so much courage about coming into the light as a horror of remaining unseen in the shadows. It didn't seem to be a matter of unhappiness masquerading as control; there was none of the tremor you get when people try to talk and whistle in the dark at the same time. Bratherton had been working out his raisons d'etre and they were as lean and fit as his body. Prostitution, he implied, should be viewed as a branch of the social services, rather than some sort of shameful secret.

But his confident display didn't just flow from the insouciance of self-possession either. There was too much pleasure in it. Bratherton,

8

Transactions that Turn Sour

The vast majority of interactions between punters and rent boys pass off smoothly. To be successful in the business rent boys must behave decently with clients and appear friendly. Some of the interviewed men said they had never had any serious problems with clients and although a majority had some adverse experience to relate, these were usually isolated incidents. Nevertheless, there is always a chance things will go wrong and both rent boy and client know this, the former having reason to fear forced subjection to painful treatments they have never agreed to, the latter risking violence, blackmail or robbery instead of sexual servicing.

The practice of luring homosexuals into situations where they can be 'rolled' is a long-established criminal con trick. In the autobiography *The Jack-Roller*, a criminological classic (Shaw, 1930, p. 85), the writer boasts of his success with this technique. 'As I'd walk along Madison Street there'd always be some man to stop and coax one into having sex relations with him. My friend and I used this little scheme to entice men into a room and rob them.' He goes on to describe how his buddy would follow and when necessary enter the room to help him subdue the victim. He felt justified in relieving of his money a 'low degenerate' who had tried to 'ensnare' him. Although he had 'yielded to them a few times' he had no liking for these 'perverts', preferring 'to have relations with girls or to masturbate alone' (op. cit., p. 89).

Regular street prostitutes may sometimes filch items from their clients or take money or goods by force if they are not paid their due, but they do not normally set out with that as their sole intent. None of those interviewed admitted ever having done so. In their favourite bars, clubs and pick-up areas rent boys recognise each other, talk together and exchange experiences. Outsiders coming along to cheat and terrorise their clients would have an adverse effect on their business. One former street prostitute (*Case 202*) explained how in his time the rent boys formed an informal collective; if anyone stepped out of line by abusing clients he would be liable to a beating, and regular punters would be warned against going with him.

The following comment from an interview with an elderly punter who

99

had patronised street workers over many years illustrates the rarity, in practice, of serious confrontations:

Case 302

> I must have been with scores of different rent boys over the years most of whom I've found in [two well-known London rent bars]. If they don't ask themselves I always ask them before inviting them back how much they need to make them happy. I believe if you treat people right they are not likely to turn nasty. Rarely has anything serious happened. One fellow gave me a good time sexwise, but got out of bed while I was asleep and went off with my wallet. Another time a well-built fellow I took back to a rented room got threatening even before we had had any sort of sex. He got hold of a beer glass and was going to break it and cut me unless I gave him a lot more than we'd agreed. I had deliberately left the bulk of my money in the car parked outside and when I told him he followed me out to get it. Once outside I managed to run away and come back for the car later. I saw the boy again in the same bar a week or so later. He was not a bit put out and even proposed coming back with me again. Another time I met a young man in the pub and took both him and an Irish boy I had been with before back home for the night. The Irish one found and took away a knife that the other boy had hidden under the pillow. The new boy let me start to have [anal] sex but then demanded I stop and take it out, which was unusual. Then in the morning the car keys were missing. I said we couldn't go anywhere till I had found them and after we had all three gone through the motions of looking all round the room the keys suddenly reappeared in the middle of the carpet. I paid the boy what I'd promised and we went off peacefully, but I realised that if I hadn't had the Irishman with me I'd have been in trouble. But that's about all that has happened to me over many years.

An article written under the pseudonym 'Cruella' in *Action*, a free news leaflet for gay men (No. 23, March 1990), blames the clients' own foolish behaviour for most bad experiences. Punters will go out wearing flashy clothes and jewellery, fraternise with youths who promise them all sorts of delights so long as they are being plied with liquor, and take on trust the offers of apparently disinterested drinking companions who offer to introduce them to a boy who 'might be persuaded'. Once the boy gets back and is sure of his fee he may prove reluctant to comply with anything but the mildest of sexual activity or decide that he has to get back home very soon. Leaving a bar or a pick-up place the punter may be too much taken up with anticipated pleasure to notice an accomplice trailing behind ready to join in mugging him or ransacking his home when they get back. An erstwhile charming innocent may later reveal his under-age status and demand appropriate compensation for keeping his mouth shut, or he may in fact be casing the joint on behalf of burglar friends who call round later. Doubtless this writer's description fits some cases, but he is wrong to suggest that such disasters are everyday incidents.

Problems are more likely to occur with rent boys who are aggressively heterosexual and despise their clients. Caukins and Coombs (1976) suggest that someone who considers himself a young, handsome heterosexual, whether he actually is so or not, recoils at the idea that he must depend for his livelihood on people he regards as queers. Resentment is natural: 'We witnessed beatings, violence and verbal abuse of the most outrageous kind.' Klein (1989), who investigated the male body-building fraternity in California, an exaggeratedly macho group among whom one might not expect many homosexual prostitutes, found the reverse to be the case. Body-builders were often under financial strain because of the effect of their time-consuming training upon their earning capacity. They also attracted gay admirers. The temptation to go along with offers of money for photographic sessions that soon turned into more intimate exchanges was hard to resist. Being under pressure to preserve a masculine image they did so by restricting the sex acts they would permit and by denigrating their clients. 'Hustlers prefer to see themselves as exploiting guys for quick money, hence they seek to get as much as possible while giving little.'

Extreme violence or actual killing of one or other participant is very rare, but the author has had occasion to examine one or two men who were awaiting trial for the murder of a punter. One was a seventeen-year-old who had been in constant trouble from an early age and had a multiplicity of convictions for shoplifting, burglary, etc. When only ten he had set fire to a car, not long after which he was put into residential care as being beyond parental control. He was currently unemployed, involved in glue-sniffing, mixing with other delinquents and generally thought of as feckless and irresponsible. He was of heterosexual orientation, but he admitted that on occasion when he was short of money he had allowed himself to be picked up by men and paid for sex.

He had met his middle-aged victim some three weeks before the killing, and gone home with him for mutual masturbation and fellatio, for which he had received money and been driven home. He met the man again by prior arrangement, but this time he took with him a borrowed hunting knife. The victim died from multiple stabbing in what was described as a frenzied attack. As commonly happens in such situations the young man claimed that he had acted in panic. He allegedly lost control when the victim tried to roll him on his face preparatory to anal penetration. In view of their relative ages and physiques he could easily have just got up and walked out if he had had a mind to do so. He left the house driving the victim's car and taking away his video and cash. Notwithstanding his pleas of provocation he was convicted of murder and given the mandatory sentence of life imprisonment.

Most European and American legal systems prohibit prostitution involving young males and punish severely the supposed seducers or corrupters of youth. Blackmailing of punters might be expected to be more frequent than it actually is. Pieper (1979) notes that few rent boys appear in court on blackmail charges and that their confessions during research interviews are much more often to do with assaulting and robbing clients than with blackmail. As a less macho activity blackmail is not something to boast about and is probably unappealing to the average street worker because it requires time, persistence and ability to communicate. Male prostitutes are unlikely to get much sympathy from authorities, so threats to attract the attention of neighbours by making an immediate disturbance are probably more persuasive than threats of calling the police.Threats of a more complicated kind, such as informing relatives or employers, to which homosexual men are sometimes subjected (Thompson *et al.*, 1985), require knowledge of the punter's situation which the typical street worker out for immediate payment may not have the patience to acquire. Whatever the reason, none of the sample mentioned blackmail although there were a number of reports of unpleasant or violent confrontations with punters.

Victimisation at the hands of clients might be thought an occupational hazard, the risk being in part related to the time spent on prostitution, much as the risk of involvement in a traffic accident is in part a function of how long the driver spends at the wheel. Awareness of the dangers was variable, some professing to be sure of their ability to look after themselves, others not. *Case 018*, asked what was his greatest worry, replied 'meeting up with a nutter'. As a lead in to this topic the question was posed: 'What happens (or would happen) if a punter fails to pay up?' The first fourteen interviewees were not asked this, but of the rest fifteen said it never happened so they didn't know, four suggested there was nothing to do but leave, nine described mainly verbal threats, but eight suggested robbery and/or violence.

In reply to a related question, whether the punter or the rent boy was generally in better control of the situation during a transaction, a majority (29 to nine) thought it was the rent boy, with twelve undecided or saying neither one nor the other. The two inexperienced men cited earlier, who had not yet learned to ask the going rate, both thought the punter was in control, *Case 019* saying 'because they're paying', the other, *Case 015*, saying 'because a lot of them are stronger than me'. After failing to pay 'they'll give you a beating afterwards'. In fact this man had had the unusual experience of a punter trying to rob him rather than the other way round. He had picked up a man of about thirty-five at Piccadilly and gone with him behind some builders' materials in an underground car park nearby. 'He sort of grabbed me and asked for my money, but I managed to get away pretty quick, but it did shake me up a bit . . . I didn't go down [Piccadilly] for a week and then I was a bit more choosy who I actually picked up.'

The more aggressive and the more experienced usually held firmly to the contrary view. *Case 016* said he was in control because 'I know the score, like. I've been around a few years and I've learned how to look after meself. And I always carry a knife when I go out to work, always.' If a punter didn't pay up, 'I stab him.' That had happened 'a couple of times and I've got the money off him afterwards'.

With one exception, the nine men who reported the use of violence against fee defaulters thought they, not the punters, were in control. *Case 039*, however, said his punters were in control at the time 'because I'm nervous, very shy. You only speak to the person a few minutes, then you're off. Don't even know him.' On two occasions when he wasn't paid, although he just walked off peaceably, he got some friends to beat up the punters afterwards on his behalf.

Violent assault is a worse risk than not being paid. It may occur to enforce sexual acts which the rent boy does not wish to comply with, or to satisfy sadistic lust, or in an outburst of irrational anger against the erstwhile partner in a guilt-ridden escapade. These are dangers well known to prostitutes of both sexes. Janus *et al.* (1984, p. 141), in their survey of male prostitutes in Boston, found that over half 'reported being raped while hustling, often repeatedly' and all of them 'had suffered some sort of violence or threat'. McMullen (1990, p. 47) points out that some men assume that because a boy is involved in prostitution he is available for anything sexual as long as he is paid. They can abuse him as they like, relieve any guilt by paying him off, and remain safe in the knowledge that fear of the police, the courts and publicity will deter the boy from reporting them. Hatred of homosexuality may induce some heterosexual 'queer bashers' to select a rent boy for victimisation. McMullen (op. cit., p. 12) quotes the case of two men who, 'for a laugh' and because 'he was a queer', stripped and tied up a rent boy for a one-and-a-half-hour torture session during which they slashed him with a knife, burnt his penis with a cigarette and made him put on nylon briefs which they then set alight. He was threatened with death if he told anyone after he was released, but he had to have hospital treatment and the men were caught and imprisoned.

Instances of anal rape by punters, either singly or with the help of accomplices, were the most dramatic and the most frequently cited examples of nasty experiences associated with prostitution.

Case 002, at the age of seventeen, when out looking for punters in Piccadilly one afternoon, met a pleasant-seeming man who offered to take him home as he had nowhere to to stay and needed to get cleaned up. The man gave him something to eat but must have put some drug in the food because, although he started off perfectly sober, he was quickly knocked out and on coming to found he was being anally penetrated.

The next thing I knew I was coming round and I was tied up, my legs and arms, and he was going twenty to the dozen. I was in pain . . .
Q. How long did that go on, how long did he have you tied up?

A. About half an hour or an hour or something. It just seemed for ever and ever, like it was non-stop.

Q. Did he just keep going at you?

A. Yes.

Q. Did he hurt you?

A. Yes, inside. He brought blood and I thought I had AIDS straight off . . .

Q. Did he beat you or anything like that?

A. He gave me a few punches in the ribs, because I was saying, 'Get off, pack it in' and calling him all bad names because he was black. He just carried on . . . I thought it was never going to end.

Q. And how did it end?

A. He just done it, untied me and said get dressed and get out. That was it. He did not give me nothing, I was glad to get out . . . He gave me crabs as well . . . I just felt so bad, dirty and different you know. It took me a couple of months to get over that . . ..I got really wary then who I was going with . . . [Nowadays] I sort of pick the ones I think are going to be OK, sort of like more weaker than me.

Case 004, at the age of sixteen, new to London, without money or a place to stay, went with a man of about thirty expecting payment. He was driven in a van out into the country and then the man 'suddenly changed when we got out into the country. He'd been nice until then . . . He held me down and that . . . didn't punch me, but you know, strong hands . . . It did hurt, he was pushing my head into the bottom of the van and saying that if I moved he'd kill me . . .. It was hurting, like, you know, sore . . . Afterwards he told me to get out and then he drove off. So I had to hitch-hike, through country roads, about 20, 30 miles . . . Getting near murdered, the first thing I was thinking was to get back to London . . . I was frightened for a couple of weeks after that.' He told no one 'because I thought if I go and tell the police they'd say that I was in the wrong for picking up men'.

Case 005 claimed to have been subjected to multiple anal rapes on two occasions during his renting career.

Q. When you were a boy, say under fourteen, did anyone ever involve you in sex activities you didn't want – against your wishes?

A. No.

Q. Has that ever happened to you since?

A. Twice.

Q. Tell me about that, the first time?

A. It'd be [two years previously] the first time. I was round Piccadilly.

Q. This was a client that you picked up?

A. Yes. He pretended to be a client.

Q. And what happened?

A. He just took me back to his place and two of his mates raped me.

Q. You were expecting to have sex just with him, but there were others?

A. Yes.

Q. You mean they had anal sex, they fucked you?

A. Yea.

Q. All of them?
A. No, just two of his mates, he didn't do anything.
Q. Why was that?
A. I don't know.
Q. And there was a second occasion?
A. Same thing, except it was Leicester Square.
Q. This was another punter? And what happened?
A. There were more people.
Q. How many?
A. Seven.
Q. And what happened then, did they all have a go?
A. Yes.
Q. Every one of them?
A. Yes.
Q. What happened?
A. Well I didn't go to a doctor or the police.
Q. You just felt sore?
A. Yes.
Q. Bleeding?
A. No.
Q. And the first time this happened to you, after they'd finished what happened? Did they just turn you out?
A. They let me get dressed and I left.
Q. Did they pay you?
A. No.
Q. And the second time, what?
A. Same thing.

It has to be said that this man is known to be an unreliable informant. A number of his statements on other matters did not tally with what he had told others and the Streetwise worker who saw him on the morning when he first described the second and more dramatic incident, which he said had happened during the night, remained unconvinced. Anticipating that such repeated assaults would leave him very sore she offered him some analgesic ointment, but he declined, saying he was perfectly OK.

Two men had actually reported sex assaults to the police, but without receiving much satisfaction:

Case 021. The victim met his assailant in a bar. He was not soliciting at the time and did not think of the man as a punter, although money was offered.

He come up to me and said, 'I'm sure I recognise your face from somewhere, I don't know if you remember me.' And I said, 'I don't think so,' and I was quite a bit drunk, a bit tipsy. So he said to me, 'Would you like to come out with me?' So I said, 'OK.' I told him I had no money and he said, 'Well, don't worry about that.' So we left the pub and went to a club till three in the morning and he was buying me drinks continuously . . . He asked me if I'd like to go back to his hotel, so I did. And umm, then he just got violent and he punched me in the face and asked me to do stimulating things to him . . .

He just sort of grabbed me by the hair, slapped me in the face and butted me and then he umm, he tried to have anal sex with me, and then he um, he told me to get on my knees and beg for mercy and then he asked me to kiss his body all over.

Q. Did he succeed in having anal sex with you?

A. No he didn't. There was too much bleeding, he cut me.

Q. But he did try and caused you to bleed?

A. He did, yes.

Q. So how did it come to an end?

A. It come to an end by me saying, 'OK, if you want to fuck me I'd like you to fuck me properly, just let me go to the toilet first.'

Q. And you escaped?

A. I managed to get out of the back window, I only had a pair of trousers on, he only let me put my trousers on. I managed to escape out of the window of the bathroom.

Q. Did you tell anybody about this?

A. I 'phoned the police. The police arrested him. They took a full statement off me and then the CID officer that arrested him and took statements from me told me that, because I voluntarily went back to the hotel with him, if we take this to court, which is up to you, the prosecution will rip you apart for voluntarily going back with him. So I said the best thing to do is to drop the charges . . . which they did.

Case 045

This happened when I was fifteen and on the run from the children's home . . . I was on the game, and once I met this guy in the early hours of a Sunday morning, who said he lived somewhere near this hospital . . . We got a cab and he took me there. Walking up this flight of steps at these flats I found out we was on top of the roof. When I turned round to find out what had happened, out comes a knife, flick, and I was [raped] there and then. I was threatened if I screamed, if I did anything, he would throw me over, he would kill me. I couldn't do nothing . . . I went over to the hospital and told them, because I was in tears and everything. Obviously I was tested by the doctors for semen, which was found, and the police were involved . . . [Weeks later he saw the man in the street and called a passing policeman] The guy was literally handled and put into the back of a police van and so was I, in the same van. I was really badly treated by the police at this time. He was taken to court and found not guilty, because they reckoned he had a good [alibi] . . . I literally caught the guy [but] the police were obnoxious to me, said, 'You rent boy, serves you right.'

Some victims were able to retaliate against abusers:

Case 011, a tough-looking tattooed skinhead with a charge against him outstanding for 'actual bodily harm' had to be suspended from the project for a time on account of racist and intimidatory attitudes. Asked about being forced into sex against his will he said:

I was standing on the corner by the pub down the road, waiting for a punter, and I got picked up by one, and he took me back to the flat. And there was another geezer there. And they forced me into sex I didn't want to have.

Q. What did they force you to do?

A. Give them blow jobs and get fucked and everything.

Q. How did they force you?

A. Well, when I came out I was black and blue.

Q. They held you down?

A. Beat me up until I done it.

Q. Did they give you any money?

A. No.

Q. Then did they throw you out after this happened?

A. No, being a real nuisance, like, I smashed a bottle and stabbed one of them with it.

Q. This was while they were doing things to you?

A. No, afterwards. I got my clothes back on, like, and they was asleep, and I just smashed the bottle on one of them, then run out of the house . . . I stabbed him twice in the stomach. There was a lot of blood and the other one woke up and shouted.

Q. Since they went to sleep while you were still there they can't have expected anything like that?

A. They was drunk.

Apart from these examples of gross violence by prospective punters, there were other stories of forced compliance, intimidation, over-persuasion or use of intoxicants to overcome resistance.

Case 039 described an incident that took place two months before the interview.

Q. You had pulled a punter, gone back to his place and thought it was just the two of you?

A. Yes. But there was another person there and they were both out to tie people down and cane them.

Q. Did you know immediately something was amiss?

A. No, I just thought he was a flat-mate, till we started undressing –

Q. Was that a bad experience?

A. Because I've never had a threesome before in my life, but I didn't know it would be like that.

Q. Did they beat you badly?

A. I had about six marks on my back. It did hurt a bit, enough to leave a mark on the back.

Q. And what else happened?

A. That's all they were into, caning.

Q. You didn't have any direct form of sex?

A. No.

Q. And did they let you go immediately?

A. Well, I had a coffee, believe it or not, then I left.

Q. Did they pay you?

A. Yes.

Case 036

I met this punter up the West End and we got in the car and I said like, 'It's 15 nicker, is that all right?' Just by sort of saying to him 'give me money' that gave him the hump, like. He didn't start talking to me and then when we got there he said to me, 'I've been ripped off by boys before, you are not fucking ripping me off.' So he had a sort of vendetta against rent boys. I've seen this sort of thing before, when punters get ripped off they start ripping boys off, or if boys get ripped off they start ripping punters off, or they rip punters off anyway. Everyone is being ripped off both sides of the board . . . He just sort of had a bit of a go at me . . . And I had another punter that held a knife to me once. That was a funny scene. He lacked respect for me 'cos I was a rent boy. He said, 'Anything's better than this.' You get twisted people like this, and he just sort of said do this and that and then he gave me my money as well. He didn't rip me off, it was just his way of dealing with it you know.

Q. Was he making you do things you wouldn't have done otherwise?

A. I might have done these things. Yes, there was no need to have the knife, you know.

Those who allowed themselves to get thoroughly drunk and incapable while with a punter were taking a special risk.

Case 030 had had a surprise offer of £100 to go back with a man he met in a gay club.

Later on, I don't know what happened, but I think I drunk too much. I passed out and woke up in a cupboard. It was horrible. My feet were like up in front of me and I had these little metal pieces all round my leg.

Q. This was in his house?

A. Yea. It was camp. Like in the morning he came to the cupboard and said, 'Are you comfortable?' And I was saying 'Comfortable! Comfortable! Bloody hell! Get your fucking hands off me!'

Q. Then what happened?

A. Nothing. He like pulled me out of the cupboard, pulled my legs down, sat me on the bed and was just staring at me, stared at me for about an hour. I said, 'Get your fucking hands off me NOW!'

Q. You couldn't do anything?

A. No, because I had my hands tied up. No, the only thing that bothered me was my legs and hands tied up. I don't like it. It freaks me out.

Q. So what happened then?

A. He was just going on, 'You're a really nice guy. I really like you. I want to keep you here for ever.' And I was thinking, 'Oh, I want to go home, where's my mum? Oh, get me out of here.' Then I thought, 'I'll play this cool, pretend I like it.'

Q. Because you didn't want any further hassle. So what happened, did he finally untie you?

A. During that time he was actually losing his temper, hitting tables and things, and I thought I couldn't abide him hitting me, because I couldn't hit back. So I thought I'll try and be nice to him, but the more I was nice the more he got pissed off . . .

Q. So what finally happened?

A. He just sort of loosened my arms and went out. He said, 'I'll see you later on.' I just got the ropes off me, got dressed and just went.

Q. Did you get paid?

A. Oh yes. He give me the money the night before, it was in my trousers.

But, I mean, I stole some more money off him as well.
Q. Could you remember what had happened the night before?
A. No, I was too drunk. He must have done it when I was asleep.

Some of the more assertive men thought they were well able to handle clients wanting more sex than had been agreed or by failing to pay:

Case 007

Someone tried to rape me once, but it didn't work . . . I picked him up in Piccadilly and we went back to his flat in Dulwich. It was a house and he locked the door . . . And he was going on, 'I'm going to rape you, I'm going to fucking rape you, I'm going down the drain pipe' . . . I said, 'Go on darling, try you bitch.' He gave up in the end and fell asleep . . . He didn't wake up, so I took all his money, it was about £250 and I thought, 'All right darling, you play that trick on me and I'll get your credit card.' I got a couple of hundred out of the card, so I made £400.
Q. So did he take you home in his car [when he woke]?
A. By cab . . . That was the one time I never asked [for payment first] because I trusted him. I never did that again.

Case 027

Q. Have you had a bad experience frequently?
A. It's happened three times. Once was where the punter wouldn't give me the money and I had to get stroppy and he got stroppy and I just had to take it in the end.
Q. What happened, did you fight?
A. Not that one. I just took the money and threw his wallet back down on his bed. The second time there was two blokes and they tried to jump me in the flat and I had to fight to get out.
Q. Did the two blokes pick you up together?
A. No, one bloke picked me up at Victoria and we went to a flat in Camden. As I walked through the door this other bloke was there and he pushed me through the door and shut the door. The one that was already in the flat was quite big . . . [and] quite young, twenties, the other one was about forty. I just barged my way out. One had his foot in the door. I had to kick his leg out of the way. I pulled the door right open and run out. There's other people who have been unlucky. The third [time] was where I had to have a fight with a punter to get my money . . . I picked him up at Victoria . . . Got in his flat, took his trousers off, took my clothes off, put it all down on one side, got into bed, done the business, got out of bed. I says, 'Can I have my money now?' He said, 'Well you wasn't good enough.' So I went to pick up his trousers and take his wallet out and he snatched it out of my hand. I said, 'Give me my money' and he said, 'You ain't getting no money. Get out, get out!' So I hit him and he hit me back, like I hit him and hit him and hit him and he hit me back and it was quite hard.
Q. You finally got the money?
A. Yes . . .
Q. How did you feel?

A. I was quite happy in the end. Because people like that, they might try to take liberties out of me, but I won't have it. There's other boys out there who let them get away with it.

At interviews with the eleven Day Centre attenders (*Cases 051-061*) not in the main sample of 50, who were seen subsequently and given an opportunity to talk at length about their experiences with punters, more descriptions of untoward incidents were elicited. These eleven may not have been properly representatve, but only one of them reported never having trouble with punters. That was *Case 059* who said, 'If you're nice to them they'll be nice to you.' He was, however, selective of his clients. 'I don't go with guys too young.' The most common complaints were of being suddenly left stranded in a hotel room or elsewhere without payment, or of having to use threats or force to extract payment, or of having to be firm to make clients desist from unwanted attempts at anal penetration. No less than four of these eleven reported violent assaults, including two strangulation attempts:

Case 051 had got into a punter's car and been driven to the deserted top floor of a multi-storey car park. 'He was massaging my shoulders and I could feel his hands going round my neck and starting to strangle me. I thought, "Oh shit! He's going to strangle me." Before he could get any further I said "Oh, quick, go – someone's watching, I've just seen someone watching." He shot off out of the car park. I said, "Stop for a minute." Then I just jumped out of the car.'

Case 056 said, 'I was doing this punter. He was wanking himself and just about to come and he started trying to strangle me. I was sat by the side of the bed with my back to him. He just sort of freaked out. I just grabbed my clothes and ran down the corridor of the flats – it was a block of flats – running round the block with nothing on.' The motive for these attacks was obscure. Sexual excitement is thought to be increased in some people by being partially strangled, but no such idea was in the minds of these victims.

One of these eleven men had been the unwilling victim of sadistic ritual and another narrowly avoided a similar fate:

Case 057 had gone with a man who said he wasn't an S & M person, but when they got back to the house he saw there were dildoes, whips, chains and handcuffs round the walls. He made to leave but the man got him to stay, promising not to do anything like that to him. However, as he was lying down, the man managed to cuff him to the bed. Then he was gagged and whipped and caned so he 'couldn't sit down for a week'. Then the man told him it was his turn. He tied the man up, gagged him, and instead of using the cane ran off with all the money he could find, which was £500. The man had locked the door, but he got out through the window.

Case 051

> I got back to this guy's and he was trying to tie me up and all this shit. He tied my hands behind my back and said, 'I'm going to fuck you.' I was really scared. He went out of the room to go to the toilet and I managed to untie myself, but I kept my hands behind my back because I couldn't get out [of the locked door]. When he come back in he grabbed me, but I just pushed him away, grabbed my clothes and went [out the door]. I actually stood in broad daylight in my boxer shorts and got dressed in the front garden.

Returning to the main research sample, an important observation was that among the totality of sexual assaults reported to have occurred since the age of fourteen, those happening in the context of prostitution were no more frequent than those occurring in the course of social contacts outside the rent scene. Evide_.tly, homeless youths accustomed to sleeping around are at risk from acquaintances as much as from punters, a conclusion which warns against the too easy assumption that street workers' social problems are attributable to their involvement in prostitution rather than to their general lifestyle.

Case 050 was asked about sex against his wishes since he was fourteen:

> A. Not so much. I mean they want to do things that I don't want.
> A. You mean you have been persuaded to do things?
> Q. Yeh.
> A. But not forced?
> Q. Well it depends how you define forced.
> A. Is this with punters or –?
> A. Oh no, not punters. I could handle them [said disdainfully].
> Q. Boyfriends or casual lovers?
> A. Casual lovers, bits of trade.
> Q. Describe something to me so that I can get an idea what you mean?
> A. Well if you think of being tied up and things like that.
> Q. By people who are into that, and you agreed?
> A. No. I didn't agree, but they tried to get me drunk and drugged me, but I weren't as drunk and drugged as they thought . . .
> Q. Did anyone, for example, fuck you when you were tied up and could have stopped them?
> A. Oh yeh. I mean, like, after a while I don't care [laughs]. I'm a real slag aren't I!
> Q. You mean you enjoyed it?
> A. Not at first, I didn't like the idea, but then I did.

Other examples of coercive sexual acts experienced apart from the rent scene included the following:

Case 033 said he had been abused by 'someone in authority'. He did not want to talk about it at interview, but it would appear from what he told others that he had been blackmailed into allowing anal intercourse by a person whose supposed authority he was afraid to refuse.

Case 037 had recently been put up for the night by an acquaintance he did not much like. There was only one bed which he had to share. He was very tired and the man waited till be was half asleep and then began to penetrate him. After that the man's mate, who had been sleeping on cushions on the floor, tried to do the same but was too drunk to succeed. Since then he has not seen either of them.

Case 042 was with a mate sleeping out on the Thames Embankment when a man who knew their names started talking and eventually offered them a place to sleep while they got sorted out. Back at his flat the man told them to take a bath:

> When I come out of the bath he said, 'I like a big one.' Actually, I didn't know what he was talking about, but it didn't take long to get what he was on about. And I said to him, 'No, I don't. You've got the wrong sort.' I actually asked to go, but my clothes were all in the wash and I couldn't. In the end we did end up by going with him [for oral sex].

Case 025, when he was seventeen, had gone for a job at a large hotel. A chef who worked there accosted him in a cloakroom/toilet: 'He just pulled my trousers down and fucked me. And that was a pretty bad experience, because I didn't know he was going to do that. I thought it was the other gentler sex, but it turned out to be the other way.'

Case 009, when he had just turned fourteen, met a man in a toilet and agreed to go back home with him. He was not expecting to have anal sex but the man, aged about thirty, forced it on him. As it was his first time, 'It was a bit sore and everything like that.' He stayed the night and left in the morning. He was 'not really' angry, but they didn't see each other again and he didn't have anal sex again until he was sixteen.

Case 028 was sixteen, but drinking in a bar, when he noticed a man staring at him. He went back to his brother's caravan and left the door open. Unknown to him the man had followed him and, taking advantage of the fact he was 'pissed', raped him. He reported the incident to the police and the man was imprisoned.

Case 012 said he had been arrested on returning from Amsterdam at the customs for drug posession when he was assaulted in a police cell.

> This copper came in with another copper. One of them was in uniform and one in plain clothes and one of them raped me.
> Q. Forced you to let him have anal intercourse?
> A. Yes, just one of them, the other was holding me down.
> Q. Did you shout and struggle?
> A. Yes, but at the time I'd been in Amsterdam and I'd been stabbed in the side and I wasn't really in much of a state to fight back.
> Q. And were you hurt?
> A. Hurt, but you know –
> Q. Hurt, but not injured?
> A. No.
> Q. Did you complain about it after?

A. No, just as soon as I got out. I was – I didn't have a lot of trust for the police.

Q. Why didn't you complain?

A. I just wasn't interested. I thought, 'Fuck it, if that's the state of the police force.' You know what I mean.

Another conclusion from the question about sexual assaults since turning fourteen was that the men who had reported sexual abuse in childhood did not appear to be specially vulnerable to sex abuse later. The eighteen who reported having been coerced into unwanted sex acts since turning fourteen (whether in the context of the rent trade or otherwise) were more or less evenly distributed between those who reported earlier sexual abuse (7 of 18) and those who did not (11 of 32). Current lifestyle seemed a much more important determinant of risk of abuse than past history.

*

Although serious confrontations may be rare in relation to the totality of contacts with clients, the potential for violence is obvious. Sexual assault is the most likely form of violence street workers may encounter and its potential for harm should be recognised. Forced anal penetration, whether by hand, object or penis, carries medical risks. Apart from a lethal transmission of HIV, other sexually transmitted diseases such as hepatitis B can be so acquired. Both gonorrhoea and syphilis may develop in the rectum and be passed on to other sexual partners without the victim necessarily being aware of his condition. Injury to the delicate lining of the bowel by finger nails or other objects may set up serious abdominal infections (Agnew, 1986).

Regardless of any medical complication, the psychological upset from a serious sexual assault can be severe. The rape trauma syndrome originally described in women is also found in male victims of sexual attacks (Kaufman *et al.*, 1980; Forman, 1982; Mezey and King, 1989). Anxiety, depression and considerable disruption of sexual feelings and sexual relationships may occur and sometimes last a long time. Obviously, some young men with wide experience and robust attitudes to homosexual acts of all kinds may shrug off the odd occasion when they have been discomforted. Others, whose self-esteem and self-confidence is already at a low ebb, can feel emotionally traumatised, as some of their descriptions showed. It is too easy to blame the victims for knowingly taking risks. Prostitutes should not be targets for abuse, least of all by those needing their services, but the reality is that young street workers are in a vulnerable situation. It is sad to learn from these interviews that they have such low expectations of obtaining help or redress if they approach authorities.

This chapter has focused on some very real dangers, but we must re-emphasise that most transactions run smoothly and that the difficulties which do occur are most often at the less serious end of the scale — rudeness, lack of consideration and avoidance of payment rather than serious maltreatment or violence. Street workers are more vulnerable than men working via agencies or on their own premises, but most still thought that they were generally in better control of the encounters than their clients, an evaluation that is probably realistic.

9

More Problems

Sexually transmitted diseases

Concern about the contribution of male prostitutes and their clients to the incidence of AIDS has stimulated a number of recent researches into the incidence of high-risk practices (anal sex and sharing injection needles) and the prevalence of HIV seropositivity (Plant, 1990). Results tend to confirm that sex workers are prone to HIV infection, but possibly no more so than other male homosexuals (especially the incautious young) who have multiple sex partners. Moreover, young sex workers seem to be as much at risk from their ordinary non-paying sex partners, with whom they are less likely to practise safer sex, than from their customers, with whom they are more cautious. Coutinho *et al.* (1988) found only four out of 32 tested male prostitutes (mostly brothel workers) in Amsterdam to be HIV positive, a proportion thought to be no higher than among the generality of sexually active male homosexuals. An Italian survey (Tirelli *et al.*, 1988) found the proportion who were HIV positive actually lower (11 per cent) among male prostitutes than among homosexual controls (17 per cent) and much lower than among a comparable sample of drug addicts (49 per cent). High proportions with HIV infection may be expected in places where prostitutes and their clients are less well educated as to the risks or generally more reckless. Pressure from clients insisting upon unprotected anal intercourse and willing to pay more for it can be difficult to resist (see p. 85). Also the use of intoxicants during sexual transactions lowers inhibitions and may render participants more reckless. In a survey in San Francisco (Waldorf and Murphy, 1990) 10.6 per cent of male street workers tested were HIV positive, but the percentage among those who were also intravenous drug users was much higher. There was also more HIV infection, 22.9 per cent, among call men, that is off-street workers offering erotic escort or masseur services, presumably because their longer time in the business and their more protracted interactions with clients had exposed them to more risks. Risk of spread of HIV infection into the community at large is greater from clients than from prostitutes because there are many more of them and because a significant proportion have female sex partners (see p. 26).

In the sample of 50 street workers attending the Day Centre 33 said they had been tested and seven of them (21 per cent) said that they had been found to be HIV positive. It may be that those more likely to have been infected are more likely to opt for the test. Another reason why this statistic cannot be taken as representative of London street workers is that men with reason to suspect their HIV status may have been encouraged to come forward by the presence at the Centre of an AIDS counsellor and a doctor from a sexually transmitted disease clinic and the ready availability of testing. One of the HIV positives was a haemophiliac probably infected before his involvement in the sex trade.

A majority of our 50 street workers said that they engaged only in low-risk acts with punters. The danger of anal sex was widely known, but many were confused about the risks of oral sex and conflicting professional pronouncements on the matter did not help (Spitzer and Weiner, 1989).

Case 049

> Really, on the rent scene, fucking is a no-no as far as I am concerned.
> Q. And that's because of AIDS?
> A. Well yea. Because of everything. It's just not worth it.

Safer sex rules might be broken sometimes, but there was a general awareness of risk and conscious attempts to limit it. As many as 21 said that they avoided anal sex altogether with punters and of the remaining 29 there were only five who said they did not use condoms. Only one of these five, however, was among the seven men who said that they had been found to be HIV positive. The seven HIV positives included four who said they used condoms with punters and another who said he did not need to as he avoided anal sex with clients. Of course their rules may not have been adhered to as firmly as they claimed or they may have acquired infection from non-paying partners.

Those who practised anal sex did not necessarily do so routinely, but criteria for agreeing to it might have little to do with actual risk.

Case 031

> I'd only fuck him if I knew he was spotlessly clean. If we were in a pokey little shit hole somewhere, then I'd think twice, you know. If it was a nice hotel or a nice flat and the man looked well off and looked as though he looked after himself, then I'd go for it.

Some had changed their sexual habits in an effort to lessen risk:

Case 009

> With my clients, lovers and things, like, I am not being screwed at the moment.
> Q. No. Why is that?
> A. 'Cos I can't. Since AIDS come out and stuff like that I'm stopping nearly everybody screwing me.
> Q. So, how long have you had that rule?
> A. About just over a year.

On the other hand there were some who ignored risks:

Case 010. This man, who was 'sleeping rough' in a nearby cemetery, had a severe alcohol and drug problem and was not very coherent at interview. He survived by begging more than by prostitution. He said he would allow anything except being tied up and usually his punters fucked him. He did not bother with a condom. He had not been tested for HIV because 'I know I'm OK.'

Case 021

> Q. Are there some things you really refuse to do with punters?
> A. Nothing at all.
> Q. You'd do anything if you get the money?
> A. Yes.
> Q. You swallow the come sometimes?
> A. I've never, no. I tell them before they come, if you are going to come tell me, otherwise it'll go all over you . . .
> Q. Do you use a condom?
> A. Never used to, no.
> Q. Nowadays you do?
> A. Usually, yeh.
> Q. What if the client doesn't want to?
> A. Fair enough, I just go ahead with it.

This was one of the two known HIV positive cases who said he did not always use a condom. He had also had penile gonorrhoea, non-specific urethritis, genital herpes and hepatitis.

Asked about sexual infections generally, apart from HIV or pediculosis, twelve of the 50 men reported having had one or more of the common illnesses, gonorrhoea, syphilis and hepatitis. Concentration on the danger of HIV may have taken attention away from other, undiminished hazards, such as the different infections linked with anal practices (Agnew, 1986). Many who denied infection had attended sexually transmitted disease clinics and a majority of the sample said they had had an HIV test. This could be taken either as acknowledgment of exposure to risk or as adoption of a responsible attitude, or both. 'Safer sex' was a popular slogan, but practical details (such as avoidance of oily lubricants with condoms) were less well known.

The data concerning sexual infections produced no surprises. As was found in a recent Glasgow survey (Bloor *et al.*, 1990), safer sex rules applied to relations with punters were often ignored in relationships elsewhere. The present findings support the conclusions of Martin Plant (1990, p. 200): 'AIDS cannot realistically be dismissed as a problem only for deviant minority groups. Commercial sex together with "unpaid" sexual activity link most of the population, directly or indirectly.'

Drug use

The prevalence of drug and alcohol abuse among female prostitutes has long been recognised (Goldstein, 1979; Weisberg, 1985). Various reasons have been suggested including a need to take something to overcome stress and revulsion to sex work, the ready availability of intoxicants at the venues where pick-ups occur as well as from the clients themselves, and the need to perform sex work to support an already established habit. Similar circumstances surround the male rent scene and surveys have confirmed the high incidence of both drug use and heavy alcohol consumption among male prostitutes and more particularly among male street workers (Waldorf and Murphy, 1990). It must not be forgotten, however, that to some extent drink and drugs is a part of the sub-culture to which most of the young street workers belong.

All save one in the sample were users of tobacco, 30-40 cigarettes being the typical daily consumption reported. The one non-smoker (*Case 049*), was unusual among this sample in having had a fairly ordinary parental upbringing in an unbroken middle-class home.

Abuse of intoxicants was reported by many interviewees and accounted for some being so short of money. Although not asked routinely, a few also mentioned expenditure on gambling machines. Problems caused by excessive drinking were described by 21 men, sometimes to the extent of being unable to stop until their money had run out. Nearly all used cannabis, although some said they took it only when it was offered to them free. A majority of 38 said they had used other prohibited, recreational drugs, and sixteen said that they were still doing so.

Many who were heavy drinkers did not see it as a problem:

Case 043 said he had always been a big drinker, but not so much as to be a problem. Nevertheless, if he didn't get a drink he 'would get very wound up, very irritable, start snapping at people'. 'Usually I have a drink when I get up, first thing I have a coke and then a Bacardi and coke.'

Case 039 said he didn't really know if drink was a problem, but 'Once I've started, have two or three, I'll just carry on, I just can't stop . . . I'll walk in one pub really sober and by the time I leave I can't walk out, I'd be falling over everywhere.'

Case 039

> Q. Do you have a problem drinking?
> A. No. I don't rely on it, but I do drink a hell of a lot.
> Q. How much per day, can you average it?
> A. Oh God, I start drinking about three pints and then I lose count how many shorts I have after that. I spend about £40 a day on drink.
> Q. You don't think that's a problem?
> A. No, it's not, because I'm not addicted to it. I'm a lot shaky in the mornings, but I'm not an alcoholic.

Drink was a substantial item of expenditure for many:

Case 019 agreed he had 'a bit of a problem'. He did not go drinking every day, but when he did he would spend £50 to £100.

Case 003 had worked in a male brothel in Amsterdam:

> Q. And how much did you earn there?
> A. £40 a time and [the agency] got £40, it was £80.
> Q. And how many times did you manage that in a week?
> A. It was about seven or eight a day.
> Q. So that's a lot of money.
> A. I mean I blew it all. After I'd finished I used to go drinking every night, and smoking, you know, dope and that. I didn't get into anything heavier than pot [cannabis].

For some, expenditure on intoxicants would have been much heavier were it not that others paid or that they made money by dealing:

Case 012 said he used to spend £60 a day on heroin and some more on 'pills' but currently he was using a lot of cannabis, and 'I do a bit of acid, but I prefer mushrooms'. But 'I don't spend so much now, probably about 20 or 30 quid a week at most. A lot of people give me stuff.'

Case 007

> Q. Do you drink a lot?
> A. Yea, I have done recently, I've been on fourteen to sixteen vodkas.
> Q. So how much do you think you spend on drink?
> A. I don't spend on drink. My sugar daddy done it for me. I call him my sugar daddy 'cos he's rich . . .
> Q. He supplies you?
> A. Yea, up the discotheque.

Case 016

> Q. Do you have any problem with drinking?
> A. Yea, I drink a lot, but I ain't got a problem with it.
> Q. How much would you say that you drink in a day?
> A. Six pints . . .
> Q. And what [other drugs] do you take regularly?
> A. Dope, every day.

Q. So how much do you think you spend on drugs?
A. Nothing at all. I sell it.

In other instances men admitted that it was their custom to go on drinking until their money was spent:

Case 010

Q. How much do you drink in a night?
A. Say about sixteen pints.
Q. So how much do you spend?
A. If I've got the money for that I'll do it, get drunk.

Case 040

Q. Do you think you've got a drink problem?
A. I have a bit, yeh.
Q. How much do you drink a day?
A. When I go out drinking I always drink a lot.
Q. So it's more the case that when you drink you overdo it?
A. . . . normally I don't drink pints, I drink shorts.
Q. How many?
A. [Shrugs]
Q. Do you just keep on going?
A. Yeh.

Case 002

Q. Do you have any problem with drinking?
A. I do drink a bit, quite a lot.
Q. How much do think you spend on drink?
A. Well if I make it I spend it on beer . . . And I'm doing me other money on the machines and smoking . . .

Case 032

Q. How much do you drink when you go out?
A. Whatever I can afford . . . If I had a lot of money I'd spend the lot on it.
Q. No limit?
A. No.
Q. You'd really get blind drunk?
A. [Nods assent]
Q. How much do you think you spend in a week on drink?
A. £90, thereabouts, £100 . . .
Q. What drugs do you use?
A. Speed, hash, coke.
Q. You use all those?
A. Acid-LSD . . .
Q. The ones you've used most?
A. Acid, speed, ecstasy, hash and poppers.

Q. So how much do you spend a week on drugs do you think?
A. Say about £100.

The histories suggested that many were heavy users of intoxicants independently of prostitution activity, but some found that after taking drink or drugs they were in a better mood to handle their punters' distasteful requirements. Others mentioned that long hours spent in pubs and clubs looking for punters involved considerable consumption of liquor. The punters also often gave them drink or drugs to facilitate the transaction.

Case 030

Q. Do they usually buy you a drink?
A. Yes, that's what they go into the club for. I mean, they're going to buy you a drink first of all, and they're going to try and get you to go home with them. And then you get them to buy you another drink and you carry on with this sort of act, 'Oh, in a minute, in a minute.' And you get them to buy you another and another.
Q. How long will you carry this on for?
A. Carry on as long as it takes to get your head completely out of it so you don't have to take notice of who you are sleeping with. So when you get home with them you can enjoy it by being drunk.
Q. So, like an hour, something like that, half an hour?
A. Try two hours for me, how I drink!

Heavy drinking was not an absolute necessity, however, since the sample included some moderate drinkers and a few abstainers. *Case 014* said he didn't drink at all and never had used drugs. *Case 029* said he drank no more than one can of beer a day. He had tried other drugs, but was currently using only cannabis on which he spent about £10 a day. In this respect he was like others who seemed to prefer alternatives to alcohol:

Case 017

Q. You don't drink?
A. I do, but it doesn't bother me if I haven't got it.
Q. How much in a day?
A. Three, four, five pints, sometimes ten ... I only do one drug at the moment and that's cannabis, that's all. I probably spend £100 to £200 a week.

Case 021

Q. How much do you drink?
A. Two pints a day?
Q. Do you smoke?

A. I smoke about ten to fifteen a day and a few puffs of the other in between.

Q. When you say puffs, you mean dope?

A. Dope, yeh.

Q. What other drugs have you tried?

A. Well I mean I've tried them all at one stage, but I've never injected, I've tried heroin on the tinfoil, chased it, and I was sick . . . Tried speed. Well that was all right, never done me any harm, but it was too much, the come down was too much, I felt rotten. Acid I've tried, dope's the only one I can say I really like . . . I guarantee I'll have four or five joints a day probably.

Q. How much do you spend on dope?

A. £7.50 to a tenner [per day].

There were some who took more easily to alcohol than other drugs:

Case 036

Q. And drinking?

A. I would say I'm a bout drinker, I have say a bender, once, twice a week, definitely once a week I get fucking quite drunk . . .

Q. So you don't take any of those [other drugs] regularly?

A. No, no. Like, if it's coming my way, a friend's got a bit of smoke, I might say, 'Can I have a puff?' Actually, the one thing that put me off drugs is the amount of fucking aggravation of getting it. Do you know what I mean, the run around. I thought I just don't want to get involved in all this, that's why I drink, because drink's a simple thing to do.

On the other hand, some moderate users of alcohol were heavy users of other drugs and some were heavy users of both:

Case 046

Q. Do you drink a lot?

A. No.

Q. Did you ever?

A. No, not very much.

Q. And drugs, you say you've tried most of them?

A. Yes . . .

Q. Which are the ones you've taken regularly?

A. Heroin and speed, and tuinal and downers.

Q. How long were you on heroin?

A. How long was I on heroin, about a year.

Q. When was that?

A. Between a period of about eighteen and a half to nineteen and a half I was addicted to it. Then I went on methadone treatment [about eighteen months ago] . . .

Q. How much were you spending on drugs at that stage?

A. About £150 a week.

Q. And you were supporting that by being on the rent?

A. Yes.

Case 027

Q. How much do you drink a day do you reckon?
A. If I go out on a drinking session I drink as much as I can drink.
Q. You get very slammed?
A. Yes. But if I just go out for social drinks, a couple of pints.
A. And how often do you go out and get really slammed?
Q. About once a fortnight. But I get stoned [i.e. on cannabis] all the time. It's better . . .
Q. So how often do you smoke dope?
A. Every day, all day . . .
Q. Are you on dope now?
A. No, but I'm going to get some though.

Case 021

Q. What would you say is your biggest worry in life?
A. Well my drug taking and things like that, and my health.
Q. So do you have a problem with drinking?
A. Yes.
Q. And drugs?
A. And drugs, yes.
Q. How much do you drink these days?
A. If I can afford it I drink seven or eight cans of Special Brew, but that's not every day, I have to afford it.
A. And cigarettes?
Q. I smoke about 20 a day.
Q. And what drugs have you used?
A. I've used heroin, coke. I've used amphetamines, valium. Valium I use [now] on a daily basis, and temazepam in the daytime as well.
Q. And cannabis, do you smoke?
A. I don't like smoking, no.
Q. Anything else besides valium at present?
A. Cocaine at the weekends, when I go out, but that's it.
Q. How much do you spend on drugs?
A. At the weekends I spend about £70.

Several others reported that they had been much heavier drug users in the past than at present:

Case 009

Q. Do you have any problem with drink?
A. No, not really. I hardly have any money to spend on drink . . .
Q. Do you use drugs?
A. I have used drugs. I was hooked on cocaine.
Q. How long did you go on using cocaine?
A. About eight months.
Q. And how did that come to an end?
A. I met a lover and everything like, and he asked me back to his place and I ended up living with him. And he helped me out of it.

Heavy consumption of intoxicants was evidently a prominent feature of the lifestyle of a majority of these street workers. As a result of their behaviour while intoxicated some had been charged with assault or being drunk and disorderly and a few had attended drug clinics. Both socially and for the purpose of finding punters the men were frequenting places where heavy drinking was usual, drug taking was acceptable and drugs rather easily obtainable, a situation of risk for anyone vulnerabe to addiction. Their stressful way of life may have contributed, although this was not a point usually made by the men themselves. Their attitudes to the dangers of addiction, either to alcohol or to other substances, were generally nonchalant.

It was remarkable that only one man was a non-smoker and 42 out of the 50 smoked 20 or more – sometimes many more – cigarettes a day, a proportion some three times what might be expected of young, working-class males in London (West and Farrington, 1977, p. 179). Since cigarette smoking commonly starts during schooldays, it probably for the most part antedated entry into prostitution. This suggests that there were reasons unconnected with the rent scene, but related to temperament and upbringing, for the observed vulnerability to substance abuse. The sample were significantly deviant from population norms for their age group in this as in other respects, but then vulnerability to substance abuse is common among the socially alienated and homeless young. Involvement in the rent scene possibly exacerbates this tendency, but cannot be said to be the prime reason for it.

Confrontations with the law

The extent of the men's activity on the streets was reflected in the fact that a majority (31) reported having at some stage been charged at least once with offences related to street prostitution, usually 'persistently importuning male persons for immoral purposes' or 'highway obstruction', the latter being a charge arising out of the habit of lingering in public places waiting to make contact with punters that does not require evidence of actual solicitation. Although some said they had been unfairly arrested at times, others described occasions when they had been warned without any further action being taken. The frequency of these incidents showed that the police are active in confronting (many of the men would say harassing) young male loiterers suspected of prostitution.

Charges of importuning normally come about as a result of police officers watching operations on the street and arresting culprits on the spot. One man, who was awaiting the result of an importuning charge, had been arrested by officers who were apparently keeping watch in a gay bar and had stopped him as he was leaving:

Case 022

> I don't know if I'm going to win the case or not. I was supposed to be going to meet somebody at Piccadilly. I was going to walk there, but they nabbed me outside the [gay bar]. They said they'd been watching me for ages, they'd wanted to catch me for ages.
>
> Q. And had you been hanging about Piccadilly for ages?
> A. No. I don't go around Piccadilly because so many people have told me not to go there because it's risky. That's why I go to pubs and clubs to pick punters up.
> Q. So you were actually going to meet somebody, you weren't just hanging around?
> A. Yes, in Piccadilly tube station, not outside.
> Q. And they just stopped you in the street?
> A. Well they were in the pub, they were in plain clothes.
> Q. They had been watching you in the pub?
> A. Yes.
> Q. Did they say that you had approached men in the pub?
> A. No, they said I had approached men in Piccadilly, when I wasn't anywhere near Piccadilly.

Male importuning is an imprisonable offence, but prosecution usually results in a fine. Even so, time may be spent in custody between arrest and court appearance, or on remand, or later for non-payment of the fine:

Case 008

> Q. Ever been in court for anything to do with the rent scene?
> A. Twice for importuning. The first time was a while back. In fact it was actually an alleged importuning. I pleaded not guilty but I got found guilty by the magistrate
> Q. Where did it allegedly happen?
> A. Two police officers said they saw me approach two males, but I wasn't aware of being in the area.
> Q. So it was totally untrue was it?
> A. Yea.
> Q. And the second time?
> A. That was true, they caught me that time, on the corner of Glasshouse Street [Piccadilly], near the Regent Palace Hotel.
> Q. And you were picking people up?
> A. Yes, I was . . .
> Q. Ever been in prison?
> A. Yes, for those two offences. Three weeks remand in custody and I got five weeks in a detention centre. The second time was three weeks remand and two years probation.

As in the last example, men often complained that they had been arrested at times when they were not actually importuning, presumably because having seen them around frequently and got to know their faces the police felt able to act:

Case 017

>   Q. How did you get caught?
>   A. I didn't, believe it or not. The police just decided to pick me up because they started to get to know me face around Piccadilly and they were just being their usual selves.
>   Q. So they just arrested you and said you were –
>   A. Yes, importuning. At the time I was, but I wasn't with anybody.
>   Q. Not at that moment?
>   A. No, they just pulled me in.

That the police should be familiar with this man's face was unsurprising. Before his conviction for importuning he had been in prison and detention centre more times than he could clearly remember for offences such as breaking in, criminal damage and drug possession.

Many of the men with experience of being arrested were deeply resentful about the testimony presented by the police at the court hearing, which they said was often false or greatly exaggerated:

Case 003

>   Q. You mentioned you had been done for importuning?
>   A. Yes, once. I got a fine. That was about two years ago in Piccadilly.
>   Q. How did you come to get caught?
>   A. It was the plainclothes police. They saw it like. And to be really, really honest – what they said apparently was that I was walking up to men asking them, whereas I'd only just got there five minutes before. And then a man came up to me and asked me for a light. I mean I knew he was a punter. He asked me for a light just to find out what I was doing. And they just ran over straight away and nicked me, saying I was importuning. I went to court and got a £200 fine. And the judge said to me – you know, I mean I was not working and I wasn't signing on the dole – we want £50 a week. I had to pay it off in four weeks. So I said I can't pay, so he knocked it down in the end.
>   Q. So you did pay it?
>   A. Yes. I think I still owe £10, but I've still got a few weeks to pay it. I kept going back.
>   Q. You said it was two years ago?
>   A. Yes, but I kept going back. You know, because I got a summons [for non-payment] . . .
>   Q. You told me about all the money you got for sex, you could have paid it off more quickly?
>   A. I could have done, but –
>   Q. How did you spend your money?
>   A. On drink and going away, 'cos I travel a lot.

The use of the charge of highway obstruction was seen as a convenient ploy to avoid having to produce evidence of solicitation:

Case 036

Yeh. Well you see, what they've got is, they've got highway obstruction as a misdemeanour, you see, and I got done for that about a hundred times.
Q. Really?
A. Right, and then I've been done once for importuning, only once. Oh, and I got done for loitering, which is when you are on the underground. If you are on the underground you are loitering and if you are upstairs you are highway obstruction, for the same fucking thing you know. Well, actually, with one loitering charge I was originally charged with importuning by the transport police. How it went was I went not guilty . . . Well, I've got to court and the transport man said to me, 'We are in a hurry to be somewhere, right. Now if we drop it to highway obstruction and offer no evidence on the importuning will you go guilty on that?' 'Cor, I certainly fucking will!' Do you know what I mean, because I didn't have a brief or nothing, 'cos I was guilty, like, the way the law is . . .
Q. What happened?
A. I got fines and then I got bind overs, you know, keep the peace for a year and I had probation thrown at me. I also done bird, I got three months right, four months, for highway obstruction . . . What happened, like, I was getting these bind overs, I've had about four of them and all of a sudden I've gone to court and that's made me break four bind overs, see, something like that. It accumulated, so they had been seeing my face a lot in this court, we'll have to teach this boy a lesson right. So they said we are going to give you 28 days for each of them, so that's an 84-day sentence. I got 84 days, but you get a third off for remission. So I've got this 84 days to do and I appealed against it, got a solicitor. When I went to Crown Court it's quite amusing. I put on the best act of my life, turned over a new leaf, I'm a reformed character, all this bollocks, right . . . I got let out. I'd spent two weeks inside . . . But when you appeal you take a chance, 'cos it can go the other way . . .
Q. What happened when you got done for importuning?
A. I got a £15 fine.

Further information about street workers' interactions with the police, obtained from eleven attenders at the Streetwise Day Centre, who were not in the main sample, is discussed in Chapter 19, p. 287.

Apart from resentment at what they looked upon as arbitrary and unnecessary interference with their trade and their complaints of maltreatment by police prejudiced against gay men, many had had confrontations with the police in other connections. A majority (32) said they had been found guilty of offences unrelated to prostitution. As many as sixteen had served custodial sentences, an indication of serious or persistent offending. Several were wanted by the police or had trial dates pending at the time they were interviewed and some had been on the run from the police when they first came onto the rent scene. Asked if they had sometimes to resort to theft to supplement their income fifteen replied affirmatively, although all denied stealing from their punters except when they had been cheated. In addition four said they obtained money by selling prohibited drugs, and as already described a majority were breaking the law by virtue of their drug consumption. Information coming to light subsequently and recorded in the case files suggested that these figures underestimated the prevalence of delinquency.

Considering the chaotic backgrounds and present circumstances of many of the men in the sample, a high incidence of rebellious and delinquent behaviour was perhaps to be expected. That the clients of the Streetwise Day Centre were a difficult and challenging group to help was demonstrated by the number of untoward incidents reported to the author during the period of his association with the project. Notwithstanding their friendly demeanour and politeness towards visitors, clients of the Streetwise Day Centre were sometimes aggressive and insulting towards staff and on occasion police had to be called to evict members who had become intimidating or refused to leave. Neighbours had also had to call the police when items were taken from communal parts of the building or people below were annoyed by objects thrown from the windows. Money and equipment repeatedly disappeared and once some members were apprehended out of hours trying to gain entry to the place by means of a ladder to the back window. Although use of drugs on the premises was supposed to be strictly prohibited this did not prevent members turning up very obviously 'stoned'. One interview had to be abandoned for this reason. Some of the Day Centre clients induced a young volunteer to participate in delinquent escapades that caused him to be convicted for fraud. Use of the telephone had to be severely restricted when it was found that some members had been using it to make contact with punters. While attending the Centre several men, including one who was in the interviewed sample (*Case 012*), were currently working in a male brothel and had to appear in court when the organisers were prosecuted.

In spite of the prevalence of criminal records, so far as could be ascertained, the men's main source of income was from prostitution rather than from other illicit enterprises. There were, however, a few exceptions where street work was apparently incidental to a criminal lifestyle:

Case 016. At the time he was seen he was awaiting trial for involvement in firesetting at a gay pub and was expecting imprisonment. He was unwilling to talk about this and did not want help from Streetwise as that would reveal his connection with the rent scene about which he felt ashamed. He was an aggressive character with several convictions and two custodial sentences for wounding and assault. On one occasion he had threatened another member of the project with a knife and another time he arrived drunk, swallowed some pills, became abusive and would not leave when asked. At the end of the interview, when asked about future intentions should he be sent to prison, he said, 'I think I'll do a big robbery and then piss off out of the country.'

Some were more deeply into offending than they were prepared to during the research interview:

Case 028. A few days before the interview he had been to court on a charge of importuning:

> Q. How much did they fine you?
> A. Well it was £30, and then I told him to go fuck his mother. So altogether I got a £200 fine for that and I was in the paper for it . . .
> Q. Have you been in trouble with the police for anything else?
> A. Entering dwellings and theft, but I didn't do the stealing though.
> Q. What about drugs, have you been caught?
> A. No. They've pinned them on me, but they can't catch me . . .
> Q. Ever been in prison?
> A. No.

A few weeks later a letter came from this man written in prison. 'I'm in for nicking cars, nicking them and stripping and rebuilding the cars again. Anyway, I'm going not guilty. They haven't got a leg to stand on even though they've caught me in the cars, but I've got one problem to sort out. My mate grassed on me and told the police that I've stole about two cars.' Back in the Project two months later the author happened to overhear a conversation in which this man said he was thinking of accepting a proposal to help with a break-in for which he would be paid a large sum.

In so far as these observations tend to show an overlap between prostitution and criminality they apply only to the street worker samples. Moreover, since the majority of those with a history of earlier delinquencies were now surviving on the proceeds of prostitution it could be argued with some justification that engagement in street work helped to divert some young men away from serious crime.

10
Attitudes and Intentions

Questioned on their feelings about being involved with the rent scene the great majority made negative comments and many declared their intention to give it up. Feelings were mixed, however, because it was clear to may men that they could not expect to obtain anything like the same amount of money from conventional jobs of the sort open to young men without particular qualifications. A few claimed to have actually ceased going with punters, or to be in the process of reducing their involvement, but most seemed unsure if or when they would succeed in complete and permanent disengagement. Obviously there were pros and cons to being a street worker and considerable ambivalence. Some were simply having a ball, enjoying the plentitude of sex and drugs and night life. Society's view of prostitution as low, dirty and immoral, compounded by condemnation of homosexuality, had rubbed off on some men who were in varying degrees ashamed of what they were doing or anxious to keep quiet about it. Others were more troubled by the health risks to which they were exposed or by their dislike of the sexual demands of unattractive punters. Some respondents felt they had no other means of satisfying immediate needs and were left with no choice.

The examples cited illustrate the considerable range of opinions expressed. The first three are typical of a general disgruntlement over dependence on street prostitution, but uncertainty about how to change:

Case 006

> I want to get out of it because it is bringing me down . . . just lowering my natural feelings about myself . . . When I turned eighteen I realised that I didn't need to do this, I could get myself a flat, get myself a decent job and be respectable.

In fact he was hoping to move into a flat owned by a friend who was going abroad, but the plan fell through and he soon found himself roofless and penniless again and without the identity papers required for 'signing on'.

Case 035

Q. What's your feeling about being on the rent scene?

A. I don't really like doing it, but it's the only way I can live, you know, feed myself.

Q. What would you prefer?

A. A job, you know, proper [job].

Q. Not be on the rent scene at all?

A. Occasionally, maybe at weekends sort of thing, or in time off, maybe the odd one . . . [but] . . . before I get a job I want to get a permanent address, 'cos it's a Catch 22 situation . . . 'cos if you go for a permanent job and say no fixed address, you know, bye, bye.

Case 016

Well I'd like to get off really. It pisses me off, the punters and the gay scene, I don't like the gay scene . . . I think I'll do a big robbery and then piss off out of the country.

Case 001

I depended on it, but after a while I got I just didn't want to do it, but I had to do it because I hadn't got anything for myself . . . I never liked it, they were all old men . . . I just think that it is disgusting that people entice young people to do it.

Some of those who felt they wanted to give up were prepared to do so only if particular opportunities came their way:

Case 044

I'd like to give it up altogether, but the situation would have to be right to do that you know.

Q. And what would be the right situation?

A. Umm. A sugar daddy you know, ideally someone who was just really wealthy, who I was amazingly attracted to.

Q. So [then] you would give it up?

A. Yea. I don't do it for the kicks.

Case 032

Q. Would you like to get out or continue in it?

A. I'd like to get out.

Q. What would you need to get out of it?

A. Mainly a lass that would understand the situation I was in.

Q. What would she have to understand?

A. That it would be hard to get out of it.

Q. Out of the sex trade?

A. Yes.

Q. But you are more dependent on thieving than on sex aren't you?

A. Yes.

Q. You would want to get yourself out of both, would you?
A. Yes.

Case 002

Q. So it's not a bad thing on the whole?
A. Yes, it's pretty good, meet people, places, company and all things like that . . . [but] . . . Mind you if I get a decent job I'll give it up then.

He was in no hurry, however. Interviewed 21 months later, when aged twenty-three.

Q. Do you want to get out of it?
A. Yes, I'm going to have to. It is no use saying do I have to because I know I'll be too old for it anyway . . . Maybe another twelve months and then I will try and get a job.

Lack of money, particularly inability to secure accommodation, was a commonly cited reason for continuing on the game:

Case 022

I'd rather give it up . . . it's boring . . .
Q. What prevents you?
A. Well it's money. And I want somewhere to live – call it a home. 'Cos where I am in the hostel it's doing me in.

Case 020. 'I can't afford to [give it up].'
Case 014. 'I'd just like to have a job to pay me money and I wouldn't have to go to those places.'

Case 029

Q. You don't want to keep doing it?
A. No.
Q. So you're going to find a way of changing?
A. Yes. It's very hard when you've been doing it for such a long time. Very hard, 'cos you're used to the sort of money that you earn and declining from what you earn and are used to spending to a regular job, earning maybe £100 a week, is very hard.

Some respondents were aware of personal difficulties preventing them from taking on other work:
Case 042. 'I think if I could get myself settled into a good paying job I'd

give it up ... [but] ... because I was homeless for so long I find it very
hard to settle down.'

Case 050

Q. What do you feel about being on the rent scene?
A. I like it – I mean I am indifferent. I mean I've got to do it whether I like
it or not, because I cannot last in jobs, I have never lasted in jobs because I
am too young to live my life [in a routine] like that. But I mean it is
embarrassing if you go out and meet someone and they say, 'What do you
do?' and you try to make up some load of old bull shit.

Case 039

I don't like going with punters, but I just do it for the money. I like gay sex
anyway, so I don't see why I shouldn't use it, the money, anyway.
Q. Do you want to get off it at all?
A. If I got a job I'd get off it, but I can't get a job because I'm wanted.
Because they do trace you through your national insurance number and all
that. I'd have to get a cash in hand job.

Hesitation about relinquishing prostitution gains altogether was
evident in those cases where men were trying to bring an end to their
dependence on punters:

Case 008

Q. What do you think about the game? Is it a good thing?
A. Not as good as it was.
Q. Have you thought about giving it up?
A. Not yet, I'm surviving on it at the moment, anyway.
Q. But you have an idea of getting a job, you said?
A. Yes.
Q. What sort of job?
A. I'd do anything. A job's a job. So long as it's got a salary at the end of it
I'm not bothered.
Q. But then would you continue to get a bit extra from the rent scene?
A. Probably I would.

Case 012. 'I don't do it any more, hardly – once every couple of months,
if I've got to pay the electric bill or something I'll do a punter.'

Case 036

Q. Are you still on the rent scene?
A. Well, I would say I haunt a couple of gay places, and if the situation
arose, through my experience, I would turn my hand to it. But I'm really not

looking for it, I'm easy about it, you know, but occasionally I get the odd punter . . .

Q. Would you like to give it up altogether?

A. Yes, I think I would actually, I think anyone would.

Case 021. 'I don't go out looking for it any more, but I don't refuse it if I happen to be in a pub and someone comes along.'

Case 034

I want to stop . . . [but] . . . if I see a punter I like I will, if he offered me [money]. If he's wealthy of course, if he's not wealthy I'm not bothered.

Q. So you're not sure really whether you will or you won't [stop].

A. Well if I see someone I like, I might, you know, think about it.

Q. What is your main reason for doing it, for money or for pleasure?

A. Pleasure.

Q. But if there's money in it you'd take it?

A. I'd take it, Oh yeh!

Case 045

Q. Would you like to have another sugar daddy?

A. No. I've had offers, just recently, funnily enough. A guy that lives in Portsmouth, he's offered for me to go down and live with him and he'll look after me. I'm very much thinking about it.

Q. You were.

A. I still am, because it only arrived last Sunday. Actually I do want to get out of the rat race.

Q. What's stopping you?

A. Accommodation . . .

Q. What's your biggest worry?

A. Bumping into my mother in the West End.

Case 031

Q. What's your feeling about being on the rent scene?

A. At first it was degrading, but like the more you get into it, the more people you get to know, you don't think it . . . I don't mind now, I'm used to, resigned to the fact now.

Q. You don't particularly want to give it up?

A. Oh yeh, I mean, like I say, over the last six or eight months I haven't gone out of my way to go and get a punter sort of thing, 'cos the money's been coming in from elsewhere and I'm working and all that sort of thing, but if I do find myself skint I think, 'Well why not go up the West End or whatever, see what's happening.'

Q. So it's basically OK?

A. Yeh, OK. I know I can go to regulars, even though I don't have to have sex to get money, they obviously like a bit to keep them sweet.

Case 027

Q. Do you want to give it up?

A. Now I've got a girlfriend, that's it [finished] . . .

Q. You have given it up, but you are out of work?

A. Well I've done one punter, I've got all the rest of the money off my sugar daddy. I've done a couple and got all the rest off my sugar daddy and some other bloke, so it's all right.

Q. Would you like to give up your sugar daddy, or is he too good in terms of money?

A. He's too good really. I could give up everything else, like.

Re-interviewed eighteen months later he had failed to live up to his intentions. He was talking of still spending four or five nights a week on street work 'regularly', 'except when I've been in prison'.

Another man, re-interviewed after almost two years, really did seem to have kept to a resolution to give up. He had been fortunate in having the help of a punter turned lover who continued to give him financial support:

Case 008

Q. How long have you been off?

A. The last time I done a punter was a year and a half ago.

Q. How does that feel?

A. It feels great, yeh.

Q. Are you glad to be out of it?

A. 'Cos I've got my sexual needs at home.

Q. How long have you been together?

A. Two and a half years now.

Q. How old is he?

A. He's thirty-three.

Q. How did you meet him?

A. [He had followed me out of a club] and he goes, 'I seen you coming out of [the club], do you fancy earning yourself some money?' So I said, 'Yeh, why not?' And I go on, 'What for?' and he goes, 'Oh, just a little play about.' I go, 'How much?', he goes, 'Thirty quid', I said, 'Yeh' . . . I took him back to my place – I was living in a hotel in Baker Street – it was over in three minutes. That was it, bang! Then he left and arranged to meet me the Tuesday after, and he kept his appointment. And we met for a couple of weeks. Then we started going steady. Then he got me out of the hotel and got me me own place.

Q. So how long after did you get out of the rent?

A. Well, I was still doing him as a punter, but once we started going serious together, that was it. I just stopped. Within a couple of weeks I just stopped completely.

Q. Where did you get your money and survival from then, did he help you?

A. He helps me. I mean he comes home every night and slips me a couple of pounds.

Q. Do you live together now?

A. No, we live separate, we've tried living together and we're always arguing. We get on great when we're living separate.

Q. But you have a good relationship

A. Yeh, we have a great one, fantastic.

Q. Do you have a job now?

A. Er, I did have, until three weeks ago. I got laid off.

Q. Are you looking for other work?

A. I'm not any more. [He went on to say that without qualifications it was impossible to get work]

Q. So does your boyfriend help you out now, still?

A. Yeah.

Q. If things didn't work out would you go back on the rent?

A. No I wouldn't.

Q. Are you sure?

A. Positive.

Q. How come you are so dead set against it?

A. Well I wasn't at first, then I realised people were actually abusing my body, you know. My boyfriend is not like that. If I don't want to do something I'll just tell him and he'll go, 'Fine', and we'll do something else.

Rather than give up prostitution altogether a few men were looking out for work in the sex industry away from the streets:

Case 028

Sometimes it's OK, sometimes I get pissed off with it.

Q. Do you mind continuing?

A. I haven't really made up my mind what to do yet . . . I want more money . . . I might go in for escorts.

Case 025

Q. Would you like to get out?

A. No, I've no choice.

Q. You are in it for the money?

A. Yes.

Q. So you would give it up altogether if you could?

A. Yea, if I could. Once someone did tell me of a certain [male strip] club, but when I went there they'd been closed down.

Case 026. 'It's just a job [but] I don't think I'd like to do it [agency work] indefinitely. I'd like to do something else . . . I'd like it if I knew them [clients] and it was on a regular basis.'

Case 037. 'I don't like it, it's boring me to death . . . especially if you don't get one [punter] for days. I was jealous of my mates last night, until I got a punter . . . I might just start going to the ——— Hotel.'

Reversion to prostitution in times of difficulty was understandable:

Case 023. This man claimed to be 'off the game', but did not seem very resolute about it. He thought he might be forced back if he could not get accommodation. The sex partner he had been staying with had thrown him out when the social security authorities discovered his presence as a lodger. He had not been prostituting where he had been staying because 'there's no rent scene down there and if there's no rent scene I don't indulge'. In London, however, he was always tempted. He would not want a sugar daddy 'because, as I understand it, they take over. The furthest I would go to that would be a house boy.'

Following this interview he was helped to get accommodation but was again thrown out. After that setback he went back to street work and was convicted for importuning. A man he had worked for as house boy agreed to take him back 'so long as there is no trouble and he behaves himself' and he in turn agreed to go back 'provided no strings [i.e. sex demands] attached'.

A minority were open about not really wanting to change their way of life:

Case 030

    Q. Are you happy to just continue?
    A. Yes. I mean, if I get arrested I get arrested and that's it, there's nothing I can do about it.
    Q. So you're not trying to stop?
    A. Yea. I will stop it. I mean I can stop it if I want to, but I like the people, the people are much better.
    Q. So it suits you at the moment to continue?
    A. Yea, because of the danger involved. I love danger.

Case 049

    Q. And what's your feeling about being on the rent scene?
    A. It doesn't bother me. I just want to do it for – I mean I know what I want out of life and this is one way of getting it quicker, that's all. . . . There's one thing, for me anyway, that being on the rent scene does, it spoils your sex life, you just can't be bothered.

Case 011

    Q. Would you like to give it up if you could?
    A. It's fun really.
    Q. So you don't really want to give it up?
    A. I wouldn't mind, but there's a good sort of income too.

In contrast, some men were only too clear that they hated what they felt they had to do:

Case 046

    Q. What's your feeling about being on the rent scene?
    A. I don't like it . . . It's just dirty, full of diseases, you could pick up anything, you don't know who you are going with or what these days.

Q. So a lot of it is physical health aspects?

A. Yes, and staying up till 3 and 4 o'clock waiting for someone to come along. You get depressed because you can't get any money. It's not worth waiting out there in the freezing cold, well I can't do it now otherwise I'd catch pneumonia . . . It changes a lot being told you're HIV positive.

Case 013. 'I'll be honest, I don't like it. Because now it's dangerous, especially with this AIDS business and that what's going on.'

Case 017

I used to be a Christian and I back-slid. I'm still back-sliding now . . . by doing what I am doing . . . It says in the Bible a man shouldn't go with a man . . . I feel the rent scene is low and degenerate.

Q. Why do you say that?

A. Because the people that do it are low and degenerate. More so the punters than the rent boys.

*

To sum up: few were prepared to say they were satisfied with street work; most looked forward to giving it up, though not necessarily completely so long as they did not remain dependent on constantly looking for punters. The sexual demands and the waiting around for clients were felt as irksome. Liability to arrest on the street and risk of contracting HIV were major concerns. Even so, the lure of easy money, in comparison with the drudgery of low-paid, unexciting jobs, was very apparent. Many had been on the game or were to continue so for long periods in spite of their declared wish to break free. Few had tried to secure safer and more regular earnings by doing sex work for agencies. Absence of a regular home base was a serious impediment and the requirement to be regularly available may have acted as a deterrent to those who found sticking to routine difficult. Lack of relevant experience and lack of a home or a job meant that many had only vague notions of how to promote themselves and escape from the social trap in which they found themselves. On the whole it did not appear that many of the men were ready or able to abandon street work in the near future. The declared aim of the Streetwise Youth Project – to empower young men involved in the rent scene to make more satisfying life choices – is no easy task. Nevertheless, workers at the Project were able to cite individual success stories of men known to them who had secured jobs and accommodation and were no longer dependent upon street work.

11

A Supplementary Sample of Street Workers

Alternative sampling

The individuals comprising the main sample of 50 were fully representative of the Streetwise Youth clientele at the time, but not necessarily typical of street workers in general. The facilities at the Centre may have selectively attracted young men with troubles of one sort or another. Since the agency has no legal right to handle minors under sixteen, and its policy is to concentrate resources on the under twenty-ones, the age range of those seen at the Centre was necessarily limited. The Streetwise sample may have been unrepresentative in other ways as well. As Mark Kjeldsen (1991), leader of the Streetwise outreach team, has pointed out, street workers may have a variety of reasons for choosing not to attend the Day Centre. Some may feel they have no need of help, some of those on the run may not trust any agency, some may be unwilling to conform to the Centre's rules and regulations, others may be disillusioned by previous contact with would be helpers or fear losing face among their associates if they admit to wanting help.

The outreach team met street workers in pubs/clubs, where they went both to socialise and to find punters, and also at their more public pick-up places on streets and stations. The outreach observations did not suggest any great diffference between the ones 'out there' and the research sample. The age range was wider and some minors under sixteen, who would not have been able to frequent the bars, were to be seen on station concourses, but in general the average age seemed about nineteen. The concerns most frequently expressed were to do with homelessness, finding food, drug use, confrontations with the law and risks of HIV infection. These were the same issues that preoccupied the Streetwise attenders, with the exception of lack of money for food, but the interviewed sample were being provided with a free meal by the Centre. The prominence of complaints of hunger by those seen by outreach workers could mean that some of them were in more desperate circumstances than attenders at the Centre. Their reports of the going rate for sexual service – £30 to £40 – were the same, but trade was often erratic and some were prepared to settle for no more than a bed and a meal when more profitable contacts failed to materialise. As with the

139

research sample, though earnings could be very large at times, spending habits, particularly on alcohol and drugs, seemed to preclude saving anything for when trade was scarce. Many were totally bereft of any legal source of income. Some were afraid to apply for benefit because they were on the run from outstanding criminal charges or fines. Others scorned the requirement to join a Youth Training Scheme, which they looked upon as slavery. Their accounts of the nature of the sexual services to punters repeated what has already been described.

No sample of prostitutes is without bias inherent in whatever method of recruitment is being used. It could be argued that Kjeldsen's sample was so similar to the Day Centre clientele because most of his introductions to outsiders came through men who were already attenders whose acquaintances would tend to be others like themselves. For the purpose of this research a further 25 men were interviewed, all of them located other than through membership of the Streetwise Youth organisation and all of them currently or previously engaged in street work type prostitution in London. One or two were obtained through introductions via private contacts and they introduced others. A larger proportion, however, were obtained with the help of one of the earliest interviewed men who agreed, for a small fee, to fraternise with clients of two bars much frequented by rent boys and former rent boys and try to enlist their agreement for a tape-recorded interview for a fee of £15 or £20. All but two of these 25 interviews were carried out by the author, one by John Friend and one by Dr Thompson. The interviews took place in a variety of locations – D.J.W.'s car, the Streetwise office and sometimes the interviewee's own room. The interviews followed broadly the same format as for the Streetwise sample.

Although older (three were teenagers, seven in their twenties, seven in their thirties, six in their forties and two aged fifty and fifty-three respectively), these 25 men were in many ways much like the Streetwise sample. They could not be compared directly, since many had been working the streets at a time when circumstances were different, when AIDS was not around and when there was less awareness of the gay scene by the public at large. Moreover they were recruited more opportunistically and the sample was consequently biased towards certain ages and types. Nevertheless, their origins and motives for prostitution were sufficiently similar to what had been found already to show that at least some of the features described were not limited to Streetwise clients. The inclusion of older men, some of whom had given up prostitution years before, helped to form impressions of the long-term social prospects of street workers, about which the Streetwise sample of younger men who were still active as prostitutes could provide no more than speculative indications. This topic is dealt with later in this chapter and again when workers in the advertised sexual services are considered (see p. 251).

Because of the opportunistic, selective, heterogeneous nature of this supplementary sample, only very loose comparison with the Streetwise group was possible, but nevertheless some useful points emerged.

Early backgrounds

The 25 men in this supplementary sample were from rather more varied backgrounds, but still most of the 25 came from unhappy, disruptive parental homes as had the vast majority of the 50 Streetwise interviewees. The following brief summaries should suffice to make the point:

Case 201. Put in an orphanage at three. Had seen his mother only once, when 'she slammed the door in my face'.

Case 202. Drunken, violent father. Frequent separations of parents. Impoverished home. Erratic parenting.

Case 203. Secure, caring, united family.

Case 204. Adopted at six months. 'Very unhappy' childhood. Never got on with adoptive mother. 'I was some kind of devil's spawn in her eyes.'

Case 205. Happy childhood. United parents. Maintains good contact with them.

Case 208. 'Extremely unhappy' childhood. Impoverished. Father drunkard. Long periods in children's homes.

Case 209. Reared by widowed 'disciplinarian' mother with whom he had a 'stormy relationship'. A 'wild kid'. Ran away briefly after a beating. No physical deprivation. Childhood neither happy nor unhappy – 'just OK'.

Case 210. Reared by grandparents after parents split up when he was five. Returned to father and stepmother at twelve. Less happy. Allowed to wander. Turned out at fifteen when father, a heavy drinker, separated again.

Case 211. 'Unhappy' childhood. Born to a single mother who had another illegitimate son when he was four. Hated this half-brother. Bad relationship with the cohabitee his mother acquired when he was nine. Frequent running away.

Case 212. Father, divorced when he was two, denied parentage and would never see him. 'Very, very unhappy' childhood. Frequent runaway. Often beaten by domineering mother who had mental breakdowns and anorexia. Stepfather had gambling problem.

Case 213. Always hated father who rejected and beat him and drove him to run away at fourteen when his homosexuality was discovered. Hated his Catholic school for the harsh physical punishments he got.

Case 214. Fostered as a baby and then adopted by his foster-parents, but adoptive mother rejected him after she became pregnant. 'Very unhappy.' Frequent beatings. Felt he did not belong.

Case 215. A 'sad' childhood. Picked on and badly beaten by drunken father. Into care at seven. Parents then separated.

Case 216. Family financially secure but bad relationship with father which was much worse after discovery of his homosexuality at fourteen. Ambivalent towards mother who was destructively domineering and controlling. Thinks nanny and boarding school were parents' ways of palming off kids onto someone else.

Case 217. Put into children's home as an infant. Doesn't know who his father is. Visited mother during childhood but 'unhappy' with his stepfather who 'didn't like me at all'.

Case 218. Reared unremarkably by own parents, but as a teenager 'they disowned me more or less'. Upset as a child by parental rows over money shortages.

Case 219. Reared by both parents. Poor but happy. 'Travelling' stock, lived in a caravan.

Case 220. 'Very unhappy' childhood. Both parents had debt and drink problems and favoured his older brother. 'Disliked' his mother and 'indifferent' to father. 'Very often' beaten. Ran away at fourteen because they were so upset to discover he was gay.

Case 221. Into care at six months, parents believed to have been killed in a car crash. Fostered from age four, but returned to children's home at fourteen because the foster-parents couldn't handle his behaviour — 'taking overdoses and walking in front of cars'.

Case 222. Following separation of parents when he was about thirteen, and their deaths soon afterwards, he spent periods in children's home and foster-home. Before then many parental rows causd him to spend a lot of time away from home. Was not materially deprived.

Case 223. In care from age three on account of parents' physical cruelty. He has no contact with them. Numerous foster-homes. Never settled. Frequent runaway.

Case 224. In care after parents deserted him in infancy. Adopted at ten years by own grandmother. Much secret sexual abuse by her then husband. 'They give me what I wanted', but 'there was no love'.

Case 225. At thirteen went to live with a friend of his mother's, a single man who saw he was last born of a large family and being neglected. His mother gambled and that 'messed up the family'. He didn't like his mother, she cared only for his sisters. Now, at twenty-one, he was completely out of touch with his parents.

Case 226. Consistently reared by both parents (save for when they separated briefly) in financially secure home about which he had no complaints. Mother had a mental breakdown when he was fourteen, which was perceived as linked to learning of his homosexuality. Parents were concerned about effect on their village business should his homosexuality cause local scandal.

Case 228. Adopted at two. Never told why. No material deprivation, but distant and fraught relations with his elderly adoptive parents. Most of childhood spent at boarding school. 'Unhappy' when at home, frequent runaway and finally put in children's home.

Four-fifths of these 25 men reported what would appear by any standard to be unsatisfactory or unhappy upbringings in spite of, in several cases, having no material deprivation. As in the Streetwise sample, a high proportion had spent periods in children's homes or foster-homes and there were several examples where the development of a gay orientation provoked a final rejection from families in which relationships were already strained.

Sexual orientation

In comparison with the Streetwise sample there was a greater preponderance of homosexually oriented men, sixteen of the twenty-five saying that they were exclusively or predominantly attracted by males, only four claiming to be predominantly heterosexual and five bisexual. Homosexual preferences had not developed through practice as rent boys. Among the sixteen gay men only one had changed from having initially an exclusive interest in girls to a predominant preference for males. Change could also go in the opposite direction. *Case 202*, one of the bisexuals, remarked that experience as a prostitute had 'made me realise that women are better for sex'. One man, *Case 213*, said he 'wasn't interested at all' in females until he was in his twenties when, to please punters, he took part in 'scenes with a guy and a chick' and 'that's how I got turned on to having sex with women'.

Two of the men mentioned having had clients of both sexes. *Case 223* said he had many more male than female clients, but he had had sex with a married woman of forty-four (he was twenty-three) only last week 'and I've got to see her next week as well . . . If she wants sex and cannot get it from her husband and then she comes looking for someone, if she's looking as a punter then she has to pay for it.' *Case 209* said his clients had been mostly men 'because I did not really like women anyway. But in the years when I was on the game I used to meet them in [a fashionable tea room], dowager duchesses or whatever, who were out of their boxes on alcohol and, basically, I was their toy boy.' He explained that though they were after him sexually they tended to make up stories about wanting to see how the other half lived or writing a book, but he was always able to exploit them for money.

The high proportion of homosexuals among these men may have been in part a result of recruiting some of the older ones from gay bars, which they were still frequenting although no longer on the look-out for customers. It is also likely, however, that the much younger Streetwise sample included some who were uncertain of their orientation or unwilling to declare their homosexuality. It is fairly evident that the majority of London street workers are gay or bisexual.

Child sexual abuse

The number who reported having been involved in unwanted sexual acts when they were boys under fourteen was nine out of twenty-five, virtually the same proportion as in the Streetwise sample. Some of the gay oriented men described early sexual contacts that had been by mutual consent, but as before these were not counted as instances of sexual abuse, even though, according to some authorities, all sexual behaviour involving boys, being immoral and criminal, should be regarded as abusive. For example, *Case 208*, at thirteen, had a sexual but loving relationship with an older man who gave him things and in whose home 'I found comfort and I found peace'. Because he was found with a record player he had taken from this man his father 'kept beating me and beating me till it came out. I had no choice.' He was forced to make statements to the police and the man was imprisoned. Thirteen years later he was still expressing guilt for having been responsible. *Case 226* said that when he was only about eight his elder brother was having some kind of sex with a girl in the bedroom and made him go in with them. This was clearly against his wishes, and in fact he complained to his father about it, making an enemy of his brother as a result. In contrast, though some authorities might consider it more serious, he 'felt quite comfortable' about a sex encounter when he was fourteen with a man of twenty-six to whom he had been introduced by a friend.

The next case was counted as 'abuse' because, when referring back to what happened the man said, 'It was obviously against my wish because I didn't know what the guy was about.' It was an unsolicited approach, when the boy was only seven, by a man who masturbated in front of him and then masturbated him, which he enjoyed. Despite some nostalgic comment during the interview, he had been sufficiently confused at the time by what was his first sexual experience to tell his mother when she asked what he had been doing:

Case 209

> I was picked up on my way to Sunday school by a guy, I think he must have been about seventeen. He took me into a building site and showed me what it was all about, so to speak. On producing his come he said, 'Wouldn't you like to do the same?' which of course at that age I couldn't. When I got home it had been reported to mother that I had not attended Sunday school and she got at me. I, being very stupid and naive, told her a bit about what had happened and she called the police . . . To this day I regret ever opening my mouth about that because I swear that that person did me the biggest favour of my life. He opened my eyes to what life can be all about if one wants to have a broad mind.

Another rather similar example, *Case 228*, was counted as abuse because 'it began against my will' although 'towards the end it really wasn't'. This was at boarding school when he was thirteen and two older boys from the senior division of the school got hold of him and 'it was really like a rape' although there were 'many other occasions when it was, of course, with my consent – very much so'.

Two other men had been assaulted at their boarding schools. *Case 216* said it happened in the dormitory when he was only seven. 'You see each dormitory had twelve boys and each had a prefect in charge and he could do what he liked with you and you couldn't do anything about it. He would just make you come into his bed and suck him off, just make you do whatever he wanted, simple as that. Because he could hit you with a stick, he could do whatever he liked, he had total control in that dormitory.' *Case 203* had attended a Roman Catholic seminary school and was much affronted when, at twelve or thirteen, one of the teachers 'came and sat on my bed and tried to touch me up. I told him in no uncertain terms to go away. Actually he gave me bad marks after that. I'll always remember the bastard.' This same man had also been offended by his elder brother touching him indecently in bed when he was only nine.

While some of the incidents were not reported as having been particularly traumatic, some were at least as violent as the ones described by the Streetwise men. Aged thirteen at the time, *Case 221* was 'on the run' from a foster-home, but not yet a rent boy. He was waiting at a bus stop and went into an adjacent toilet. Inside he was grabbed by two men, stripped and anally raped. It was 'very painful' but he told nobody. 'I just didn't think anybody would believe me.' *Case 215* was already in the habit of seeking sex encouters with men in a local public toilet when, at the age of thirteen, he got picked up by a man with a van who offered to take him home with him. Instead, he had his clothes ripped off in the back of the van and was forcibly penetrated. It was his first experience of anal sex and it was both 'sore' and 'bloody', but he never told anyone about it and it did not put him off male sex. In fact 'I had to experience it again'.

One man, *Case 224*, said he had been habitually abused by his stepfather from about the age of seven till fifteen, when he left home. It started by having his genitals handled when he was being given a bath and progressed to anal penetration on occasions when he was taken out to go swimming. This made him 'very sore'. He had actually mentioned the incidents in the bath to his grandmother, but she just told him to keep away, possibly not understanding what was really happening. He wasn't much upset at the time. 'To be quite frank I wasn't aware of it, I didn't understand it.' Later on he came to regard the behaviour as exploitative, but at the time he liked his stepfather because he 'gave me quite a lot of presents and cuddled me'.

It can be seen that, as with the Streetwise sample, the abusive incidents occurred most often when boys had run away, were allowed to wander unsupervised or had been sent away to residential schools. The conclusion that the many stories of child sex abuse reflected the type of background from which street working prostitutes tend to come was further supported by these additional cases. The association between boyhood sexual abuse and becoming a rent boy is not a matter of direct cause and effect.

Starting and continuing

As with the Streetwise sample the great majority (eighteen out of 25, 72 per cent) reported their ages at the time of their first act of prostitution as having been in the later teens, that is fourteen up to nineteeen inclusive; two were at thirteen and the youngest was at eleven.

Men who entered the rent scene for the first time as adults were unlikely to be encountered in the Streetwise sample, given the age limit imposed by the organisation. In fact, among the 50 interviewed, the two who reported the latest ages when they first got money for sex had been twenty and twenty-one respectively. In contrast, among the 25 street workers from elsewhere four described their first prostitution experience as having occurred in their twenties at a time when they were coming out into civilian life after a period in the services. *Case 202* started when he was twenty-two. For no clear reason he had failed to return to duty after one of his leaves from the army. He came to London deliberately to look for punters, having read in the newspapers about the possibilities. He very quickly found some. *Case 201* was twenty-four and just out of the navy. Some former navy men told him what pub to visit 'to earn a few bob'. *Case 224* quit the merchant navy when he was twenty to see another side of life, came to London and being in his own words 'a good-looking lad' soon found customers. *Case 203* left the RAF at twenty-one and was enjoying life in London when he was picked up in a gay bar by an American who began to pay him for sex and companionship on an extended holiday. It was after this man left for home and he found himself without ready cash, but unwilling to admit to his family he had squandered his severance pay, that he decided to join the rent scene. None of these four could be said to have been under intolerable pressure when they made a deliberate decision to try out their fortunes as prostitutes and they were all fairly well informed about what to expect.

Those who first took money for sex when they were still children already knew something about the rent scene. *Case 204*, when he was eleven and truanting from school, used to visit an amusement arcade. One day he was there without his usual mates and a man approached him, gave him money to play on the machines and invited him home 'for a drink'. There had been talk among the boys about 'poufs' in the arcade, so he already 'knew what was meant'. The man got him drunk and gave him pills and had anal sex. He 'quite enjoyed it' and 'made money'. After that time he 'didn't go back to the arcade to pick up anybody else', but 'used to go and see [this man] a couple of times a week'. He was always given money. The arrangement continued till he was thirteen when, the man having told him where to go, he ran away and 'headed straight down for Piccadilly'. *Case 218* was already active in meeting men at bus-stops and elsewhere and going back with them for sexual pleasures when, at the age of thirteen, he happened to be in Piccadilly Circus during the school holidays when he was on an errand for his father. He saw an attractive man leaning against a car smiling at him. He got in without hesitation, went back to a flat, had 'wild sex', which he enjoyed a lot, and was handsomely paid. He kept the money secretly to himself and got clothes and things he wouldn't otherwise have had, but that time money was not the main motive. 'I'll tell you exactly what it was, I took one look at him and got an instant erection.'

Consistent with the fact that so many of these 25 men identified themselves as gay, relatively few of them found their first prostitution experience shocking and some positively enjoyed it. *Case 212* was a fourteen-year-old runaway to London. 'I met some kids who were skint and hungry and someone suggested Piccadilly Circus . . . I stood at the station and a man walked round and I noticed him looking at me. A lot of people were looking at me, I was very pretty. The man made a motion with his eyebrow and I followed.' He went back to the man's place, had oral sex, which was enjoyable and 'exciting', was given money. He was then driven back to the West End where he 'went out and discovered London'. *Case 209* had been very active homosexually with his schoolfellows. In his later teens he left home to go to live with a gay man in a neighbouring town and begin a promiscuous life in which 'it was just a gradual involvement that I expected older men to pay for me'. At the age of nineteen he got bored with the job he was doing. The man he was with decided to go to London so he did the same. On arrival at Victoria Coach station he was soon picked up by a gay man who gave him temporary accommodation while he was supposed to be looking for work. Instead, he joined the Piccadilly rent scene 'which was much more open in those days, with geezers hanging over the railings of the old meat rack'. This case, (like *Case 204* above) displays a not uncommon pattern. A boy goes looking for gay sex, finds it with an older man, gets rewarded and the link between sex and profit is made.

As with the Streetwise sample, many were runaways at the time, were not out looking for pleasure, but were under pressure to find money for survival and prepared to agree to sex whether it was pleasant or not. *Case 213* was sixteen when he first went to Piccadilly and got picked up. He was very hungry and was given something to eat before going back to have anal sex. The man was rough with him and 'I didn't like the way it was done. I didn't mind my boyfriend doing it, but I didn't like the approach he had.' *Case 228* was fourteen and a runaway from a children's home when he came to London and met another youth in a West End amusement arcade who explained the rent scene to him. 'This friend of mine, he always had loads of money in his pocket and it was so easy to do, so fast.' The sex performances were 'on many occasions indifferent, on odd occasions it would be frankly distasteful, but fortunately also a few times when it was very pleasurable for me'. *Case 216* was sixteen, he had left home because he was unhappy and he had very little money. He was walking around near Piccadilly when a man of about thirty-five came up and asked him if he wanted to earn some money. He went back to a hotel for a short session of masturbation. 'I suddenly realised this was the easiest way to make money . . . I don't think I had any feeling. I just had this need and it was easy to fulfill.' *Case 208* was fifteen when, following the exposure of his homosexual involvement with an adult male, his father told him, 'Well get out, you are not a son of mine.' He wandered around begging, spent some time being looked after at a Catholic refuge until eventually, at seventeen, he came from Ireland to England, gravitated into London and took to picking up punters around Piccadilly. He survived in this way until he was twenty-three. Sometimes he made enough money to go into gay clubs and make friends with young men he liked, but he was ashamed of being on the game and always tried to hide it. *Case 226* was eighteen and short of money when some friends introduced him to a man who offered him money for a sex session. He agreed and enjoyed the sex. He could have got money otherwise 'but not as easy as what I did'. After that he moved to London, was even more short of money and so started making use of pubs that friends had told him were places where could find punters.

Men who identified as heterosexual were more likely to recall their first prostitution experience as repugnant. *Case 210* was fourteen, truanting from school and already under a probation officer. He was hitch-hiking and a driver asked him if he was gay. He asked what that was and on being told he asked the man if he gave money for it. He had to fellate the man and he 'felt a bit sick about it' but he wanted the money badly as his father wasn't supplying pocket money. The man gave him a phone number and so after that he used to meet him once a week. Later, at seventeen, it was through this same man's introduction to a male photographic modelling concern that he came to London and 'couldn't believe how easy it was to get money' from prostitution. *Case 223* had come to London from a children's home but had nowhere to live. He was eighteen and had rejected some homosexual propositions until 'one day I was so hungry I didn't know what to do and a bloke come up to me, asked me and said he'd give me £60'. He 'felt really sick' about what he had to do, 'but if you want to earn money that's the way to do it'.

One man, *Case 225*, was unusual in taking to prostitution to test his own sexuality. He was seventeen, wandering about on his own, staying in a hostel and drinking in a gay bar hoping 'to make new friends' when a man bought him a drink, invited him back and asked him if he was on the rent. He wasn't sure just what that meant but said he was and in the morning, after they had slept together, the man gave him £30. After that he went with others and gradually got into the habit. It started more as an experiment, 'to find who I really was', than for the sake of the money. He decided he was bisexual.

In summary, it seemed that the circumstances and motives leading to the start of prostitution were much the same in this second sample as in the Streetwise cases. In both samples the majority, even of those who were quite young, had entered the game knowingly, many at a time of leaving or running away from unhappy home backgrounds. Pressing need for money was the most often cited motive for selling sex and ease of obtaining it the most common reason for continuing to do so. The main differences from the initial Streetwise sample were the greater preponderance of self-declared homosexual predisposition and the presence of a few who had not started in prostitution until their twenties and then more from deliberate choice than dire need. This last group was necessarily omitted from the Streetwise sample on account of their much younger age.

Most of these 25 men had continued in the prostitution business for long periods, sometimes till a much later age than the young men of the Streetwise sample imagined was possible. Although at the time they first started they had not all been in such desperate circumstances as had most of the Streetwise sample, the discovery that money could be made so readily motivated them to continue. This had had the almost inevitable result of diverting them from more conventional careers. *Case 202*, who absented himself from the army to enjoy the money and freedom afforded by the rent scene, thereby ruined his chances of a military career, which he later regretted. He was obliged to continue on the game without legitimate employment because he was 'on the run'. He gave himself up after a few years and served a term in a military prison only to return to street work subsequently. *Case 213*, following his first prostitution experience, 'saw it all in a different light and just went out with the sole intention of prostitution. I'm still doing it.' He gravitated from Piccadilly to Mayfair and to the gay bars and then worked for an escort agency. He left after two years because clients were always wanting new faces and he was getting older. Also the agency was raided and he was convicted of assisting in the running of a brothel. After that he worked as a self-advertising masseur from the flat he shared with a lover, but they split up and he went back to the street work. 'I think I'll end up by topping myself. I don't think anyone's going to want an old queen at forty.'

The chance of easy money had lured some men away from other possibilities for making a living. *Case 214* explained: 'When I started I would do between four and six men a night. It was easy money, so therefore it became a regular habit.' *Case 222* had visited the Streetwise Youth Day Centre for 'a day off, company and quiet', but only twice, because 'Rent work gets in the way of everything. I work days and nights, everything.' He was only twenty-one, but had moved to London to get more money, having already begun prostitution in the provinces. Return to an ordinary job was seemingly not on his agenda. He had left several jobs because 'I can't stand being told what to do.' *Case 215*, after first being given money when he was fourteen, thought, 'Oh, this is easy', so 'when I left school I used to go down there and get money for it'. He continued the practice after joining the army, but a policewoman caught him in a parked car with a man he had met in a toilet and so he was discharged. The scandal got into the local newspaper and so annoyed his father that he had to leave home. He resolved the situation by coming to London and loitering in the station toilets where he soon found a client. Thus began a prostitution career that was to last for a dozen years. *Case 220* had first tried picking up punters on stations and in Piccadilly when he was only fourteen. He had heard about it from a gay member of staff at his children's home, whose advice to keep clear of such places had had the opposite effect. In subsequent years he got work as a chef and also had a period of army service, but always he returned to the rent scene because, 'I have got expensive tastes in life . . . I like gambling on horses and just basically having a good time, going on holidays and things like that.' *Case 205*, at the age of thirty, also felt the need to supplement his income from legitimate but low-paid catering work. 'I enjoy having sex with a bloke, but sometimes I don't like having to do it for money because I like to have a friendship with a person . . . If I had money on me every day I wouldn't need to do it. OK, I suppose I would occasionally, but I wouldn't go out of my way to spend hours looking for it.' He had left a school for slow learners with no qualifications. As a boy interested in male sex he had discovered early on how to make contacts in local toilets and to get paid for it on occasion. Prostitution fitted in with his promiscuous inclinations and his partiality for socialising in gay pubs. If he didn't much enjoy a session with a client he would go out later looking for a younger partner.

One implication of these histories from an older sample is that, for some people at least, disengagement from street work proves difficult and can take a very long time.

The prostitution experience

Contacting and serving clients, joining that segment of the London gay scene where rent boys flourish and forming occasional sugar-daddy relationships was much the same for these 25 men as for the Streetwise sample. A few differences were noted by the older men. At the time they had been active in the seventies AIDS was unknown and participation in anal sex relatively free from anxiety. *Case 224*, for example, said his clients nearly always used to have anal intercourse with him; in fact he liked being penetrated and was disappointed if it didn't happen. *Case 211* had practised safer sex for a reason unconnected with HIV. He used to use a condom 'only with kinky rubber people who had a fetish for them . . . and sometimes if I thought they were a bit licentious and they wanted to fuck me. Because I remember a friend of mine telling me about gonorrhoea and saying maybe it would protect you.' *Case 215*, until a couple of years ago, used to have anal sex, both ways, and never used a condom. *Case 209* said he believed in experiencing everything. He had often had either active or passive anal sex with clients and had done many other things as well, including fist fucking. Things he learned from one client he could charge extra for when with another. For some men, reluctance to have anal sex used to be a matter of personal preference. *Case 210*, who emphasised his heterosexuality, said he disliked anal sex but if he wanted the money badly enough he would agree to either active or passive intercourse. 'We never knew nothing about AIDS in them days, it wasn't mentioned.' *Case 211* had 'never gone in for' anal sex, though he liked passive fellatio and 'in the old days before AIDS' he would swallow the ejaculate. Once he had contracted pharyngeal gonorrhoea. *Case 214* did not use a condom 'in those days', but would allow clients to have anal intercourse with him. He would not reciprocate, however, for the unusual reason that 'the guys that I would go with were, in my head that is, better equipped than me'. The younger men and those still active in prostitution generally avoided unprotected anal sex and only one man out of a total of eighteen who reported having been tested said he was HIV positive. It would seem that nowadays most male prostitutes successfully avoid HIV infection.

As with the Streetwise youths these men had participated in a multiplicity of sexual activities with clients, but most had certain things they would decline; being tied up and thereby losing control was refused by nearly all. *Case 217* was exceptional in liking to be tied down and caned. 'I do get a sexual satisfaction in being caned and also in caning young boys.' *Case 210* was very willing to whip clients or beat them up if they wanted it – 'I don't get a sexual turn on, I just enjoy it, don't ask me why' – but he refused to stamp two gerbils to death for a client, even though offered an extra £30 to do it. *Case 212* was willing to fist fuck clients but wouldn't do anything that drew blood. *Case 215* would do almost anything to punters but would not let them urinate or defecate on him.

Only four men reported any assault during their prostitution work. *Case 212* was 'in France and went back to a hotel with an Arab guy. We were in his room and he pulled out a knife and held it against my throat. And then half a dozen other people came in and just used me, they all fucked me, I just had to give in. I was paid, but I was very upset and I came back to London . . . It was just very painful and I was bruised.' *Case 216* recalled a punter who proved to be a sadist: 'He was fucking me and he just got very, aggressive and then he started to hurt me. I said, "You're hurting me" and he said "That's good, you've got feelings." I managed to get away.' In fact he fled without having been paid. *Case 213* described an incident early in his prostitution career when he was 'coming up to sixteen'. 'A guy I picked up in Piccadilly Circus took me back to his place, and when I got there locked all the doors and four of his friends from another room walked in and all five fucked me . . . It was very upsetting because it was painful, and it also destroyed my whole outlook on everything.' After they had done with him he was thrown out without payment. 'What could I do? I was under age, I couldn't go to the police, I knew that if I did I'd get deported back to Ireland. My boyfriend wanted to kill them.' *Case 223* reported one bad experience with a punter which was very serious. He met the man in a bar, agreed to go with him for masturbation for £25 and went with him to a park. The man wanted to be masturbated on and on for hours. When he finally refused to continue and asked for his pay the man drew a knife and 'started putting it in' his abdomen. He was found by the police lying with blood everywhere and taken to hospital by ambulance. His greatest fear was of meeting up with another murderous character. As with the Streetwise sample, not all of the sexual assaults described had happened during prostitution work. For example, *Case 203*, at the age of nineteen, he went to a party on board a ship. 'I had had a lot to drink and I woke up feeling awful pain and realised this guy was fucking me. I turned round and hit him. That gave me more pain, incidentally, turning round while he was still in me.' *Case 212*, had gone back with someone he met in a bar (for pleasure, not for payment) when three others, 'kind of rough people', came in unexpectedly and all wanted sex. He managed to bluff and struggle his way out.

The differences between a regular client (who expects to receive the same service for the same price again and again) and a real sexual friendship (engaged in for mutual satisfaction) or a sugar-daddy situation (in which the younger partner has no sexual motive but receives consistent material support in return for minimal sexual servicing) may seem subtle, but they were clearly distinguished by most of these men. Presumably because they were older than the Streetwise youths they had more and longer sugar-daddy relationships to report. *Case 201*, aged forty-nine, described how three different older men, formerly regular clients, had each gone on subscribing small gifts for some years after sexual contacts had ceased, but they had all ceased eventually. *Case 212* had had 'two at once actually'. One was killed, the other 'was very good to me for about a year' but 'I got bored with him. I mean he is a very rich man but I suddenly decided that the guy was a fascist and I would not see him any more, even though we had holidays together and he was very wealthy and bought me things.' He distinguished these relationships quite clearly from a long-standing affair he had had with a man friend somewhat older than himself.

In some cases prostitution practice continuing in later years led to increasing dependence on the patronage of former clients who had become sugar daddies. *Case 215* was working as a street prostitute after being discharged from the army when an older man picked him up and gave him a home, but secretly he continued prostituting in toilets and bars. When his friend found out what he was doing he was turned out and had to depend on more casual punters. He kept being taken back, however, because 'he could not do without me and basically I can't do without him'. At thirty-six he was still there, but 'it is only temporary. He is not the sort of person that I want to settle my life with. Nothing really [against him], he just ain't got enough money.' *Case 202*, at forty-five, was still having his rent paid and receiving other perks from a former punter whose sexual requirements had become negligible. *Case 210* had accommodation in the house of his elderly friend and was already making plans to start up a business as soon as the old man dies and leaves him the property. *Case 219* depended on an old man whose sexual demands and jealousies greatly irked him, but who had come to his rescue on numerous occasions, taking him in when he was temporarily disabled from injuries sustained in a fight and again when thrown out by his wife.

The disadvantage that some sugar daddies tried to limit their freedom, especially their sexual freedom, was pointed out by several. *Case 203* thought that rent boys 'just tolerate the sugar daddy sexually. I'd say it's just market forces that keeps it going. Often it comes to an abrupt end. Either the sugar daddy or the boy who is being kept brings it to an end. Quite often it's the sugar daddy, because of the boy's wishing his independence. For example he will want to carry on going to gay bars, going with people his own age, etc. This creates a possessive situation and then there is a row and they split up . . . If the boy has just lived solely on the allowance he's been given, then of course he has nothing and he's got to start on the same scene again, which is usually the case.' There were some who were clear that they had never had and would not want a sugar daddy. *Case 211* had never had one and said, 'I've always liked to support myself, not to rely on anybody else.' *Case 214* responded, 'No, I don't think so' when asked if he would have liked one. In contrast *Case 215* said 'unfortunately no', he had never had one but would have liked to have one 'very much'.

The impression left by these varied recollections from a different and older sample was to confirm that the nature of street work is basically as decribed by clients of the Day Centre, and that it has not changed fundamentally over the past decade or so.

Social problems

The findings from this supplementary sample reinforced the impression gained from the Streetwise clients that men working as prostitutes in streets and bars display a range of social problems, such as excessive use of drink and drugs, delinquency and inability to settle in conventional work. Although most had a place to live, only four had any regular job at the time of interview and, apart from when they were working as prostitutes, most were chronically unemployed or unemployable. *Case 217*, aged forty-one, said he had once worked in a hotel, but it was 'very long ago' and lasted only 'about four months'. *Case 213*, aged thirty-seven and unemployed, had once held a job for as long as two years, but that was exceptional. He had walked out of many jobs. 'I am very temperamental. Very, very restless, I can't be tied down.' Asked what sort of work he might like to do he said 'I don't know, to be honest with you.' *Case 215*, aged thirty-six, unemployed and recently out of prison, said he had walked out of 'hundreds' of jobs. 'I've not got patience with people, I just can't let people tell me what to do, I like to be my own boss.' *Case 214*, though currently working as a dustman, said he had walked out of jobs, 'many times, mostly through boredom and frustration because I was never given responsibility and believed I could do something better'. He had also been dismissed 'many times for lateness, fooling around, not getting on with the job'.

Added to handicaps of temperament and lack of training the demands of prostitution work further limited the chances of obtaining alternative employment. One man, *Case 203*, was quite eloquent on this point. 'It can lull you into a false sense of security. There were several times when I have been taken abroad by punters, and certainly to all parts of the UK. That prevents one from being able to manage oneself properly. If you are away, obviously you cannot do anything, you cannot get a job, you cannot keep a job. Plus you are living quite well and it becomes problematic. You can literally be eating at the Savoy one day and starving the next . . . When one fills in an application form for a job one has to account for the period of time [on the game]. One has actually to lie in one way or another. I think most rent boys are totally untrained and some have never worked in their lives, so they don't have a very good chance.'

Several men suggested that their exposure to the sub-culture of drink and drugs in the specialised gay bars where they went to find punters had contributed to the acquisition of intemperate habits, the sheer cost of which helped to entrap them for longer in the rent boy way of life. For example, one young man, *Case 221*, who said of his rent boy activity, 'We know it is wrong', had ideas for obtaining legitimate work. He was most unlikely, however, to be able to earn enough to maintain his present level of drug consumption which was costing him £300 a week, several times more than what he was paying for necessities such as rent and food. *Case 208* was drinking 'vast' amounts while working on the streets. 'I would do a bottle of scotch a night.' In the clubs he started taking drugs – LSD, cocaine, amphetamines, cannabis, valium. 'It just seemed the thing to do.' Then, somewhat less than two years ago, he was arrested for carrying drugs. In the cells he felt his whole world caved in. He was put on probation and went to a hospital for help. He went through a bad period with 'some severe withdrawal symptoms', but met up with a sympathetic friend, enlisted a priest's help in obtaining local authority accommodation on grounds of his recuperation from alcoholism and has since been living on welfare payments.

There seems to have been in recent years an increased acceptability of drugs and corresponding increased temptation. *Case 211*, aged thirty-seven, remarked 'Lately a lot of rent boys are on drugs, why I don't know. Maybe it's just the stress of living the scene they are living now, because it's a lot harder now than when I was a lad. The cost of living has gone up and therefore the boys are asking for more. A lot of them are not getting more, they're getting into trouble and looking to drugs to relieve their frustrations.' Nevertheless, there was a minority who had successfully resisted such pressures. *Case 225*, aged twenty-three, said a pint of beer a day would be the most he took. 'I drink cokes. I can't enjoy myself and I'm no good to nobody if I'm drunk.' His only drug intake was the occasional cannabis joint, usually when on offer from a friend. *Case 226* was unusual in taking no drink, drugs or tobacco, but he was nineteen and had only recently come onto the London scene from the provinces.

The deleterious effects of heavy usage of intoxicants, having had longer time to develop, were more obvious among these men than in the Streetwise sample. A majority, fourteen, reported serious problems with drink, and twelve were or had been regular users of prohibited drugs other than cannabis. The well known tendency to gravitate from so-called hard drugs to alcohol in later life was evident among some of the men. *Case 209*, aged forty-three, admitted, 'I do have a rather bad drink problem. I spend £20 a day on drink.' And as to drugs, 'I have used nearly everything at one period of my life. Nowadays I take anything that is available if I can afford it.' He had been notorious as a drug peddler and served several prison sentences. He was probably still engaged in that activity. He was interviewed in his own room by the author. He asked for a lift afterwards and as he was preparing to leave he was seen to stuff some white powder into a plastic envelope. *Case 228*, aged twenty-seven, was still a heavy drinker and user of drugs, but had been more extreme in the past. 'When I was in Amsterdam [working in a brothel] every night of the week I was drunk and on drugs. There was a time when I was very, very heavy on heroin. During the period of eighteen years old until about twenty-one I must have been doing £1,500 to £2,000 a week on drugs.' He had finally got off heroin with the help of a friend who literally shut him away and tied him down while he was going through a withdrawal. These assertions were rendered less incredible by the fact that, unusually for a street worker, he had had a superior education and been able to attract very wealthy patrons. *Case 212*, aged thirty-one, had been a registered heroin addict and had gone through a methadone withdrawal programme, but was still using the drug on occasion, spending about £70 a week to get black-market supplies. *Case 214*, aged thirty-nine, had worked for some time as a delivery driver, but the year before he had lost his licence for driving under the influence of amphetamines. *Case 202*, aged forty-five, had been a massive consumer of alcohol all his adult life until forced by liver damage to stop. He too had had a period of dependence on injected heroin. *Case 203*, at forty-two, was under hospital treatment for alcoholism. *Case 224*, aged fifty, said he used to spend £200 a day, which he got from 'hustling my arse', on injected heroin. When he could no longer find the money for heroin he took to barbiturates. Finally he got scared. 'I looked in the mirror one day and thought: What am I trying to do, kill myself?' He had been off drugs for six years but drinking 'quite heavily, eight cans of strong lager a day' and often going home drunk. *Case 210*, aged thirty-two, said he had given up prostitution because the money he got did him no good as he was spending it all on booze. He still went on periodic binges after which he would have to go and stay with a friend to dry out. 'I am an alcoholic. It's not a problem to me. To other people it may be a problem.'

As with the Streetwise sample, many of the men were or had been involved in delinquent activities unconnected with prostitution, for which eighteen had a criminal conviction history, eleven of them serious enough to have served one or more custodial sentences. The convictions were mostly for property offences, such as shoplifting, fraud and burglary, sometimes for violence and occasionally for drug offences. Although about one in three adult males in Britain may have some kind of criminal conviction history, relatively few include custodial sentences, so the figures show the present sample to be in this respect significantly different from the ordinary population.

There were no well organised, professional criminals; the offending was generally fairly petty and sporadic and geared to meeting immediate needs rather than providing a long-term income. *Case 223*, during long periods of unemployment, occupied himself, other than by prostitution, knocking on doors asking for odd jobs. He had been imprisoned for a series of housebreakings. His nickname derived from his facility for squeezing through small openings. *Case 224* had a conviction history for taking cars, which he used to do frequently 'out of frustration' for a thrill. *Case 225* had never had to go to prison, except for a short time for non-payment of fines, although he had convictions for stealing and for receiving stolen goods and selling them in pubs and for 'actual bodily harm' to a man he caught in bed with his girlfriend. *Case 219* admitted to one term of two years imprisonment for violence. He had been working on a fairground roundabout when 'a couple of coloured started taking the mickey'. He swung round on the machine, 'knocked them both flying with my feet and broke their noses when I stood on their heads'. It was learned from a conversation with his elderly 'sugar daddy' that he was also notoriously 'light fingered', picking up any cash he could lay his hands on from punters or anyone else, but for this he had not been prosecuted. *Case 228*, aged twenty-seven, had what was probably the worst of the criminal records. He had been in trouble with the police from boyhood and had served several custodial sentences in borstal and prison. He did 'everything from burglary to robbery, everything'. One of his prison sentences followed a revenge burglary of a wealthy Arab punter who had given a friend of his a bad time, 'spiked him up really bad and just gone to town on him'. His last imprisonment, at twenty-two, was for 'post office things, I mean it was several charges of armed robbery. I only got three years because they could only get me guilty on one armed robbery, a pretty minor one, it wasn't even guns.' Now he was resolved 'never to break the law to the point where my liberty will be at risk again – never, ever'.

Drink or drugs played a prominent part in some of the offence histories. *Case 209*, in addition to his convictions and imprisonments for other matters, had been prosecuted for gross indecency in the street with another man, a friend not a punter. It happened when 'this friend and I were out of our mind on drugs'. *Case 210* named a detention centre, a borstal and two prisons for adults as places he had served sentences. 'They've all been for violence, or something like that. It's mainly through drink.' His most serious offence was 'Attempted murder, knifing a geezer that was. They dropped it to malicious wounding. It was a gay club and they wouldn't let me in. But instead of just not letting me in he pushed me, so I lost my temper and I just grabbed him by the throat and stabbed him in the back.' *Case 201* had only one conviction, the result of an assault on two policemen when he was drunk. *Case 212* had no conviction history save for two arrests for drug possession for which he had received a fine and a suspended sentence of imprisonment. *Case 204*, who had only one conviction, and that for shoplifting, had been charged with going 'equipped to steal'. The case had been dropped and he was saying he had been 'fitted up', which was not altogether unlikely as he had been buying a lot of drugs for others as well as himself. *Case 218*, aged forty, had only one conviction, which was for larceny at the age of seventeen when he was sent to a detention centre. At the time he was interviewed, however, he was on bail for an alleged assault that had occurred in connection with a quarrel over illegal drug dealing. *Case 221* was fined for an assault in a pub. His victim was one of his punters who had made him angry by accusing him falsely of stealing money.

The men were also at risk of being prosecuted for the specialised offences connected with prostitutional activities. For instance, in addition to the eleven men imprisoned for other things, two more had served prison sentences, one (*Case 205*) for 'pimping', that is living on the immoral earnings of a male, the other (*Case 217*) for repeated importuning. *Case 213* was given a suspended prison sentence for brothel keeping. *Case 215* had been twice convicted for importuning. The lower incidence of convictions for importuning or obstruction in this sample compared with the Streetwise sample suggests that police are taking action more frequently nowadays.

Attitudes to the rent scene

As in the Streetwise sample views varied, but many were critical of the rent boy scene and regretful of their own past or present involvement. *Case 210*, who was particularly insistent about his heterosexuality, said he had given it up because 'I just got sick of gays. I still don't hate them. I just didn't like it.' *Case 211* had an opposite reason why he 'just got fed up. I started to go away from older people and started fancying boys myself. I become a punter then.' *Case 203*, who had a lot to say on the matter, was critical of the commercialisation of relationships and of the inconsiderate treatment experienced by rent boys. 'There is an exchange system where punters will put you onto another punter and even suggest the price to pay and what to expect, which is to me just a cattle market. I really believe that it destroys the characters of young boys. They come down from the provinces, they're totally naive to these things and there are some evil men in the West End of London.' He went on to argue that 'hustling' is no lasting solution to social problems. 'Some do not wish or know how to work. Others are simply not able to do the jobs demanded of them in our modern society. By paying them and giving them money, food or even the means to stay in one place for a while, the punter is actually just prolonging the problem.'

Some of the men were only too well aware of the disadvantages and dangers of the rent scene, but they had come to rely on it too much to give it up easily. *Case 222*, for example: 'I'd like to be less dependent on renting, but it's one of those jobs where you need it but you don't need it, because it's money always coming in, but you don't need it because you know what it's doing . . . If anything is going to kill me it's this. It fucks up your head and you become too reliant on it. I don't worry about AIDS because I practise safe sex all the time, but if I was to get AIDS then there's nothing I could do about it.' *Case 228*, aged twenty-seven, who was cleverer and more enterprising than most, remarked, 'I'm still doing it, but not to the extent that I did it in the past. I'm only seeing clients that I've known for years. As to whether it's a good or a bad thing, it's both, you know. It's like any job in this respect – there's perks, there's times when you enjoy your work and there's times when you are fed up with it. My greatest worry would be to wake up at thirty-five years old with nothing behind me.' *Case 212*, at thirty-one, was still in touch with some of his regular clients from years ago, but he would like to be able to give it up altogether 'Because I would like to settle down. As I get older I think I approve more and more of a monogamous situation.'

There were some who seemed to suggest that the life suited them in spite of its disadvantages. *Case 214* thought that AIDS had spoiled the scene, but 'when I started in the late sixties until the eighties, provided you kept your wits about you, you could have a lot of fun. You got taken places and it was fun. I mean, there was a lot of fun people out there.' *Case 225*, aged twenty-three, who had been on the game in London for five years, said, 'I like to think I am offering a service and that the punters are happy with it. I'm quite friendly with all my regulars. I've been seeing one of them now for about three years.' He thought he had a good reputation and was 'highly recommended'. He had got into the habit of renting gradually: 'It was a sort of experimenting thing to see how I took to it and to find out who I really was. I'd say I'm bisexual, I know that definitely now.' He had lived with a girl for eighteen months, but 'it was on and off really, I wasn't around much'. The relationship broke up because 'she couldn't take it, me being out all the time'. He had never had a real sugar daddy, but would like one and was 'working on one'. He was picking up in clubs and pubs rather than on the streets and was pretending to be an 'escort worker', because he could get more out of punters that way. He had no settled address, he mostly stayed overnight with punters, or with friends, occasionally he booked into a cheap hotel. He agreed he had a certain wanderlust – 'I don't like staying in one place long . . . I'm reasonably satisfied. When I make my millions I'll be happy.' In the long run he thought he might start his own legitimate business in the security trade, of which he had some experience. *Case 209* was frank about his enjoyment of the rent scene for the sexual experience – 'the promiscuity of it, of meeting people, but once one gets to know a person it is often not the same. Hence the reason why I started pimping, in other words making money by introducing other boys.' *Case 220* was even more positive: 'I don't mind it so long as I make enough money to keep me going. I mean I live quite happily off what I make. I don't mind doing it at all because I'm a hundred per cent gay, but there are young guys coming to London with no money or anything . . . basically getting forced into it.'

Overt expressions of guilt or remorse about their involvement were rare. One man, *Case 208*, who had given up renting several years previously, was still feeling guilty because he believed he had been responsible for the break-up of the marriage of one of his punters. He had gone home with this married man a number of times and then, on one such occasion, the wife had returned and appeared shattered. At that stage 'I could not see what I was doing or what was going on. I was blind to the whole lot, I was riddled with alcohol.'

Case 216, who had himself since married and become successful in legitimate business, was clear that whether prostitution was good or bad depended on the individual. 'It can be very stunting. If you're making enough money to get by and you just keep getting by and you keep doing the same old thing and you actually hate it, but you've got to do it, then it's bad. But if you're having a whirl and enjoying it, then it's fun and it's different. I don't think it's so terrible if it's just a phase you go through. We prostitute ourselves all the time anyway . . . working for somebody else. It makes very little difference whether you are cutting up potatoes or sucking somebody off.'

Conclusions from the supplementary sample

Since this was effectively a convenience sample it would be wrong to generalise from it too readily. All the same, since many of the features noted among the sample of 50 Day Centre attenders were repeated among a differently acquired group this does support the view that certain observations are true for the majority of street workers. For example, the majority of both samples gave histories of deprived or defective upbringing. The proportions who reported histories of homosexual assault when they were boys were similar. Most of the men in both samples were homosexual or bisexual in their habits before they came onto the rent scene. The most frequently cited reasons for beginning were similar, namely practical necessity and the opportunity for quick gains. In both samples attitudes towards clients were often critical, but violence from clients was rare, though on occasion serious. Reliance on a sugar-daddy relationship was fairly common. Substance abuse and involvement in delinquency were prevalent in both samples.

The supplementary sample was on average much older, and it became clear that street work sometimes starts in the twenties and not just in the teens and that it may carry on into the thirties. From the recollections of men who had been street workers decades before, it seemed that the West End rent scene had not changed fundamentally. At least one of their favourite rent bars was still going strong, although the largest and best known, situated on Piccadilly Circus itself, had long since changed. Before the advent of AIDS sexual transactions were much more often expected to include anal intercourse. Street workers had been able to practise more freely in the days when street policing was less vigorous and readers of the tabloid press were less informed about homosexuality and homosexual prostitution.

12

Later Careers of Street Workers

To explore systematically the long-term prospects for participants in the rent boy scene would require a study that followed the lives of a sample over many years to see what happens to those who are involved for short or long periods. Subsequent developments may depend upon personality and circumstances before entry into prostitution. The later careers of prostitutes should be compared with those of males of similar ages and backgrounds but without prostitution experience. Impressions gained in this research from opportunistically assembled samples, with no strict comparison group, must therefore be treated with caution.

The histories given by the Streetwise Day Centre sample, few of whom had yet fully disengaged from soliciting in streets or bars, provided no secure indication of what might happen later on. Some of those who said they had left the rent scene were known to have returned to it not long after and others who said they had left for good were not very convincing. *Case 043*, for example, who was aged twenty, said he had stopped two years ago. He maintained that he was still living on savings from three years of prostitution. 'What I did, I used to like saving money. A lot of these people, and in a way I feel sorry for them, they get between £30 and £60 and put it all in a fruit machine. Now what I was doing I was saving it up over the years. I could save £50 a week or whatever . . . At least then you have got some money to fall back on when you pass your sell-by date – which I've done already.' He was, however, still unemployed and still frequenting the bars and clubs where he was well known to the managers and the punter clientele. His boast that 'I treat them mean and keep them keen' sounded more like a rationing of his services than complete withdrawal.

The histories obtained from older street workers and former street workers in the supplementary sample may have given a biased impression, since this group included men who continued to frequent their old haunts and maintain links with old associates and former punters. Men who successfully sever all links with anyone connected with prostitution are naturally more difficult to locate and interview for research purposes.

Fictional romances about prostitutes finding love and riches usually refer to women. One novel about an East End male prostitute's escape from poverty is set in the nineteenth century (Hunt, 1986). Neither literature nor research publications are much help in determining what is likely to happen to real rent boys of today. Anecdotal evidence of success and failure in individual cases points to a varied outcome. Some French journalists interested in the fate of children who come under the control of care authorities (Boulin *et al*. (1977, p. 145) reported having received letters from both men and women, now socially stable and respectcd and often married, who had been inmates of children's homes and who had prostituted themselves while still children. They had been neither more nor less unfortunate than others who had been kept in children's homes, but most of them, thanks to the money they had earned from prostitution, had been able to establish themselves subsequently.

It has to be acknowledged that the gloomy prognostications commonly made about the future fate of rent boys were well illustrated by interviews with former street workers who were found to be in serious and continuing social difficulties or existing on the margins of society. Some of their social problems have already been cited in an earlier chapter (see p. 115ff.), but further information on the course of their lives over a period of years suggests that some will never be able to attain a satisfying social adjustment. It would be wrong to conclude, however, that involvement in street work is necessarily responsible for subsequent disasters. The histories given by some of the men suggested that they would have been problem personalities in any event and that involvement in street work was incidental to the disaster-laden course of their lives. Underlying personality problems may contribute both to choice of street prostitution in an attempt to solve immediate difficulties and to the continuance of social malaise after prostitution activities have ceased. As will be described later (see p. 251), these stories of social failure were in marked contrast to impressions gained from the masseurs and agency workers who were interviewed, some of whom were making realistic provisions for their future while they were still active in the sex industry and some of whom had retired into profitable occupations of a conventional kind. With more favoured upbringings and better education than was common among the street worker samples they were much better placed to make the transition.

Some summary life histories from retired street workers who were interviewed follow. Only the last two are success stories. The others are men with serious social or personal problems for which embarking upon street work proved no solution. Inability to extricate themselves from drug or alcohol addiction was a prominent feature in some cases.

Case 217. Aged forty-one, he was contacted in a gay bar where he was reportedly a regular and frequently inebriated customer. He was of dissolute appearance and slightly tipsy during the interview. He was currently threatened with eviction from the flat in which he was squatting, which had belonged to his recently deceased sexual partner. He came from a typically deprived background, never having known a father and having spent much of his childhood in children's homes. He had attended a school for the educationally retarded. He started street prostitution at seventeen. 'Being gay myself, being very gay, I knew that London was very attracted to young boys. That's why I come over . . . In fact, when I was a young boy I was getting £20, £40, £60 even £100. I was being caned and everything, but it was nice, you know, I enjoyed it.' He had been convicted five times and imprisoned once for street and lavatory importuning. He continued with street work 'on the quiet' even when living with an affair (regular partner), until he got 'around thirty' and was 'too old'. He had never worked at a regular job and was now dependent on welfare.

He was preoccupied with finding a young man for sex. 'Although I'm forty-one I'm quite attracted to young chickens, like nineteen, twenty. I've actually come down here to pay for a chicken . . . I don't want another affair because I wouldn't be able to pick up young boys, which I want to do . . . I get £75 a fortnight from social security, so obviously I can afford to pay £10 here, £10 there, 'cos I don't pay rent . . . I have earned a few bob today [for the interview] . . . If I've got the money they'll come back to bed with me.'

Case 201. Put into an orphanage at three, for reasons unknown to him, he remained there until he was sixteen when he joined the navy and served as an able seaman for nine years when he was finally discharged 'unsuitable'. 'I disobeyed orders, wouldn't do anything right.' On shore he would get drunk every night when he had the opportunity. He was attracted to both sexes but contacts with men were more frequent. From the age of twenty-five, when he discovered the rent bars in London that were often patronised by sailors on leave, 'I used to go with a different bloke every night.' He did some labouring jobs at the same time, but 'I kept getting sacked and walking out. I didn't want to work, I was making easy money without work.' He had some gay friends he could stay with at times and he also made friends with several regular clients, older men who gave him small sums of money when he was in need, but now he was forty-nine and it had been a long time since any of them had wanted to see him. Being on the game 'wasn't bad', he had had no 'bad experiences', but he had stopped it a long time ago.

His heavy drinking continued all the time he was a street worker. He remembered lying prone and swigging a punter's whisky while the man was enjoying anal intercourse with him. At the age of forty he fell ill with 'voices' and 'thoughts that the cops and the IRA were after me'. He went to the police about it and was hospitalised and diagnosed as having paranoid schizophrenia. He had been on depot injected anti-psychotic medication with depixol ever since. 'I can't do without the injection [otherwise] I get messages over the radio, juke box, television. I know it sounds stupid but I can't stop it. I don't know whether I'm coming or going. I get as if I could shoot myself.' For years he had been living a solitary existence in a bed-sitter, suspicious of being watched or talked about. He was on welfare, but occasionally doing a little casual work cleaning up in the local bars where he spent most of his time. Through lack of money his drinking had moderated, save for occasional binges, on one of which he had been taken into hospital unconscious, but he had no memory of the circumstances. He had a fraught and intermittent relationship with a middle-aged alcoholic woman for whom he ran errands, but she refused sex and had recently rejected him.

In this man's case, work shyness, uncontrolled drinking and finally mental illness seemed more powerful determinants of his fate than the time he had spent as a prostitute.

Case 224. From an unhappy home background this man joined the merchant navy at an early age. Sexually attracted only to men, he was often picked up in bars, for pleasure not for money, and this led him to decide, when he left the sea, to try his luck as a rent boy in London where he soon found he had no need for other work. He was not very bright – he had hated school because he 'couldn't keep up' – but prostitution was easy. Unfortunately for him the readily availability of drink and drugs led rather swiftly to serious addiction, aggravating his social problems.

At the age of twenty-seven he married a black girl of seventeen and lived with her off and on for five years until she got fed up. She knew he was gay and they did not have a normal sexual relationship. 'I would take drugs and I would get large dildos and things like that and I would get her to fuck me.' At the time he was living on social security and doing 'a bit of work here and a bit there'. His wife did not get on with their male lodger with whom he was having an affair at the time.

His various gay love relationships had never lasted and he was now on his own living in a hostel. He had given up drugs but taken to spending every penny on alcohol. He was living on welfare that 'lasts me two days and then is gone'. After that 'I just hope that somebody buys me a drink or buys me a meal'.

He said he had a 'nice body' and could still get customers. He no longer liked the gay bars because 'you've got young boys that want to sell their bodies for £100. I just go round the straight bars.' When pressed to describe his last paid contact it had been with a man older than himself who had picked him up on a railway station a year ago. He insisted on providing the interviewer with his address, insinuating that he could be available for sex as well as talk.

In reality he was a fifty-year-old social derelict of dishevelled appearance, with pock-marked face and swollen lip, who was located in a gay bar frequented by the rougher type of rent boy. He was anxious not to leave for too long the friend he was with who was 'spaced out' on drugs. They were accustomed to helping each other home when intoxicated. He was interviewed in the author's car. He seemed to want to cooperate, but some of his responses were confused and he was ill at ease and twice had to step out of the car to urinate in the street in the middle of busy Soho.

Case 202. In youth he had been heterosexually promiscuous and fathered at least one illegitimate child, but he was to some extent bisexual and in his twenties, during the years he was active on the London rent scene, he had no problem enjoying himself sexually with some of his gay friends and punters. He was still mildly involved in that scene when, approaching thirty years of age, he met a girl much younger than himself, fell violently in love and married her. At that time he had little trouble talking himself into jobs when he felt like it, although he rarely stayed for long. With a wife and a baby on the way he became more serious about finding work. When he could not earn enough legitimately he stole from cars and removed metal fittings from unoccupied houses for sale to fences. His young wife wanted more than he could provide and, although their sex life was happy, she proved restless and unfaithful and several times left home taking the baby with her. When he found work and accommodation on a farm, which he liked, she became bored and nagged him. He quit their tied cottage taking with him the contents of the electricity meter. He expected her to rejoin him in the West End, but instead she left for good and he became depressed and made a serious suicidal attempt with drugs. He mourned the loss of wife and child but felt it was useless to try to get them back.

After this he never again made much attempt to maintain a regular job, but subsisted on social security and what he could extract from one elderly punter. His life continued to revolve round heavy drinking and socialising in bars frequented by drug users and rent boys. He had been stopped and searched by police many times and had a number of convictions for possession of cannabis. In spite of severe bronchitis he also smoked cigarettes. In the past he had been a heavy drinker but now, due to a damaged liver, drinking made him ill. He had also been addicted to injected heroin, but after a drug clinic had advised hospitalisation he had managed, slowly and with a number of relapses, to wean himself off the drug. During his phase of heroin use he had cohabited briefly with a girl who was involved with a criminal gang of drug dealers, but he took fright and fled the area when they wanted him to take part in robbery with violence.

Seen at the age of forty-seven, he had given up trying to get work and was subsisting on social security supplemented by hand-outs from his aged punter. He had given up socialising in bars, was living alone and friendless in a small bed sitter and spending most of his limited income on cannabis which he smoked in solitude. His situation was not due to lack of abilities. He liked reading and was strikingly fluent and expressive, but spoke of feeling depressed and apathetic and being no longer confident in company. He agreed that the material support provided by his elderly punter over many years might have sapped his motivation to provide for himself.

Case 203. This man, who was in his early forties at the time of this research, was followed over a two-year period. It had been hoped he would assist in word processing tasks, but he was an alcoholic and could not remain sober long enough. He provided some insightful comments on the rent scene, some of which have already been quoted. His history suggested an underlying emotional instability. Neither the ending of his dependence on prostitution, nor his subsequent marriage and securing of profitable employment, had prevented relapse into alcoholic invalidism.

He was bisexual and had fathered a child when he was still on the game. At the age of twenty-seven, at a time when he was beginning to feel prostitution a 'no go situation' he married his child's mother. Before this he had been staying in the home of a married punter, but he left there because his necessarily secretive sexual relationship was causing unbearable tension in the household. He did not, however, immediately give up either his prostitution activity or his liking for sex with young, effeminate males. He spent some time in London getting money together so his wife and child could join him. At this point he had a rich punter who took him on a trip to France, paid him well and even made a promise (unfulfilled) to provide a flat for him and his wife.

He suspected his wife knew of his gay relationships. 'I'm sure she must have done. She was quite promiscuous herself – extremely so. We used to have orgies and things. We had a good time, but we never actually loved each other, I don't think . . . Before the wife came I stayed in London with a young boy. Then I split with him and moved in to share a flat with homosexuals. At the time she came down I was away knocking it off with this chicken, so I wasn't at the flat when she came. I got back in the morning and as I was walking down the road she came out with this queen who was carrying my baby. I then escorted her back to the station. About a week later I changed flats and she joined me.'

During this often strained marriage he secured some training and obtained well-paid work as a telex operator in a bank. At the age of thirty-three he deserted home and children and went to live with a woman of nineteen who was working in the same office. He had long had an intermittent drinking problem and 'through guilt about leaving the kids I hit the bottle for two months and had to go into hospital for two weeks'. After this there were rows and periodic separations from his woman friend during which he would have gay sex contacts, although 'by this time I'd given up the rent scene completely'. During his time with this woman, whose brothers were professional criminals, they engaged in credit frauds and with the proceeds moved out of London to set up a retail business. Soon he fell ill with Hodgkins Disease, and when he was due for release from hospital she declined to have him back. As the property was in her name he was left to subsist on a disability allowance in local authority accommodation in a very poor tenement block. His drinking bouts got worse and he was spending days on end indoors, stuporose, surrounded by bottles. He was also addicted to valium, for which he blamed the medical profession. A former punter helped him obtain better accommodation and he found work, but both home and job were soon lost and he had to be hospitalised to dry out, only to be re-admitted as an emergency with a haemorrhaging duodenal ulcer doubtless brought on by his drinking.

This man had received considerable material help at different times from several punters, but like the previous case he had not been able to make use of it to improve his situation in fact, also like the previous man, he was inclined to blame punters' generosity for exacerbating the rent boys' problems:

Q. Have you known some of the rent boys in their later years?
A. Yes, I certainly have, and in all cases none of them has been any way what you would call a success. Each one I have met since has a problem. I think that what happens is that the punter, by paying him and giving him money, food, or the means for food – the means even to stay in one place for a while – is actually just prolonging the problems of the hustler.
Q. Can you give me some examples?
A. Yes. Some do not wish or know how to work and therefore give up [trying]. Others are simply not able to do the jobs demanded of them in our modern society and therefore they're unable to cope. There's not one rent boy that I knew in the late sixties, early seventies, who has actually made anything of his life . . .

Case 210. This man had hopes of settling down with money he expected to get from his elderly sugar daddy, but the prospect seemed doubtful as the support he had so far received had done nothing to improve an irregular lifestyle punctuated by wild alcoholic binges. Aged thirty-two, he appeared in Hell's Angels gear, denim deliberately unwashed and slashed with many sewn-on badges (one showed an eagle with the legend 'no remorse') and sporting a multiplicity of tattoos. He was illiterate and declared he hated blacks. The interview took place in a council flat in central London which he said he used when he was too drunk to get back to the rooms he occupied in North London in the house of his sugar daddy. He insisted on his heterosexuality. He said he had had girlfriends, 'but they've all been on the game as well' and 'I've put a couple of them on the game myself'. He was married once, briefly, when he was twenty-four to a girl of sixteen, but she was a glue sniffer 'and I couldn't handle that'.

He was the product of a particularly disrupted early upbringing. He had not needed to run away from home because he was anyway allowed to come and go as he pleased. He was the toughest guy at his school, truanted constantly in his last years there and left without taking any exams. He had done many unskilled jobs, but never stayed long, usually walking out through boredom or through drink.

When he first came to London at seventeen he very soon found he could pick up punters in West End bars and get paid £20 or so several times every day. 'I earned a lot, but I got nothing out of it, 'cos every penny went back on drink, or back on – well not drugs so much – drink, giving it away, buying fags, you know, picking up girls. So I never got nothing out of it. I went on like that till I was about twenty-six.'

Some punters had been good to him: 'I've been [taken] to Spain, I've been to Morocco, I can't complain. I've got a house out of a punter. When he dies, that is. He's seventy-four now. I'll own that place, it's worth a couple of hundred grand, plus whatever money he's got knocking about, which ain't much. I never sleep with him, but that's how I first met him. when I was seventeen. He wanted me to move in and everything, but I said, "I ain't moving in if you want sex every night, no way." He said, "I just want you to move in." And he's still my friend.'

For the time being he was doing any sort of job that came along, working on building sites, house painting, introducing rent boys to punters, selling drugs – 'not for myself, but if a person wants them I go and get them . . . If you want heroin, if you want fucking, I know where to get it . . . I earn money that way, just enough to tide me by to get a bit of food, bus fares, whatever. Money's no good to me. I just spend it on drink . . . I like drinking and I like being drunk.' He said he was about to get a job as a bouncer in a well known gay bar. He thought he would sell the house when his sugar daddy dies and set up a guest house business with a friend who would work the business and give him a wage. 'All I want is a bike and sidecar again. He can do all the business.'

Case 209. Like the man just described, this forty-five-year-old was eking out a precarious livelihood with the moral and partial financial support of a sixty-five-year-old sugar daddy with whom he shared a flat. He was seen in his own spectacularly disordered room that contrasted starkly with that of his orderly flatmate. He wore jeans open at the knees, long hair and a beard and had multiple tattoos, including 'true love' across his fingers. He looked like a left-over hippie from the Sixties. He explained that he had known his flatmate from years back when he used to procure gay youths for him. 'We don't have sex, but we have a very strong affection for each other.' He said he still 'gets a hit out of having sex for money', but since his flatmate's recent retirement there had been squabbles between them because he no longer had the place to himself to bring his pickups back unobserved.

Soon after he first started street work at the age of nineteen he met a punter, a married man, who 'did contribute a lot to my life as, one might say, a sugar daddy. He died when I was doing three years in the nick for drugs, but it went on for a good fourteen years.' This man set him up in a flat to allow him to make money by renting rooms. It became a virtual brothel with other rent boys (including *Case 202*) living there. 'I also happened to have clicked with a middle-aged leather queen . . . We used to call him Alice, because she was sort of like the mother of the place. She did all the washing and enjoyed cooking.' He recalled this time with obvious nostalgia, but he gave it up when he started an affair with an Australian man with whom he planned to emigrate. That didn't happen because they 'fell out while we were doing Europe'. By then his present flatmate had come into money and was able to provide a place for them to live together. He continued to be active on the rent scene and also to have affairs that were not strictly commercial, friendship and business tending to go together.

For him business included drug dealing. He boasted a conviction record 'as long as your arm' and four sentences of imprisonment for theft and burglary as well as for drugs. He had been a heavy consumer of LSD himself, as well as heroin, and thought this had made him reckless and easily caught. He had long been a heavy drinker as well. He used to drink 'because it was sociable', now he has to drink 'to become sociable . . . I spend about £20 a day on drink.' As to drugs, 'I take anything that is available if I can afford it . . . I sometimes wonder where I find the money.' He was officially unemployed and receiving sickness benefit but probably still drug dealing.

About his plans for the future he said nothing definite. He mentioned that his tattoos, acquired 'when I was in the nick' had prevented him getting jobs because people think it means he is a burglar and had discouraged gay clients from taking him back to their places. He reiterated, however, that he could still get paid for sex on occasion.

Case 218. This was the older man, aged forty, with whom one of our earlier interviewees (*Case 204*) had been living. He was yet another with multiple problems which would probably have been little different if he had never engaged in prostitution. He was a rough, tough-looking character wearing a heavy overcoat, army boots and torn jeans. He spoke with a pronounced East London accent. He was seen in Cambridge having fled there and landed on the doorstep of a social worker friend. He had quit his East London local authority flat to escape from some 'heavies' he believed were pursuing him. He admitted to being a heavy user of amphetamines and to having supported this habit over many years by dealing in drugs, including heroin. He was intensely preoccupied with his fear of further assault from men who had entered his flat and attacked him and the youth who was with him at the time and stolen his drug cache. He was not very coherent about it, but he seemed to think that the intruders were from rivals of the big-time drug dealers who were his own suppliers and that they suspected him of having been instrumental in informing against one of their gang. He said he was himself on bail for an assault charge on the sixteen-year-old son of a neighbour whom he thought was in league with the men who had attacked him. Probably as a result of the drugs he had been taking, including a lot of alcohol from his friend's house, he was in an abnormal, paranoid mental state, imagining he was being followed everywhere.

On matters unconnected with his immediate problem he was quite lucid. He identified as gay, and was estranged from his family on that account, though he had been married briefly to a lesbian and had considerable heterosexual experience. Now his interests were 'mostly males, but my eyes still wander'. He had begun rent boy business very willingly in his teens. His first client paid him well and 'introduced me to one or two other people who also gave me money. They were all pretty well heeled.' From then on till he was eighteen or more 'I was seeing four or five guys each week and bringing home between £50 and £100 a time. They obviously thought it was worthwhile . . . After meeting these people over a year I ended up living with one or two guys or they provided me with accommodation elsewhere.'

While on the game he undertook over a period of years part-time college training in interior decoration. He was skilled at this and also at mechanical repairs and general handyman tasks. While on the game 'I made a lot of money and I was careful. I banked most of it.' He paid for his training out of it and 'by the age of nineteen, twenty, I had an awful lot of money, enough to start me up in a small business interior decorating. For quite a few years I did quite well.' He was living with a lover. He took on a business partner 'who was a wizard at books and I am useless with books'. Unfortunately this man embezzled the funds, left big debts, the business collapsed and 'when the business broke [my lover] could not stand the strain, I could not stand the strain, and we split'. Their menage at the time was highly unorthodox. It was 'a very crazy time'. Living together were the mother of his children, another woman, himself and his male lover. Then the women 'decided that they loved each other a lot more than they loved me and they sodded off with the kids'.

After this he had a succession of stormy homosexual love affairs, the longest being with *Case 204*. He was a possessive and jealous lover and he fought with and injured this young man several times. He was also subject to mood swings that may have been connected with his amphetamine habit. His drug taking had started when he was on the game. Some of his love affairs were with adolescents under sixteen. On one occasion he narrowly missed prosecution when one of them ran away from home leaving behind compromising letters from him which were found by the parents and handed to the police. He was suspected of having done away with the boy and was interrogated roughly, but the boy returned and craftily denied any sex in their relationship. He had had trouble with the police for other things. At seventeen he was given three months detention for larceny. 'I have been very close to being arrested for drugs and managed to wriggle out.' For driving under the influence of drink or drugs he had lost his driving licence more than once; on the latest occasion losing his job as a motorcycle dispatch rider. He admitted he was still spending £200 a week on amphetamines, cannabis and the occasional treat of 'acid' or 'coke'. Over the past decade he had had numerous short-term jobs and attempts at self-employed building and decorating and motor-cycle repairing, but in spite of his technical competence he could never stick to anything consistently and successfully; moods, intoxicants and stormy relationships continually got in the way.

As his two children: 'One is eighteen and I believe [is] a student. He is doing very well for himself. I wish him the very best of luck. They know who I am, I have seen them, but it is best if we stay apart, I am too much of a bad influence.'

It would seem that this man's life problems had little connection with his period on the rent scene. He had been better off then than at any time since.

To set against these disastrous histories we did locate some more successful men who had once been prostitutes. Among the group of 'miscellaneous' informants was one who proved to be a former street worker. He had been introduced by *Case 301* (a previously interviewed client of rent boys) as someone who could tell us a lot about the rent scene. The conversation was informal and not tape-recorded, so it has not been counted as part of the properly interviewed sample, but it is worth mentioning as an example of a street worker from an unfortunate background who had partially made good.

Case 304. This man was in his mid-forties and was running a seemingly profitable small car-hire business. His upbringing had been disrupted. He had been adopted by parents who 'found they didn't want children'. IIe was put into a boarding school where he met up with a pederastic house father. He was 'puzzled' at first, but 'went along with it' and the man became 'everything, friend, mentor, father figure'. Nearing fifteen, he was interviewed for a routine job, but by then he 'had other ideas' and ran off to London, losing contact with his parents for fifteen years. He was picked up very quickly by a 'rich sugar daddy' who kept him in luxury and successfully evaded the authorities. By the time he reached sixteen he was 'fed up with being virtually a prisoner' and broke off the relationship to become a street working rent boy. He developed a friendship with one of his punters who supported him with pocket money so he could make use of the bars and provided him with a bed when he didn't find one elsewhere.

He thinks that the fact that he was bisexual and also never shy of doing a job of work encouraged him to abandon the rent scene. His jobs remained on the fringes of the scene. For a time he was 'bouncer' for a large gay club and he had also at one time 'run an escort business from a friend's place' but had given that up because of police hassle. 'They wanted to know the names of clients in return for protection.' He admitted that he had been using his car to transport prostitutes of both sexes and had been questioned by the police in that connection. He was aware of advertising companies and hotels that introduced rich clients from abroad to escort agencies. There was little doubt that he was still acting as a go-between and was putting punters and rent boys in touch with each other.

Circumstances did not permit any closer inquiry into his lifestyle, but he did mention having been married three times and there were strong hints that he was living dangerously on the fringes of criminality by combining his legitimate business with pimping.

The next two examples are of former street workers whose success in after careers was indisputable. Both were unusual for street workers in coming from materially secure backgrounds and having a good education.

Case 216, who was interviewed at the age of fifty-three, had at one time been a street worker. He had had unhappy, conflictual relationships with his parents, but he had been brought up in a financially secure, middle-class, two-parent home and educated at boarding school. However, 'When I was fourteen my father found out I was having a relationship with a boy who was about seventeen and he found out through a letter the boy wrote to me. He found out and took the letter and locked me in my room and wrote to the guy saying if you ever see my son again I shall contact the police. That was the most devastating thing he could have done really, because the relationship never had its normal time to pass through, so it remained in my memory as perfect. Consequently I spent many years looking for that [again] and of course could never find it.' He was a self-willed, independent-minded boy and on reaching sixteen his parents agreed that he could go to London. 'I think they thought they would never be able to hold me.'

In London he attended a technical college learning catering, but the allowance his parents sent him was so small it left him nothing to live on once his fares and rent were paid, which was why he took so readily to selling sex. 'It was something that seemed obvious. Here's a man who is older, a man who's got money and you haven't, and the very fact that you are sixteen and there's a guy double your age . . . a perfectly presentable man and he says, "I want to do something with you and I'll give you some money", it seemed perfectly simple. I didn't have any money and he did.' He started picking up on the street but soon found a convenient West End coffee bar open all hours. 'I didn't do it nightly, only once or twice a week, if I needed money to go to college, or if I needed to buy a bit of clothing. But then I moved away to having regular clients . . . [met] through a guy that I was very friendly with, a man much older than me who was charming. He was retired and he took on a rather fatherly role.' This senior army officer was gay but made few sexual demands. He was happy to be seen with me, taking me around, because, as it happened, I was extremely handsome . . . He had a lot of very rich friends and some would ring up and say, "Would you like to come to the theatre or to dinner?" . . .

[Afterwards] I would go back to their place, do something with them and they'd give me 20 quid. I liked it, most of them were very nice men, very interesting, very educated. I mean they were educating me in taste, style, fashion . . . I got fucked most of the time, safe sex was unheard of . . . The price was not negotiated, just something that happened.' Usually he got about £20, whereas on the streets it had been in those days only £5.

He worked as a rent boy from about the age of sixteen until, at twenty, he started an affair with a young man and they set up in a flat together. By now he had a regular job so he neither needed nor wanted to continue. In any case he had never been desperate or homeless. 'I did have some money coming in from my parents, so it wasn't so bad and I could be choosy . . . If it was somebody I didn't really like and I didn't need the money I wouldn't take them up on it, but if I got to the situation where I really needed the money I had to put up with it, but I made it as quick as possible . . . It was normal for me to have some money behind me, so if I got 20 quid from this guy tonight I'd spend £5 and put £15 in the bank.' While on the game he drank a lot, but it was no great problem. 'I used to get quite pissed, but I wasn't addicted.' However, he did sometimes go with people he wouldn't have gone with had he been sober.

His relationship with a man lasted some eight years, after which he had relations with both men and a woman. In his late thirties he had a period when he himself patronised and enjoyed young rent boys. By the time he was interviewed he had been married some eleven years and was running his own business. He liked sex with a female. Looking back on it he thought he had had relationships more often with males because he was 'oversexed' and young men were so easy to pick up in bars.

Several features distinguished this man's story from the less fortunate histories of other former street workers. He came from a relatively privileged background. His resources as regards accommodation and basic finance and his self-discipline in saving money enabled him to exercise choice in selecting clients. His relationships outside the rent scene, both personal and occupational, were stable and he had no great difficulty deciding when to quit the scene.

The next and final example suggests that there are some who can experiment with the rent scene for short periods of their youth, but without becoming permanently dependent on prostitution and without it affecting their future prospects. Such cases are usually inaccessible to a research survey, but this man's cooperation was secured via a colleague's personal contacts. He was interviewed by Buz deVilliers, but without the use of a tape-recorder. Being American, he was not included as one of the supplementary sample of 25 London street workers described in Chapter 11.

Case 229. Untypical of most London street workers, he came from a close-knit, supportive, tolerant middle-class family. He made normal progress through school and eventually university and obtained a degree.

He was thirty at the time of the interview and had spent all his working life as a writer/journalist. Hard-working and successful at his job, he was in London on secondment from his American employers. He was an almost total abstainer from both drink and drugs.

His bisexual interests had begun by the age of ten. He reported having had 'hundreds' of relationships with males and 'dozens' with females, the former tending to be one-off contacts, the latter more long-standing affairs. His sexual life had been uninhibited and unproblematic – he was open about his bisexuality to his family and others, though reserved about it with work colleagues. In youth had felt free to have fun and experiment as much as he liked, but this changed in his early twenties, following several doses of gonorrhoea and growing awareness of the risk of AIDS, causing him to abandon anal and oral sex.

From the age of about fourteen to sixteen he had a lot of anonymous sexual contacts in toilets. On one occasion a man prevailed upon him to go back with him to a hotel room and gave him $20. This he found exciting and it may have aroused his interest in paid sex. At seventeen to eighteen he was having a full sex life on college campus and also visiting New York City's gay bath houses. He made the acquaintance of an attractive young man who, unknown to him, was a hustler. He was taken to a bar occupied exclusively by younger rent boys and older punters. He soon realised what was going on and returned about six to eight times to try out the system. Picking up would begin with a relaxed chat over a drink. The punter might just say, 'OK, shall we go.' At this there would be a quick agreement on price ($50 was the average), discussion of the sex required being left till they got 'home'. The money was an incentive and the sex was easy and he generally enjoyed it, except on a couple of occasions when he had to resist demands for anal sex. The novelty wore off after a while and he gave it up when he felt it no longer suited him, though it was good and interesting at the time. He found he couldn't identify with the other hustlers he met. He regarded them as 'shattered'. Some of the clients he regarded as pathetic, like a pot-bellied priest who only wanted to be hugged. He didn't like having sex with men he didn't care for and he disliked having to do things on the clients' terms, like leaving in the middle of the night. There were nights when he had no success, which he thought was due to the fact that his age (eighteen) was about the upper limit of interest to clients. He was not ashamed or regretful, he felt he had gained insight into another facet of life.

He would like a wife and family, but in an open marriage that allowed for casual sex as well as the security of a permanent relationship. Meantime he feels somewhat frustrated and has been having some paid sex, both heterosexual and homosexual. He has found female prostitutes in London rather jaded in attitude but has enjoyed visits to a male massage parlour. It was fresh and clean and for £30 you got a good massage, considerate sex (using his own condoms) and the workers were affectionate and generous with their time.

*

These case histories show that male street and bar prostitution may appear attractive to vulnerable individuals lacking in education, training, self-discipline and social or family supports, but it provides no real solution to their life problems. By its nature, the trade and the lifestyle that goes with it can provide only a temporary means of survival and the longer it is pursued the more difficult it becomes, especially for men who have never had proper work experience, to make the transition to conventional employment. The added complications of involvement with drugs and petty crime increase the likelihood of permanent social alienation. The success stories cited involve men who had alternative means of supporting themselves, who had never severed their links with the wider community and who were able to disengage from the trade when it suited them to do so. They had in addition the requisite temperament, determination and ability to succeed in an ordinary career. The student in the last example was aware of the difference between his own situation and that of other 'shattered' bar hustlers. For the typical street worker from a deprived or non-existent family the prospects are more bleak, but of course they might be equally bleak if he does not take up street work. Although some former street workers remained delinquency-prone, none of those interviewed showed an escalation of criminality during or after their involvement in prostitution. In fact one of the examples quoted was of a man who seemed to have been less of a law breaker during his street working period than at other times in his life.

Finally, the present research has unearthed contrasting outcomes, but the proportion of street workers who may eventually achieve social integration after leaving the rent scene cannot be realistically deduced from this kind of survey, in which failures are always more visible and accessible than successes. Workers at the Streetwise Project assured the author that they knew of some former street workers who, given requisite help and encouragement, had found satisfactory jobs or places in further education.

Part II
Advertised Services

13

The Scope of the Male Sex Industry

Non-contact services

Rent boys working in public places comprise only a tiny part of the male sex industry. Workers of vastly different background and character from those found on the streets are employed in a variety of services, some of which are organised into large and profitable business enterprises. Sex industry activities range from the production and distribution of pornographic videos, through strip shows and sex talk over the telephone, to agencies advertising 'escorts' that are actually supplying prostitutes. There are also self-employed men, working at home and advertising themselves as masseurs, who are actually purveying sex in the shape of masturbation and other forms of release. 'Escort' agencies also provide similar 'massage' services to callers at their premises, which effectively become male brothels. Most of the advertisements appear in gay magazines and papers whose readers are under no misapprehension as to what is on offer. Some of these services have developed relatively recently, others have long been available but are now advertised more widely and with less subterfuge, and others again, like the cinemas specialising in homosexual pornography, are no longer a feature of the London scene. Before discussing our inquiries among workers who have direct sexual contact with clients, who are the main concern of this research, some mention of non-contact services may be of interest. These are of relevance if only because, by offering what may be cheaper, safer and more accessible enjoyment, they are in a sense in competition with the ordinary prostitution trade.

Britain imposes more restrictions on these alternative outlets than do most European countries. In Denmark, Holland, Germany and Spain magazines and videos are openly sold containing material, either homosexual or heterosexual, that would be considered obscene in Britain. The production and distribution of pornography is now a technologically sophisticated and well capitalised industry catering to an enormous public demand.

In England only so-called soft porn is legally available and it is supposedly restricted to specialised sex shops licensed by the local authorities. Videos for sale have to be submitted to the British Board of

179

Film Classification which grades them according to suitability or otherwise for viewing by the young. The most restricted grade may be sold only through sex shops, but as these are thin on the ground or entirely absent from large parts of the country the legitimate market is discouragingly small from the point of view of those in the business of making videos. In any event, homosexual pornography does not enter the legitimate video market. Whereas videos of heterosexual intercourse will obtain a certificate, provided hurtful violence or humiliation is avoided, explicit representations of male homosexual intercourse are either totally excluded (as being susceptible to prosecution under the obscenity laws) or are never submitted to the censor.

Male striptease acts are allowable in England provided they are limited to nude exhibition without masturbatory activity. Performers are hired for women's outings, public house entertainments and by some gay bars for the benefit of their interested male customers. Until recently there were small cinemas in the Soho area of London exclusively devoted to the showing of gay pornographic films or videos. A good description of the type of venue and the behaviour of the audiences at these shows appears in the novel *The Swimming-Pool Library* (Hollinghurst, 1988). At least one Soho facility selling gay pornography used also to provide a continuous male strip show. A succession of naked youths would dance, or prance, on a small platform shielded from the audience by a transparent partition. Small openings in the screen encouraged the more enthusiastic watchers to 'post' money into the arena to mark their appreciation of the dancers. With recent crackdowns on pornography such facilities have vanished.

Cinemas that were once well known to the initiated as places where homosexual activity went on in the auditorium are no longer available. The notorious Biograph cinema in Victoria, long since demolished, used to be patronised by rent boys as a convenient resting place with the added possibility of finding the odd paying client (West, 1977, p. 140).

The use of the telephone system for the transmission of obscenities is illegal, but this has not prevented the proliferation of 'chat lines' and other services of a quasi-sexual nature which enable callers to engage in saucy conversations with strangers. Those of interest to heterosexuals are advertised in the national press. The gay newspapers advertise their own brands of service. Callers to 'hot lines' featured in such papers as *Capital Gay* can listen for a modest fee to pre-recorded salacious stories. Some include extremely explicit descriptions of genital activity, others, like the following example, rely on innuendo and double meanings:

> Hi there. Welcome to my hot line especially catered to suit all you gay guys of varied tastes. But I have to warn you our lines contain really explicit material, so you have to be over twenty-one. And the call will cost 25p a minute cheap rate and 38p at all other times. Be prepared to have your

senses stimulated and your blood pressure raised. Do you think that you are ready for this? Oh good! Then we shall begin.

[After a snatch of music the voice changes]

Ah so! You have been a naughty boy haven't you? And that's why you've come to me so that you can be punished and have all the cockiness knocked out of you – and believe me you will too. I know a lot of cocky guys, like you, but they all respond to six of the best from a good strong cane. It seems to give them a sense of *relief* to know that they have been punished for their wrongdoings. They just seem to *explode* in gratitude after caning. And I try to see to it that they are fully satisfied when they leave . . .

Yes, I can feel it. You are getting excited now. I can feel your rising excitement very clearly with you pressed against me like this. Let me just get a bit more comfortable. If I move my hand a bit and slip under here. Yes, that should do it. Ready for it. [whack] Oh yes! You are rising to the heat of the moment aren't you . . .

More explicit messages are scarcely suitable for reproduction, but a summary of one example will give an idea of the quality. Beginning with the usual warning that the listener should be over twenty-one, the story-teller describes a visit to a tattooist who is tough, muscular and very attractive. He lowers his trousers in preparation for tattooing on the hip, but the tattooist shaves his belly. He becomes sexually aroused and the tattooist responds by licking his genitals and fellating him to orgasm.

Organisations using the telephone system that most closely resemble a homosexual prostitution service are those which employ men on chat lines to have uncensored 'heavy' conversations with callers prepared to pay for the privilege. An advert in a gay magazine read 'CALL [X] Live. The ultimate in safe fun'. When the number which followed was rung the following recorded message explained the system:

Hi! Thanks for calling. My name is [X]. They call me big [X], but I'll have to tell you why when we speak person to person. That's the object of this message, to tell you how you can speak to me, just the two of us, for half an hour, live, uncensored conversation. I want you to dial a certain number and then you can find out more about me when we speak together. I'll give you a few small facts now, if you like. As you know my name's [X], I've got blond hair, twenty-two, quite stocky, skinhead – well, kind of skinhead. I like going out down the pubs and that. I'll tell you more about myself. What you've got to do, like, is dial ******* so that we can talk together. When you dial that number you can book the call. Ask for [X], nobody else, I'm the best, right. Ask for [X], give the receptionist your credit card details and I'll phone you back within 10 minutes. So within 10 minutes you'll be hearing from me and the call won't be charged to your phone bill because I'll be phoning you. So if you want to speak to me you've got to dial ******** and remember to give your credit card details to the receptionist and then it will just be you and me, 10 minutes later. You can ask me what you like, I'm not shy. I'll answer any of your questions and maybe ask you one or two as well. I enjoy doing it. Nice and natural, nice, heavy, strong phone conversation to get us both worked up . . .

On calling the number given the young lady answering the phone quoted the price of a conversation with [X] as £29.90 + tax.

Immediately above this advert appeared the following notice:

> Advertisements for telephone services will not be accepted if such advertisements explicitly suggest or imply that obscene conversations are possible, contrary to the British Telecommunications Act.

Date lines provide another form of service, assisting people who want to find others with similar sexual interests. In the gay press they are advertised under such titles as Man-2-Man and Blind Date. Several telephone numbers all beginning with the 0898 code are displayed in each advert. One is for calling in to record a message giving particulars of oneself and of the sort of person it is hoped to contact. Others, linked to descriptions such as 'gay men', 'gay women', 'BI/TV/ALT', 'Slaves and Masters', indicate which number to call to hear messages from the desired category. These systems are run by substantial and established business enterprises. The fact that they are so flourishing points to a widespread demand for sexual contact that is not being met through ordinary social channels.

From time to time these telephone services attract unfavourable media attention. One report (*News of the World*, 14 Jan. 1990) told of a dating line being sued by a well known disc jockey for using his pirated voice to introduce its recorded messages from people seeking sexual partners. Another time, under the heading 'Sadism lurks on the end of the phone' (7 and 14 July 1991), the same newspaper named as 'perverts' a barrister and a vicar tracked down through their advertisements by investigative reporters.

A student who was doing temporary, part-time work for one of these companies agreed to be interviewed and supplied further information about their operations. He explained that the company who employed him advertised under several different names targeted at different types of client.

> Q. When people leave the messages about themselves and what they want do they give their own telephone numbers?
> A. Some do. We have a filtering system whereby we take their name and number, because we can either give the number out directly to people who ring up wanting to contact them or the number can go on the collect system whereby we don't give the number out but take the name and number of the person who wants to contact them and pass that back to them. They have to phone in once or twice a week to collect the numbers . . .
> Q. Where does the profit come from?
> A. What we do is we master the tapes and post them off every day and British Telecom put them on their computer for that number. You pay £1,000 a year for the right to have that number, the 0898 number . . . The callers are charged at 25p a minute off-peak and 38p a minute peak time.

Q. That's more than the [regular] price isn't it?

A. Definitely, yes. The company averages £25,000 profit a week. Telecom will take their normal rate and the company gets everything above that . . .

He went on to explain that all operators, who work in shifts to man the phones, receive £4 an hour. They have to work the computer that locates the details from each recorded message so that they can quickly tell the caller what number to ring or whether he must leave his own number.

Q. You were saying that you have special lines for homosexuals, transsexuals, fetishists?

A. Yes. We've got about fourteen specialist lines ranging from leather interests to mud and oil, PVC, construction workers, bikers.

Q. Anything else?

A. A rubber line, a master line, a slave line.

Q. Are these all both heterosexual and homosexual?

A. They're all homosexual. We had heterosexual slave and master lines, mistress lines, etc., but they proved really unpopular.

Q. So most of the kinky ones are homosexual?

A. Definitely, yes.

Q. Which suggests that homosexuals are more interested in kinkiness than heterosexuals?

A. Or else more blatantly overt about the fact that they have got those interests. One of the major problems of the company is that we can't get enough heterosexual women to use the service. Millions of heterosexual men, but no heterosexual women . . . We have a policy now for the staff to get £1 bonus for every recording they make if it's from a heterosexual woman . . .

Q. Is most of the custom homosexual?

A. The majority of lines are for homosexual men . . . It's a general trend through the whole spectrum of telephone dating. You look through all the magazines, even the free weekly magazines like *Miss London* or whatever, the telephone line adverts are mainly homosexual . . .

Q. Now this is a sort of contact thing, it's not prostitution?

A. No, and many would argue it's not a sex contact thing, but I believe it is.

Q. So officially it's a friendship line?

A. Yes . . . A heterosexual prostitute was using the service to get clients and we got complaints almost immediately. People were phoning her or she was phoning them and she was telling them what she was going to charge. I'm not sure how much, £60 or something. We immediately withdrew her tape.

Q. You haven't had any of that trouble with the men?

A. Not that I know of. I mean mainly because no one has complained that any of the people who have placed messages are rent boys.

Q. The example I told you about of the telephone service to ring for a man to call back and talk sexy, that is a different kind of service?

A. Definitely, yes. It's more Americanised than we have here at the moment . . .

Q. So that's a kind of telephone prostitution?

A. Definitely, yes, telephone sex. One of the reasons our 0898 numbers do so well is that people phone up and listen to them and masturbate while they are listening. We make more money from people listening than from people phoning back the office . . .

Q. Now also on the 0898 numbers advertised in the gay press there are these recorded stories. Some of them are pornographic. How does that work with British Telecom?

A. Well, recently the company got a letter from British Telecom warning us that if we didn't tone down the explicit nature of some of our messages they'd shut us down. We know that a rival company got the same letter. Their lines are far more explicit than ours anyway. Since then all staff have a memo on their desks of words and phrases that just aren't allowed to be used, usually ones that refer to violent sex or violent interests. Now we ask the client to repeat the message before we record it so we can tell them what they can and can't say. What we do now is we have colour codes. Each member of staff has a colour code of handkerchiefs that a lot of gay men use to refer to specific interests. So now some of the messages can just refer to colours rather than interests. Blue for fucking, red for fist fucking, black for S & M, grey for bondage, I think pink for dressing in drag. There's loads of them.

Q. So you must keep an index?

A. Each operator has a little file with the index in.

Q. You hope that listeners will know what the colours mean?

A. If they don't it's hard luck. When restrictions come along the company just thinks of something else to keep the revenue coming in . . .

Q. I know that there has been some legal trouble about some of these services. Do you know anything about that?

A. There have been two articles in the papers recently because three ex-members of staff went to the newspapers and sold their stories, saying tales were false, messages were false, on lines that were not particularly busy.

Q. How do you mean?

A. Staff had recorded messages on the collect system and when people phoned in to reach them they took the person's name and number but never phoned them back. It was a system being used when opening new lines when no one had been placing messages. You fill up the line with false ones until it gets busier. Now, since the revelations in the paper, that's stopped.

Suspicions that some telephone services are being used for buying direct sexual contacts with rent boys were allegedly confirmed by reporters from the *News of the World* (28 Oct. 1990). In answer to a call to a male telephone dating line advertised in the *Pink Paper* a rent boy aged sixteen called back and offered hand relief for £25 or full sex for £50. After being given £50 he described how the system worked. He paid the agency £12 every time he went with a punter and double if he had full sex. He said that the offices operating chat lines and a prostitution service were situated on the floor above an apparently legitimate but suspect employment agency for young people. An investigator posing as a rent boy infiltrated the office and was shown a computerised list of prostitutes and told that all tastes were catered for – gay, lesbian, bisexual, transsexual – and that the organisation would give him an appropriate image and find him work.

Erotic massage and escort services

The so-called 'working girl' need not be a street walker; she may ply her trade in a safe house or brothel, she may advertise herself as a 'masseuse' providing sexual release in her own or the client's home or in a massage parlour, she can offer herself directly or via an agency as a 'model' for 'photography', or she may work for a firm providing an 'escort service' that includes sex. Off-street male prostitution services are similarly organised and advertised using the telephone for initial contact with clients and avoiding the need for street solicitation. The American term 'call boy' aptly describes the arrangements, though it is not favoured by London workers.

The operations of one London escort agency, as they operated in 1981, have been described by Salamon (1989) who was able to interview the owner/manager. He was gay but married, as were most of his clients, but his agency did not restrict its advertisements to newspapers and magazines for gay readers. It had on its books 50 female as well as 170 male escorts, so not all of its clients were seeking a homosexual companion. Moreover, its respectable location, away from blue movies and sex shops, was intended to make it more attractive to men not wanting to be seen in those places. The owner thought of himself as running a legitimate business. The fees he took were for introductions and most of his escorts were qualified masseurs. The client had to pay the escort directly for any services rendered, but the owner insisted he did not 'pimp' on those transactions. He was fully aware, nevertheless, of the sex activities that were involved. In fact he would guide the client in choosing the model most likely to fit his requirements while they both browsed through the agency catalogue. The photos gave hints of the kind of activity to be expected. For instance, some of the male escorts were shown in black leather or military style gear, others in diaphanous negligées. The owner would help out with questions such as 'Do you give or take?' Then he would recommend accordingly.

Escorts were told not to fix appointments with clients other than through the agency, but often they broke the rule. Any who did not attract custom were soon deleted from the catalogue. Introductions were by Christian names and anonymity was preserved. Everything was geared to the protection of the clients from exposure of their homosexuality which, since most were family men, could be disastrous for them.

In contrast, the American male 'model' agency described a decade earlier by Pittman (1971) was effectively a brothel, since sex with clients could take place on the premises. It was situated in a respectable residential neighbourhood and run discreetly by a gay 'male madam' or manager who prided himself on guarding clients from robbery, blackmail or exposure of their homosexuality. The reception area and the bedrooms were lavishly decorated, featuring queen-sized beds and lubricant and towel arranged on nightstands. The manager occasionally advertised 'models for hire', giving a phone number, but most clients were introduced by already established customers. Strangers were vetted in a personal interview with the manager.

The models, nearly all in the age range eighteen to twenty-six, consisted of sixteen who gave full time to the work and 20 who had other jobs but were supplementing their earnings in their free time. When he was recruiting the manager rejected any who did not identify as gay or bisexual or any whose homosexuality had come to the notice of police. He favoured the young and genitally well-endowed, since these features appealed most to customers, and he gave preference to those prepared to be 'versatile', that is agreeable to both active and passive oral or anal sex. Prospective employees had to demonstrate their erectile ability in front of him.

The manager arranged all appointments and took 30 per cent of the fee, although models were allowed to retain tips. They were instructed to perform a professional job without becoming too friendly or emotionally involved with clients. They were not to see the clients except at the official appointments. They had to maintain a smart appearance, wear clothes suited to the client, be prepared to respond to calls at unseasonable hours, accept whoever wanted them and attend to appropriate personal hygiene – such as deodorants and rectal douches.

The call boys working for this establishment often started with the idea of working there very temporarily, but finding it well paid and initially exciting stayed on for months or even a year or two before getting bored with the job or losing their popularity with customers as they became older or more jaded. Often the sex was enjoyable and many customers were wealthy and pleasant personalities. During sessions the call boys usually accommodated themselves to the sexual acts most wanted by the clients, but on occasion it could happen the other way round. In the long run, however, commitment to the job interfered with their desire to set up with a sugar daddy or with the development of their own private sexual and social relationships.

According to a survey in Chicago by Luckenbill (1986), based on interviews with 28 male prostitutes aged from eighteen to over thirty, agency 'escorts' were regarded as better placed and better protected than street hustlers, or even bar workers, because the agencies screened prospective clients for troublemakers or under-cover police officers. Some agencies promised bail and legal aid in case of arrest. They also arranged fees and dates and the details of what was expected by way of 'sex and other agreed upon activities, such as having dinner', so the call boy did not need to haggle. Agency clients paid better and the appointments system permitted the call boy to plan his own time, to obtain a steadier flow of cash and to undertake non-prostitution work so that he was not so dependent. Agency employees were thought to enjoy better incomes and more stable lifestyles. In order to be accepted as employees, however, they had to be over eighteen, to maintain an attractive, stylish appearance, to keep to the financial and other rules laid down by the agency and to be proficient at their work so as to generate rather than discourage business. Some of them thought it a disadvantage that they had less choice in selecting customers than when they were operating in the gay bars. Many had started as hustlers when they were under eighteen and so had no choice but to work off the streets initially. They found that less agreeable because of the greater risk of arrest, the embarrassment of being exposed to the public gaze, the cheaper type of prospective customer and the restricted opportunity to avoid undesirable types when answering a driver's signal to jump into his car. As one man said, the driver might have a knife under the seat. 'You're just in a bad situation.'

Nowadays gay magazines and newspapers in the UK contain numerous advertisements for personal services which, though not represented overtly as sexual, give broad hints, readily understood by the gay readership, about what sex is on offer. Scrutiny of a sample issue of *Gay Times* (April 1990) reveals two pages containing 166 small advertisements for models, escorts and – the largest category – masseurs. The classified advertisement section is prefaced by a notice that includes the sentence 'No advertisements intending or appearing to intend to solicit for sexual purposes will be accepted'. In addition, the list of masseurs is headed by the statement '*Gay Times* only accepts masseur advertisements if they are accompanied by genuine certificates of qualification'. The wording of most of the entries, however, puts greater emphasis on the physical attractions of the masseurs than upon their qualifications, and some of the additional particulars given concerning such items as jocks, videos, leather and corrective treatment are fairly easily translated by those with relevant interests into the kinds of satisfaction on offer. Here are some examples:

> Handsome straight looking guy (24), tanned, offers complete massage in comfortable, discreet appartment. Also body shaving. Central. In/out calls. (24 hours).

> Come on! Hot experienced leather man is waiting to service you. Tanned, blue eyes, dark hair and moustache. Can visit.

> Ex prison officer. The firm escort you'll remember. Leather room.

> Young student (21). Slim, smooth, athletic, short blond hair, gives warm, sensual full service in his own flat. Shower, videos, central.

Fresh faced (22), sports wear model, stunning looks, firm well defined physique, offers intimate full service in private flat with shower, oils, rubber and leather.

Cain. Handsome, tough ex-prefect gives corrective treatment. Beats the rest and the best.

Beautiful, firm, smooth body (21), 5' 11", fair cropped hair. Complete, stimulating masage. Sports gear, video, shower. Friendly, complete, unhurried service. I also visit.

21 year old qualified masseur, boyish looking, short dark brown flat top, height 5' 9", waist 29", chest 38", offers a full safe massage in jocks, briefs, shorts, rubber, leather etc. Private flat. Duos available.

The advertisers all provide Christian names – invariably male – and telephone numbers for prospective customers to contact them. Prices are not normally given until an inquirer telephones, and they may vary with the time of day or night and whether 'specialised' services are wanted. When the age of the advertiser is included it is usually in the early twenties, but never under twenty-one. As a rule it is only a few of the 'leatherman' advertisements, suggestive of sado-masochistic activity, that state an age in the thirties.

An amusing account of some visits to advertisers of 'massage' is given in an article in the *Pink Paper* (a freely circulated newspaper for lesbians and gay men) by an author who tried out several (Burn, 1989). His first visit was to a rubber specialist who turned out to be disappointingly middle-aged. He had been in the business six years and charged £30 for a 40-minute session. He ordered the client: 'Get down on that bed' and, after absenting himself for a few moments, returned covered from head to toe in rubber. All pretence of a massage was soon gone and as the client lay naked, except for clamps on his nipples and a gas mask over his face, the masseur perched over him tugging at a bootlace that had been tied round his penis. In contrast, another masseur proved to be a stunning looking twenty-two-year-old who received his customers dressed in just a jock strap. He was clearly into sex rather than massage, remarking, 'That's what you all really want.' During a visit to a 'duo', who charged £55, the pair showered the client before placing him on the bed and beginning their stroking. Soon they got to chatting together, sniffing amyl nitrite and carrying on with each other, leaving the client to watch them, although watching an exhibition was not what he thought he had paid the fee for. Only one of the masseurs visited performed literally as advertised. He kept his clothes on, avoided intimacy and had a picture of his girlfriend on display.

The recent proliferation of masseur and escort advertisements in the gay press suggests that the trade may be in a boom period, but the gay masseur service is not a new phenomen n. An article in the defunct magazine *Gold* (1978) described visits to masseurs advertising in a tobacconist's shop window and in a gay newspaper in such terms as 'Attractive slim guy gives relaxing massage' and 'Male massage service – visits arranged.' It seems the style has changed little although prices have at least doubled. For £15 the writer received a half-hearted five minute back rub quickly followed by the removal of his underpants and the masseur, himself by this time naked, climbing on top of him with 'all real pretence of qualified massage forsaken'. A second masseur reported having been beaten up recently by men who telephoned him while sober and then turned up aggressively drunk. Now he was doing out-calls only with first-time clients. He appeared at the hotel as requested dressed in a sober suit that would not attract unfavourable attention from the doorman. He said he was twenty-two but looked and talked like someone eighteen or nineteen at most. He charged only £10 plus his taxi fare, started to undress as soon as he had been handed the money and happily stayed overnight.

Apart from the usual escort/masseur adverts there are others wanting or offering a diversity of services, such as 'house boy' and 'holiday companion' into which might be read a hidden sexual agenda. Here are some examples:

Young attractive houseboy 21-25 needed for busy guy to help look after pads in UK, overseas and afloat. Wages, travel and fun guaranteed.

Gay males and females required by film production company to take part in 18 certified adult videos.

Young amateur photographer seeks young bodybuilder or stripper (21+) to perform for my camera.

Looking for security and affection? Home, friendship and employment offered . . .

Limited time and resources have prevented exploration of these less common types of advert. A search of British and American publications failed to turn up any relevant information. None of the interviewed men mentioned having tried answering such advertisements, although they would seem to offer scope for obtaining lucrative employment for men willing to accept payment for sex. One French writer (Hennig, 1978, p. 201) quotes the experiences of a man who inserted advertisements reading something like this: 'Homo. 25 years. Seeks employment. Personal secretary for preference. Possibility of extras.' None of the numerous respondents proposed real work. He sent them photographs of himself – one nude – and met various buyers. He found it a lucrative way of getting money for sex, better than having to spend hours on the street, sometimes without any client turning up. He found one not too demanding fat guy in his fifties who gave him lots of money for a sex visit just once a week.

One gets no more than a tantalising glimpse of the world of gay escorts/masseurs from their numerous advertisements or from the few scattered accounts of their activities that have been published. The chapters to follow attempt to fill out the picture by means of first-hand accounts from both workers and clients.

14
Agency Operations

Impressions of London massage parlours

The advertising pages of papers such as *Gay Times* include extensive announcements by agencies offering to furnish escorts, masseurs or both and smaller notices from individuals offering themselves for similar services. Many mention both an 'in' and 'out' service, according to whether the client visits the advertiser or has the advertiser visit him. Visiting an 'escort' seems a contradiction in terms, but in practice escorts generally perform massage and the distinction between the two services is hazy. Visiting an agency generally means calling at a massage parlour equipped with several rooms or cubicles and a selection of young men waiting to perform. In some adverts the telephone number given appears to be personal but is in fact the number of an agency. When the client rings up he thinks he is making arrangements with the advertiser direct. Actually, he is talking to an intermediary who subsequently contacts the rent boy who most nearly fits the advertised description from among those available, telling him where to meet the client or when to expect his arrival and what kind of service is likely to be wanted. Clients calling at agencies offering an 'in' service are given a choice of which of the 'boys' currently on the premises they want to have for 'massage'. Since these arrangements amount to brothel keeping, for which the managers would be liable to imprisonment, they have to operate cautiously and there is a chronic fear of being raided by the police. According to a survey (*Simon's Word*) published in 1986 by a gay group (see p. 227) most London agencies are owned by the same few people and some are 'caught up in the twilight world of crime and other things' and so attract visits from the police. They are not too particular about the trustworthiness of the young men they employ and their relations with their workers, who are often transient, are beset by paranoid suspicion that clients are being seduced away to private assignations. Some agency employees or ex-employees were interviewed and in addition several gay men agreed to try out some masseurs and massage parlours in London and comment on the services. Presenting themselves in the guise of ordinary clients, the information they gleaned depended upon the talkativeness or otherwise of the operatives they met.

Sexual servicing took place in six out of seven visits to massage parlours, often with minimal attempts at a preliminary massage. One masseur, whose suspicions were aroused by the visitor's probing questions, maintained that sex was not allowed, but another visitor calling at the same massage parlour a week later got the full treatment. Here are some extracts from our volunteers' reports, with the two just mentioned quoted first:

Visit 504

[After phoning] I arrived at a basement flat in a rather pleasant residential street and went in as the door was open. The doorman introduced himself as Bob and asked if I wanted tea, coffee or orange juice. He said he only had four or five boys there at the time as several probably had got drunk the night before and were late coming in. He was rather off-hand, didn't ask anything about me and pushed me to choose a boy long before I had finished my orange juice.

I was given the choice of five 'boys', four behind a one-way mirror and one out working with the doorman. The masseurs were as follows: two English (one had a migraine, supposedly, and was curled up in a corner looking rather ill), one English-Mauritius, one English-Jamaican and one Italian. The choice was not impressive. The decor was all right but not warm, and the entire ambience and the attitude of the staff wasn't impressive – more off-hand and uncaring. I chose the well Englishman.

The masseur was Sandy from Somerset, medium height, dark hair, with a lower-middle-class accent and a tattoo on his arm. He asked nothing about me except had I been there before. He would talk and elaborate on his answers to my questions, but volunteered very little. He told me at least three times that he was currently the most popular masseur at the parlour due to his schoolboy looks. I believed everything he told me in his blasé but unhesitating manner, except the information on sex in the parlour. I had an agenda of what I wanted to find out . . . I started within the context of 'What a good massage you give, where did you learn?' I just let the questioning flow from there in a hopefully casual manner with long periods of no talking.

Sandy said he was a bar manager in the West Country but came to London six weeks ago because he was 'bored'. He worked for a week at a massage parlour in Earls Court but didn't like it as it was 'clinical' and 'sordid' , 'mirrors on the wall', and there were too many masseurs there for the business. He started work here two weeks ago. About ten masseurs work here, but they have only four or five on duty at a time because there are only two massage rooms open now. (There was a leak in the third.) He is so popular he works ten hours a day seven days a week. He lives nearby, so he is one of the few that can get there by 1 p.m. (They open at noon, but there is seldom business before 1 p.m.) He's so popular he is allowed to work seven days a week. His typical day is 1 p.m. to 11 p.m. with some nights on out calls till 2 or 3 a.m.

The massage is £40. The parlour gets £20 and the masseur £20. An out-call is £70 an hour. The parlour gets £22, the masseur £48. The masseur has to pay his transportation from his fee. If the out-call is very far away the client is charged £80 and the masseur gets the extra £10. Last week he had fifteen clients, including two out-calls. This week (4½ days) he has had six so far. The busiest times are lunch times through to early evening. Saturday is the slowest day. Sunday is mainly busy between 3 and 7 p.m. when the pubs are closed. The clients are probably mostly married, at least the ones who come during the day. Gay men tend to come in late in the evening and on Sunday afternoons. All ages come in, from late teens to early sixties, most forty to fifty.

The money is 'all right, but not enough'. He wants to move on soon, get a regular job. One would only stay at one parlour for two or three months. By then the clients are used to the masseur and his business falls off. One has to move on to where one is a fresh face. When he had applied for a position at the previous place the only criterion for a job was 'youth and beauty'. He was asked his age (because they supposedly will hire no one under twenty-one) and his nationality. He was good looking and had a good body so they hired him. He was going to be shown what to do when a client came in, asked for him, and he had to start working immediately. He had some experience (one week) giving massage and he had practised on friends.

The massage was good, almost professional, but not totally so. Sandy said he was gay. He was dressed in jeans and a pair of socks the entire time. He volunteered, while speaking of clients, that he always kept his jeans on except for regular clients, then he would give the massage in his shorts. He said some clients were difficult and had the wrong idea about the place. When queried, he said they would start talking dirty as soon as they came in and often tried to become 'physical'. He would pleasantly and firmly let them know what was expected and what was done in the place. My massage lasted at least an hour and was boring towards the end. I said I thought it was to be a full body massage. He said it was. I explained why it wasn't. He apologised three times, said he was sorry I had the wrong idea. Said several times that the other was against the law and that a gay massage parlour had to be very careful because of the police. The police come around once in a while. Just before he started to work there a policeman had come in for a massage, pretending to be an ordinary client. If that happened to him he would know it was a policeman because he could spot one the minute he got on the massage table. I said that surely he didn't think I was the police. He said that he wasn't saying one way or the other. As I left he hoped that I had at least enjoyed the massage.

Visit 512. A somewhat younger volunteer visited the same parlour a week or two later. He rang at 2.30 p.m. and was told to ring back later as there were no masseurs in at the time. After ringing again at 4. p.m. he was given the address and told to call. He was surprised at the dinginess of the place compared to the luxury of another parlour he had visited nearby. He was given juice to drink and a choice of three boys. Two were behind the one-way mirror, a black youth and a very rough bovver-boy type; the third, a tall young man making a hot drink in the reception area was the one he chose. He asked to go to the toilet, which he found in a mess, for which the man at the reception made some light-hearted joking excuse.

He undressed in a dark room that was not very clean or well furnished and had weight-lifting equipment on the floor. When the masseur came in he looked about twenty or twenty-two, very much the young gay disco type. He was friendly but not very forthcoming, conversing at a social, superficial level in what seemed a middle- to upper-class accent. He explained that he had been not long awake, having not got to bed till 9 a.m. He said he went out dancing after work each night and that that was 'all that we live for'. He mentioned that he was soon to go on holiday abroad for three weeks with the manager of the parlour, but was having trouble getting his birth certificate due to a combination of red tape and his own lack of attention to the details wanted by the authorities. He made some leftist comments on current political issues. Business had been slow the day before, with only three clients. Asked about the music that was playing he said it was what the 'weirdos' played, referring apparently to the other masseurs.

As the massage progressed he soon worked round to the client's genitals, then stripped off his own clothes, presented an erect penis for fellatio (which was discreetly declined) and finally pressed their two penises together, masturbating both simultaneously until both ejaculated. That he did so surprised the client who felt he had not been very responsive to the masseur's overtures. After providing a damp towel to clean up he surprised the client further by asking him, a non-smoker, for a cigarette. After another orange juice the client went to reception and paid by credit card a fee of £50.

More information was obtained about this particular massage parlour subsequently; one of our interviewed men (Case 228) happened to be a lover of one of the staff. There was no question but that it existed to give a sexual service. In fact the manager had been convicted a few months earlier for brothel keeping.

Visit 507

The telephone number of the agency was given in *Gay Times*. I rang on two occasions. Both times the answer was friendly but guarded, without giving a name or number, just 'Hello'. I was given an address and instructions how to get there, but in a foreign accent I found hard to follow. When I asked if I would get a 'full service' I was just told, 'Come along, you will find it very good.'

After going through the entrance door of a basement flat one entered a lounge with a desk on one side. The lighting was low and there was a very oriental ambience. I was served coffee from a choice of tea, coffee or orange juice and had a little friendly chit-chat with the man who said he would lead me back to see the 'boys' after I finished my drink. We went back to the end of the flat (two massage rooms on the left, bathroom on the right). The 'boys' sat in front of a TV and many were talking. I could see them through a one-way mirror as the head man told me their names. He also said he too was available. There were eight 'boys' in the room. It turned out later that three were Thai, one was a black man, I believe from the West Indies, one from Argentina, one from Switzerland, one from Liverpool and one from Birmingham. I chose one from among the white men called B, who turned out to be Swiss. I was then taken to one of the massage rooms, told to undress and told B would come soon. Overall the premises were comfortable, warm and clean, I was impressed.

B was short and well-built with decent muscles and a warm and pleasant smile. He was more than willing to talk . . . He saw himself as gay. He said that the 'boys' (this was his and the head man's term for them) sat around watching TV and drinking coffee while waiting for a client to come in. Some days B would get no clients, some days three or more. Most 'boys' work at the parlour for two to three months. Many go off to live in 'cheaper-than-Europe' places the rest of the year, such as Thailand or Brazil. The price is £40 an hour, shared half and half between the masseur and the parlour. Sometimes clients have given more, but he has still only to give the parlour £20 and can keep the rest. One man gave him £100. The clients are 'fairly young' to about seventy. Some may come because they want to try out sex with a man. One client this week was about twenty-one years old and sat in a chair looking at B for 30 minutes. He didn't take his clothes off or touch B and after 30 minutes paid £40 and left. Two men had wanted him to do things he refused to do. One wanted to whip him. The other brought in women's clothes and wanted him to dress up in them. Some of the clients were bad. (He seemed to mean personally unpleasant and physically unattractive.) When an ugly client comes in (old, bald and fat) they all hope they aren't called out, but they have no place to hide because if they go to the shower they can be seen through the one-way mirror.

For the massage I took off my clothes and B removed all his except a pair of striped boxer shorts . . . [He began] a reasonable massage, but I'm certain he wasn't a professional masseur . . .

The massage soon developed into mutual fondling and masturbation during which the masseur was highly aroused. He also made flattering remarks about the client's physique, was very solicitous throughout the session and almost seemed to be wanting affection.

Visit 509

I saw an advert in *Gay Times* for 'a young masseur who commands respect at all times. You'll find me fully equipped for rubber and leather in discreet luxury apartment.' I rang his number twice, once to ask if he would be working today, again, at his suggestion, to say I was nearby and ready to call. The voice did not sound the same the second time, but I could not be sure it was a different person. Both times there was a slight hiss on the line which made me wonder if the call was being recorded. I said I had seen his advert and asked the price – £35. I asked if it would be a *firm* massage and was told, 'Oh yes, certainly', and was given a street name and number and told to ring the bell on the brown door.

The street was one with large, multi-occupancy, late Victorian type terraced houses typical of the area. The 'luxury apartment' was not a private flat. It was in a building at the end of a mews that looked to have been converted from old stables. The door had an entry phone which was answered promptly by a young man in his mid-twenties, dressed in jeans and T shirt with bare feet. The door led onto a stairway to an upper floor that consisted of a corridor with several rooms leading off it and a toilet at the end.

I was shown right away into a small massage room containing a table to lie on, like a hospital trolley, a chair and a covered-over chest of drawers. Some bottles of oil etc. ready for the massage stood on a shelf. As there was no other place I piled my clothes on top of the chest of drawers. While I was undressing the masseur took off his shirt and jeans leaving on some black jogging shorts. He did not ask for money up front but asked if I knew 'our pricing system'. It was £35 for straight massage, anything else was extra and 'at our discretion'. He asked if I had been before. I said not to this place and explained that I had expected to meet somebody at their own flat. He said there were two boys working there this afternoon. I said I knew of massage parlours and knew there was one somewhere nearby called [X] and was this it? He said it was a branch of it.

He was polite and friendly, but not communicative, answering only when I put some direct question. The massage started off in silence. I lay face down on the table while he went on with a slow, sensuous stroking. Then he pressed his thumbs over the spine, moving from one bone to the next. I said, 'That's nice, where did you learn that?' He said he had been to a massage course and that this helped relaxation. He had been working for the agency for only a few weeks – since Christmas.

After some time, while he was leaning over me rubbing my chest I commented on his hairy chest, touching it. He smiled encouragingly and asked if he should take off his shorts. He then did so and asked, 'Is there more I can do for you?' He said a wank would cost another £25. I said I hadn't brought much extra money with me and suggested £10. He agreed, but then said, 'Make it £15.'

While dressing afterwards I asked if he was busy. Friday and Saturday were busy but Sundays, like today, were unpredictable. However, he would be 'on duty' till 10 p.m. While still polite he seemed eager to end the session and show me downstairs to the door, with no suggestion of a drink or chat as had happened with other private masseurs I had tried. It had all been quite clinical and I saw no sign of the advertised rubber/leather equipment. Intending to try another masseur I rang up a different telephone number taken from *Capital Gay* where, under another name, a man was advertising a 'hard to beat service' in a 'private, discreet flat'. When I was given the address it was the same place as before and I turned it down.

Visit 505. On the first of two visits to this massage parlour our informant noted that it was a basement flat in a smart residential area with its own individual entrance. This seemed to be a favourite arrangement for these businesses. As well as a couple of massage rooms there was a reception area that served as a lounge and, as usual, a room with a television where the masseurs waited for clients, in this instance with a viewing window rather than a one-way mirror. T, the staff member present, was talkative. He said he had been working at the place two months and that he was from abroad and had not been able to get a work permit. He said he had a degree in communications from a university in his own country and was intending to return to work there in television. He had applied for courses in London so he could remain here and learn practical skills in set design or something similar that would be of use in television. He was pleased to be working for the moment as receptionist as he did not enjoy doing the massages. He listed the 'boys' at hand, most of whom were foreigners. One Englishman was a college student working during his vacation. There was a big turnover of masseurs, partly because of the need for new faces, most clients wanting a different boy each time they came. The longest masseurs stayed was about two months.

The masseur the informant picked was from France and said he had come to England to learn English, but was trained in hotel management and was intending to return to his own country very shortly to take up a job he had lined up. He had been at the parlour for just one week, since the end of the term at his language school. He had also worked at another parlour for two weeks some months earlier, at a time when he needed money. He used to be a swimming champion and gave what he called 'a swimmer's massage' which was 'excellent'. He said that some straight men came to the establishment to have just a massage. He can usually tell if they are gay and want sex, but if there is any question he gets close to them and if they look like they can be kissed he then kisses them. If they respond he then gives them a 'full' (i.e. masturbatory) massage. He had heard that a few women come there for a massage because they feel they can 'trust' a gay masseur, but he hadn't seen any himself.

The masseur was 'very assertive sexually, with much tongue kissing and mutual masturbation, and he got on top of me for a fairly long period of body rub.' 'When he leaves for Paris he doesn't plan to be a masseur ever again.'

Visit 513. This was a second visit to the parlour just described (*Visit 505*). As before, the staff were very open and talkative. This time D, a twenty-two-year-old Englishman, was acting as receptionist, but unlike T he said he was looking forward to getting back to doing massage when the manager returned later that afternoon. He seemed enthusiastic about the job, which he had been doing for three months, longer than the others there. He mentioned being invited to the country by clients for weekends, which he enjoyed. He had also accepted an invitation from a wealthy man from Saudi Arabia to go and stay in a flat there for six weeks and was excited at the prospect. He was somewhat embarrassed to have to explain that since the last visit the charge had gone up from £40 to £50. During this conversation another client arrived, 'about sixty-five, tall, thin, dignified looking and dressed in a very expensive and conservative suit. He looked nervous. When he was asked if he wanted a drink he said he would rather go directly to the back. When D returned after arranging the massage for this client I said the client seemed in quite a hurry. D said that some people did not like to be seen by other clients and were not

comfortable coming into the parlour. The "city types" were the most likely
to be uncomfortable.'

The informant chose T for his massage, which soon progressed into
sexual contact. 'There was considerable body rub, much mutual
masturbation and he masturbated himself to the point that at one time I
was afraid he would come over me . . . A pleasant but uninvolving
experience.'

In addition to these visits inquiries were made at some more
'up-market' agencies, but were not followed through on account of the
relatively high cost. Here are two accounts of what happened.

The agency is in a small two-room office on the third floor of a building in [a
West End shopping street]. A man came from the inner office to greet me . . .
After explaining that I had heard about their agency through a friend and
was considering using an escort he explained the set-up. I could look at their
book of escorts with no obligation. If I chose an escort they would give him
my telephone number so he could contact me so we could arrange between
us the price after I specified what services I wanted. My introduction fee to
the agency would be £45, once the escort and I agreed to meet.

I was given a blue-covered book containing information on each escort
and his picture or pictures. The man, who never introduced himself, gave
me coffee and a piece of paper to take any notes I wanted. He was friendly
and pleasant, but I got an idea he was a bit hard and brittle. He did say he
assumed I wanted the blue book (containing men) rather than the one
containing women.

There were thirteen escorts in the book, several from England, others
from Denmark, USA, Ireland, Spain, Greece, Cyprus, Portugal and
Yugoslavia. The photographs were of good quality. Most showed the escort
dressed well, one or two were very 'arty', . . . only two or three were
provocative, none were in the nude. Against the photographs was given first
name, age (all between twenty-one and twenty-five), nationality, hair
colour, eye colour, weight, height, chest size, waist size, hip size and
interests (typically film, theatre, sports, travel) . . . I went to the inner office
door and said I would think about it and was told that was fine, it was all
right if I rang tomorrow, next week or in a year.

Another agency advertised escorts/masseurs between the ages of thirty
and forty-five:

I rang the number and the phone was answered with the usual 'May I help
you?' I asked and received a 'yes' to the question 'Is this the —— Agency?' I
said I was interested in a massage. The man, who was very businesslike,
asked what kind of man I was interested in. I said someone in his mid to late
thirties. He said he had someone available now in Hammersmith. I said
that was a bit far from where I was in central London and he said that all
the other masseurs were even further out. I said Hammersmith would do
and asked the price. When I was told £60 I said that was a little expensive.
He answered, 'That's what you can expect to pay through an agency.' I said,
'No thanks' and rang off.

These reports provide proof – if any were needed – that the agencies exist to provide a sex service. Over the telephone, with an unknown inquirer, they try to avoid direct reference to sex and employ euphemisms like 'full body service'. Agencies providing massage rooms on their premises cannot so easily distance themselves from their workers' sexual activities as can those providing only out visits to clients' homes or hotels. Once staff feel confident they are dealing with a gay customer it is openly accepted that he is there for sexual pleasure with the 'boy' of his choosing. At the 'massage' session the worker will respond to any gesture of sexual interest from the client, who will sooner or later be brought to climax. Most masseurs permit mutual stimulation, often becoming much aroused themselves. On the whole clients depart satisfied, having been treated with consideration – perhaps more so by the workers than the managements, whose attitude was sometimes less friendly. Some of the men working in massage parlours were well educated and some claimed to be doing the job only very temporarily pending taking up a different career.

There were indications of some conflict and suspicion in relations between agency workers and their employers. From the charges made to clients it would seem that the amounts agency workers receive for a session are not necessarily any more than the sums street workers can get from their punters. Agencies vary in their policies and business practices from those enforcing 'squeaky clean' rules to avoid any legal complications to small, unregistered, untaxed, back-room enterprises run by marginal characters. The names of some eight advertised agencies were searched in the register at Companies House without any being located. Business names were not observed to be displayed in any of the massage parlours visited by our informants. Several occupied premises in residential zones where one would not have expected business use to be permitted. Inquiry was made at the relevant town hall about two of the addresses on the excuse of being interested in acquiring flats in those buildings. Assurance was given that no business was registered at either place.

Workers' impressions of agencies

More information about how the London male escort/massage services operate was obtained from interviewing men with experience of working for them.

Workers all agreed that most massage sessions end with sex, but agencies cannot be frank about giving a service that is against the law. Dr David Tomlinson, a clinician and researcher in sexually transmitted diseases, telephoned agencies advertising in the gay press to ask if they would display a notice about HIV and testing. They all declined, saying that sex was not involved in the activities on their premises. However, when he telephoned individual advertisers, some of whom were working for agencies, they made no such pretence and a high proportion turned up at his clinic for screening.

The methods of recruiting and paying agency employees were also varied. Some charged the client for the introduction and left the rent boy to negotiate his own fees. Some agreed the price with the client, had the rent boy collect it, but required him to turn over an agreed percentage. Additional payments – 'tips' – received by the employee over and above the pre-arranged price were sometimes matters of dispute. The interviewing of a prospective employee might or might not include detailed questioning about the sexual acts he was prepared to perform, a complete bodily inspection or a practice massage under supervision. As *Case 514* explained bluntly, agencies pretending to be purely for escort work still want to know 'your height, the general description of yourself and as a rule they tend to want to know what you have got between your legs as well – strangely enough if they are supposed to have nothing to do with massage'. The interviewed men included workers from six identifiable agencies. Their accounts reflected the differing scale and practices of these enterprises.

Agency [A] was an establishment run in a relatively discreet manner, in the guise of a health club, and with rather more regularity expected of its employees than suited two workers from there who had since become private masseurs and were interviewed by the author:

Case 114

I was living with an infamous rent boy who had been involved in lots of scandals and I got a lot of information off him. His boyfriend had worked at [A] and so he told me about it. I telephoned in and went to see them. [They hinted at but were not explicit about sexual requirements.] The thing is, if you go and say somebody told me to come, and they know who it is, then they know the score. They asked did I know what the situation was and I said yes. They asked how old you were and would you be prepared to take a massage course, which I did, and things like that, basically.

It is a small gymnasium, there is a sauna and a Turkish bath and there is a TV room, a sun bedroom and a lounge. I don't think they actually advertise, I remember talking to them about it. It is very established. Clients go in, they have to be members, and they book a massage, I think they can book half an hour, three-quarters of an hour. I think an hour is £24, half an hour £15. They book a time and have a number. You get told the number and you go into the club with two towels shouting their number. Some just book blindly, but they do have some choice of masseur. Some of them go round the club first and ask your name. Most people attend there every day and some of them know who is there. When they go to the massage room they have a towel and they take it off, so they lie down on the bench on two towels, naked. You tell them what to do. I just say, 'Lie face down and I will give you a massage.' And then you say, 'Would you like extras?' That means, like, a hand job. And they usually say, 'How much?' If they don't, you say, 'It will be £25, is that OK?' You have to check. I don't know what other people do, but all I ever did was masturbation and they could suck me as well . . .

You work shifts and get a basic wage, like £2 an hour, [keeping the money from the extras]. The number of customers for massage each day varies a lot, from two to as many as fifteen, twenty I have had. Some shifts you have to do a lot of cleaning as well. You get harassed quite a lot about not cleaning or not turning up on time. They try to run it so.

This man was working at [A] together with his flatmate (*Case 113*). They both left when the flatmate had a violent quarrel with the owner. 'We were not very popular with [him]. I mean he liked having sex with me, but we were not very popular. We are too vivacious and too intelligent and creative. But the punters liked us a lot, I was very popular.'

Agency [B], the up-market and well-established enterprise called upon by one of our helpers, but not used because even the preliminary introduction cost £45 (see p. 198), operated a policy different from all the others in that it provided no massage on the premises and worked basically as a contact service. One former employee (*Case 514*) put it this way:

[B] is actually an escort agency as opposed to an up-grade massage parlour. The way I see it the difference is the fact that an escort is somebody who goes out with you for a drink or a meal or whatever. Sex does not actually come into it at that point, it is the company you are paying for. If you wish to pay for sex, then you offer a different deal over and above. In fact [B] used to stipulate that you are being paid for your company. If you have sex with the man it does not matter, it is nothing to do with [B]. They do not in fact encourage you to charge extra for sex because obviously that would be illegal, whereas escorting is not. At massage parlours everybody knows full well that 90 per cent of the masseurs cannot perform an adequately good massage, in fact they know nothing about it. It is merely the five-minute trick – get them turned on and turn them over and get them out.

Even though they advertise as escorts most are massage parlours with massage done on the premises. Although they will send workers on out calls to clients 'you do not expect an escort from a massage parlour to go out for a drink with you'.

What [B] does, they would ring me first, give me the client's name and I would then ring him and say something like: 'I am ringing you because the agency gave me your phone number.' Normally this would only be about two or three minutes, just basically going straight down to mercenary details and where they were planning to take me, or whatever. You would not discuss chances of sex or anything like that . . . When you go out with a client it tends to be with a sugar type person . . . You think you are there to keep them company and have a conversation to make them look good. Because they have got a young man with them obviously everyone thinks they are interesting . . . I have done two clients for [B] and slept with one, but he in fact paid more on top . . . I was on something like £200 for the [overnight] jobs I did for [B]. £200 is not much when you compare it with street work. On the streets you would expect a boy to be with you for approximately two hours, including any travelling time, for about £50. Knowing that you are on a better grading as an escort £50 per hour is not that bad.

According to another former employee of [B] (*Case 515*):

They are really the very plush end of the market. They are the most expensive. A discreet service. You tend to get MPs and businessmen and so on, who will only occasionally use other agencies, all signed up with [B]. What they do, they take photographs of you and they put them in an album. If the punter sees someone in the photo book that he likes they charge him £45 introduction fee. Then he gets the lad's number, what day he is on, and he makes all the other arrangements with the lad direct. But the lads are told to ask for a minimum of £100, which goes to them . . . They will fix up calls over the phone, but most of the time with regular clients they will use the books [at the office] . . . You had to ask for £100, but that was a standard minimum price. It's very much this end of the market. [B] always likes you to turn up in a suit . . . What you do is you sign up with them. They don't want people who are working with any other agency. A lot of agencies don't mind if you are working for two or three others but [B] only want people working for them. You pay a deposit. They take a deposit off you, which is about £100, which they hold until you leave. So if you do a runner after the first job they have got £100 held from you . . . Once you have agreed to sign up with [B] they expect you to be prepared to see clients five days a week. They expect you to go into the office and sign in and then, for the rest of that day that means that you are on call, so you have either got to hang about the office there or have a bleep. If you don't mind taking the phone calls at home they will give the guy your phone number . . . They didn't have premises, but now they have a few flats and you can rent a flat off them while working for them and they will send clients round to the flat. They never used to do that. If you could accept clients at home that would be great, but otherwise you just did out calls.

They ask you as a matter of interest when you join what you do. They liked to keep a record of this sort of thing, but their automatic response to people over the phone, unless they were regular customers was, 'Oh, we don't do that.' [B] doesn't really deal with S & M at all . . . If anyone rings and asks for S & M they say, 'Well you can have a word with the boy and see what he wants', but their official policy is just straightforward masseur jobs . . . If you phoned up and said on the phone you want somebody who will be fucked their automatic response on that will be, 'Fuck off, this is a respectable agency, we do massages, anything else you can have a word with the boy about, other than that, Get lost!'

None of the men interviewed had much good to say about the agencies they had worked for. The last two informants were distinctly critical of Agency [C], a large concern with more than one office and several flats where masseurs can receive clients. It was said to advertise in the gay press under a variety of names. *Case 515* was particularly critical of the management of Agency [C]. Having set up an agency himself in competition he knew what he was talking about, and any bias in his comments would not be due to lack of information.

They are very big and owned by a rather dubious character called M. He is apparently a millionaire. He operates on a scheme whereby he takes you on and you work twelve-hour shifts at a time and he gives you £50 for that shift. All the money that you make – and you may do only one client or as many as six clients on a shift – all the money goes back to him, basically, except any extras that you make out of it. At the time it was the first agency I had been to, so I didn't know that usually you get substantially more money, normally 60 per cent of the punter's fee ... Although he would guarantee several shifts a week, if you wanted it, he would only give you in advance two or three shifts, whereby you start in the morning at 10 o'clock or at night at 10 o'clock. But he would also dish out bleeps and say, 'I can't guarantee you any more than two or three shifts, but you may get a couple more this week if you keep your bleep on at all times so we can bleep you at some time this week to do an extra shift if we have a call on.' It was insecure, because some weeks there wasn't much work and you didn't get the shifts you were guaranteed, but most weeks you did. He had at least one person working there and the phones were covered virtually 24 hours.

[At the interview for the job] he asked me to take my clothes off, which I did, strip right down. And then he wanted to – he had some idea about tying me up, which I wouldn't ever do. So then he got me to tie him up, which I said was fine. He is very kinky, very kinky and weird ... I didn't get a hard on at that time, but he did and he came ... He ties up with most people. He usually suggests first of all that can he tie them up, then if they say, 'No', then he says, 'Well, you tie me up.' I found out later that if they are very good-looking boys, but don't go along with that sort of interview, because they have had enough experience to know that not many agencies would do that, then he will take them on anyway. But he will usually try it on first. Certainly, in a lot of cases, if people won't do anything then he won't take them on ...

The thing about [C], as opposed to other agencies, he used to train the people who were operating the phones to find out first of all where the client was ringing from and to judge what he sounded like before they offered a price. If he sounded like a straightforward punter it would be just £40 for in calls, £80 for out calls. But if he sounded American or something, or in a big hotel, then the price could immediately be put up to double that for an hour, or in excess of that if they wanted no time limit. On that first night I only did one punter and he was charged £250 for two hours, which I collected by cheque, but I still got only £50 ... When I first went to work for him he only had guys that were employed as masseurs. He would use us while we were on shift to do other things, like taking it in turn to answer the phone and he would get people to tidy up the place. He had two massage rooms on the premises. Later he did employ somebody as a PA and he had actually employed a full-time telephonist.

There are a number of things nasty about him, like he has about fifteen private escort ads, all on different numbers and different names ... all supposed to be individuals as opposed to the agencies ... He actually gets most of his business through the private masseur columns . . . In just a few years he has become a millionaire. I knew the people who were doing his accounts for him. I even helped him with his accounts once . . . He is not paying tax. He has a couple of cover outlets which are up front. That's how he came to accept credit cards. He had been accepting credit cards for about a year and had loads of back slips, but couldn't actually put any of them through. I mocked together on a computer a complete set of three years' worth of accounts so he could accept credit cards . . . I could see that he was giving us a lot of work because he was spending a lot of money on advertising, but he was still making gross amounts for himself. He expected you to hand over half of any extras that you got, and no other agency asks that. Needless to say, hardly anyone did hand over extras, because it's like a tip. It was better working for him than going on the street, I guess, but people weren't getting a fair deal . . .

One other thing I didn't like, he would send out virtually anybody to do any job. If he got calls for body-building jobs – and he hardly had any body-builders because they wanted more money anyway – he would just send anybody. If he got somebody who was obviously into chickens – sort of twenty-one maximum or something – then he would say, 'Go and say you're twenty-one.' Things like this. It's amazing, most of the time clients tend to swallow it. I have been out on jobs for twenty-one-year-olds and they have taken me . . .

Case 514 also criticised the deceptive stratagems used by [C] to pass off employees as private masseurs. 'You are supposed to be pretending that it is your own flat. A lot of the time [others] would have to go and hide in the bathroom so that the client did not think there was anyone else there apart from the masseur. Because a lot of clients are very nervous, do not want to be discovered.' The client may not be given what he expects. 'Clients go by the description that has been given in the paper which might have included somebody 6 foot tall in black leather and in fact they might turn up and find somebody 5 foot 6 and looking ridiculous in leather. They are advertising falsely on a lot of occasions. They might have somebody on their books who looks like that, but if they are not available at the time they will put somebody else in instead.'

Case 506, who had also worked for Agency [C], gave substantially similar information. He had been approached in a gay club by a man who asked if he needed to make money and who gave him the telephone number of the agency to ring for an interview.

I was asked a few questions on what I would be willing to do with escorts. I was asked, you know, my vital statistics and how far I would go with them and if I would mind doing duos and all these things. They definitely said at the time that their policy was that there would be no fucking, but then the same night they were on the phone asking me would I fuck this bloke or could this bloke fuck me . . . They set up a few lads in a flat, twelve-hour shifts each we used to do in this flat. They would phone up for each lad, whichever the client wanted, and they would ask would you fuck him or can he fuck you . . . If people wanted us to go to their house or hotel, if there was enough of us, then one would go. If not, they had what they called freelance masseurs that they could page at any time of day. They would be given their hours when they would be on call. Instead of getting a set fee, like we got, they would get a fee every time they went out on a call. If you did a twelve-hour shift at the flat you got £50 plus 50 per cent of all your extras. Their agent used to fix a fee with the client when he phoned. They would phone us up to tell us the client was on his way, because all the telephone numbers in the magazines go to one place, which was not even the flat we were working from. For example, you know, adverts for Butch Billy, Bobby the Biker and Public School Terence, all different numbers but all going to the one place. The agency would tell us the name, who we were supposed to be, what was wanted and how much had been quoted. So in the flat there would be what they called the coordinator, who would write all this down. Some of the clients, who are regulars, would get to know it was an agency, because they end up going to the same flat. You get told who you are supposed to be, but if you do about ten or fifteen clients it is quite hard to remember . . .

I never did meet the guy who ran the agency. Apparently they wanted to set me up in my own flat, but I was never there very long, only five days actually, which does not sound very much, but when you are there for twelve hours a day for five days it is long enough. The main reason I came out was because the police, CID, were there the night that I left. They were outside and people were coming in and telling us we were being watched. So I more or less sneaked out. One of the guys who'd been on the day before, during the day, had said that he had been followed home. The agency actually put people to watch the people who were watching our flat, so they used to give us warning phone calls about clients being followed and things like that.

He was scared but needed his money, so he went round to the agency's office where he had been interviewed and managed to get a cash cheque out of the organiser working there. 'As I went in everything was packed, all in boxes, like the telephones were all being unplugged. He said to me to hurry up and get out of there because the whole street was absolutely crawling with CID.' Be that as it may, some months later it was noted that Agency [C] was still advertising and apparently continuing as before.

Agency [D] was a more run-of-the-mill example of a massage parlour, established a long time, but with numerous changes of address, employing about seven boys at a time working on shifts and having a steady clientele. The system was described by a Swiss student (*Case 503*) who had been working there for a short time. He and a friend, another gay man, had answered an advertisement and gone to [D] for an interview at which they were asked to take off their shirts so their torsos could be inspected. Then he was taken into a massage room where a boy lay on the table and the manager showed him how to do a massage, ending with masturbation. The manager has a large flat above and runs an expensive car and makes a lot of money out of the boys, who don't like him. They believe he has a hidden camera in the TV room where they wait for customers. One reason for their suspicion is that the manager runs in whenever two of the boys, who are lovers, kiss or show affection to each other, which they are not supposed to do while they are there. The TV room has a one-way mirror through which clients can see them and choose who they want. There are some orientals among the masseurs and the manager seems to favour them, letting them into the reception area so customers see them first and may think they are the only ones available. Otherwise there is little competition between the boys, which is fortunate as they have to spend ten or more hours together each day. There is a rapid turnover of masseurs and of fifteen currently working there all but two are foreigners. He himself is working there illegally without a permit and of course paying no tax. The busiest times are lunchtime and early evening on weekdays – times convenient to married men. The boys are selected by clients with roughly equal frequency except for one big, muscular, heterosexual Scotsman who is particularly popular, perhaps because the idea of having a heterosexual turns people on.

The massage fee is £40, out of which he gets £20. He sits in the TV room from 1 p.m. to 11 p.m. daily and does some fifteen massages in a week amounting to £300. Only once did a client leave without having sex. Normally he waits for the client to look excited and then begins to masturbate him. If the client wants oral sex he does it with a condom and asks £10 extra, which he can keep. He refuses anal sex. He finds the job OK but the long hours are boring and he wouldn't want to work there for too long.

Agency [E], as described by *Case 511*, appeared to be one where employees were receiving an unusually small percentage of the profits and were also liable to experience more demands from clients than the managers led them to expect at their initial interview:

> He had a lot of questions, he had a questionnaire, he had to know your age, how tall you were, the colour of your eyes, the colour of your hair, and how big your dick was and all that, personal questions. A lot of agencies ask you to strip off so they can see for themselves. Some people exaggerate the inches . . . There were questions about what I would do. I said I would only do messing about, wanking and sucking, I wouldn't go the whole way and let them fuck or anything. He said, 'Well that's OK' and asked if I could have people at my house. I said I couldn't 'cause I was living at home.
>
> It mostly involved sex, say 90 per cent . . . We were supposed to time the session, an hour and 20 minutes. I was always there a good 2½ hours, because I did not want to rush away. I just sat there talking to them. The sex would take half an hour, top whack. They'd offer you a drink, before and usually after.

The standard charge for an out call of 1 hour 20 minutes was £65, of which he got £15, plus a similar proportion of extras charged for additional sexual acts. Clients usually handed over the money that they had agreed with the agency to him at the end of a session. What he collected he would take in to the agency at the end of the week, £1,200 or £1,400, of which he would get back £300 or £400. Although he had set limits to the sex acts he would do the agency would sometimes send him out to people who had asked for and been promised more without telling him. Sometimes he would relax his rules a bit. Once he had to rub a client's genitals with nettles, which he didn't like doing at all and which stung his own hands in the process. An extreme example was one occasion when, 'They said it was just a man on his own, what you expect, anyway, and there were there five fellows there. They all wanted to fuck me, do everything to me, you know, use me like a sort of guinea pig. As soon as I walked in I said, "I'm sorry, I think you've got the wrong person." And I took my £65 as well, because they had called me out all the way to be fucked about. I was in there about fifteen minutes. I called the agency and said, "The job you sent me for was a fucking joke." He said, "Oh, I never knew." I said, "You must have known, because the fellow said he'd told you exactly what he wanted." He said, "I'm really sorry, it won't happen again." He was hoping that I would have done that job.' Others, more desperate for money, might have gone along with it.

Agency [F], which one of our interviewees (*Case 515*) helped to run for a time, was an example of the less stable type of business set up for personal gratification, without proper financial management and prepared to risk open discussion of sexual transactions with strangers over the telephone.

I did in some degree get talked into opening up an agency by this friend of mine from the [C] Agency who had got a sugar daddy of his to put money up. Had it not been for a lot of persuasion from him I guess I would have gone completely independent [as a masseur] and not bothered with an agency. I have always been a bit political in my ideas and I wanted to form a cooperative, an escort cooperative. This friend of mine had been involved in a bit of left-wing politics and I thought he might like that idea, but later he turned out to be a total bread head, compromising his ideals all the way along, but that's where the idea started. We kept wondering about how much money we would actually need. I spoke to a few escorts. Then he got his sugar daddy to put the money up for a full agency. It was obvious to me that this sugar daddy was into this friend of mine. I told him so and said, 'He is just trying to buy you full time.' That's always a danger with that sort of thing, like repeated calls. Street rent boys get into that situation and it's worse if they are very reliant on the money from those clients. Obviously my friend had got quite involved with this client and he had seen him a few times before he said he would put the money up, but he didn't want it to be a co-op, he wanted it to make money. At first I was against the idea, but my friend said to me, 'Well, you can employ friends there and give them much better conditions than at [C]' . . .

It all got quite complicated because the agency ran up a total of £15,000 worth of debts, of which, I guess, he only paid £5,000, the rest he actually did a runner with, both the partners ended up doing a runner. The agency should never have cost so much to set up in the first place. I was warning about this all the time. They rented two flats, one over the other. One was a private flat and the downstairs one the agency, both under the name of [X], the company they set up. I thought it very expensive and unnecessary having a flat over the top, but I thought, 'What the hell, if this guy is prepared to throw money into it.' We spent an absolute fortune on advertising, much more than we should have done, just basically to compete with [C].

We did some market research by phoning around a lot of other agencies. There was a lot of competition with new agencies that kept setting up and there was a lot of fluctuation in the prices, particularly on out calls. In calls stayed around £40, but there were some agencies offering to do out calls for about £50. For out calls one was taking £30 and giving the boys £20, which wasn't good at all, but they have gone. I don't think it generated a lot of business for them, because it doesn't work like that. We refused to cut our prices down [from £40 for in calls and £80 for out calls] . . .

My friend had only worked for [C], so he wanted to set it up on similar lines. So he had 30 phone lines put in, which cost an absolute fortune, a bill which was never paid, and all the time they were notching up expenses setting up a really salubrious agency in [an expensive area], running more adverts than necessary and having this private flat. I couldn't go back to operating independently because I had had to vacate the flat and the new flat [shared with a new boyfriend] couldn't be used [on account of domestic friction] . . . The agency was spending far too much. On good days it was averaging £600, I guess, but out of that we had all the expenses. We had some people employed on a shift basis, but they would only work an eight-hour shift at £60. Because the agency was fairly quiet a lot of the time they only did one or no clients at all, but would still get paid. We also had workers on the usual agency percentage basis, which was 60 per cent to the boy doing the job. We had about ten different boys who shared different shifts between them. Then about another twenty who were lined up to be used occasionally on the percentage basis . . .

[The other partners wanted to lower the fee for shifts.] They were less philanthropic than I was and gradually it entailed my getting into arguments with them . . . When it first started I was virtually living there full time doing the phones. I wrote all the adverts for it and so on. I said I would not be into a system where I was employing people and exploiting them. During the course of the agency they had taken in about £10,000, which had been paid into a bank account that they just took. I was supposed to become a shareholder once it started making a profit, but for a while I was on a salary of £300 a week . . . then a couple of my salary cheques bounced and I started getting heavy. Then, as I say, they both disappeared. I lost about £1,000 in total. I guess they did lose some money, but they probably broke about even. So many of the debts were not paid, about £15,000. [I wasn't personally liable.] I didn't have anything on paper at all. I was specific about not wanting anything with my name on it down on paper or anywhere. I was happy dealing with the advertising and the interviews and doing the phones and occasionally I would go out and do clients, regulars, or some I thought might be difficult, but most of the time I was on he phone . . .

Agency [F] was set up in an extravagant and unbusinesslike way, but even a modest enterprise would need some considerable outlay and organisation. *Case 514*, who had worked for several agencies in his time as well as having been a street worker, began to realise this when he was considering the possibility.

Yes, I thought of getting a flat together, say a two- or three-bedroomed flat, preferably three, one set up as an office with switchboards and the other two as a bedroom and a small lounge, in such a way that obviously the people can't hear. You have to soundproof the phone room, so that it is not heard by people coming in and out. As far as they are concerned all they see is one live telephone and that is it on the table, just for calls coming in. Whereas most of the calls will be coming through the switchboard. In that way they would see a flat, a normal person's flat, not a masseurs' agency. People get put off by the professional look. They do not like it to look like they are going to a massage parlour, but they do like to go to one. I know that sounds like an anomaly . . . The thoughts are there, but it is the practicality of carrying it through. With one room as an office and two others as working rooms, you can always put a bed in the office if you have got to sleep there. You could leave the other two rooms as working rooms so that anyone who wants to use the house as a place [for work] can. A lot of the street boys find they will get somebody and the guy will just announce, 'I am sorry, I have just not got anywhere to go either.' But the boys, well those that were older, and those that needed it, could use that room for a small fee. I would only expect a tenner or something from them. What they want to say to the punter is a different matter, if they want to say £25 they can. I would also, of course, be having people I would be finding contacts for who would ring in and ask for somebody. I would then ring [a boy] and say, 'Look, there is somebody wants to come over in an hour's time, will you be here?' Again they could use the room. For that I would take the same tenner out, possibly, as the standard price for a full body massage is about £35 in the masseur's flat – a body massage but nothing else. Most clients do expect to be brought off manually. If they want any [other] sex they need to be charged extra. It is fair enough for me to have a tenner off so long as they do not use the room for more than half an hour – I can't prove they have done any extras. But they have got to pay me another tenner for every extra half hour they use it. To use a three-bed flat you would have to put in with other people, you would have to get others in partnership, in fact.

An interesting point emerging from these accounts was the difference in size and managerial competence of the agency businesses and the suspicion that some of the larger ones were being run by wealthy entrepreneurs with scant attention to ethical considerations. The large amount of money changing hands and the number of different agency advertisements appearing, including advertisements for workers, shows there must be a substantial market for gay sex and a large number of men prepared to pay for it.

Working with agency clients

The ready offer of sexual gratification reported by visitors to agency massage parlours was also described, from the other side of the fence as it were, at interviews with men who had worked in these places. For example, *Case 514*, who had experience of working in the flats provided for the massage workers employed by Agency [C], described how the opportunity for sex is typically presented, but his comments about the absence of sex in 40 per cent of sessions and the substantial extra fees when sex was included are unusual:

It is fairly plush. The lighting is pleasant. You would ask him to undress completely and lie face down. First, it would probably take five minutes rubbing the back down. This varies. You usually do it gently, rub the baby oil in or something. Most people don't realise if you do it gently it is not going to do any bloody good anyway, but they do not like you to do it too hard. So after five minutes or something like that you would ask them to turn over. Obviously you would take a quick glance down to see if they have got a hard on. If they had you would then continue up to the shoulders and mention it, usually making a wisecrack that they are obviously enjoying the massage, and gradually stirring the conversation round towards the idea that they want you to do something for it. If they want you to do anything other than a hand job then it is time to start doing cartwheels, because it means you are going to get some money out of it. If they are not too experienced you will normally tell them that £50 will get them a hand job. If they are fairly experienced then they will normally turn around and say, 'Well I normally get it included.' This is when I say, 'OK, I will agree to this, I did not realise. OK, I will let you off with that one.' But you then try to get them back to the £50 for oral sex. Penetration would be £100. If you managed to get them up priced for a hand job, because they did not realise what was going on, then you bunged it up to £70 for oral sex . . .

Some have just a massage, but I would say that 60 per cent at least have sex. Don't get me wrong. They are offered sex. In a lot of cases you turn a guy over and he has not got a hard on and he is not going to have sex, is he, so it is not worth even discussing the fact. You can sort of give him a bit of stimulation around his thighs to see if that brings him up. If it brings him up you can discuss it. [As to penetration] I am not particularly butch myself, anyway, I would be the first to admit that. To be quite honest I prefer being fucked myself, but I won't do that for business. The normal way of talking around it would be to suggest how much you would like to do oral sex with him . . . You might talk about what a wonderful time you had fucking with your boyfriend the night before or you say, as another way of introducing a double act, what a wonderful time you had fucking someone while you were in front of another client. And he says, 'You mean you get other people to come in as well?' . . . I have in fact done it, fucking, using two condoms, I am not absolutely one hundred per cent bitch.

Sex on massage parlour premises was generally more limited than activities on out calls to clients' hotels or flats which were, like the street workers' encounters, less structured, allowing a wider range of sexual practices, more scope for negotiation and more opportunity for social interchange. By the same token there was also greater chance of meeting up with an abusive client, although the threat of being blacklisted by an agency might be some deterrent. Agency workers who had been or still were working also as freelance rent boys on the streets and in bars dealt similarly with direct contact and agency customers, except that agency customers tended to be more affluent and expect better service.

Case 511 expressed a robustly cynical attitude to the work relationships with his clients. Only once had a client taken him out for a meal. 'It sounds good, you know, escort agency, but that's a load of crap. It's just down to sex, it *is* sex ... 90 per cent of times sex is involved.' As a cue for starting sex, 'Sometimes they would put their hand on you. After a while you would think, "For fuck's sake get on with what we've got to do ..." I might have another job to go to so I'm thinking, "This has got to be over and done with." I'm no massager, I used to get bored with it, really fed up. I'd think, "This is really stupid, just get down to it, I know what you want." ... One man wanted me to wear ladies knickers, which I did and I felt very stupid. I mean I'm gay, but I don't ever try on women's clothes ... But that was what he wanted and it doesn't hurt to put on a pair of knickers.' He was particularly insistent on his ability to refuse what he did not want. 'Some of these boys on the street, it must be dreadful, they've got to do it, otherwise they've nowhere to go to sleep for the night, so it's a different ball game ... It was easy for me to turn round and say I'm not doing it any more and go back to work in the pub.' He would never allow clients anal sex. They might say the agency had promised it, or offer more money, 'up to £155, but I never rose to the bait'. He would get them excited in other ways so they would ejaculate and cease to press him. 'There was some people had to wear leather or rubber. They would get more money. I wasn't in it for that ... When it comes to wanting to hurt one another, funny things like spanking, I don't like anything like that.' The weirdest thing he had agreed to do was to beat a naked man with nettles. 'It turned my stomach a little bit ... He was saying, "I want you to hurt me" and all this. I felt silly. I'm not an actor ... I couldn't really get into it because I'm not that way inclined.' He was cautious in other ways. He would never drink with clients. 'I can't handle drink and I am much better when I haven't had one.' Likewise he took no interest in drugs, though they were much used in the gay clubs he liked to visit. He thought he had escaped AIDS because he had always practised safe sex with clients.

Case 026, one of our original Streetwise Day Centre sample, who had gravitated from street work to work for a massage parlour, said he liked agency work better because there he was 'relaxed, prepared to do just what I was supposed to be doing'. This amounted to masturbation and fellatio only. He waited for the client to make the first move before starting sex, but the whole session lasted only about fifteen minutes. He had answered an advert from the agency and was attending their premises on a shift system, waiting in a TV room, along with others, for the arrival of customers. He was working weekdays only by his own choice. He saw ten to fifteen customers in a week, taking £30 from each, half of which he turned over to the agency. He was signing on as unemployed and the £200 a week he pocketed, plus tips, was more regular and profitable for him than street work. He liked what he was doing, liked meeting people, but he rarely ejaculated during sessions because there was insufficient privacy, with people moving around just outside the door of the massage room, which made him nervous.

On the issue of sexual practices some men expressed little enthusiasm, stating their reluctance to become too involved themselves or emphasising sessions that did not include any sex. Others mentioned agreement to variant activities not just for extra money but because it meant less physical contact.

Case 514 liked swift, businesslike transactions, especially when he did not need to ejaculate. 'With agency work you're fairly lucky because you can call round and say, "I've already done three today and I've come already." . . . The whole point is they are supposed to enjoy themselves, not the masseur, so it is OK . . . I make sure that they come, then it is fair enough, I have served my purpose . . . When I come myself it is usually with a lover or someone I actually fancy, so the actual money does not make much difference.' He saw agency work as having the disadvantage that 'When you get a client you can't really refuse him. On the street you can always walk away or tell the client to go take a hike if you don't trust him or whatever.' Even so, he had never been forced into anything. 'It is an illusion that I try to keep up that the client is in control. In fact you can always, basically, tell the client that you will not do this and you will leave now. In a lot of cases the agency wouldn't like you to do this, but you did it anyway.' Like most agency workers he had clear rules about what he would agree to do. 'I will not take pain and I am not keen on the idea of anything to do with bodily wastes. Dressing up is fine. If they want to see me looking stupid, fine! Unfortunately in leather gear I look like Peter Pan in drag.'

Case 513, who worked for a another agency, had different attitudes and experience. He said there was no sex in about a third of his encounters. 'Some clients are just lonely, insecure people who want somebody to talk to.' After an arranged rendezvous in a quiet pub, 'They normally buy you a couple of drinks, take you out for a meal and then, if they want to, take you back . . . I normally get on really well with them, we just get to be friends and that, you know. So I normally stay the night.' If they wanted sex he would ask for more money. 'I have my own personal charges from when I used to be a rent boy in Birmingham, so I know the charges, £30 for a blow job, £20 for a wank and £50 for anal sex, [but with] a condom, lubricant and everything.' He would not agree to kinky things like water sports, bondage, photos or S & M.

Agency clients often wanted kinky sex. *Case 501* actually preferred such clients because it meant he did not have to have actual sex with them. 'There was one I had to wrap up in bin liners, but they had to be blue. Then, on top of that he would dress up in this bondage gear and I'd just have to leave him and go back in half an hour and I'd have to learn a script where I'd talk to him as if I was his wife . . . It was like a play really, which I suppose was his fetish.'

Satisfying kinky desires could be very profitable. *Case 506* mentioned that 'sometimes we would have to do CP, corporal punishment. But it depended, I mean I would only take light, I did not want them to mark me, but I would give it to them as hard as they liked, the harder the better. We had to do different things. There was one guy, I was out at a hotel, and he made me put a bag over his head with amyl nitrite in it and tie him up to his bed, tie something round his balls and just pull on it. And I just had to come over him. I got over £200 from him for myself, plus the agency fee, which was £90.' Over a short span of five days working for this agency he got £1,200.

This same man had had one frightening experience. 'This guy asked me all the questions about what I would do and I said yes and no to whatever. It seemed all well and good. I went back with him and he had some friends there who all tied me up and tried to fuck me.' They had not tied him securely and, 'Once I realised what was happening it could not have taken me more than fifteen seconds to get out of it. You know, they had not tied me up really well . . . I just sort of smashed the place up on my way out, just to frighten them, because I was scared, but trying not to act as though I was.'

Evidently working for agencies did not altogether eliminate the risk of assault. *Case 102*, currently a private masseur but with past agency experience, described one out call for an agency during which he began to feel uneasy and was actually about to leave when 'three other guys walked in and I started running'. He failed to get away and 'I was dragged to the bedroom, had my clothes ripped off, chained to the bed and they just did what they wanted. They stuck bottles up me and everything. And they threw me out with no money. I just had my shirt and jeans on, I couldn't even get my underpants and socks. I had got there about 10 at night and was thrown out about 4 or 5 in the morning . . . I'm a hard faced cow and it didn't hurt me [physically] . . . I was more hurt that I had got myself into that situation and even more that I didn't get any money for it . . . It's an occupational hazard, something I had to accept.' He reported the incident to the agency and the man who had booked him sent in £10 for him. Having had no previous trouble with that customer the agency did not accept his story, so he stopped working for them.

When the agency system permits the worker to negotiate with the client by telephone he can sometimes avoid potential danger. *Case 515* complained: 'The trouble with escorting is there is no laid down strategy, it depends on what the person sounds like on the phone.' If they are brash and ask straight out about fucking he would think they might be obnoxious and would not take them on. 'If they sort of worked up to it and said how much for a massage and will you fuck me and that I would say, "Yes, but that will be £25 extra." But I mean I would never get fucked by clients at all.'

Except for the method of payment, workers who received agency clients in their own flats were in much the same position as privately advertising masseurs. Some combined both systems. At one stage *Case 515*, together with a boyfriend, was also advertising a personal service independent of his agency clientele. 'I mean, I could probably have stopped working completely for agencies at that stage. I was doing 200 to 300 quid a week at home and if I had stayed at home completely instead of going to the agency I could probably have got 400 or 500.' For kinky things he would charge extra. He had done 'fisting' only on out calls and for that, 'I would charge £100 right away.'

Case 516 had his own comfortable quarters and like others similarly placed was satisfied with the system and considered himself safe from the law. 'I never worked in a massage parlour, it was far too tacky! I am privately based [with clients] arranged by the agency – all licensed and legal. Everything I was doing was legal, so it seemed quite the normal thing to do.' He had to give 30 per cent to the agency. As the service was supposedly for escort, he was often taken out for meals, but there was nearly always sex as well, usually masturbation or fellatio. He would never allow himself to be anally penetrated, but he would occasionally perform on a client if he found him attractive. Like most others he would agree to the dominant role in S & M rituals, but not the reverse. He didn't mind the job because he had always been sexually permissive. It was profitable and he had had no trouble with clients, some of whom had become friends with whom he mixed socially. People he met were impressed that he could make money through his good looks. He believed he was performing a useful service keeping people from looking for sex in public conveniences, etc.

The contrasts between agency work and street work that emerged from these descriptions were mostly in favour of the former. It meant a steadier income, less risk from police, more personal choice and independence and a certain amount of job satisfaction, but a lot depended on the quality of management of the agencies and the nature of their clientele. Agency premises ranged from the luxurious to the seedy, and some agencies showed concern for the welfare of their workers although there was not much they could do to provide protection. Working practices varied from the blatantly overt to the discreetly cautious. Most agency managers were unwilling to discuss sexual acts over the telephone and the masseurs at some agencies were careful not to make the first move towards sexual contact with a client in case he was a policeman out to trap them. Masturbating the client – hand relief – was the usual and often the only sexual service provided on agency premises, but on home visits there was more scope. Workers' earnings and the prices charged to clients were maintained fairly high in spite of increasing numbers of competitors and complaints of a saturated market. The share of profits retained by agencies was considered by some workers to be extortionate. By means unexplained workers were often able to receive payment without being officially registered as employed or having to pay tax.

Agencies for photographic models

Adjacent to the many adverts from masseurs and escorts in the gay magazines are a few from models. For example:

> Bodybuilder is available for private modelling work. Ready, willing and able to drive you crazy . . . [Measurements and Box number followed].

As in the case of the female trade, male models for 'photography' and their suppliers are often assumed to be operating a thinly disguised prostitution service. Such advertisers have not been systematically visited or interviewed in this survey, but one of our volunteers did try replying to an advert in an ordinary (i.e. non-gay) magazine with interesting results. He received back a circular notice from which the following paragraphs have been extracted:

> Whether you are an amateur, or professional photographer; artist; sculptor or simply an admirer of the naked male form, we have a whole bunch of guys spread right across the country, ready, able and willing to take their clothes off for *YOU!!!* . . ..
> This is how it works:
> For just a small ONCE-OFF outlay of £25 we will send our new catalogue of currently available models winging its way to you, complete with a FULL COLOUR *NUDE* PHOTOGRAPH OF EACH MODEL! Usually over 20 guys, yes TWENTY, guys prepared to strip for YOU! We give you the COMPLETE run down of each model, vital statistics, which part of the country he lives in, likes and dislikes, in fact the whole works!
> Simply pick out which lad or lads you require for your own private sessions and write to them PERSONALLY, initially through our office, and arrange the details and dates direct with the models of your choice! The models will reply personally, and you mutually arrange the finer details between you!
>
> EASY AS THAT!

We don't get involved in the organising, so NO AGENCY COMMISSIONS OR FEES! You simply sort out the fees and expenses with the model direct! GOOD HUH!

The list of photographic sets on offer makes very clear to what kind of interest they are intended to appeal. Just one quote suffices:

ECSTASY! This is the sizzling Full Colour Portfolio that we have all been waiting for! On his 18th Birthday PAUL positively INSISTED on unveiling himself for you, but AFTER his party! He invites you to join him on his bed, in what surely is [our] most thrilling, exciting and EROTIC Portfolio to date! Ten fabulous photographs follow delicious, stark naked, PAUL as he kneels to say his prayers, like a good little boy, showing off his shapely curves. Then tantalizingly sits on his bed, offering his open invitation not only with his dazzling eyes! He thrusts his loins forward, for easier appreciation. With his soft foreskin pulled back, AND forward he writhes and nuzzles into his pillow displaying himself to the full! There follow even more gorgeous photographs, front AND rear of Paul ... Join passionate PAUL in his EROTIC ECSTASY!!

A cheque for £35 was requested for the Model Agency Catalogue, but 'We also accept postal orders and these major credit and charge cards: American Express, Diners Club, and ALL VISA CARDS.'

The catalogue was bought and one of the models was selected. The legend against the picture read: 'Hirsute and cute with it! Slim, young, he is more than willing to strip and pose nude for you, or anyhow you fancy.' The usual data on eye colour, weight, height, waist and inside leg measurements followed. A reply came back giving a telephone number and suggesting dates, mentioning that he was available only on Sundays. An appointment was fixed which the author kept in place of the volunteer.

When he arrived the man was told he would receive his normal fee, but that all that was required was a confidential talk about how the modelling system worked. He appeared quite willing and confiding, though somewhat ill at ease at first, and he apologised that his information was limited. His picture had only recently been inserted into the catalogue and this was almost his first assignment. He said quite firmly that he was not a gay man. He was twenty-eight and had got into nude modelling through the practice of naturism which he had taken up when he was living abroad where nude beaches are more common. He had picked out the agency's advert for male models from the well known naturist magazine *Health and Efficiency*, which is not a publication directed towards gays, though he had since found out that the agency advertises also in the gay press. Initially he had applied to the agency for employment as a model for advertising clothes and other goods as he knew that the organisation supplied models on assignments to large companies. There was no place for him in that line at the time so he obtained details from them about work as a freelance nude. He did it to get extra money. He was in a restaurant job, but he had a mortgage to pay.

The agency made their profit from sales of the catalogue of photographs. He did not have to pay to have his picture included. The agency forwarded him letters from prospective clients, opening them first to see that there was nothing out of order. After that it was strictly up to him to negotiate. When he applied they asked if he was gay and told him that most of the clients would obviously be gay, but many would just want to take photographs. If he wanted to go any further that was up to him, but the agency did not want to be involved at all and did not want to be associated with pornography. The models were all males, but he was told that not all of them were gay. The agency had given him some rules to follow; he was to ask for the money before doing anything and to watch the time work began so as to know when the agreed period was up. The fee is for straight photography. 'If they do want to go further it's up to us.' With the money in advance he can walk out. He implied that he himself would not agree to sex, though he had nothing against gays having known many in the catering trade. It was left a little unclear whether he could be persuaded by the right person and the right price. He did not know how much extra would be paid for sex.

It seemed fairly clear that this agency knew full well that some of its models were giving sexual service, but kept itself distanced from what happened after the initial introduction. In any event this aspect of their business was probably only a sideline. On seeking an appointment with another of the advertised models a letter came back explaining that the contact service was closing 'for lack of support', but a further circular indicated that the sale of photographs of nude males was continuing.

The overlap between nude male modelling and prostitution is hinted at by sex masseurs' advertisements that cite the photographic magazines for which they have posed. Mike Arlen, a well known producer of albums of photos of young males in erotic poses, is quoted as saying that there is a huge market in pornography and that many individuals jump at the chance to lead a life of vice. No one has to be persuaded to make a sex film, otherwise they wouldn't be waiting to peel off for the camera (Merewood, 1990). His models seem to share many of the characteristics of street workers. Writing in the introduction to one of his *Mike Arlen's Guys* picture collections (Vol. 5, undated) he explains that 'one major mistake' was 'when I started standing bail for my models . . . More than a dozen of my past models have been writing from British prisons this year asking for anything I care to send' and 'quite a few who stay out of trouble are equally unpredictable'.

15

Self-Employed Masseurs

Visits to private masseurs

Information about self-employed sex workers who operated independently from private premises was obtained from reports by volunteers who visited them as clients and also through systematic interviews carried out by the researchers, mostly by Buz de Villiers. These interviews were secured by direct contact through the masseurs' advertisements or by introductions, usually from one of those already interviewed. A total of 27 masseurs were either visited (sixteen cases) or interviewed (twelve cases) one man being both interviewed and visited. There was no way to check whether some of the ostensibly private masseurs visited could have been former or even current agency workers, but at least none of the flats visited appeared to be communal.

In all cases the visits were arranged by telephoning the numbers given in adverts in *Gay Times* or *Capital Gay* or, in one instance (*Visit 115*), by phoning the number given on a note stuck inside a public telephone kiosk offering 'Male Massage. Bondage. CP.' Conversation over the telephone when making appointments was usually brief, without mentioning anything explicitly sexual, simply explaining that the caller was responding to such and such advertisement and seeking a 'full massage', 'firm treatment' or whatever other euphemism the advert had used and asking the cost. The volunteers did not, as some clients are reported to do, seek further details of the masseur's physique or specify particular sexual requirements. Several reports commented on the brusque manner masseurs adopted on the telephone. For those advertising 'leather service' etc., this may have been part of their pose for the benefit of clients wanting 'masterful' handling. There may also have been an element of defensive reserve, since the volunteers were strangers to the masseurs, calling up as prospective new clients. Two masseurs wanted to call back before making a definite appointment, and one of these was rather abrupt when the caller explained he was in a public kiosk. He apologised later, explaining that he had had trouble with callers from public telephones. All inquirers were given a private address and a time to call, but most masseurs were unwilling to make a booking more than an hour or two in advance. Usually they asked the caller where he was, gave instructions how to get to a nearby tube station or other landmark where there was a public telephone, and told the caller to ring up again on arrival when he would be given the precise address. Masseurs thereby avoided the difficulty of having their availability blocked for other requests in the event of callers having second thoughts and failing to turn up, a frequent nuisance. In two instances (*Visits 121* and *118*) visitors followed the instructions, but on arrival at the nearby telephone were instructed to call again half an hour later. Presumably the masseur had taken on a different client in the meantime. In one instance a session failed to materialise, the visitor obtaining no response in repeated attempts to telephone from nearby as requested. The calls to advertisers were mostly made in the afternoon or early evening. Sometimes half a dozen different masseurs were called before obtaining any reply, other than from an answering machine, suggesting that either trade was brisk or, more likely, the masseurs' working hours were limited. It is, of course, virtually impossible, and certainly life-restricting, for one man to try to man a telephone over a 24 hour day.

The visits, and those formal research interviews with masseurs that were conducted at their place of work, found them operating in varied accommodation, usually in their own flats. Arrangements ranged from the distinctly seedy, through youthful disorder to carefully contrived and sometimes quite luxurious gay chic. Prices were from £30 to £50 for massage with masturbation (sometimes mutual) and £50 upwards for 'specialised' sex. The citations are summary abstracts from the original reports.

Visit 122 was to a luxury flat in a much sought after block in Chelsea. The visitor, who was given tea after the sex session, noted the sparse but expensive antique furniture and was told by the masseur that he had just moved back into the place and had not yet got everything together. It appeared that he was also in the business of 'doing up houses' and owned other property. He apologised for having been short on the telephone because his secretary had been in the place at the time and he did not want her to overhear. It was clear that for him sex massage was a sideline which he liked doing. In fact he said he was gay and 'you can't do this properly unless you enjoy it'. He specialised in mild sadism, body shaving and enemas. For the session he made use of a double bed in a well furnished bedroom.

Visit 127 was also to a smart location in West London, but to a basement flat with a large sitting room that looked as if it was being used as a study, with papers and writing materials strewn about and weight-lifting equipment in one corner, a stereo in another. The masseur, in the course of conversation over a cup of tea, explained that he had secured a place at university (he named the college) and was intending to become a student of classics and archaeology while supporting himself with the massage business. He too mentioned he was gay and thought that it would be very difficult for a man who was not gay to do the work and that it would be unfair to the customers who would soon realise the fact. He charged his customers a basic £35. He rolled out a thin mattress on the floor and stripped to his briefs for the commencement of the session.

Case 106, another of the more up-market masseurs, charged rather more, £40 for straight massage, £50 for sado-masochism, £90 for a duo performance in which a friend who liked it would be flogged by him in the customer's presence. By an unplanned coincidence he was visited by a volunteer client and also interviewed by a researcher. Both were impressed by the elegance of his arrangements:

> When the sex was over I was invited to take coffee and biscuits in his expensively furnished parlour. He had two very elegant long-haired cats, an impressive music centre, luscious upholstering and drapes. He spoke of the high cost of buying his flat and of his efforts to make things nice. He fussed about a small patch of damp hidden behind a flower display which had damaged the costly wallpaper. He made disparaging comments about masseurs who work in grubby little places. Several telephone calls came through during the short time it took to drink the coffee, one of which he said was from someone ringing from Paris. He said he had customers from many different countries through advertising in *The Advocate* which had an international circulation. His talk on the phone was short and businesslike, using phrases like 'I give full service' which avoided sex words. He said some callers were useless, they just wanted to talk dirty without coming for massage, but he knew how to recognise them and put them off.

The research interviewer noted: 'His flat is situated in a row of terraced houses in middle-class suburbia in West London. Obviously he spends a lot of time and money on the flat which was expensively decorated and beautifully kept ... He has a separate massage room, extremely well equipped with proper table and all extras, including dimmed lights, soft music and en suite bathroom/shower.' This masseur inserted adverts under two different names and numbers, one offering massage, the other a leather room service. The volunteer, who had rung the second number, saw an additional room. 'I was led up a movable metal ladder into a strange attic cubby hole lit by lights shaded by traffic cones where I was told to undress ... Then he pulled aside a black curtain and ordered me into an attic room with black walls and a ceiling with mirrors so that one could watch oneself lying on the table in the middle. It had fittings for wrist and ankle clamps. I noticed lots of straps, chains and a leather sling. The lights were dim at first but changed at different stages from bright to total darkness.'

Visit 117, in contrast to the last case, was to a man advertising himself as a twenty-two-year-old skinhead who in fact fitted the description. His flat was on an upper floor of an old Victorian block in the East End, largely inhabited by immigrants from the Indian sub-continent. The place was reached via a stone staircase and the massage room was bare save for a mattress on the floor and a stand in the corner containing a bunch of canes. His manner throughout was brusque, the session was short and on leaving the visitor was invited to donate a 'tip' on top of the stated fee. *Visit 126* was to a rather similar venue, the top floor of a tower block on the outskirts of the East End. The visitor was warned over the phone that the place looked 'rough' but would be OK once he was inside. In fact it was notably quiet and private, kept neat and clean and comfortably arranged inside with good quality modern furnishings.

Case 114 was interviewed by the author in a small flat near the top of a council-owned tower block in South London. The stairways were bare, the lifts primitive and adorned with graffiti and there was a heap of junk in the passage outside the entrance door. The flat, which was shared with a friend and fellow masseur (*Case 113*), consisted of two bed-sitting rooms and a small kitchen and bathroom. Everywhere was sparsely furnished and chaotically untidy. The beds were mattresses on the floor, both unmade, and the only available chairs were piled up with clothes; some of the garments looked distinctly theatrical. It was effectively a student type slum, deliberately unkempt but not poverty stricken. Bits of art work and art materials were strewn about and the walls were covered with photos, murals, cartoons etc., some slightly pornographic. The pictures showed lots of nudes, mainly male, but cleverly arranged in inventive situations and poses using trick photography. An expensive looking camera and a modern dictionary were among items lying about the kitchen. It was explained that some of the pictures were part of pop video productions which both masseurs were working on. At the interview, which was conducted in the bedroom used for massage, there was no special equipment visible and we both squatted on the bed for the purpose of the tape recording. The windows were obscured by material pinned to the frames and the light was almost too dim to follow the prompts on the interview schedule of questions. In the middle of the interview the second masseur came in, rather agitated, turning over the piles of clothes to look for a missing bus pass. Failing to find it, he borrowed some change from his colleague and arranged to meet him later in the evening at a gay bar.

Most of the venues were more nondescript. *Visit 119* was to a masseur in a small back room in a terraced house in a quiet suburban street in East London. 'He said it belonged to a friend who let him use it. He normally worked only during daytime as he liked to go home in the evening and have his own life elsewhere. A chair, a small table with miscellaneous leather gadgets spread out on top, and a bed covered with a dark sheet more or less filled the space. He said the leather things belonged to his friend and he didn't know how to use them himself. I asked to use the bathroom, which was next door. It was small, but clean and unremarkable.' *Visit 118* was to a flat on the top floor of a large Edwardian town house in a fashionable residential neighbourhood of North London. 'I was shown into a fair-sized living room at the front of the house and was sat down on a large black leather settee. A stereo was playing softly and on a low table a selection of gay magazines was on show . . . I asked him in the course of conversation if he had any problem with the neighbours and he said he didn't, and he didn't know if they realised what he did, he might be running any kind of business. Had he been a woman with lots of men callers they would have twigged at once.' *Visit 110* was to an address in an unfashionable quarter of North Kensington in a house towards the end of a very long row of Victorian terraced houses. 'He answered the entry phone promptly and showed me into a first floor front room where a large colour television was turned on. The room was almost filled with a big three-piece black leather suite of sofa and chairs. He was in his early thirties, dressed informally in jeans and trainers. He sprawled in a relaxed pose on the sofa, legs wide apart with one dangling over the arm and one on the seat. He had shortish, slightly thinning hair with an artificially bleached blond patch on top. [After drinks and 'chit chat'] I was taken into a small, darkened bedroom at the rear containing a wardrobe, a rolled-up mattress which he spread out on the floor and a rickety chair on which to place clothes. A small table stood in the corner of this otherwise barren room and on top of it one tall white lily, probably artificial, and a modern silvered candelabra with three very fat, ornate red candles which he proceeded to light. I felt it all a bit comic.' *Visit 112* was the top floor of a tall building on a main street with business premises on the ground floor. 'I called the number, quoted the ad and asked if R was free. He said "Yes" and agreed I could come round in half an hour. The charge was £35. The names on the door were faded and unreadable in the dark, but I counted three from the bottom as instructed and the entry phone was answered quickly. I was told to come to the top floor. I had to grope my way up several flights of narrow, unlit and litter-strewn stairs and landings. I was shown into a small room, well heated with an electric fire, but with little else save a mattress on the floor. R. apologised for the unfinished state of the flat, which was being done up. He was sharing it with somebody, because he had to go out of the room "to ask my friend for change" when it came to paying. He stripped off completely to begin massage. He was exactly like the description in his ad – young, with a lithe, athletic body and a prominent tattoo.'

Of all the set-ups described, the dingiest was the one advertised via a telephone kiosk. It was a ground-floor flat in an old tenement block probably used by the local authority to house poorer people. 'A bag of bones hung intimidatingly on the entrance door. The masseur said it was for a pet dog. He answered the door in a bath robe. He looked still in his thirties, but was much overweight and pot bellied with a hairy torso. The small sitting room was dimly lit with a red light. There was a TV, a video, a low-slung settee and a single bed for the massage that had old fashioned metal bed ends. There were leather belts and lengths of rope hung around. The masseur excused himself for a minute while I was left to strip off. He returned, took off his bath robe, pushed down his quite dirty underpants below the genitals and started rubbing his penis. He asked if I liked his big cock. There was no other introduction and no pretence that I had come for a massage. I went along with it, but I was a bit revolted and contented to ejaculate quickly and get away. It cost £30. He invited me to come again anytime. He said business was up and down and a bit slack.'

This masseur's approach sounded particularly abrupt, but in every case some sexual activity took place and there was never any suggestion that the client had come for anything else. Of course, the visits were made by gay men who responded appropriately when masseurs asked what they liked, so it was not a test of waiting to see who would make the first move. The report from *Visit 118*, for example, stated 'I was sat down on the settee and offered coffee. The conversation began with questions about where I had seen the ad and whether I had been to a masseur before and then got onto what scene did I like and finally whether I would like a massage first before other things.' A similar approach was used at *Visit 110*. The client was sat down and given a generous helping of whisky, and asked in conversation what gay magazines he was familiar with. Some of the visitors' accounts of the commencement of sexual activity, however, suggested that masseurs who felt confident they were dealing with a gay man could be more forthcoming about initiating sexual contact than might appear from the descriptions of more cautious approaches given by workers during interviews with researchers. For example, the report of *Visit 112* stated, 'After very little preliminary I was told to get undressed. The only question I was asked was if I had been to a masseur before. He started undressing at the same time and when I pulled off my briefs he did the same. I was told to lie face down on the mattress and he wet his hands with scented lotion and began to rub my back, sitting astride me with his penis rubbing against my buttocks. As this went on he developed an erection and changed his position to one side with his erection pointing over my shoulder towards my face . . .' At *Visit 117*, the young East End skinhead made a few insinuating comments: 'What is it makes you like skinheads?' 'You must have had a lot of experience.' Then, seeing no reluctance, told the client, 'Take your clothes off', did the same himself, exposing a large, half erect penis and commanding, 'Kneel down and suck it.' *Visit 127*, after a brief chat about how the client found his way, began with a little stroking and nipple play while both were standing on top of the mattress on the floor. He then removed his pants and presented a penis for fellatio without any preliminary massage.

Owing to an understandable reticence about their own contributions to the sexual interchanges, some of the volunteers' reports lacked precise detail, but all reported being stimulated to orgasm, in one instance by means of a vibrator. In all but one instance (*Visit 126*) the masseurs worked at least a part of the time in the nude or with genitals exposed and most of them allowed or encouraged the client to masturbate or fellate them, but usually not to the point of ejaculation. Condoms were never introduced, but in no case did anal intercourse take place. One masseur encouraged a client to lick his anus, another performed inter-femoral intercourse, a third pressed an erect penis against a client's buttocks and might have penetrated had the client not moved his position. A fourth, who had been flicking his client with a cane, used it to probe the anal area and effect some penetration.

One of the volunteers, who was not averse to sado-masochistic activity, was encouraged to answer adverts mentioning 'leather room', 'dominance', 'firm treatment' etc., and at these visits, six in all, there was no actual massage. The operators proceded directly to administer slaps, caning, nipple squeezing and rough genital manipulations, the client being nude and mostly under some form of restraint, such as being tied spread-eagled to a frame or handcuffed with wrists fixed behind the back or neck. One operator offered enemas and shaving of perineal hair. These higher charging 'specialists' usually wore high quality leather gear and had a considerable amount of expensive looking equipment available. Other signs of affluence were noted. At *Visit 123*, while the client was dressing at the end of the session the sex worker put on an impressive leather jacket and cap, gathered up a car telephone and, after accompanying the client to the door, hurried across the road to a smart car which he drove away at speed.

Apart from *Case 106*, mentioned earlier, the most elaborate set-up for S & M activity was encountered at *Visit 121*. The operator was working in a large ground-floor room in an exclusive block of flats in central London. He was young and very well-built, as his advertisement had said. In addition to the electronically operated door to the main building, equipped with entry phones, the door to the individual flat was guarded by an iron swing gate. The visitor was led along a corridor to a darkened room facing the street with heavy curtains drawn. Not much of the rest of the flat was visible, but it looked very smart in a traditional manner. The bathroom was luxuriously equipped and well supplied with bath towels. A fan-shaped bath with shower above, which the visitor was invited to use, fitted into one corner.

The sex playroom had a high ceiling and in the middle of the floor was a large four-poster bed construction, built from scaffolding, from which hung a leather harness sling and chains of different sizes. I said I thought it a clever thing. The masseur seemed pleased, said one had to be inventive and asked me if I had seen any other places like it and how they compared.

Along one wall I saw a row of large black military style boots. I think the cupboards probably contained uniforms of different sorts. The masseur had mentioned leather and military uniforms in his advertisement and he began by asking me what kind of thing I would like him to wear. I said he didn't need to wear anything, so he immediately took everything off ... After the session, which cost £50, he drew the curtains a little so the window did not look closed up from the street some feet below, but not sufficiently for people to be able to see the unusual contents.

The one sex worker who did not undress for his client (*Visit 126*) was a young S & M specialist who wore an ornate leather suit and advertised himself as a 'biker', kissed the client uninhibitedly, performed genital manipulations and was friendly and intimate in manner, but without ever exposing himself.

None of the S & M operators were seriously violent or did anything to pierce or break the skin, although one was noted to be wearing metal ornaments suspended from pierced nipples. Only once did a client come away with visibly bruised buttocks. The operators would make comments such as 'You'll take what I give you', or 'You're my slave now', but they were generally careful not to exceed what the client would tolerate. With clients wanting fiercer or more exotic treatments they might possibly have behaved differently.

Several of the S & M operators were particularly insistent that they couldn't do their work properly if they did not themselves have a taste for it. One or two mentioned having similar kinds of sex with non-paying contacts. At *Visit 124*, the occasion when a client was bruised, the operator said the sight of a guy tied up and writhing excited him. He used to do it for pleasure until about three years back when somebody suggested setting up in business and he began to advertise. He thought most men enjoyed something a bit harder and different from what they normally got from their partners. A lot of his customers were city types he saw in the daytime. They liked to be home of an evening. One of his regulars would bring his wife with him. She enjoyed watching her husband's punishment. Some customers wanted anal practices which he didn't like. Another S & M specialist (*Visit 126*) was sniffing amyl nitrite while attending to the client. He said that he had no other job at the moment and so was available evening and daytime, but he did not take on more than two clients a day as then it wouldn't be the same. He had given up a good job in business because he was finding it a strain and he liked this better. He already had a collection of leather gear when he began. He was thinking of going to [a well known leather men's club] later that evening. He liked the clients who came to him. 'You would be surprised how nice the people are who go in for this.' An older sex worker (*Visit 111*) explained that he had started advertising massage and leather service after his lover's death. He found it a better way to get the sex he enjoyed than hanging about bars. Another leather man (*Visit 120*) was sharing his flat with a gay motor cycle enthusiast. Erotic pictures of leather men posing with motorbikes hung around the walls. They both belonged to a gay motor cycle touring club and sometimes there would be groups of them staying in the flat having lots of sex. He mentioned that he had been married and was glad to have had heterosexual experience because 'completely gay people lose out on things'. He had parted from his wife in a friendly way because she got fed up with his gay interests. He had had training in therapeutic massage for relaxation purposes and when his business failed he decided to cash in on that experience.

The S & M specialists were older than the others, probably because age was less important to their clientele (Robinson, 1990, p. 11). The nature of their activities was immediately evident from the equipment and pictures openly displayed. *Visit 126* was an exception. This man's rooms looked ordinary, his equipment (including a moulded rubber face mask with evil looking features) was stowed in different places to be brought out bit by bit as needed. He showed the client out furtively, looking through a spy hole before opening the door to the outer corridor and explaining that he didn't want to speak once it was open.

Except for some being older than expected, the masseurs' physical appearances and their charges tallied with their advertisements. Payment was generally not asked for until the end of the session, although some volunteers offered it at the outset. Masseurs were generally friendly and polite and on about half of the occasions clients were offered a drink, mostly non-alcoholic, either before or after the performance. Some chatted freely about themselves and their circumstances, others did not, but of course this must have depended partly on the visitor's demeanour. Although the accommodations varied in the comfort provided, most of the privately operating masseurs were described as furnishing a pleasant, relaxed and, from the clients' perspective, effective sexual service. Oils and lotions were plentiful, but more elaborate arrangements, such as proper massage tables and professional style massage, were exceptional. Except for the grubby man who advertised in a telephone kiosk (itself an offence), there were no other complaints of misleading advertisements or disagreeable experiences.

The impressions from this cursory sampling of masseur services were confirmed and supplemented by an interview with a man in his late sixties (*Case 306*, introduced by a friend of *Case 206*) who had used sex masseurs frequently over the past decade without encountering any bad or unpleasant experiences. He lived in the provinces and answered adverts from male masseurs appearing in local papers. Their prices were often only half what was charged in London. They all gave sexual relief, although some were not prepared to have customers manipulate them. He preferred men who included genuine massage to purveyors of pure sex, whom he thought of as prostitutes. Some were middle-aged and married and working at massage as a sideline. One man he visited fairly regularly charged him only £8, saying he enjoyed it too. After their sessions he would join the man's wife for a cup of tea. He had also contacted masseurs by inserting adverts of his own in the 'wanted' columns. These had produced some varied reponses. One rather ugly man, insistent on meeting him, was married and wanted him for a threesome with the wife. Another was advertising under different names and numbers a massage service, an escort service (which offered callers prepared to come to his house 'any kind of sexual service' for £25) and overnight accommodation for truck drivers.

This informant also produced a publication, issued from an anonymous West End box number address in 1986 entitled *Simon's Word* Issue 1. Apparently there were no subsequent issues. It was essentially a small consumer guide produced by customers comparing notes on London masseurs. The services were graded on a 10 point scale according to such criteria as telephone information correct and polite, accessibility of location, friendliness, cleanliness, privacy, unhurried service, quality of massage ('if one given, which was frequently not the case'), sexual satisfaction (all gave some sexual service) and charges, including 'extras'. Of the fifteen masseurs listed four were given the maximum awarded score of six, seven were scored five. This seems faint praise, but only one really bad experience (a cheque book lifted) was reported. The man who got the lowest score of 1 was said to be about thirty-five, very bald, running to fat, vague in manner as if drugged, hopeless at massage, clock-watching all the time and money-oriented. At the time most were charging £25 to £30. Versatility in meeting customers' sexual requirements, especially if at no extra charge, earned points. It was reported that some masseurs were working through agencies and their advertised descriptions did not always tally. One masseur was listed and scored twice as he advertised under two names, the second for speciality S & M activity. Some had jobs and did massage only in the evenings. Some shared accommodation with other masseurs. Clearly the masseur system has not changed much in the past five years.

Some aspects of self-employment as a masseur

Information about how self-employed masseurs organised their work was obtained from interviews with twelve men who were working from a private base and providing a sexual service under the guise of a massage or escort business. Similar issues about dealing with clients were raised at all the interviews, namely how contacts with clients were established, how payment was secured, what sexual activity took place and whether they had had any unpleasant experiences. Attitudes to being involved in a sexual service were also explored. In all these respects the responses were different from those of street workers, if only because these men were generally working in a freely chosen occupation, under circumstances less often subject to police intervention and operating a system that gave them better control over the selection of clients and the activities they would permit.

Most were obtaining clients through advertisements in the gay press giving details of themselves and their service and a telephone number for clients to ring. Some typical examples were cited earlier (see p. 187). Adverts were sometimes put in periodicals with a more general readership, which could lead to misunderstanding when the innuendoes had to be toned down. *Case 104* had used a popular magazine, but found that he was obliged to reword his advert. 'When they phoned up to say they wanted to change the wording I was very indignant. I said, "Do you doubt my genuineness?" They said, "Oh, no, not at all". But obviously they realised that through their columns people were advertising a sexual service as well ... I was happy with the wording they proposed, but I said, "I want the insert for men only." I was insistent on that because I didn't want lots of women phoning up. And so they agreed. As far as I am concerned "For men only" is implicit, it means one thing ... Only once somebody came to me for a genuine massage, or I think he did. He got an erection after I massaged him and I started slowly masturbating him and he suddenly got up and got dressed and left. He seemed a little surprised and I was a bit apologetic.'

Case 104 explained the way he handled telephone callers. If pressed, he was prepared to be quite explicit, but unwilling to give out his address immediately. He had an answerphone which he switched on when he was engaged or going to bed.

Typically people phone me and say I saw your advertisement in *Loot* or whatever. Sometimes they just say, 'I saw your ad' ... They usually say, 'How much are you?' or 'How much does your service cost?' And I say, '£35', and then I say, 'That's inclusive.' Some don't ask any further details, some say, 'Inclusive of what?' and then I say, 'Well I do offer a very good, thorough, relaxing massage' – which I do. But some of them want to know more details. They want to know what I look like and how old I am. If I offer a description and people say I still sound attractive they'll come along, but sometimes they say they'd like to come along and then they don't. It's because they can't say over the phone, 'I'm sorry, you're not my type.' Sometimes they say, 'Oh, I don't think you're my type' and put the phone down. Sometimes they'll put the phone down without saying anything. They are just very rude. Then I get even more explicit questions, people asking what I'm into. Then I do say, 'I offer a massage and masturbation at least. If we like each other I am prepared to go further.' I think that's only fair, because some people that come here – old, fat, ugly and smelly – they want to go further than the masturbation and I'm not prepared for that, so I put that clause in, a safety phrase ... I wouldn't compromise myself by having sex with or letting somebody get off on me, you know, by me undressing, when I'm just totally repulsed by them. [If] then some of them say, 'Fine, I'd like to come round at such and such a time, can I come round, where do you live?' I don't tell them my address, I tell them to come to a telephone box at the end of my street and to ring me from there. Then at least I know that they are genuine. Because quite a lot of people are phoney callers and then if they don't turn up it's all right, they don't have my address.

Workers who preserved the image of a legitimate massage business with tax returns and accountancy tended to exercise greater caution about what they would discuss over the telephone. *Case 108*: 'When asked, "Do I offer extras", I will say, "What are you looking for specifically?" They will say, "oral' or "intercourse" or something like that and I will say, "I don't discuss it over the phone" ... From my understanding of the British Telecom system it could be bugged at any time and it's illegal to discuss those things over the phone. If you are going to discuss things like that they might just be sitting at the other end having a wank. I am not interested in getting somebody like that on the phone and not getting paid for it.'

The use of a personal telephone number provides some protection because the sex worker need not disclose his identity to callers he suspects he would not want to deal with. The ritual of preliminary massage could be used as a defence against unwanted intimacies. Some masseurs exercised a good deal of discretion both in accepting clients in the first place and in deciding what they were prepared to do with the client. *Case 107*, for example, maintained a strict reserve with most of his clients:

With telephone work most of the potential hassles are sorted out on the phone prior to seeing them. They can, of course, try to pull one on you when you see them, but I am able to be in control all the time. I was taught to do this by [an agency], in one of their main training sessions. Let them think they are in charge, but keep control. I have been taught massage, so I know how to do that. You start on their back and then try to get them turned over as soon as possible and get them to come as soon as possible. That is the aim really of what you are doing and most of them are that horny that is all they want. The bit of massage at the start is just to relax them. So there is no real problem, unless they can't come, which can be tiring. Those who want to get straight onto sex usually turn over immediately. With the rest I wait till they are relaxed and only then get them to turn over and then, in the shortest possible time, give them maximum energy to make them come quickly and then be nice to them afterwards and get them out. So it is a real routine in that way. It's better not to mess around, this way we both know where we stand ... There are three things I don't do with customers, partly to keep my distance from them. I don't ever have an orgasm, never have, though I suppose I might if I really liked the person. I never kiss and I don't like talking during sex. These are things I keep for my personal sex with lovers. I don't get fucked and I don't do corporal punishment. Sometimes I suck and have to spit afterwards, very rarely do I get sucked. These are things I only do when I really cannot get out of them. So it's really being as horny and athletic as I can without doing anything risky.

Case 108, besides being cautious about explicit sexual conversation over the telephone, also made use of the opportunity to weed out unwanted clients. 'It depends what they sound like on the phone. Some people sound genuine enough and you don't worry about it, you give the address out and no problems. Other times they sound a bit iffy and I tell them to come to the station and give me a call then or when they are just about ready to leave the house. Sometimes they try to book two or three days in advance. I don't normally do that unless they are a regular client . . . When I was advertising in *Capital Gay* people would come out after reading a copy in the pubs or clubs, ring up drunk, want a dirty phone call, make an appointment and then not show up. So after midnight I want credit card confirmation as well, because I am not going to get out of bed and then the person not show up. If they don't show up I can charge their credit card account for a cancellation fee.' Like most other masseurs he felt he was in charge of what form of sex would take place. 'It is my place, they may be paying the money, but it is only if they happen to be very, very cute and I am very attracted to them that I would allow anything else to really happen . . . Basically, [I offer] a wank. If they want to play with me and they give me a bit of a blow job that's OK, but it does not mean I am going to reciprocate on them. I never have done intercourse except with one or two clients that I particularly fancied and then only afterwards. I have taken them into the bedroom and that is out of the business time and into my personal time. As far as I am concerned that is not work, it is my own pleasure.'

Financial management by the private masseurs, who were maintaining accommodation suitable for receiving visits, was necessarily better than by the often homeless street workers. Some talked about their use of conventional business facilities, such as accountants to help with tax returns. *Case 108*, for example, occupied an extremely comfortable rented apartment in West London, shared with a friend and fellow masseur with whom he occasionally performed duos. They had two bathrooms, two bedrooms, a lounge/diner, a roof-top patio as well as a well equipped separate massage room with proper table, lighting, sound, video, and en suite bathroom. He was registered as self employed and said he had 'brought in about £45,000 in twelve months', he did not know exactly because, 'my books are with the accountants at the moment'. He said business expenses amounted to about £60 per week, for telephone, advertising, oils, heating, laundry etc., plus rent of the flat. 'But then if I was to pay myself for the time I spend on cleaning and everything else you could add more to that.'

Case 106 was another masseur operating in comparatively luxurious surroundings, but with an even more businesslike approach. 'To keep me going I have to clear £400 a week by the time I've got my mortgage, my endowment, my pension plan, my private health plan, my advertising, my insurance on the building, my cleaning bill each week – I have a cleaner – and I have TV and video rentals. It's all part of the business because people want to see videos sometimes . . . I have to make £400 a week to pay myself and break even . . . One room is purely for business, so I can get tax deductions . . . I have an accountant, I feel much more secure with that . . . I am a business, I have a business name, I have a business accountant.'

Obviously, there were some who made a lot of money they did not declare for tax purposes. *Case 116*, before the law overtook him and he was billed for thousands of pounds of unpaid tax, used to receive clients in a luxury appartment. 'I saw everybody in my flat, when it came to sex, because it was a safe environment.' He had been a street worker, but £3,000 advanced by a wealthy punter, plus some introductions to other wealthy clients, had enabled him to set up his own flat and telephone. He had advertised himself for the first few months only. After that he found he had a sufficient clientele of regulars and new clients mainly obtained through personal contacts and introductions. 'Most of my clients would suggest that they had friends who they knew would like me and would I be interested in going out to dinner and things like that.' He wore very expensive, fashionable clothes and jewellery and catered to high class and lavishly paying clients. He would be with them 'about 4 to 5 hours, which would probably be an hour in bed, the rest would be entertainment, like going to the theatre or dinner or cinema, whatever they wanted me to do'. At the peak of his business he said he had been taking enough to pay out £1,500 a month in rent, £1,400 to two employees, male friends who acted as 'minder' and 'maid', and £600 for car hire. 'The maid was there when the clients arrived. If I had another client "she" would entertain that client till I got though.' The hired limousine he used when calling on clients.

Some of the masseurs were operating at much lower levels, but still very differently from most street workers. *Case 114*, aged twenty-four, in addition to his main occupation as a masseur, had some income from 'unofficial' work cleaning business premises and helping with pop videos, but he was not registered as employed. 'Officially I don't exist, I have not paid tax since I left college.' Nevertheless, like other masseurs who were not exactly businessmen, he was getting by. He commented spontaneously on the less fortunate situation of street workers. 'I am lucky. I have probably had more advantages in life than a lot of rent boys, because I think that they live a much harder life than I do. I have had it very easy and I think it very sad and I would hate to have to do some of the things some of the boys I know do to live, but I don't have to.'

These interviews, as well as the reports from clients' visits, showed how varied were the masseurs' arrangements. Some were running well organised and profitable home businesses, some were dabbling in their spare time, some were operating in a primitive way without resources or equipment, some were fairly crude and others quite sophisticated in dealings with clients. There was potential for a gay man to make private massage a reasonably pleasant as well as profitable occupation, which was more than could be said of street work. As in any occupation its successful performance called for a certain natural endowment and certain skills. In this case, in addition to physical attractiveness, it called for skills in handling telephone inquiries, dealing with clients pleasantly, setting limits without offending and avoiding conflicts with neighbours or the law. Most of the Streetwise sample could never have met such requirements.

Working with private clients

Privately operating masseurs with their own facilities for hosting clients had ample opportunity for extended sexual activities and for becoming intimately involved with clients, but there was individual variation in how far they were prepared to go, though most were clear about what they would or would not do. As with street workers and agency workers the majority of sessions involved masturbation and/or fellatio only. Most found that they enjoyed sex with some of their customers and disliked it with others, but they varied in their emphasis on likes and dislikes. Insistence on safe sex practices was the general rule.

Case 114 was one who reported rather little enjoyment. Sometimes 'the best I can do is have a hard on. But a lot of people say if I have a hard on that is good enough . . . I don't really do special things, just basics. All I do is hand jobs and let them suck me. Because I have got a very big cock that is why I can get away with not doing anything else. It is easy for them just to suck it and that is enough . . . I have only tried to fuck one punter and I could not get a hard on so I gave it up.'

Case 113 was more amenable to customer requirements and more often able to obtain pleasure himself, but he would not let it interfere with his own social life. He would ejaculate with them 'sometimes, all depending on how I felt, who I was meeting later on, what I wanted to do.' He would agree to it, 'If people wanted to fuck and they were good looking enough, but that would be extra.' He would insist, however, on the use of a condom for either active or passive anal sex. He had taken part in dressing-up scenes and in pornographic photography.

Case 108 went further with some clients but 'unless they specify otherwise they get a hand job'. The client is made to ejaculate but he does not usually do so himself. 'I could not do that all the time.' As an added attraction 'I am just going to do some new ads now which state that I have videos. If they want to watch while they are being massaged they can. Moreover, 'with the right person anything goes so long as I am in the mood for it [and] if I see someone whom I like and I am attracted to them and they are attracted to me and we are getting along OK. I have actually made a couple of very good friendships out of clients. I currently have a lover who was originally a client . . . When he turned up at the door I just couldn't believe this person was coming to see me. Not much massage went on that day.'

Case 109 limited his sexual transactions with clients to body clasping and mutual masturbation and passive fellatio. He avoided ejaculating himself because 'it is easier to keep going if you don't, if you've got somebody else coming in later'. He refused all other sexual activity, including anal sex, so never went outside the limits of safer sex. He had never got friendly enough with clients to see them or have sex with them outside the paid sessions.

Case 106 offered a variety of services, but exercised strict rules according to his own preferences and the needs of safe sex.

What I actually do is a very good stress reduction massage . . . It's also what I call an erotic massage that gets you horny so it's nice to have a wank at the end, and that's it . . . [But] I don't like just sort of saying, 'Right, you've just come, now let's have the door.' I hate that, hate that! Usually I will try to get them to come a quarter of an hour before the hour is up and then I will have a chance to wipe them clean, have a laugh . . . I only do safe sex. Them sucking my dick is harmless. Even if I do that to someone, which is very rare, that is low risk. If I fuck them I always use a condom and I never come inside them anyway, even with a condom . . . I never kiss clients. I'm just revolted by it, it's just one of my rules. With the right person I love to kiss, but very, very rarely with a client . . . As soon as they have come I have to get a towel and wipe my hands clean . . . I always wash my hands in medicated soap and Dettol, it's like a ritual with me, and if they've sucked my dick I wash it in medicated soap four or five times.

He would never allow clients to have anal intercourse with him and rarely did it to a client and then only if he fancied them. He would do things to clients like strapping, caning, bondage and even fist fucking if they wanted it. He didn't mind dressing up to please them and had a colleague who didn't mind him being strapped if a customer was prepared to pay a double fee for a duo.

Case 104 expressed what seemed to be a regret that his sexual relationships with clients were too distant.

My rules for safer sex are fucking with a condom. I wouldn't actually ejaculate in anybody's mouth, but I would let somebody ejaculate in my mouth, because I like that, that really turns me on . . . I believe it is relatively safe, unless I have bleeding gums. I mean it depends on what you believe about what safe sex is . . . I tend to fantasise about having quite a close relationship with some of my clients, especially with those who are regulars, but I've been disillusioned. Maybe I'm just a romantic, or just not a realist. Because sometimes they come and then the session's over and they're not bothered about me, whether I've come or not, which is OK, I'm not sore about that. But it is one of the things makes you sit up and think, 'This is just a business.' I'm offering a service for money and people are just after their own satisfaction.

The feeling of being able to manage interactions with clients in ways that suited themselves, which was a prominent feature of the independent masseurs' situation, added to the caution that came naturally with their greater maturity, meant that safer sex rules were observed much more strictly and consistently than was the case with street workers. If relaxation of rules was to occur it would more likely be in relations outside paid sessions with clients.

Private masseurs, considering the extent of their practices, rarely experienced unpleasant confrontations with clients. The feeling that on their own territory they were in control was expressed well by *Case 108*: 'It is my place. I know what is going on and I can be pretty forceful if I want. I am not an eight stone weakling, I can throw my weight around if I want. And I know where the knives and the rolling pins are. I have never had any real problems, just that one guy who bounced his cheque . . . I am taking him to the petty debtors' court for that.' *Case 109* denied having had any significant hassles from clients, either over payment or making him do anything he didn't want. 'I am usually in control.'

Not all potentially unpleasant encounters can be predicted from the client's manner over the telephone. Difficult to spot in advance, but potentially dangerous to the masseur, are those clients who are ambivalent about their homosexual urges, wanting to obtain release, yet feeling guilty about it afterwards and tending to blame the worker. One such client was described by *Case 104*. 'A very rugged man, very butch, macho and upper working class, a van driver.' He had a girl friend and he kept on saying he was not gay, as if to reassure himself. 'I masturbated him, that's what he wanted, but he was confused . . . The next day I came home to a message on my answer phone from him saying, "You fucking AIDS bastard", and he was really angry.' A couple of months later he returned and this time had more intimate sex, fellating the masseur, but he insisted he just wanted to find out what it was like, it was an experiment and he would not come again. Yet he did come a third time and persuaded the masseur to take a bath together and have more sex. *Case 103*, who was at fifty-three the oldest of the working masseurs, was aware of this same danger but had been able to handle it. 'When guys who have had too many [drinks], they play around and then once they have become sober, or they have come [to orgasm], they get a tremendous sort of guilt complex, especially the straight ones, and that can be a bit of a

hassle. But I have only had the problem once. He calmed down in the end
. . . just a bit obstreperous. I don't have any trouble with gay people, they
know what it is all about.' *Case 101* described a similar but more
ominous-sounding experience. The client, after being massaged for about
half an hour, went to the bathroom. Unbeknown to the masseur he picked
up some scissors from there and on returning to the massage couch
secreted them under the sheet. The massage continued for a long time but
the client never touched the masseur and didn't get a proper erection.
Feeling uneasy, and wondering how to bring the session to a close, the
masseur benefited from a call from the landlord on the floor above to tell
the client he would have go, keeping very quiet. The client paid up and
went quickly and then the masseur found the hidden scissors. This
masseur said he would 'almost never' visit clients in their own home or
receive new clients late at night because 'I found it a bit too risky if I
didn't know them'.

    Case 102 had had 'only one really bad experience [with] someone I had
been seeing for a while. He'd been drinking too much. Because I knew
him I tried to be polite and thought I'd not ask him for the money first. So
we did what we had to do and I asked him for the money and he said he
wasn't paying because we hadn't come to an arrangement beforehand. I
said, "Well I'm sorry, but you can't leave until I get paid." I'm quite
prepared to stand and fight for my money if I've worked for it. We did
fight and a friend of mine came in and grabbed the bread knife. He took
the knife off my friend and attacked me with it and I've got a couple of
scars on my arm.' The man called the police and the masseur fled and hid
on the roof because he thought the police would inevitably believe his
accuser. This was the most violent incident reported by any of the
masseurs, but this particular masseur had been a street worker for many
years and was untypically reckless and disaster-prone. He was well
known to the police for drug dealing and importuning in drag.

    Even in the absence of any actual experience of violence masseurs were
aware of the potential risk and several mentioned it as an anxiety.

Case 106

I never know who I am going to open the door to. It is more and more pushed
to the back of my mind, but it is a worry – am I going to have trouble with
this client. I mean it has only happened four times ever, but it is a constant
sort of worry. On an out call, when you are going to someone's home, are
they going to drug my drink and beat me up, is there someone else sitting in
the other room waiting to mug me. It has never happened but it is a
constant worry. [Some of his phone calls had been unpleasant.] You do get
weird people, you do get lots of abuse on the telephone . . . You always get a
call at 5 a.m. just to wake you up and mess you around. You feel like
screaming down the phone, but that does not do any good, you are just
achieving exactly what they wanted.

Case 104

> I've heard a horror story I got from another masseur who told me that this guy – I don't know how true it is, he could not verify it – this client had asked if he could tie this guy up, and this guy said yes and he tied him up and he cut off one of his testicles. He actually threw the money onto the bed when he left, leaving him tied up there. That's pretty horrific, but I've never had any trouble. Like once or twice I've had one or two odd people who've been eccentric . . . But the worst thing that I have actually anticipated is that somebody might come to the flat when I am not here and rummage through it and take things.

As in the case of street workers, sexual assaults were not necessarily linked with the prostitution business. *Case 113* had never been forced against his will by his massage clients but it had happened when he was nineteen and payment was not at issue. 'I went back to a man's house because I wanted to have sex with him. I didn't fuck then. I did not enjoy it, did not want it, but he wanted it and he was twice as big as me and made sure he got it.' It was a nasty and very painful experience. 'I mean I bled for about a month, but I did not go to the doctor.'

*

These descriptions showed that although street workers often expressed confidence in handling clients, the masseurs had much better control and reported fewer bad experiences. Some, however, were concerned that their activities could attract the attention of police, that they might be 'raided' or that a new client might turn out to be a potential police plant. Incidents of the sort will be cited later in the section on legal controls (see p. 297). They could choose whether to be friendly or distant. They had more opportunity for personal satisfaction and were more likely to find their clients agreeable as people even if not physically attractive. Those who had a mind to do so were able to find social companions and even sexual partners from among their clients.

16

Characteristics of Advertisers: Personal and Social

Backgrounds

In social origins, in motives for prostitution, in attitudes to the trade, in their avoidance of drug dependence and crime and in their intentions for the future most of those advertising a sexual service under the guise of escort or massage, especially the self-employed, home-based masseurs, clearly differed from the generality of our street worker samples. Whereas very few street workers had come from happy or secure parental homes, eight of the eleven agency workers interviewed and seven of the twelve interviewed masseurs had no seriously adverse comments to make about their upbringing. Of the three agency workers who came from unfortunate backgrounds two were cases located at the Streetwise Day Centre (one belonged to the initial sample of 50). Their attachment to agencies had been recent or intermittent, either following or interspersed with long periods working the streets or bars. They may not have been typical of those whose experience was limited to agency work. Two of the interviewed agency workers had both disengaged from the sex industry a long time before and made a successful social adjustment since (*Cases 501* and *511*, see p. 252). Both had come from seemingly unexceptional homes, one of them had never worked on the streets and the other had done so only very briefly when his agency work fell through. The five masseurs who complained of unhappy childhoods were from broken or emotionally fraught family set-ups, but none of them had experienced the destructive combination of emotional, material and educational deprivation so common among the street worker samples. The following examples, the first describing a happy childhood and the second an unhappy but materially secure situation, typify the majority of the early histories of the sex advertisers.

Case 109 grew up on a farm in what he described as a very quiet family with no evident problems. He rated his childhood 'very happy' and said he had loved both parents and got on well with them. He had been in full-time education up to the age of twenty, first at school and then at technical college, in each case passing out with appropriate examination qualifications. He then came to London and took up holistic massage because that interested him. Although he was gay and enjoyed sex contacts he had not at first intended it to be a sexual service, but finding that customers wanted it and that it suited him he continued. He was then aged twenty-three. Because his family was in Ireland he had not told them about his gay life, but thinks he would have done so had they been living nearby.

Case 104 enjoyed introspection and talked at length about his early relationships with his parents. From an outsider's standpoint his home background might have seemed satisfactory, but he viewed it very critically. He had grown almost to hate his father because he was so passive and undemonstrative and distanced himself from his children's concerns. He was much attached to his mother, who was the dominant figure in the home. His father had a well-paid job in a bank, there was no lack of toys or other material things, but he felt unhappy. There were tensions between his parents, his mother wanting his father to be more decisive, then becoming angry when what she thought were the wrong choices were made, but these things were largely hidden from the children. He was made more unhappy by dislike of school, caused in part by the onset of his gay tendencies and partly because he disliked subjects like maths and science which he was forced to learn. Nevertheless he was successful in leaving examinations (university entrance equivalent) and subsequently got a job in his father's bank. It was not until many years later when he was thirty-six, working as a mature student and struggling on a small grant that he got into the sex massage business to supplement his income. He had had some previous training in massage, was aware of the sex industry from a rent boy escort agency worker he knew and also from a masseur friend. Although money was his prime motive, he thought also that perhaps he had wanted the experience to boost his confidence in intimate dealings with people.

Among the minority with unfavourable early histories one of the saddest was *Case 102*, currently a masseur, who had been for most of his life a street worker and occasional agency worker. He came from a family that was not poor, but 'my mother has got a beautiful house but is very mean with money'. His parents were divorced when he was seven and he was not allowed to visit his father. His mother called him a bastard like his father and beat him frequently. For seeing his father secretly 'I had to have stitches in my head'. He disliked his stepfather who was 'a nonentity'. He was a 'desperately unhappy' child. 'It was a rough area where I came from, I was always picked on a lot. They used to spray "X is a poof" on the walls of houses.' His mother didn't mind gay people at large, but hated a gay son on her doorstep.

Together with other schoolboys he began meeting men in a local park toilet and going back with them for unpaid sex. He was fifteen when he first got money from one of them for anal intercourse. It was painful and he didn't enjoy it, but at the time his mother was taking off him all the money he got from a Saturday job. At sixteen, when he left home, he came to London inspired by a recent television programme *Johnny Come Home* in which 'there was this queen saying he was earning £80 a night, which was a great deal of money in those days . . . I knew I was going to do it'.

The link between unhappy background and prostitution, observed among street workers and emphasised in many previous surveys, was much less apparent among agency workers and not at all among self-employed masseurs. The connection, therefore, is not between background and prostitution in general, as has often been suggested, but between bad background and the population of rootless young men who have gravitated to life on the streets and who are the source of most street working prostitutes.

Child sex abuse

It was suggested earlier (see p. 51) that the high incidence of sexual molestation in boyhood, reported by the street worker samples, was probably related to the circumstances of deprivation, poor supervision and institutional placements that so many had experienced as boys. Since many of the agency workers and self-employed masseurs came from better backgrounds it was to be expected that fewer would have experienced early sexual assaults. This was in fact the case, although a firm statistic is difficult to establish because of the difficulty of definition of 'unwanted' or coercive sexual experience. Nearly all these men identified strongly as gay and were apt to recall their early homosexual encounters as at least partly consensual, as in the already cited *Case 102* who used to meet men in toilets when he was a schoolboy. *Case 104* was another who described what others might consider classic child sexual abuse but which he viewed in an utterly different light. 'I was about eleven and we had this teacher and he actually let a group of us masturbate him. I never regarded that or him as perverted. I never regarded him as a child molester in any way. I think I regarded it as an honour that you could do that. I mean I thought it was nice that he would actually break the barriers and let us get close to him. For him to let us masturbate him to me was a nice thing to do.' *Case 116* remembered an incident at the age of five. 'A baby sitter got me to jerk him off. I enjoyed doing it at the time.' *Case 107* mentioned an incident which in any event fell just outside the childhood age range: 'It was all voluntary. I lost my virginity at fourteen . . . I was there with my parents when I met this guy. He took me out in the country in his car and we had really nice sex, it was so exciting. When we got back he went to the library and I went to the hotel, but as my parents had gone out I went to drag him out of the library and took him to the hotel and asked him to do it again. It was so nice and I was so happy for the next few days. There wasn't any penetration, I was just so horny to be with someone.'

Case 105 was thirteen when he was paid by a man for sex, but his motive for participating was not financial. He had got into conversation with a man of forty exercising dogs on the neighbouring common.

> We started to talk and he said, 'I have some videos at home.' I was quite intrigued because I'd not actually seen a porn movie ... I knew that there was a suggestion of sex there, I was not completely ignorant ... I went to his place and he put on the movie and I got a hard on and so did he, and he started playing around with me. I did not stop him. I guess if I had wanted to stop him I would have, but also I don't know if I really wanted to stop him because maybe I was frightened of what might happen. I was in his place ... and he was much bigger than I was and I was frightened of getting hurt so I went along with it ... I got excited and he pulled my pants down and gave me a real good fuck, not good in the sense that I enjoyed it, but in the sense that it was quite rough. He had not used much lubrication and it did hurt quite a bit, but he did give me some money, like 20 quid, and when I was thirteen that was a lot. When I left him I felt really dirty, really weird. I went home and went to the bath ... He really had been a very inconsiderate lover. He knew that he was hurting me, because I was crying out, but then I did not want to pull away and make a scene because I was a little bit scared. But then I went home and thought about what we had done and I had a wank. And, you know, the idea grew and I went back three or four times after that ... Anyway it was a strange experience and I guess it was quite a valuable experience. I don't know about long term ... it is like water under the bridge, I don't think about it.

Case 516, on the other hand, who was an agency worker who had come from a distinctly unhappy home, provided a classic example of intra-familial sex abuse. From the age of five to fifteen his father 'used to force me to give him oral sex'. He reacted to it 'with confusion. Misguided parental love, I thought at the time – then I didn't know much about it.' Later 'I became more aware that I was being used as a sexual object [but] nobody ever knew, I never told anybody.' He had one sister, younger than himself, and he thought to protect her by being interfered with himself. He felt even worse about his father when marital infidelity began and 'I was quite happy when they were divorced.' His childhood was very unhappy, he became rebellious and violent and was often beaten by both parents who 'were both frustrated by the situation and I was the target'. At ten he was sent to a child psychologist. [Presumably the issue of sex abuse was avoided.] His father had a contemptuous attitude to things 'poofy' – 'which probably brought me into homosexuality'. He had sex with boys at school and at sixteen 'I moved to London with the main object to find somebody older to take care of me – not a form of prostitution, but a

form of being taken care of'. It was not until he was twenty-five, after he
had been working in the fashion clothes industry, that he contacted an
escort agency because he needed to make money quickly:

Q. What's your position now?
A. I am a prostitute now.

The impression gained from these accounts was that histories of
unwanted molestations were no more frequent than might be expected of
any group questioned on the topic and that other situations in which
contacts between adults and boys were described were no different from
what is reported by the generality of homosexual males growing up in a
society that obliges them to be secretive about their sexuality. The
statistical link between child molestation and prostitution appears to be
limited to street worker types and to be characteristic of the deprived
populations from which they are drawn.

Motives for entering the business

Coming, as many did, especially among the self-employed masseurs, from
relatively affluent and supportive backgrounds, the decision to enter the
prostitution business was often a matter of choice and calculation taken
after several years of experience of other ways of making a living. Their
choice was influenced in most cases by a homosexual orientation. One
agency worker (*Case 003*), a man from the original Streetwise sample,
claimed to be heterosexual – although he said later that he enjoyed sex
with males and females equally. Apart from him, all the other agency and
self-employed workers who were interviewed, or who mentioned their
orientation during visits, identified themselves as predominantly gay,
usually quite emphatically and exclusively so. One of the masseurs, for
example, *Case 105*, said, 'I look around heterosexual boys of my age and I
really think I am having more fun.' One of the agency workers, *Case 511*,
said, 'I'm gay and that's it. When you're already gay you are only doing
what comes natural really. You're not really doing anything abnormal. It
would be abnormal if you was gay and you was going to a woman to fuck
her. Me, I wouldn't like to do that because I'm gay, I don't fancy women. It
must be like that for a [heterosexual] to do it to a man because they've
needed to feed a drug habit or to get a roof over their heads or food in their
belly.' Among the masseurs who were visited but not formally
interviewed several mentioned that they could not do the work properly
were they not gay and able to enjoy it. At *Visit 111* the man went further,
explaining that since his lover's death he had found advertising as a
masseur a better way to find sexual pleasure than having to cruise the
bars. It seems probable that men who advertise their services, either

personally or through an agency, have a greater commitment to the sex industry and include a higher proportion with a homosexual orientation than among rent boys who are restricted to work in streets and bars.

It was only among the minority who came from unhappy backgrounds that feelings of having been obliged to take to prostitution were expressed. *Case 102* was an example of this kind. 'There was nothing else I could have done if you see what I mean. Much as I wanted to do it, I was also thrust into that situation because of home life. I had to earn money somehow and to me it was just easy money. I dearly wished I could have been in a position where I could have stayed at school. I wished I had done well, that is what I really regret.'

The following examples illustrate very different sequences of events from the pressurised experiences of homeless street working youths who had much less power to control the course of their lives. As in *Cases 104* and *109* (cited at the beginning of the chapter) there were many who described an easy, unforced decision of convenience.

Case 108, aged twenty-seven, had left Australia a year and a half ago because he found it 'boring' and wanted to travel. He gave up a job he had had for 5½ years in order to do so. He had been working for a company engaged on government contracts that 'gave me a lot of training in computers and dealing with the public and cash, money management and all that sort of thing. So it was all through that company that I got my experience.' He had also had three years' experience in partnership with a lover running a cleaning business that had contracts with hotels and employed five permanent and 32 casual staff.

His parental background was emotionally secure in spite of the death of his father when he was eight. His mother remarried 'a very nice man' whom 'I love dearly'. There were financial problems, but no lack of basic necessities. He had a close relationship with his mother who had 'always known' and accepted that he was gay. He had never run away or truanted and he thought his childhood 'quite happy. I would not really change any of it.' For financial reasons he had had to leave school at fifteen, but he had always managed to support himself in a variety of work, including non-sexual massage, for which he had had some training. He had had only relatively brief periods 'on the dole'.

On arrival in England he was 'house sitting' for someone and looking for work. 'I wanted to work with computers here, but I realised what the wage was going to be and the way I liked to live would not match up. I have always liked doing massage so I just had a look through the gay papers to see what there was and X had an ad running that he wanted a [massage] partner so I went and saw him and just started working for him. He told me what was involved and I just thought there is no problem with that, I could give them a hand job while counting the lines on the wallpaper or something . . . Once I had worked for him for two months I realised how much money could be made out of it and I thought I might as well go in for it myself. There was room for competition.'

In fact he was doing well. 'It gives you a very good lifestyle. It enables me to have a nice apartment and to have nice clothes and to buy the food I want and if I want to go to Europe for five days I can take five days off and I don't have to think.' He estimated he had 'brought in £45,000' in twelve months. 'I will probably only be in this house another two months as I have just been offered a flat in [West London] that's being done up and I will be moving over there.' Nevertheless 'I don't actually intend on staying in it as a lifetime profession . . . What I am trying to do at the moment is set up an import business, but the red tape in this country is absolutely crazy.'

He was moderate in his personal habits, an intermittent smoker, a light drinker save for exceptional occasions and no more than a very occasional user of recreational drugs. Poppers he would pretend to inhale when customers wanted it. He had stopped going for check-ups for sexual infections as he no longer practised anything unsafe.

He was well aware of the contrast between his own situation and that of some street workers. He did not regard himself as a prostitute, any more than most people who are being paid for what they can do. 'For me, prostitution is basically where you stand on the street corner selling your butt for £10. You know, doing anything for £10, whereas me, no matter how much they were to offer I would not bend over.'

Case 105, aged only twenty, was described by the interviewer as 'friendly and cheerful, from a middle-class background, well-spoken with a public school education'. He himself said his childhood was 'very, very, very happy. Materially I was fine, I never wanted for anything . . . I adore my mother so much because she really did give my sister and me the best in life and, you know, we had a lovely time . . . We lived in a lovely house and I went off to [a well known] public school.' His parents had divorced when he was an infant but his mother 'had this boyfriend who we lived with for seven years . . . We were always going to hip places and we used to have little VIP passes.' He still sees his mother once a week and goes out to theatre and dinner with her. 'We have a very, very good relationship.' With her he had 'always been able to talk quite openly. She is very broad-minded.' She knew all about his gay affairs, but he thought she would be 'disappointed' if she learned about his prostitution activity. He had visited his natural father, who was a wealthy man, but 'not at all interesting as a person'. Of the man who was effectively his stepfather he said: 'He was lovely, more than a father.'

His introduction to the possibilities of the sex industry came though falling in love and going to live with a man who told him he had been a rent boy. 'He is very good looking and has been all over the world, travelled enormously . . . He lived in a squat and, you know, hung out and took mind-expanding drugs and all the rest of it. I was in complete awe of that man, really respected him immensely and thought he had an extremely interesting life ... So, anyway, I adapted to that way of life quite readily, and it was quite fun. I had a good time and met different people and coming from this middle-class background, although I had always met interesting people I had not actually met street people, as it were, you know drug dealers, pimps, prostitutes and all the rest of it ... About four months after we had met he told me what he wanted to do, to go for this [massage] job in the [health club, since closed following newspaper publicity, see p. 296]. He told me that was what he wanted to do and I really freaked out.' He talked to two girls in the house. 'What am I going to do? He wants to become a whore and I can't possibly stay with him.' She told him she had been a whore herself and it was not so bad. So 'it took on a different light' and when his friend got the sack the first day, but brought home a lot of money, 'the seed was planted [and] I thought I would give it a shot'. He was eighteen at the time and finding his conventional employment with an advertising agency 'deathly boring ... having to get up at eight on a packed tube, commute there, commute back ...'

After some months his affair began to go wrong. Both liked picking up other young men and there were 'horrid, jealous scenes. It got to the point where we were just doing it to spite each other. Then we started taking drugs, going out less and just staying in and fixing and getting out of it ... The quality of life was pretty abysmal ... I just thought enough is enough and I went to live in Paris.' There he continued to make money as a prostitute. After some months he was able to return and set himself up in a flat near the city where 'there are an awful lot of guys who are dying for it. The phone starts ringing in the morning about nine as soon as they get into the office.'

As a masseur he was making three times as much as his former pre-tax earnings of £150 a week.

> Q. You sound as if you are glad you made the change?
> A. Oh, completely, yeah.
> Q. And from everything you've said you sound as though you enjoy your lifestyle?
> A. Yeah, I do.

Having broken with his drug-abusing friend he was now using only cannabis and was a moderate drinker. He was already thinking of saving enough money to be able to get into better paid conventional work (see p. 258).

Social problems

The unconventional occupation of sex worker is likely to attract unconventional personalities, gay men with liberal notions of sexuality prepared to embark on a risky business that is frowned upon by society.

Their lifestyles might not conform to orthodox ideals, but most of those interviewed seemed to be coping adequately.

Although substance abuse, gambling and reckless spending were more characteristic of the street worker samples, some of the agency workers and masseurs had similar problems, although not usually to such an extent as to lead them into similarly desperate circumstances. They were usually better placed and better able to manage an unconventional lifestyle. For example, one masseur (*Case 105*) had been heavily into injected heroin, but said he had had no need to worry about infection as he had always been able to buy clean needles from the chemist. Another user of injected heroin (*Case 107*) was able to break the habit when he left the lover who had introduced him to it. *Case 506* found himself repeatedly and hopelessly in debt, but finally solved the problem by accepting help from his father. Aged nineteen, he was the son of well off and loving parents. He described an 'extremely happy' if rather spoilt childhood. He enjoyed expensive living – travel, smart clothes, gay clubs and lots of drink – but his family were getting fed up with having to pay off his debts. He had been in the forces but bought himself out because he had already discovered the gay scene and done some modelling in his spare time, and he thought he could do better for himself in civilian life. When he was in a gay club recently he had been approached by a man who asked if he would like to make money working for a male escort agency. Being in debt he agreed readily, but he had just left the agency because he was frightened by police surveillance. He had no settled address and was staying for a day or two with a wealthy punter who took an interest in his circumstances. He could go back to his parents, but did not want to. He was hoping, however, that they might pay for him to get training for a legitimate job as the sex industry now seemed less glamorous than he had once thought. In the event, soon after the interview he accepted a job in one of his father's businesses and might be said to have retreated from a lifestyle he had not the ability to sustain.

Some of the interviewed masseurs had started as street workers, but it can be difficult for street workers to break into regular sex industry employment if they have no place where they can be contacted by telephone, unless they can be taken on as shift workers at a massage parlour. *Case 514* thought he had been lucky. He had struck up an acquaintance with an older man who let him 'stay on the front room floor, sort of thing and use the phone . . . As we got to know each other better it increased from just using the phone, so that I could receive [agency] calls and go out to somebody, to being allowed to use the flat on occasions with a small fee.' Many homeless street workers never get such a break.

It was noticeable that those who had entered the world of advertised sex after a period of street working were the ones most likely to pursue lifestyles leading to the sort of disasters that were common among the street worker samples. *Case 003*, one of the original Streetwise Day

Centre sample, had been recruited by a gay acquaintance for work at an agency in Amsterdam, but this had done nothing to change his uncertain circumstances. 'It was a flat and they did out calls and six or seven boys lived in the flat. I was the only English one there. It was £80 a time, I got £40 and they got £40, doing seven or eight a day, but I mean I blew it all. After finishing I used to go drinking every night and smoking, you know, dope and that.' At the time he was interviewed he claimed to have virtually ceased prostitution and in fact he did secure a flat, a job and a girlfriend. Soon, however, he was seen by a Streetwise outreach worker on the streets again, trying to taste once more the thrills of drugs and easy money he had been missing. The following year he was seen still haunting one of the stations. He had been identified by an ex-punter and caused to lose his job. He was by now feeling too old to 'rent' himself, but existing on the fringe of the scene, passing punters onto others, pimping and drug dealing.

Case 102, as mentioned earlier, came from an unhappy home. He was contacted at the Streetwise Day Centre although, at twenty-nine, he was too old to be accepted as a regular attender there. He was a heroin user, but with a different story from those masseurs who had been able to maintain control of their drug habits. He said that, although he was earning £2,000 a month from prostitution and was able to keep up appearances with smart clothes and a well-set-up massage room, he was forced to resort to street work in addition in order to support his continuing and very expensive heroin habit. He had served a prison sentence for drug dealing.

The last two examples illustrate the undoubted overlap between the street working types and employees of the wider sex industry. They do not, however, contradict the conclusion that off street sex workers, especially those who have never worked on the streets and have entered the profession at an age when they are capable of managing their lives successfully, are as a general rule less prone to social problems and personal disasters than the typical street worker.

Currrent attitudes

During the interviews men were encouraged to enlarge upon the advantages and disadvantages of being in the sex industry. While acknowledging its profitability some had reservations about its effect on their personal relationships; others, however, found it suited their gay lifestyle. Some acknowledged they were engaged in prostitution, others distanced themselves from the concept, reserving it for street working rent boys with whom they felt nothing in common. Some took a certain pride in performing a helpful service, others with less commitment seemed to regard it more in the light of a money-making racket. The following quotes from agency workers illustrate some of these contrasts.

Case 511 was sure people did not work in the sex industry for pleasure. 'There are enough clubs where you can go and get sex as much as you want . . . You can get a job somewhere and enjoy doing it, like a pub job, where you can do an extra couple of hours for nothing and enjoy it, but it wasn't like that, it was just basically for the money. You just went, done it, got the money and you went. That was all there was to it, just money.' When in the business, 'I felt like a prostitute, I felt just like a rent boy, I was no different from anybody else working on the street or for an agency. I just had that bit more security than working on the street . . . I knew what I was going into. I didn't have these visions of grand hotels and out for dinner every night of the week.'

Case 514 saw the job as work like any other. 'I perform a service and that is it, that is the way I look at it. It should be a legitimate service, it would be a lot better if everyone could accept that.' He did not like the word prostitute. 'It does not sound correct. I am an escort as far as that goes.'

Case 516 was one who saw himself as doing a useful job. 'My feeling is that you're giving people a sexual release that probably they can't achieve elsewhere, or if they did achieve it elsewhere it would probably cause them problems legally . . . Sometimes it's like giving therapy to people because sometimes they just want to talk in a relaxed gay atmosphere where they're not stuck in a heterosexual world, so therefore I feel I'm providing quite a good service . . . Basically, I think that escort agencies provide a good service, provided they don't take on anyone under age, which they shouldn't. It affects people in different ways. I think if you're young and vulnerable then it is a bad thing to do, because it can affect you mentally in the long run. But someone like myself . . . I don't think it has affected me badly at all. I'm still the same person I was before I ever got involved.' Moving, as he did, in gay circles he had no need to keep his work secret. 'It didn't seem to bother anybody really . . . It gave me a lot of available cash that I didn't have normally.' Several of his clients had become personal friends.

Case 515 saw agency work as less soul-destroying than being a hack writer for advertisers. 'I find physical prostitution less damaging to me than creative prostitution . . . All work is prostitution as far as I am concerned. The job is physically a bit messy, like most types of work, but you clean up afterwards and there is not much of a problem . . . I generally used to say that I was a rent boy, because it fitted in more with my street cred than escort, even though I was never doing it off the street . . . It didn't really have any bad effect on me, not more than doing any other job. In fact I was making more money and having more spare time . . . But then I did go through money a lot quicker and seemed to want to use the club scene more than I had done before, which could mean to a degree that I wanted to escape – by taking ecstasy and things – from what I was actually doing, though I didn't really feel that at the time.' He was

finding the work bad for his relationship with his boyfriend. It was a
strain also coping with the 'mind games' of clients trying to seduce him
into sex acts he did not want or had not been paid for.

Case 506 agreed that money was the only advantage to the work. As to
disadvantages: 'There aren't any really, except getting caught.' Even so,
he wanted to be out of it, but 'I am in an incredible amount of debt.'

As might have been expected, the self-advertising masseurs, working
in their own place independent of agencies, more often expressed positive
attitudes, but still there were some who found the work not always
pleasant. There were differences also in their assessment of the
advantage of greater freedom than in ordinary employment balanced
against the disadvantage of possible interference with their private lives,
both social and sexual.

Case 116, who styled himself 'a high-class whore' said, 'It was a
business, but the hours are much more adaptable and the wages are
much better and there was an awful lot of fun in it.' He believed 'life is for
living' and liked to spend lavishly when he had the chance. He loved 'all
the suits that I had, all the shoes, all the watches, all the rings . . .' His
sex work did not prevent him from simultaneously forming consecutive
monogamous sexual partnerships, one lasting a year, the other six
months, but between times 'I was a slut.'

Case 108 was conscious of his personal life being circumscribed. 'I am
tied to here and I do not have a lot of time to myself. I am not free to go to
the West End and do what I want to do when I feel like it. If I don't make
enough money I don't go out.' He was 'quite happy' with being in the
business, which he saw as lucrative but short term. 'Some people may be
able to do it for five or ten years. Good on them if they've got the strength,
I have not, I enjoy my night's sleep.' Also, 'it does affect my idea of a
relationship'. He had a lover, but 'I am going through a bit of a rough
period because he knows what I do for a living and he is not happy about
it . . . He is being quite understanding, but if I was not going to try to get
out of it I would have seen the back of him a long time ago.'

Case 106 was appreciative of his freedom to organise the work to suit
himself. 'I can work when I want to. I don't have to wait in the rain for
buses in the morning . . . I have a very good income basically. I do meet a
lot of people, I make a lot of acquaintances in my job.' On the other hand,
'Being at home all the time to answer the bloody phone is lonely, gets on
your nerves sometimes.' It certainly interfered with the acquisition of a
lover. 'I think the hardest thing for me is the emotional side of not having
a lover and if I did he would not be able to cope with it. If I met somebody I
was really very, very in love with and it was reciprocated and I knew he
hated it, then I would really have to think very strongly about quitting.
But then I would also think, "What the hell am I going to do that pays this
kind of money?" . . . I get very depressed with what I do sometimes, but
then I sort of bounce back again. I think most of my depression is based

on the fact that I am not in a relationship, but then again I hate all the jealousy and the possessiveness . . .' There was also the problem of satiation with sex. 'You do lose your desire because you get sort of bored. When I go out when I am horny I am just looking for sex and in the bar I never find it, because I have such strong likes and dislikes. Because I have clients who are so cute and so lovely, what is the point of going to bed with somebody who is not in the least as nice as them.'

The problem of having little energy left over for making personal sexual contacts was mentioned by another masseur (*Visit 118*) who told the client that he used to think sex work did not interfere with his private life but had come to feel differently. It was actually tiring. He had a friend, also a masseur, with whom he went out to gay clubs, but often they would both find themselves too tired to look for sex. *Case 104* made a somewhat similar comment. 'I am reappraising where I am at now and this work and casual sex in general impinges on something else that I need around relationships. If I am putting energy into all these dissipated one-off relationships then I simply don't have the time or energy to give to main relationships. So if I do want a relationship then my behaviour at present is perhaps not the right way for me to go about things.'

As regards a regular sex partner, not everyone found the masseur business an impediment.

Case 108 was sharing the flat he used for massage with his lover. 'You see we have got an open agreement which works out real good. He plays around and I play around . . . [With] the job I do we could not have any other arrangement.'

Worries about what other people might think about their involvement in the sex trade were brushed aside by some, but others were at pains to justify themselves. Reluctance to admit the label 'prostitute', either in thinking about themselves or in talking to others, was much in evidence. The fact that they had freely chosen what they were doing was often cited in this connection.

Case 109 agreed his job was a form of prostitution, but it suited him. 'I am not willing to give up eight hours a day of my life to do something I don't want to do. I enjoy this, it earns money, I work when I want to work and if I don't want to work I can tell them to go away . . . What other people think about it doesn't bother me really, because I know what I am doing and I choose to do it and the only effect it can have is a positive one. I can tell people [about it], I do tell people, I just don't tell everyone.'

Case 107 was interestingly ambivalent. He recognised but disliked the idea of being classed a prostitute. 'I suppose the word evokes a meaning of selling yourself for necessity, something degrading which is forced upon you, whereas what I do is through choice. It is a voluntary exchange, which is not the same as prostitution on the streets if you are homeless with no money and are forced into it though you don't want to do it – then you are prostituting yourself . . . Women sell themselves in advertising where sex is used in the market place to sell anything. Even in a gay club you sell yourself through sex before you even get to talk to anyone . . . People prostitute themselves all the time, which is something I really object to and fight against, which is ironic as I am doing this so that I don't have to prostitute myself! . . . I now don't do anything I don't want to do except for very short periods of time for large amounts of money . . . I suppose the word prostitution evokes a meaning of selling yourself through necessity, something degrading which is forced upon you, whereas what I do is through choice, it is a voluntary exchange.'

In reality it had not always been like that for him. 'There is something before then I had forgotten to mention . . . I did not have any money and I was walking around Soho and went into a male strip joint that existed at that time. I walked in and asked if they needed a dancer. They got me to come back at 6 p.m. and said, "You're on!", and I was petrified. There was a stage and tables all around where the clients sat . . . You just took all your clothes off, perhaps rubbed body oil on, and just danced. If you wanted to make more money you would have to dance close to them to let them touch you and they'd give you money and you would put it down your sock. Eventually I got into it and quite liked the sleaziness of it. It was an interesting experience and gave me a lot of confidence, I mean sexual confidence. If I was being paid for what I was I no longer felt the need to prove myself by sleeping around.' Later he worked for an agency. 'I liked it. I had a lot of work zipping around London from one crazy, fabulous bedroom to another, around hotels, being given drinks, meeting lots of different people. It was a challenge, because you had to suss them out very quickly and act in the way that would please them. It was like a test. You can judge how well you've done by the time you leave. You work hard at it and you get results and you're paid for it, a decent wage. I didn't feel exploited at all, I was enjoying it.'

For all that, he did not like to get personally involved with customers. 'I've never had a sexual relationship with a client on a non-business basis. And I've never formed any sort of friendship with any of the clients. I've also never had a sugar daddy.' He was uncomfortable when he went with a friend and fellow masseur to stay the weekend at the rooms of one of his friend's regular patrons: 'I felt strange. It's more of a compromise than what I do, because you have to keep up a stance for a longer time and in a way that's more dishonest. I prostitute my body, not my mind. In that situation they want more than your body and the distinction becomes blurred.'

Case 103 was asked about friends knowing he was doing sex massage. 'I don't sort of shout about it. It's not the thing to do. I don't broadcast it among my friends because they are not going to be my clients anyway, so what is the point of telling them.' He was very clear he was doing it by choice. Taking up massage 'was the best thing I ever did, I should have done it years ago. It is very job satisfying.' He did not regard himself as a prostitute. 'No, I don't at all because I charge for a massage. That is what people come along to you for and that is what I am prepared to give them. If they ask for anything else while they are here then that is, you know, another story as far as I am concerned . . .' His idea of a prostitute was someone soliciting on the street. 'Could you imagine me standing out in the street and going up to a guy and saying, "Look, do you fancy –?" Come on, it's ridiculous!' Unlike *Case 107* he was not averse to mixing business with pleasure and having continuing sexual and social contacts with clients. 'A lot of guys I've made friends with. That's the problem, make a friend, lose a client!' Some clients he found all too attractive and when massaging them, 'I get carried away and really have a good sort of play around. You know, I can get so worked up.'

Case 104 was another who expressed somewhat confused feelings. 'I am not a prostitute, I am a masseur. It's money for massage and the fact that we have sex is by the by. When someone does want the full hour's massage and I have to give all that physical and psychic energy to it then I do feel completely justified in charging £35 for it. This really is the service I have offered, whether sex follows or not. But yes, of course, massage work that involves sex is a form of prostitution. Sometimes I do feel like a prostitute and sometimes like an out-and-out slut. It's ironic that I am in Soho where I am surrounded by brothels and prostitutes and I may be carrying around derogatory thoughts about them when I am in exactly the same position.'

The abiding impression left by the different views expressed was of a certain unease at being in the sex industry which went beyond practical concerns about fluctuating income, protection from abusive clients, or legal status. It was not that many of them had moral scruples about what they were doing for a living, but rather that they did not like to identify their actions with the label 'prostitute' that carries with it so much social disapproval. This revealed itself in some convoluted rationalisations or an unwillingness in some cases to acknowledge their occupation openly. In some cases anxiety that prospective sexual partners would disapprove was one reason for the feeling that private sexual relationships were being sacrificed. It seemed that personal pride in providing a valued service and achieving high earnings and sometimes obtaining simultaneous sexual pleasure was insufficient to prevent some ambivalent feelings about their situation.

Future prospects

As already mentioned, two former agency workers who had given up prostitution were interviewed. Both were contented with their current situation and lifestyle and had no regrets about having once been part of the sex industry. Unlike the vast majority of street workers, however, they had come from happy and stable homes and their circumstances at the time they first started agency work had been relatively unproblematic. Their stories are quoted at some length because they illustrate a point, missed by research focused exclusively on social problems, that some individuals see sex work as a positive and valid choice of occupation for a particular phase in their lives.

Case 511 reported a 'very happy' childhood. There was no financial hardship, he 'had everything' and was 'quite a bit spoilt'. He was an over-active, mischievous boy, but although often in trouble with teachers he attended his comprehensive school regularly until he was sixteen, after which, his parents being publicans, he himself went to work in pubs while continuing to reside at home. In fact, he stayed with his parents more or less continuously till 'the first time I seriously lived with somebody' at the age of twenty-five. He was still visiting them once a week. 'I think they were very good parents, very supportive as well to all of us in our own way.' They know he is gay and though they don't talk about it much 'they just treat me as their son, nothing different'. It was only 'Mum', however, that he was able to tell about getting money for gay sex. He had been a steady worker. 'I've always stayed in jobs, I haven't gone from one to the other. Even the cleaning I stuck for two years, but I enjoy it, I liked both jobs, pubs and cleaning.' He had stayed in one pub for seven and he had never been dismissed. When interviewed at twenty-five he was in a steady relationship with a man. 'I feel more stable knowing that we're together, not just a casual affair. We are trying to make a go of everything, get a home around us and just be together, we're happy together.'

He started to work for an escort agency when he was twenty-two. He had never before been paid for sex. He was on holiday when one of the friends he was with revealed that he ran an escort agency, gave him he address and suggested he was a suitable type to work there and that he should give it a try. The money sounded attractive, it seemed he could make £150 a day, and it was implied that the sex was only masturbation. On his return he went for an interview, was asked questions about his physique and what sex acts he was willing to do. He said he was prepared only for masturbation but they engaged him all the same.

It was because he was temporarily low in funds that he decided to try agency work. He had just given up his pub job because 'they messed me about on holiday money and everything and it was getting nearer to Christmas and I thought about presents to buy and everything . . . I had no money to spend, I was living at Mum's, signing on and they were giving me a pittance. The pub had rung me to come back, but I was so annoyed at what they'd done and I didn't really want to go back there and this sounded really good [pay].'

He remained living with his parents while working for the agency. He had no overheads or 'responsibilities'. Having made a deal, the agency would ring him to give the punter's number and leave him to phone to arrange a visit to the client's flat or hote'. 'When the person phoned he used to say, "I'm David", and Mum and Dad used to think it was the close friend I had who was also called David.' Eventually, because he had often to go out late in the evening when he had a call he had to explain to his mother what he was doing. She was shocked – 'knowing your son is a prostitute is not very nice really' – but remained cooperative.

He had never thought of prostitution as a long-term career. 'It isn't really normal and it's really not a living because it doesn't last for ever. You get old and no one wants to know . . . I just saw myself getting out of it with a few quid.' He enjoyed having lots of cash. He spent much of it giving treats to his mother and his friends. Originally he had intended just to tide himself over Christmas, but he carried on doing it 'basically for the money. You just went, done it, got the money and went. That was all there was to it, it was just money.' In addition, 'it was a bit of an escape for me because I had been tied down'. After he finished 'a job' late in the evening there was still time to go to a gay club, enjoy himself, have enough money to get a cab home and then stay in bed till mid-day. 'It was fun . . . I wouldn't say to anyone, "Don't do it" – if they want to then try it, but be careful.'

He had ceased work for the agency four months back. He finally decided to make a clean break because they had found out he was seeing one of their 'very big punters' privately without paying commission and had stopped referring so many clients to him. He had become fond of the punter in question, who was a married man whose family was abroad on holiday. He was now in a close relationship with a gay friend. He was sure he would not return to agency work. 'If I ever get hard up I'll sell something and get money that way.'

This man, who had resumed legitimate work and was contented with a much quieter lifestyle, contrasted with the typical street worker in his supportive family background, his avoidance of intoxicants, his prudent relations with sex clients, his opportunity to switch back to previous employments and his ability to make unpressured choices.

Case 501 was introduced by a social worker who was a personal friend of his. He was seen at his home, a tasteful country cottage near a university town. He was thirty-four. His manner was cordial, his speech was educated and he said he had nothing much to complain about with his current way of life. He was an artist, supplementing his income with part-time clerical work. He described a 'happy' childhood and a 'good relationship' with both parents. They got on well together and he had kept in close touch with both of them until their deaths. As a boy he had enjoyed material comfort. His father had been self-employed in an antiques business. He had been an average scholar, but left school at fifteen because he wanted to start work. At first he had 'various jobs', but then settled into a porcelain studio where he learned to paint the wares.

He had always been attracted sexually to men and so he decided to move to London where he shared a flat with a gay friend. He obtained work from a photographic modelling agency, mostly for selling fashion clothes, shoes and so on. It was a large and legitimate concern, 'a syndicate really', but it had 'another side, an escort agency ... They didn't really need to go out of their way to get good-looking young men, they were already there, and it was a way for the guys to earn a bit more money and keep them there ... I wasn't desperately short, but I always felt that I could do with a few more bob in my pocket.' So he and his friend, who was also working for the agency, decided to try. He was then eighteen or nineteen years of age.

'Initially we were led to believe, you know, that we'd be taken out and won't need to have any money. We said, "Yeh, if it entails going out to supper with somebody, then fine." The appointments were arranged by the agency. The clients had already been there and sort of picked out [one] from the photographs ... There were about ten or twelve of us going to various appointments.' The client would make clear he wanted to have some form of sex. 'You see, he had already paid his fee, the agency fee, and if you wanted to make a few more pounds then you, as an individual, would come to some sort of arrangement with the client.'

One client, 'was ugly, pretty grotesque, and I thought this isn't all that much fun. I was being paid, I had my fee, but it just wasn't particularly interesting.' He 'made absolutely clear from the start' he wouldn't have anal sex and he was never forced into it. 'I just wanted space between them and myself ... A friend working for the agency said, "Well, why don't you go in for kinky work?" ... There were things you had to do to various clients, but they didn't hassle you, they didn't touch you, didn't make any physical demands on you. So that was an area that I got into, which was fairly easy, provided you switch yourself off ... I had to tie them up, sometimes with ropes or chains or stockings. There was one I had to urinate on him, which, again, I just switched myself off.'

He continued supplementing his income through this work, mostly doing kinky jobs, for about eighteen months. One of the things that decided him to quit was that one of the escorts disappeared, possibly killed according to rumour, and this made him anxious. 'After leaving the agency I did carry on seeing my clients, which was, looking back on it, a bad move. Some other boys who were still operating were watching the houses where I was going and I was beaten up a couple of times, probably by heavies that the agency employed.' He changed his address, but 'I was still pursued, so [after three months] I decided that enough was enough. Had I got away with it, then maybe I would have carried on a little longer.' Because they owed money to the landlord he and his boyfriend resorted for a few weeks to picking up clients near toilets in Piccadilly and Victoria. After that he returned to his home area and began looking for legitimate work.

Like other sex workers who had never been mistreated by clients his only experience of sexual assault w.s in other circumstances. At twenty-five, long after he had given up prostitution, he was the victim of a brutal anal rape when hitch-hiking. The driver stopped miles from nowhere and 'he was a big guy and he just jumped on the back of me and forced my head down . . . and drove off after, leaving me . . . I had to have stitches.'

Asked how his time selling sex had affected him he said, 'I think that I've had some great times, looking back on them. I've also met some very odd people. You'd be earning a fair bit of money and you could do an awful lot of things with it. I spent it, went clubbing, went out for meals. You didn't really need to do very much. If you wanted your room cleaned you just picked up the phone. When I finished it took me a long time to adjust, having to earn money which was less than I was accustomed to. There were times when you think, "Maybe I could get a train up to London and earn myself some real money," but I didn't, I was very nervous about going to London again.'

Like the previous case, this man was from a supportive, middle-class background. He entered the sex business out of deliberation and opportunism rather than desperation and was circumspect and choosy in his dealings with clients. After withdrawing from the scene he missed the expensive lifestyle that went with it but did not try to go back. One can appreciate the greater temptation to return experienced by street workers whose only alternative ways of making a living are fairly unattractive.

Some men who were still working for agencies had clear plans to do something different before long:

Case 515, aged twenty-eight, was another man from an unproblematic middle-class home. In adolescence, however, 'I started to get very punkish and anarchic'. He dropped out of a university course, but was able to support himself in work as an advertising copy writer. He was never on the streets, and it was only when he was twenty-six that he decided to seek work with an escort agency. 'I was doing it mainly for money to get a flat and things together.' He gave several reasons why he intended to stop soon. 'For one thing, I have only got a couple of years before I started looking too old . . . For another thing there is this boyfriend. I am quite in love with him . . . I have started writing again and have written some articles for a film magazine a friend of mine is the editor of and I am starting thinking in terms of doing a bit more freelance journalism.'

Case 503, a twenty-two-year-old Swiss, had come from a close, intact and solidly middle-class background and had had training in accountancy. He had not told his parents, but he had come to feel he could only be totally happy living as a gay man. He had a passion for travel and was wanting to learn English and make some money and go to the US or Australia where he might find a job and a lover. He was obviously attached to his parents, was intending to visit them in a few weeks' time for Christmas, and said if they fell ill he would have to return from abroad even if it meant prison for skipping military service. He had attended a language school, but his money ran out and his parents were unwilling to continue supporting him in England because they wanted him to continue his education at home. To support himself he got a job without a permit in a restaurant and then, more recently, at a massage parlour. He felt guilty about the work he was doing, disliked it and intended to do it for only a few months until he had the money to travel. He drank very little, did not use recreational drugs and struck the interviewer as serious-minded and honest about himself. There seemed no reason to doubt he would carry through his intentions. Agency work can be attractive as a temporary expedient to some young gay men with an open attitude to sex at times when they are simply 'passing through' London or anticipating fresh career openings a little later.

Prospects were less rosy for some, particularly for those who had gravitated from street work. Of the two agency workers who belonged to the initial Streetwise Day Centre sample one, *Case 003*, soon lapsed back into street prostitution and pimping (see p. 246) and the other, *Case 026*, while working shifts at a massage parlour was still signing on as unemployed. Although aware that at his age they might not want him much longer he had no definite plans for obtaining another job. *Case 514*, not in the initial sample, but interviewed at the Day Centre because he was for the moment working for an agency, planned to stay in the sex industry, partly from choice and partly because it would be hard to find other work 'having been out of it so long'.

The self-advertising masseur/escorts who were still working when first interviewed generally had realistic plans for the future and their circumstances were such as to make it seem probable that they would succeed. One reason may be that so many of them had attained mature years and a degree of social stability before deciding to embark on sexual servicing. Some had relevant experience or training in other work to fall back upon when the time came.

Case 101, aged fifty, occupied his own modest West End flat, where he was interviewed, and said that although he still saw one or two of his long-standing clients he had given up advertising his service eighteen months before and was effectively retired. He was living a quiet, orderly life, supported by a disability allowance on account of asthma, doing casual cleaning work and spending a good deal of time on voluntary work with an agency befriending people with AIDS. His habits had always been abstemious, he was a non-smoker and did not drink or use recreational drugs. He came from a middle-class background, his father having been an RAF officer. His upbringing had been more stable than that of most of the street workers but he had not had an entirely happy childhood. His mother died when he was five and he spent most of his boyhood in a boarding school. He did not get on with his father too well but became very fond of the stepmother who appeared when he was twelve. He defined himself as completely gay with no wish to be different. 'I've got lady friends, but they don't turn me on. I find ladies like me, but that's as far as it goes.' His work history was unremarkable. After a period in the services he returned to the parental home but felt bored there, moved to London and worked steadily in various jobs in retail trade.

He had never worked the streets or bars and only got into the massage business when he was thirty-nine. He discovered that a younger man with whom he was having an affair was doing sex massage at his flat. He was told what was required and persuaded to join in. He liked the idea, the money was good and for a year he helped out his friend in this business. Then the friend went abroad, so he took a massage course and began to advertise himself. He ran a rewarding, undeclared and untaxed business for some eight years. It allowed him to get some little luxuries 'like videos and cameras'. He was content to give up now because of his age and the AIDS scare.

It would appear that this man's interlude of unofficial work as a self-employed masseur, save for providing some extra material comforts, had scarcely changed his already settled way of life. He used to frequent gay bars and he maintained various gay sexual relationships of his own apart from clients. He was still in touch with a former sugar daddy, now aged seventy.

Case 103 was another who had started in the massage business at a surprisingly late age, forty-five, after retiring on a pension following 23 years of army service. He was a gay man sharing a flat with his 'other half' and using massage as a way to supplement his pension, pay the rent, run a car, give suppport to an aged mother and maintain the lifestyle he liked, which included much socialising in the leather/motor-cycle scene. He enjoyed the work and wished he had started sooner. He thought of himself as a man who ran his business from home and paid his taxes. It suited him. He needed to make money and older people are considered unemployable.

Case 106, aged thirty-four, had a very professional attitude to his massage business and was clear about what he needed to make to secure his future. He had got together the money to start by working for escort agencies which he found 'dreadful, really . . . They always undersell you, expect you to go all around the world for £40 and you have to pay a third to them. But in six weeks I saved a lot of money . . . [Then] I rented a flat . . . I worked and worked and worked on my own. I was lonely, but I worked, and eventually . . . bought the flat and I've just gone from strength to strength.' He was saving money through insurance because he realised he would not be working as a masseur indefinitely [though judging by his good physique and the age of some others still in business he had a long time to go] but 'I have always been a survivor, I have always bounced up . . . If, in five, ten years' time I can't do this any more I think that something else will crop up.' Given his obvious determination and efficiency, his university education and his creditable work record prior to entering the massage business in his late twenties, it seemed unlikely that retirement would bring collapse in this case either.

Case 104, aged thirty-seven, was another who had started massage at a mature age, only two years previously. He was already looking to a future elsewhere, allowing his advertising subscriptions to lapse and resolving to adjust to a return to the work he was trained for, albeit at a lower income level. 'I think I've given it a fair stint of two years and I think that's enough. It doesn't feel right, on an inner level, to continue. But I'm still going to keep on the regulars for a time.' He was aware that 'I won't have to spend what I do now on little luxuries like food, going to the theatre, opera, restaurants etc. . . . [At present] I am living above my earning capacity as a social worker.' On inquiry a year later he was in fact employed once again in social work, had given up massage as planned and was seemingly happy and settled.

Even some of the younger masseurs were looking to a more comfortable future based on savings from their sex business. *Case 105*, though only twenty, already had a varied experience of working as a masseur in a health club patronised by gays, as a street worker in Paris and finally as a self-employed, self-advertising masseur. In addition, he had built up friendly and rewarding contacts with several elderly but socially well placed and interesting gentlemen punters in various parts of Britain who liked to have him to stay as a guest. He was well educated and had some work experience in market research and as a translator. He had this to say when asked what he thought about the future: 'This is a question I am often asked, my mother for example, and other people, my regulars, the guy in Scotland, the guys in ——— and ———, they are all quite concerned, but I have always been fending for myself as it were, I have always been very lucky and things have always gone my way so far . . . What I want to do now is to be clever in this job, be clever with the money I am earning and, you know, hopefully build a base on which to branch out into other things . . . I visit the theatre, I visit the movies, I am quite interested in art, I am intelligent and I have intelligent things to talk about. I buy books, I buy videos, I read all these things, it all costs money to do. I have a high standard of living and I intend to keep it that way . . . If I let all this money slip through my hands, then I am a complete jerk and on my head be it.' A few months later, having worked for a time in a market research firm needing a French speaker, he had been accepted for further training at a polytechnic and given up sex massage. Sadly, some symptoms caused him to seek an HIV test which proved positive and changed all his plans.

Case 107, who was also quite young, just twenty-three, had recently relinquished agency work in favour of a self-advertised, home-based service. He was clear in his own mind that he would be getting into a different way of supporting himself shortly. He feared that 'they are soon going to stop me from signing on here, what with compulsory training schemes and all; that would just kill my brain. I want to get out before I lose my freedom. I feel I can start again somewhere else and do so intact. I only started this in order to get myself out of the [debt] I was in. It's not something you can do when you are older and I don't want to get hooked on this and eventually disposed of. I have always seen it as a temporary thing. I now sometimes find it hard to do. That's why I've stopped work with the agency as I can no longer do it always when they want me to. I can control it better through the [advertising].' He intended to continue long enough to pay off his debts and pay for a language course so that he could take a job abroad.

Case 109, another twenty-three-year-old, said he was doing 'what I wanted to do, I wouldn't do it unless I wanted to. As long as I enjoy it I'll keep doing it.' He was confident he could give it business when he felt like it and in fact was thinking of doing so shortly when he planned to emigrate. In his case, however, there was some doubt about it because 'I am not willing to give up my life to eight hours a day to do something I don't want to do. I enjoy this, it earns money. It is not like other work, I mean I am not very good at working, I can't hold down a job for very long.'

Case 114, aged twenty-four, had already begun some legitimate contract work and was expecting to let the massage business tail off. 'The future is looking good for me.' He had had warm and supportive parents and was aware that this gave him better prospects. 'I am lucky. I have probably had more advantages in life than a lot of other rent boys. I would never associate myself for one second with some of them. I think they live a much harder life than I do. I have had it very easy.'

There were exceptions to the relatively unproblematic future envisaged by the majority of the masseurs, as the following cases illustrate.

Case 102, at thirty, was advertising himself as an 'escort' and having clients telephone him and come to his room for a sex session, though more often he visited their hotels. He was much less sanguine and less stable than most of the others and his personal history of early deprivation was more like that of the typical street worker. In fact, he had started on the street at the early age of fourteen, having fled from an unhappy home, and had been a prostitute ever since. He had many stories to relate of disastrous experiences including assaults by clients and spells in prison. He was still reverting to street work at times when custom was poor. He had a drug habit, but 'not as bad as it was. Now it costs me £100 a day, which is a lot of money I know, but it used to be £200 or £300.' He was distinctly pessimistic about his future. 'I have had a lot of money, so much money it's not true, but when you're in that situation, making such a lot, well you just spend it. But I've got to the age now where I'd like to stop . . . There is no future, there isn't anything, you just take it day by day. There's not a lot to look forward to, especially when you get to my age.'

Case 116 described a highly profitable four-year career as a very up-market prostitute working from a home base and building up a clientele largely by word of mouth. He had been a rebellious child from an emotionally fraught family background and had started in street prostitution at the age of twenty, following dismissal from his job for taking drugs. One of his clients advanced money to set him up in an apartment and introduced him to a number of wealthy customers. Soon he had built up a thriving business. Although he 'didn't have to rely on that any more, I'd go up the West End and maybe pick up a client, just because I've always liked the West End . . . I get a real kick out of it.' He described himself as 'a recreational drug addict'. At gay bars and clubs 'if you've got something like acid or coke or speed you get into it much, much more and that's what I like.' Obviously a risk taker, he ignored the AIDS scare, continued with unprotected, passive anal sex and became infected with HIV. His activities attracted a police raid and he was charged with keeping an immoral house. Since his release he had been very ill with AIDS. He was for the moment partially recovered but unemployed and living on state support in a flat provided by the local authority.

Such clues to the future prospects of one-time sex industry workers as can be picked up from these histories seem to support the old adage 'to them that hath shall be given'. Those who start off with advantages in the way of education, money, family support, maturity of purpose and a compatible sex orientation, and who do not need to start off on the streets in order to find clients, are likely to thrive. Those who enter the trade with deliberation and out of informed and free choice, after rather than before they have established some social stability, are able to make a relatively smooth transition back to conventional living when they decide to do so.

Part III
Social Issues in Commercial Sex

17

The Clients

Previous research

The sex industry could not exist without a substantial demand for its services. Consideration of customers' needs and motives is essential to a proper understanding of the rent scene in its wider social context. Knowledge of the clients of female prostitutes is scanty and often speculative, but information about the customers of rent boys is even more meagre. Gibbens and Silberman (1960) reported some observations from a sample of clients of female prostitutes taken from men attending a sexually transmitted diseases clinic. They identified several types. There were many young men beginning sexual experimentation. Others were inhibited and sometimes mother-bound characters who had difficulty forming heterosexual relationships. Some were aggressively promiscuous, alternating between prostitutes and casual affairs. Members of roaming occupations (travellers, sailors, etc.) and men away on business were also much in evidence.

More recent research in Birmingham (Kinnell, 1989), in which both female prostitutes and professional outreach workers interviewed clients, found that the vast majority were residents of the town or surrounding areas, tourists and travellers being the exception. Over half were without a current marital partner. Very few required unusual sexual acts and there was hardly any anal sex. In 70 to 80 per cent of encounters vaginal sex occurred and condoms were used successfully in 85 to 90 per cent of such occasions. The commonly stated reasons for paying a prostitute were a desire for sex without emotional commitment, insufficient sex otherwise and a wish for oral sex not obtainable elsewhere. Based on the men's frequency of visits and the number of different clients serviced by the women it was estimated that something like a tenth to a fifth of the local male population used prostitutes, many of them doing so regularly over a period of years. The researchers concluded that 'prostitution has an entrenched place in the sexuality of our society'.

One might expect the demand for commercial sex to feature even more widely in male homosexual society, given the legal and social impediments to sexual relationships between men and the fact that, homosexual activity being a minority interest, potential partners are fewer. A counter argument suggests that there are so many patrons of gay bars and discos on the look-out for a companion for the night that the need to pay should not arise. This reasoning overlooks the facts that such venues are plentiful only in the centre of large conurbations, that they do not appeal to the more closeted gays and that they serve mainly younger people.

Child sex abuse has been blamed for producing clients as well as prostitutes. Lew (1988, p. 187) believes that victims are put off sexual relationships and tend to confine themselves to the purely physical activities provided by prostitutes, massage parlours and lavatory sex. Without invoking child abuse, however, it is not unlikely that clients of male prostitutes bear a resemblance to men who haunt public toilets for anonymous sexual activity. From what is known of men caught in such situations and brought before magistrates on charges of importuning or indecency it appears that many are married and many are men of respectable social status who have hitherto been able to conceal their sexual propensities from their colleagues in business or the professions. Similar observations were reported by Humphreys (1970). He tracked down a sample of men seen using a public toilet in a park in St Louis for sexual purposes. A majority (54 per cent) were married and living with their wives. Some of these, whose marital sexual relations were unsatisfying or non-existent, were basically homosexual, but others were bisexual, valuing their healthy-looking marriages, but enjoying homosexual experiences 'on the side'. Among the never-married gay men (38 per cent), some were 'closeted' gays, fearful of their employers, colleagues or families finding out about their sexuality; others were 'open', mixing freely in gay circles and using the lavatory scene with sophisticated discretion as an additional opportunity for promiscuous sex. The majority of users, however, were men who, by virtue of their social or marital situations, were attracted to the brevity and anonymity of lavatory sex. One man summed it up neatly (op. cit., p. 154). He used the toilet 'for sex – not friendship'. Being committed to wife and children he had no 'time, energy or money to invest in anyone else'.

Another factor was age. The median age of the Humphreys sample was thirty-four, and of course some were considerably older with presumably decreasing opportunity to secure new partners otherwise. Humphreys believed that the risk of arrest for sexual behaviour in public acted as an aphrodisiac. 'Some of the older men said they were no longer able to reach orgasm outside the excitement of [lavatory] encounters' (op. cit., p. 151). An obvious overlap between this population and the clients of prostitutes was illustrated by one of the men Humphreys interviewed, a socially isolated, closeted gay who used both outlets (op. cit., p. 128). He used the toilet facility in question because it was near to his place of work but he preferred to go to places frequented by rent boys. 'I just want to love every one of those kids', he said. He was later murdered by one of his teenage pick-ups. Rechy (1977, p. 88) finds pitiful those men who, even though rich and famous, continually fall in love with rent boys who cannot reciprocate.

Brongersma (1990, p. 72), reviewing studies from the European Continent, concludes that most clients are middle-aged men, often fathers of families and in socially advantaged positions, who preserve both their reputations and their psycho-sexual equilibrium by using rent boys. Some do so because they are insufficiently attractive or confident to secure a partner without paying, or because they prefer adolescents. A French example is described by Hennig (1978, p. 265). Aged thirty-nine, he had patronised rent boys since he was twenty-five. Feeling ugly and pot-bellied and having lost his hair early, he found it hard to obtain unpaid sex. He cruised toilets and stations, knowing there were tricksters out to mug or to steal papers for blackmail. He believed that rent boys did get sex pleasure as well as money. He met most only once, but liked repeat sessions when those who had at first refused might agree to anal sex so long as their mates didn't hear about it. This man's attitude, typical of many clients, is summed up by an older gay character in a recent witty novel about the contemporary London rent scene who exclaims 'How else am I going to get the company of handsome young men!' (Beadle, 1990, p. 81).

Observers have remarked upon the power games played out between client and rent boy (McMullen, 1987, Cates, 1989). John Wayne Gacy, serial sex murderer of 35 boys and young men in Chicago, is quoted as looking upon rent boys as 'greedy little bastards', 'little shitheads with sick minds' who have to be outsmarted in a game of wits in situations where jack rollers will perform if they have to but run if they can get the money first (Cahill, 1986, pp. 113, 153). Some of our interviewees resented the power of the client's money to force compliance. Equally, some clients resent being held to ransom by the power of the rent boy's sexuality. A small sample of 20 clients were interviewed in California by Caukins and Coombs (1976). Most were middle-aged and physically unattractive. Their sometimes brash or sarcastic manner concealed resentment at not being desired for themselves and being forced to pay for impersonal sex. One rich but lonely man, with no hobbies and few social skills, regarded the rent boys he had to use as 'dregs and opportunistic pigs'. He liked to choose two of the more arrogantly masculine types and pay them enough to make them swallow their pride and perform together while he watched and called them names. Most clients' favourite fantasy, however, was of having sex with a super-masculine sex object. A domineering hustler could often obtain satisfying confirmation of his self-image as a masculine stud while pandering to the client's illusion. The handing over of money helped the hustler to disavow emotional or erotic involvement, sanctioned taboo activities, protected the client from the pain of rejection and softened the guilt attendant upon the exploitation of vulnerabilities. Guilt was lessened further for the client if he resolved not to employ the same rent boy a second time, much like the man who indulges the luxury of confessing things to a stranger on a train because he knows they will never meet again. The authors cited one young man who literally begged a rent boy for sadistic servicing and then, as soon as he achieved climax, warned the boy never to speak to him should they meet up on the street.

Many clients demand anal intercourse when they find a willing rent boy. As in the present research, a pilot survey in Glasgow (Bloor *et al.*, 1990), found that only a minority of street working rent boys said they would agree to anal intercourse, but every one of eighteen clients questioned said they had had anal sex with a rent boy in the previous twelve months. The fact that some workers are sometimes willing to agree means that anal intercourse can occur quite often. The fourteen clients in the Bloor study who gave frequency estimates reported a total of 141 instances of anal insertion over the year with a condom used in only 60 cases. Evidence of even more reckless behaviour was found by Morse *et al.* (1991) who studied 211 male street prostitutes in New Orleans together with fifteen clients. Reports from sex workers and clients corresponded fairly well. The clients said they liked having sex without the complications of continuing emotional involvement. They agreed that drinking together or sharing drugs was a quite common feature of the sexual transaction. All fifteen demanded oral sex and a majority wanted anal sex. They never used a condom for sex with a regular partner and only rarely when with a prostitute. In fact ten of them said they would seek another prostitute if condom use was made a condition. Whereas the prostitutes had judged two-thirds of their clients to be homosexual, most of the clients questioned said they had regular sex contacts with women.

Doubtless these depressing reports of selfish client behaviour are true for some, but certainly not for all. As has already been shown in this research, transactions between punter and rent boy can include respect and affection and do sometimes develop into long-term friendships largely independent of sexual considerations. Richie McMullen (1990b, p. 47) has put it rather well: 'Some regular punters become close friends with certain rent boys and despite the misconception that all punters are bad apples, I have seen them often take great care of a boy, clothing him, finding him work, helping him with his education and so on. It is too convenient a social notion to think of all punters as bad. Without many of them, God knows what would happen to some boys.'

The potential benefits to the socially or emotionally deprived of having a stable relationship with an older patron who provides moral and material support can outweigh the disadvantages of a sexual commitment. Paradoxically, boys who begin to sell sexual services to paedophiles when they are very young may obtain greater secondary benefit than older rent boys because they are still of an age when the learning of social skills and the development of good personal relationships comes relatively easily. Drew and Drake (1969, p. 157), describing the effects of having been prostitutes as young boys, report that many 'feel eternally grateful for the "lift in life"' gained from contacts that opened horizons that they had never dreamed of and provided money that enabled them to extend their education and ultimately obtain rewarding jobs, 'often helped in this by their men friends of the past'.

Claims about the benefits derived from clients are suspect, being often linked to arguments favouring permissiveness towards sexual contacts between adults and pre-pubertal children and challenging the belief that such contacts are generally harmful (O'Carroll, 1980). It can hardly be denied, however, that some adult men, both heterosexuals and homosexuals, who have had an affectionate and sexualised relationship with a paedophile when they were boys, look back on the experience positively and feel continuing gratitude towards the man who helped their emotional and social development. The homosexual paedophile Clarence Osborne kept an intimate diary of a lifetime of relationships with hundreds of boys, none of whom ever complained to parents or police. After his death a sociologist contacted twelve of his former friends and all spoke of him warmly and with respect. Heterosexual development had seemingly not been impeded (Wilson, 1981, p. 46). Brongersma (1990, pp. 67, 312), in his mammoth work *Loving Boys*, cites similar examples, both contemporary and historical. He even quotes instances in which uncontrollable runaway and delinquent boys have been weaned away from their antisocial ways through being placed with or forming an attachment to a well-intentioned paedophile. As evidence that such relationships can have an educative value, both morally and intellectually, the example of Ancient Greece, where close attachments between youths and older male patrons received some cultural support, is often quoted (Eglinton, 1964; Dover, 1978, p. 91; Davidson, 1970).

Older youths, especially if they have had years of immersion in the culture of the streets, are likely to resist the efforts of middle-class patrons to bring them into line with their own values and attitudes. The example described in the classic German novel *Der Puppenjunge* (MacKay, 1985) has alreay been cited (see p. 94). As some experiences at Streetwise Youth have shown, it is a difficult task to try to help youths with personalities already formed in a distrustful, egocentric mould. One is reminded of the determined efforts of the criminologist Clifford Shaw to help Stanley the 'jack-roller' (robber of drunks and of gays lured with the promise of sex). Shaw found him an understanding foster-home and, although Stanley was choosy about the work he was prepared to do, Shaw provided him numerous jobs, most of which he quit in a week or two. Shaw helped him further when he got married and was making some effort to settle down, but both this and a subsequent marriage broke down. In his seventies Stanley was still struggling against a tendency to uncontrolled anger at minor slights (Snodgrass *et al.*, 1982).

Information from sex workers

The research included very few interviews with punters and only limited impressions of their clients were obtained from the sex workers, but the information is presented for what it is worth. The street working rent boys were often very critical, agency workers and self-employed masseurs rather less so, but most were agreed that there were good and bad among punters.

The men we interviewed were, almost without exception, post-pubertal when they first began selling sex. Some described consensual sex contacts with adults which they had had as children. One man, *Case 208*, had had a continuing loving relationship, but the fact of their being in the sample meant that they had not been thereby diverted from prostitution. Most of the descriptions of early sexual experiences with adults that were obtained through direct questioning were, as noted earlier (see pp. 35-49), unpleasant encounters with sexual molesters when still under fourteen.

None had been extricated from their bad situations in boyhood by paedophile lovers, but we have already seen described how some of the older men interviewed, who had once been street workers, had received considerable material and emotional support from punters over the years, without any great beneficial effect on their way of life. *Case 202*, in spite of having been helped over many years with money to pay his fines, secure him accommodation and boost his wages during times when he was working, remained, at forty-seven, apparently permanently unemployed. *Case 203* had had a job arranged for him many years before by his regular punter, a well-off married businessman, but he failed to turn up and 'disappeared' without explanation. This would-be benefactor was seen in the course of this research, shortly before his death from cancer. He was still expressing concern about his former protégé – evidence, one might think, of care beyond the call of lust. The existence of such well-meaning individuals demonstrates the strength and duration of the attachment to a rent boy that some punters develop. To divert into a more regular way of life sensation-seeking individuals who have long been used to acting on impulse without thought for long-term consequences is often beyond the power of well-meaning sugar daddies. At the time help is on hand boys are often unready to settle down. One of the Streetwise sample, *Case 027*, aged eighteen, had a well-off sugar daddy who took a real interest in his welfare 'not like these blokes that when they see you they only like you for your body. This bloke doesn't bother if I don't go to bed with him for months.' He spoke of approaching this man to help him out get started in a business. When seen again over a year later this idea had been forgotten and he said he was too young to think about getting legitimate work: 'If you want to go out to work you should do it when you are thirty or forty.'

Punters who became regular clients and struck up friendly relations did appear sometimes to have a moderating influence on the rent boys' prostitution activity. *Case 006* said he had finished with prostitution except for one client. 'He is my friend who is into S & M. I've been a regular with him for a year. I know him as a friend now. It's not the money side of it, it's more friendship.' *Case 016*, a heterosexual who disliked the gay scene, was pleased he did not have to go with different punters very often because, since he was fifteen (he was now seventeen) he had had a sugar daddy from whom he got money without him having to perform sexually. The man enjoyed going clubbing with him and got his kicks from being beaten.

Clients of male prostitutes are popularly thought to be selfish exploiters of vulnerable youths, misusing their money to have their lustful whims satisfied, then discarding the young man who has served them as if he were some sullied and disposable object rather than a person whose feelings and welfare should be respected. It has been shown that this is by no means always the case, but still there were many among the street workers who had little good to say about most punters.

Case 017 thought the rent scene and the people in it 'low and degenerate, more so the punters than the rent boys'. His views were based on religious precepts rather than actual experience. Mixed feelings were more typical. *Case 007* thought: 'They're sick people, half of them, with what they want to do.' He had told one man, 'If I was starved I wouldn't go with you.' Yet he described how he enjoyed being taken out to dinner by wealthy American clients, mostly theatre people. *Case 203* was more reflective:

I categorise punters in three ways. One is the lonely and normally married chap who has no other method, being bisexual, no other method of picking up, or doesn't know the situation of how to pick up. Two is the foreign visitor who finds it more convenient. He gets it through his gay guide and knows what pub to go to to pick up, and it's more convenient for him just to pay a few pounds for a pick-up. The third one is what I call the professional punter, as there are professional hustlers. The professional punter, as far as I am concerned, is carrion. He just preys on boys for their cheapness. He will get his pound of flesh . . . I always remember one occasion. It was winter and I wasn't living anywhere at this particular time and I had, I think, influenza or some kind of infection. This chap picked me up and he lived in a place in North London. He emphatically stated to me, because I'd said to him that I'm not well etc., and he emphatically stated, 'It's all right, I shall look after you.' He took me back and the next morning, quite early, I think 7 or 8 in the morning, he gave me 10 shillings and told me to go. We had had anal intercourse and he was the active partner. I gave him no reason to be aggressive towards me . . . In my estimation these types of people could not have relationships with anyone for very long, either because they do not wish for them or [because] they are such unlikeable people that you'd have to have a very peculiar partner to find for them to live with.

In the supplementary interviews with Streetwise attenders not in the main sample comments about their punters were much the same: some favourable but most derisive. *Case 54*: 'Some of them will take you to shops and buy you clothes and put you up in hotel rooms. Some of them are really good, give you a helluva lot of money as well . . . [but] I don't enjoy it really – I don't know them – most of them are very ugly.' *Case 55*: 'Some of the geezers are genuinely nice guys and I like to talk to them sometimes 'cos some of them have interesting things to say [only] there are very few of those to tell the truth.' *Case 56*: 'Punters are sick . . . the police are cunts.' *Case 58*: 'He says, "I want you to come to America." He's a right genuine geezer, he says, "I'll pay for your flight and like your visa and everything." I said, "It's a bit difficult at the moment", 'cos like at the time I was jumping bail so I couldn't get a visa.' *Case 52*: 'The person doesn't matter to me. When I go to bed with them they're not a person, just a walking wallet . . . As soon as I get my money I'm away.' *Case 51*: 'I think punters are just dirty old perverts, all of them, just dirty old men paying for sex. I hate it when I see somebody really young, like a sixteen-year-old rent boy, getting into a car with an old man.' *Case 61*: 'I make them feel as if I'm their boyfriend and then, when I get out, I say, "Fuck him" sort of thing.'

Many of the complaints about punters, such as their unattractiveness, the fact that 'they were all old men' (*Case 001*) or their peculiar sexual interests were not so much criticisms of their behaviour as resentment at the situation in which money is expected to compensate for unpleasurable sexual contact. Nevertheless, clients obviously varied in the coarseness or delicacy of their approach and the extent that they showed consideration for the rent boy's feelings. *Case 025* was more or less typical of the majority of gay orientated street workers in saying, 'I enjoyed it with the ones I liked and with others it was just ordinary sex, and that was it, just for the money . . . There was a few really nice people who don't give you any hassle.' With them he would 'talk a little bit, just take a bit longer time, enjoy it while you can'. *Case 048* said the typical punter was 'fat, horrible and old' but 'I've got one now that I enjoy going with . . . He's like a friend, but he realises that he is still a punter, but he is a nice guy and he likes talking [and] I actually like talking to the guy.' *Case 036*, aged twenty-three, one of the older members of the Streetwise sample, had lost his initially good impression of punters: 'When I was younger I was a bit naive, so I honestly thought these people really liked me, you know, and I needed a bit of affection.' A few street workers were exceptional in having a more generally favourable impression of their customers. *Case 026* said he was not choosy about punters, but he had had no bad experiences and he 'quite enjoyed' the sex because 'they are so nice'. Later, when he was working in a massage parlour, he again found his clients agreeable, but explained that he sometimes got very aroused with the customers but he was nervous about having full sex with them because he did not feel securely private with people walking about outside the door.

Spontaneous expressions of appreciation were more commonly made about clients of agencies and private masseurs. *Case 513*, a seventeen-year-old, pretending to be eighteen and on the books of an expensive escort agency, said of the clients he visited, 'I normally stay the night, because I normally get on really well with them. We just get [to be] friends and that, so I normally stay the night.' Sometimes he arranged to meet them again apart from the agency appointments, but 'secretly, because if the agency find out they will sack me . . . I ring them up if I want them to take me out for a meal or something . . . I have got about six like that. I don't really class them as clients any more, they are more like good friends who help me out. After a bit you get to know them well and I class them as friends more than anything, but I still take money off them.' The money is usually for sex and you charge your own rates for that. The clients have to pay 'a hell of a lot' for the escort service, but 'with these clients money never seems to be any object to them. I mean they always seem to live in really, really nice areas of London in really nice flats and everything, so they have got to be really well off . . . They all say they have not been married, but I have spotted a few wedding rings that have been on their fingers which they have forgotten to take off.'

A different impression of the social position of clients was reported by *Case 103*, a middle-aged man advertising massage at £20 in the gay press. 'I find that most guys charge very high rates for the service they do, and I don't particularly agree with it . . . I advertise in the gay press so the majority of them would be openly gay, but they don't want to broadcast it because of their jobs and society . . . Generally they are sort of hardworking types with sort of lower income, middle income. I don't get calls from professional people for some reason . . . I go to a lot of guys' homes in the West End which are very nicely appointed, but generally they are hardworking types that have come up, sort of self made.'

Case 107 had some interesting ideas as to why gay men needed to pay for sexual servicing. 'On the whole [clients] are nice and have good reasons for paying for sex, like they may not want to use the gay scene, they may be older, it can be harder for them to cruise all night in a bar or whatever . . . Gay people have less guilt about sex, they don't mind casual sex and it's not such a big deal whether they cruise for it or pay for it. It's less stigma, it's just one option for them, particularly when London closes down . . . They tend to be between thirty and forty, which I don't think of as old . . . When I work from home over the phone it costs them less [than through an agency], but they have to be able to afford it, so they have jobs.'

But some have to save up and they are not all middle-class at all. But most have a decent job and it's recreation for them.'

Comments about some clients' need for companionship as much as sex were quite frequent. *Case 511*, describing escort clients, said the agency 'used to call me the Samaritan. They used to say I shouldn't spend all this time talking to them. I just didn't want to rush in and rush out because I did feel sorry for them ... [I liked them] as people, not as lovers or anything. They were just nice people, but shy. A lot of people ask if they are closets, but they didn't strike me as being that, they just seemed to be very, very shy. At that time there wasn't so much of these chat lines that you can phone up now ... Most of them were just [unmarried] gay men that lived on their own. They really wanted to know about you and not really to talk much about themselves. They was interested in you, I think just as someone different to learn about. Also you're gay and they can relate to what you're telling them.' *Case 116*, who had run for a brief period a very up-market sex business and had been able to reject clients he found unattractive, remarked, 'I would like to think that most of my clients regarded me as a friend as well. Some of the things we talked about I wouldn't talk to people about unless they were my friends.'

Such comments echo the sentiments of the gay rent boy interviewed by Allegra Taylor (1991, p. 111), who felt sorry for his clients when thinking about their loneliness and the lies they had to tell, and who often came away pleased at having made someone happy.

Customer experience

Among the former street workers interviewed were several who had become punters themselves and might therefore be expected to provide different insights into the motives and relationships involved and to be more sensitive to the sex workers' feelings.

Case 216, the fifty-three-year-old former street worker who was married and running his own business, recalled that for a couple of years when he was on his own and aged thirty-eight to nine he would occasionally patronise a rent boy. When wanting sex he would go to the same traditional gay bars that he used to frequent to pick up clients and if he did not find a companion he would take home a rent boy. He would stand outside the bar at closing time and one or other would come up and talk or he would start a conversation himself. They usually had some reason to give for needing money. He felt quite good about these contacts 'because the feedback I got from the boys was that it was brilliant because they made love and then they went to sleep and that was it. They said that normally they never got left alone all night long, guys just want so much for their money. I just didn't do that. I just had one decent session and that was it. I fed them too. One has a sense of decency towards the guy you know. They are really nice little guys.' This man's positive feelings to the boys were unsurprising considering his declared attitude towards rent boy activity in his own earlier years. 'I just thought it was the easiest way to supplement my income, to be honest . . . I think that an enormous amount of friends and guys that I knew in gay life were doing the same thing.'

Another former street worker, *Case 211*, aged thirty-seven and living on a disability allowance on account of epilepsy, was in no position to provide rent boys with much money. He was an inveterate drinker and spent most of his time in a bar in the West of London (since closed by the police) where he was contacted for interview. It was well known as a haunt of drug users and rent boys and he fraternised with the latter freely. He had his own little flat where he could take back young men who had nowhere to sleep for the night. 'I give them a bed and let them stay – why I get on with a lot of them I suppose.' They would sometimes ask for money as well 'and I'm soft enough to give it them'. He agreed that over the years quite a few of the rent boys in the neighbourhood 'I've got to know personally. Round the corner . . . I know that family quite well. The son is on the rent scene.' He'd only been ripped off twice 'out of years and hundreds [of boys]'. The last time was three years ago – 'TV and video gone, while I was asleep actually. Both times I'd had a few drinks.' He was generally sympathetic to the boys, thought they were having a hard time, and that many gay bars were nasty to them 'but the landlord there now is very good. He understands the scene and he doesn't stop boys coming in.' He was wary, however, of some of them who 'are not gay. They are in it just for the money and they go out for a drink with you. I know some of them that go in [the bar] there do it. You go home with them and they wait till you are flat out with the drink and whoosh they are away . . . I can spot them a mile off, I can now, through experience.' He thought it bad that anyone who was not gay should be a rent boy. It was obvious that this was a punter from whom the rent boys had nothing to fear even if they had not much to gain.

Apart from these former street workers, two elderly middle-class men obtained through personal contacts were interviewed. Both had been regular patrons of the sex industry. (The volunteers who helped with visits to masseurs were not otherwise regular patrons.) Their views were informative and supported the notion that some homosexual customers form complicated relationships with their prostitutes.

Case 302 was seen informally and notes made subsequently of the information given. His experiences of S & M services in Amsterdam are cited elsewhere (see p. 303). He counted himself exclusively gay, having been aware of erotic attraction to males from well before puberty, though it was not until around twenty-one, after finding attempts at sexual relations with girls unarousing, that he came to that conclusion. He had had eroticised friendships with fellow students, with ideas of setting up a marital-type gay relationship, but his romantic ideas were not reciprocated until, nearing thirty, he met a younger lover and they set up home together. In the meantime, while working in London, he had had much casual sex with men encountered at Speakers' Corner, at that time a well known venue for cruising. He had not knowingly encountered any prostitutes at that stage, a meal and a bed usually being sufficient to secure a partner for the night.

His lover proved possessive and jealous and disapproved of his urge to continue picking up men for casual sex. There were many rows about this, but he persisted in the habit secretly, visiting West End bars when his lover was away and bringing young men home. As he had a need to restrict his activities to brief, clandestine meetings, and was anyway no longer youthful, he soon found himself paying men younger than himself who were prostitutes and willing to fit in with his requirements. He tended to seek out the same prostitutes repeatedly and came to look upon them as friends, even trying to persuade his lover to receive some of them in that guise. Apart from the sexual satisfaction, he got a kind of relaxed pleasure from their company and on occasion took one or other of them with him on trips abroad. His behaviour was disapproved of not only by his regular lover, who continually threatened to leave, but by acquaintances who considered he was allowing himself to be sponged upon by unappreciative parasites. He himself was aware that his 'friends' were work shy and materially demanding, but he could not bring himself to sever contact completely. He regretted not being in a position to make any radical alteration in the lives of those he got to know well and he was inclined to blame himself for providing just enough material support to remove the incentive to change. Gradually, after much emotional upheaval, he became sexually cold with his lover, although they remained otherwise bonded together. His visits to pick-up places became rarer and his few regular prostitute friends, now no longer young, drifted away. He began to respond to adverts and visit male masseurs for sexual release. He found them friendly and obliging, but the impersonality of the transactions could not for him fully substitute for the enjoyable times he had had with the rent boys, for some of whom he had felt real fondness.

Over the years he had had encounters with scores of prostitutes and never had any serious disaster (see p. 100). He attributed his avoidance of any worse trouble to the fact that he would not go with anyone whose demeanour suggested ambivalence and that he treated politely those he did go with, took a genuine interest in what they had to say about their situations, always asked them in advance how much they needed 'to make them happy' and never gave them anything less. In his earlier years most of his encounters had ended with anal sex, either active or passive, with no suggestion that a condom was needed. He had had one episode of syphilis contracted anally, but that was from an acquaintance not a prostitute.

Case 301 was a professional man of some distinction, a bachelor in his sixties who had had dealings with male prostitutes over many years, some of whom had become regular callers or even 'close friends' and holiday companions. In spite of having once been engaged to be married he had been exclusively homosexual in habits since his early twenties.

I think it was in 1951, when I had money, that I got into the paying situation, because I met guardsmen then. They used to come to the flat I was temporarily occupying in London and one always paid them £5. Even as late as 1951 they were often in uniform and one used to pick them up in places like Tattersalls in Knightsbridge – which was the principal place one found them, or on the streets. One found them also at Victoria Station. They used to troll and I would follow them around, pick them up and it was £5. 'Put it in my cap Sir' or 'Put it on the chair by the door' would be the kind of thing that was said. Guardsmen were considered fashionable among grand homosexuals because they were always considered to be clean. Gonorrhoea and syphilis were the worries. Guardsmen were always medically inspected, it was supposed, so they were OK. They were also very good fun in bed, but it was a fiver a time. I think they are well paid now, so it doesn't arise much . . .
  I think most of them were, I suppose, to use a very loose and rather silly term, bisexual. Most of them are probably now married men with children. I think most of them were in it for the lark. If I had questioned them I think a lot of them would say, 'Well, it's a wank, isn't it?' . . . Certainly my young guardsmen liked a lark, they liked a bit of fun, physical fun, and if they got five quid for it so much the better. It was not the sort of problem that X [a well known writer] described. He struck me as being the most cynical and wicked of men. I mean he would talk about 'Oh, you should have been in Vienna just after the war, when they were so poor, they would do anything for a cigarette.' When I heard this remark from that man I hated him, it struck me as an appalling attitude, and I have hated him ever since.

Asked why he went in for paid sex rather than having a regular relationship, he explained:

I think if I'd wanted to form or been good at forming permanent relationships I'd have presumably got married in the days when I was still uncertain whether I was heterosexual or homosexual. That's one part of the answer, a very superficial answer. The second thing is, and this is where one does have to speak totally selfishly, these people and their conversation and what they can tell me about their lives do provide to an extraordinary degree a kind of relief for me from my style of life. I find their conversation and their company very endearing and attractive. It gives me something totally outside my normal range of social intercourse and associations. It gives me something new and fresh . . . I can be at a grand dinner party meeting extremely interesting and eminent people, whose conversation is of course fascinating, and one feels privileged to be with them, but my mind wanders to what I might discover later in the [gay pub] if I can get away before closing time. Because that's where I'll find my relief . . . It's a selfish way of relief and escape from the society in which one is normally straight-jacketed. [Sometimes he would just chat without any intention of sex.] If they are going to talk to me and relieve me and relax me in that way, well they deserve something. I mean I have in such circumstances given a boy a tenner and said, 'Here you are lad.' 'What's that for?' 'Well, because I've enjoyed your company.' It's as simple as that.

He explained that although he worried about it, he felt on balance he was helping rather than taking advantage of the youths he patronised.

One of my worries about liaisons of this kind has always been that there must be a certain degree of mutuality. I'm not a sadist. I'm not a domineering person. I've no desire to use or exploit people for my pleasures, whether my physical pleasures or intellectual pleasures or a combination of the two. If I have guilt feelings now, as indeed I do have about some of my associations, it has come to this – Was I pretending that I was being kind to him when in fact I was exploiting him entirely for my own satisfaction? . . . It may sound rather pompous, but you must understand that all this is mixed up with my particular kind of religious feelings and indeed upbringing. I am a Christian and follow, as such, a Person who, as you know, welcomed prostitutes. So [kindnesses] I regard as my moral duty, especially if I've been immoral with them. Obviously these are people who ultimately – although they wouldn't see it like this and their pride would be hurt if they heard me saying anything so patronising – perhaps need someone like me more than I *should* need them.

He had experienced theft only twice, both small articles of value.

I've always appreciated the fact that I have been lucky. I've had no threats, but that has been partly because, if I've ever had anybody alone in my house I've generally been very careful that they have been vetted by this friend I brashly call a procureur who would not allow me to pick up anybody he thought would endanger me in that way . . . Of course the great dread of the lonely older man is the bang on the head and the theft or indeed of the blackmail tactic. I've always had it worked out that if there were any threat of blackmail I'd go straight to the police, take the initiative, but I've never had to.
    [As to criminality:] I'm afraid that a very large number among those I've met – among the casual pick-ups, if we want to categorise them – they've generally done a spell either in a borstal or in some kind of approved school or a prison where, incidentally, I think they have learned a lot about what they are now up to. [In fact he had letters from some of those he knew who were now in prison.] Two of them, they write. In the case of D, he was being visited by a boyfriend of his. I would help this boyfriend, who was not very well off, to make a fortnightly journey to the Isle of Wight to see him. But D's letters were insistent that I should in no circumstances visit him there. The other boy, there was no question of my visiting him, but he would write occasionally because his great plea was that he had nobody, so I did send him occasionally cigarettes and I did send him once a portable radio and occasionally a little cash. With D, when he was in prison, he was an avid reader, so I did send him things like the English translation of *Les Miserables*, a jolly good long read for him.

These last two stories show how male prostitutes help to fill an emotional as well as a sexual void in the lives of some of their clients. In spite of having made many attempts to help their rent boy contacts materially and with friendly advice, neither of these men had had much success in changing the lifestyles of their protégés and both of them, more especially the latter, still felt doubts about whether they had done harm or good. In their many years of contacts with criminal types neither had ever been significantly hurt by any of them. Information was obtained from a third punter, an American, also of mature age and long experience, who likewise recalled no serious trouble beyond petty pilfering (see p. 307). It seems that punters with manifest good intentions towards their rent boys and with some discretion in their selection are at low risk of harm.

*

From the scattered information garnered about the clients of sex workers two points emerged most clearly:

(1) Clients, like sex workers, are of many kinds, they can be from any social class, married or single, selfish or considerate, brash or inhibited, wanting only sexual release or trying to relieve loneliness, wanting ordinary sex or seeking special rituals.

(2) Clients' motivations vary, but many feel a strong need for sexual experience which they cannot or dare not obtain except by contact with a sex worker. So long as a male sex industry exists it will never lack custom.

18

Child Prostitution

Paedophile victims

There were some topics which this survey could not include simply for lack of material. The visible rent boy scene in London is the the domain of adolescent and young adult males. Child prostitution and child sex rings, despite tabloid attention, would appear to account for a very small proportion of the male prostitution scene and were outside the experience of nearly all our informants. It was not unknown for boys of fourteen or even younger to turn up at the Streetwise Day Centre, but legal considerations prevented their being dealt with at the Project or becoming part of a research sample. Two adult callers at the Centre who had relevant experiences to report were interviewed. One was a prospective volunteer who wanted to rescue boy prostitutes. He was not accepted, but he subsequently misrepresented himself as working on behalf of the Project. The other was a sometime street worker who was himself attracted to young boys. Their sharply contrasting approaches gave food for thought.

Case 305. This twenty-three-year-old man presented an emotion-laden story of having been forced into sex and prostitution by the age of twelve by two men who sexually abused him and rented him out to others among a small network of about a dozen men. He got the courage to break away from them when he was sixteen and did not engage in prostitution after that. He found it distressing to talk about his early abusive experiences and gave a somewhat vague account of how he had been forced into collaboration over several years. He was still feeling very bitter about it and although he could not identify them he seemed to be threatening to do something to the two main culprits. 'I just want to see them off the face of this earth, and that's it . . . I should have gone to the police at the time, but you see, where I was brought up, I was taught never to go to the police . . . Now I've got no evidence, so I can't go to the police. I've got to sort it out my way.'

He described an unhappy upbringing. He was about five when his father was released from prison and his parents divorced. He went to live with his father and never saw his own mother again. He was eight when 'all of a sudden we were lumbered with a stepmother that we didn't know.

278

She had kids of her own as well ... It weren't fair on us and we just couldn't handle it.' His father 'had this drink problem and 'cos I was the eldest he had to take it out on somebody, so I decided not to hang about'. From eleven he started running away and staying out nights on end. At thirteen he was placed in a children's home as beyond parental control. He stayed there till sixteen, but he hated the schools he was sent to because he was always being ordered about. He was a frequent absconder and was often caught and brought back. Finally he was expelled. Since leaving school, 'I've had plenty of jobs, but I just can't seem to hold them for some reason.' He would walk out when given orders he didn't like. 'I was employed as a store detective, but she was telling me to hoover the floor, I don't do that, I just freaked out ... I picked up my wages and went.' At the time of the interview he was unemployed and staying with his grandmother, but 'I'm never really there, I'm out most of the time.'

It seems that initially, when he was only eleven or twelve and a runaway, he was pressed into sexual service in return for food, shelter and clothes by two men, one about twenty-two and the other thirty-five. 'I was forced into it, 'cos I told them to stop what they were doing ... It's like a bad memory ... After that they forced me to go with others and everything, like I suppose they were getting money for it ... It was orchestrated by these two ... They were the only two that forced me to do what I didn't want to do ... They never hit me, I'll give them that, they never beat me or nothing ... They used to frighten me with violence, like threaten me, and I believed them ... All the rest, if I didn't want to do something, they just said, "All right, fair enough, we won't do that".' He wouldn't fellate them, but they could fellate him and have anal intercourse. 'All of them insisted on that, you know, otherwise they used to grass on me to the other [two] guys and I'd have to answer to them.' The children's home used to send him out at weekends to stay with his grandmother near King's Cross. She didn't like him hanging round the house and didn't care if he stayed out at night. 'Them two geezers were always around, they always knew where I was hanging out and that, it was just weird. Sometimes I was with them and they wouldn't let me go back [at night].'

He always felt it was somehow his fault and he was doing something wrong, but at sixteen 'I decided then and there, I'm gonna stand up for myself ... He tried it on me again one night and I just said to him, "Enough's enough", but he weren't having it, like, so I just picked up the broom and whacked him over the head and that was it, I was off. I haven't seen them again to this day.' After that 'I went out, see me social worker and she put me into a bed and breakfast. But I went out and I robbed somebody one night, spent a lot of time on remand, got sentenced and by the time I was back on the streets I was getting on for eighteen.'

He was still having sexual problems which he blamed on his abusive experiences. 'I tried a couple of relationships with girls and it don't work and that . . . We was always rowing and everything and splitting up, so I decided just to leave it till I could sort it out properly. So I thought I might have been gay, you know what I mean [after] what happened, so I tried all of that as well but nothing seemed to work. It was like I was aroused and that by them, but as soon as it came to the undressing part I didn't want to know.'

Apart from his obsession with the two abusers ('I know exactly what I'm going to do, I'm just going to get rid of them, that's going to help me out.') he felt his other mission in life was to save other street boys from perverted men, which was why he had approached Streetwise. His history was difficult to establish, given so much emotional overlay, but it was clear that his early exposure to unwanted sex, whether paid or unpaid, reflected his chaotic upbringing. He was encouraged onto the streets and into the company of delinquent gangs by family conflicts and violence and by the assumption of the children's home that he had a satisfactory place to go for weekends. His resistance to authority, at school and later at work, cut him off still further from normal socialising influences. As a rootless street wanderer he fell easy victim to dubious offers of conditional hospitality. He let himself be used by men in return for money that enabled him to get by while on the run.

It is well known that paedophiles, whether individually or in 'rings', behave differently from punters looking for older rent boys. They are at pains to cultivate the acquaintance of boys they meet up with in the ordinary course of work or leisure activities, giving them presents, taking them on trips and gradually insinuating sexual practices. In this instance the abusers were more brash, though they did provide the boy with a refuge of sorts, but their sexual demands could not by any stretch of the imagination have done other than add to his difficulties, particularly in regard to his own sexuality and perhaps to his continuing unsettled emotional state.

Once he was old enough to break free, his aversive experiences put him off any idea of earning money that way again. This runs counter to the commonly held view expressed by one policeman: 'You're not born a rent boy, you're made it because you're corrupted . . . rent boys are at the end of the process, and if you go back into their earlier history you will find, I'm sure, in the majority of cases, tales of abuse' (Redding, 1989).

Victim becomes predator?

It is often suggested that victims of child sex abuse grow up to become abusers themselves. It is true that in early adolescence the young man in the next example had been seduced into committing acts of prostitution with an older male, but the connection, if any, between that and his own sexual interest in boys was unclear. His caring attitude, so unlike that attributed to the abusers in the last example, did not in the least fit the image conjured up by the notion of victim turned predator:

Case 303 was a Canadian, aged twenty-four, working in England and supplementing his income by prostitution, as he had done earlier while in Canada. In spite of much delinquency during his adolescence he had managed to secure some further education and was maintaining independence of state welfare and even hoping to gain entrance to polytechnic courses. He proved an intelligent and fluent informant.

His father, who died when he was fourteen, had been a violent drunkard who failed to support his family who were dependent on welfare. 'He was an animal. He would take all the money and when he was living there he would beat her up and then send her to the beer store. One time it was closed and he made her go around door to door to the neighbours.' 'I wanted to kill myself to shake up my old man, because he didn't really know I existed.' 'He moved out and eventually he died as a skid row sleeping on the street . . . I refused to go to his funeral. I would have killed him if I was big enough.'

By the time he was fifteen he was a tough juvenile delinquent and street prostitute. 'I would wake up at noon and scour the streets looking for anything to steal. We used to rob trucks, we used to wait until factory workers had gone off for lunch and break into their lockers and take their wallets, things like that. If I had a bad day I would eventually make my way down town to get my dick sucked behind some stairway for $10, $20 or $30, depending. I would tell my friends I had robbed this person and as I was a thief as well I could always justify having a large amount of money [but] it was the sex money more often than not.' His mother had always been good to him, but she could not tolerate his way of life. 'I was drinking heavily, I was doing a lot of dope, I was doing acid and coke and a lot of things like that and she just kicked me out.'

He had first got paid for sex as a boy of thirteen. He was one of a small group of boys who got money for doing errands for old people. One man in his sixties used deliberately to leave money and whiskey about for the boys to steal in order to get them a bit tipsy and keep them sitting with him. One time the man suggested he visit on his own so he wouldn't need to share out the money for the errands. At the risk of a fight with his mates for cheating on them, he agreed and so 'it started . . . He just touched me up and stuff. I was half drunk. I just lay back on the bed and let him give me a blow job. I can remember sitting up and seeing his head there and I was going to punch him in the face. And yet I had a hard on and was just about to come. It was weird. I never went back there for a long time.' He did go back eventually. 'This time I just charged him money out and out . . . I said, "I want 5 bucks." You know, being tough, give it me up front and then let him do it, the same thing. Afterwards I had to go home for a bath. I had to. I just felt so awful. Then, within a week I forgot about the awful part and went back and did it again.'

This was the start of a part-time career in prostitution which was still active. In the years following he had some enjoyable heterosexual experiences, but gradually came to realise that males attracted him much more and young adolescent boys in particular. 'I never had sex with a man without money involved until I was probably eighteen . . . I mean, especially at first, it was such a strong, conscious effort on my part, I did not want to admit I was gay at all.' At sixteen he was visiting the streets where rent boys 'flaunt it, dress up in tights and put make-up on. I wouldn't want anything to do with them, especially at that age, because I was still denying it to myself and still saying to myself I am not one of them. I come down here but I don't like the sex that much, I need the money . . . I would stay on the outskirts of the thing, I just wouldn't hang out with any of them.' He appeared to be struggling to come to terms with his sexuality. He still disliked mixing with gays. 'I always thought that I was a unique case and there was something, sometime that was going to change . . . I just cannot see myself as being a gay person. I want to be a family man, I want my own kids and just want to have a normal existence and I don't know if I ever will.'

After leaving his mother at fifteen he went to live with a family where there was a boy some six years younger than himself. They developed an 'incredibly close' relationship and although there was a separate mattress provided they would share the bed together and he would become sexually aroused. 'Sometimes when he was asleep I would feel him up a bit, but because I knew he didn't want to do that I wouldn't risk the friendship and make him think lowly of me, because I was like his hero. I took him everywhere, camping, cycling, I'd see him every single day.' They remained good friends for many years. Some five years later he started another man-boy relationship, this time overtly sexual. 'I met him in a washroom when he was twelve years old. He was letting some absolutely disgusting skid row slut give him a blow job. When I walked in I thought he was being attacked or something. I was going to college at the time and I had my hockey stick with me and I just cracked this guy in the face with it. The kid came out nonchalantly and said, "I was just getting a blow job, what are you doing?" I mean I just freaked right out. This cute little blond kid! I had a continuing sexual relationship with him, at his insistence all the time, because I was starting to feel real guilty for it, obviously. But I thought this is the best thing that ever happened to me. Here's a kid, twelve years old, that loves to have sex. Perfect! But I was so guilt-ridden the first couple of times . . . I said, "You don't have to. I'm still going to be your friend if we don't have sex. I'll still help you, give you a bit of money." He said, "No, no, I like the way you give a blow job." He was just like that and he still is.' He preserved intermittent contact and when the youth wanted to leave his unhappy parental home he arranged for him to stay with a 'boy lover' he knew. 'This man now has three different kids that sleep there . . . One is basically the guy's lover for the last couple of years, since he was fourteen.

So it's the kind of place that's good for this kid. He's sort of hanging around with them. And he has his own, basically, lover who's sixteen too. But you know I'm still very close to him, but I don't restrict what he does. I tell him experiment, but just do it in the right way with the right people. He knew all about washrooms and money and the whole bit at the age of twelve, and that was three or four years before I did, and I thought I'd started young.'

He described other relationships with boys. 'I am most definitely interested in young boys, like thirteen to sixteen. If it's sex, like I said, I'd love to, if it works out, but quite often I just know that it can't and I just don't even bother bringing it up. But I've had so many friends and kids that I've helped . . . I've always had this feeling that if I was to be struck dead and there was a Goddamned God there was nothing wrong with what I've done. I still believe that. It's so frustrating to know that you have all this desire to give love to someone and it's just not looked upon, you just can't do it. You have to play games, you have to lie, you have to sneak around, it's terrible.' Speaking of the murder of the rent boy Jason Swift he said, 'I remember that. I swear I got close to being violently ill. When things like that happen it just absolutely kills me . . . From what I gather about the story he had gay feelings as well. Do you know how many men there are out there who would really and truly love a kid like that? If there was at least the ability to be more open about these kinds of things he wouldn't have died.'

He had come to admit that his commercial relationships with older men did sometimes give a certain enjoyment. 'It is a totally different enjoyment from what I would get with a younger person, just a different thing. I kind of like knowing that I turn a guy on that much and then that kind of turns me on too. I don't want to explore his body, you know, but I can enjoy what he does to me   With a younger person I like to lay close, touch, feel, explore, everything.' With his own age group 'it just doesn't work out at all sexually. I just don't have the same strong feeling. When it's an older person and they are really into you it's easier and you don't have to work at it.'

As with other cases, irregular home circumstances as a boy might be blamed for turning him onto the streets and thereby exposing him to a culture in which trading sex for money from older men was familiar practice. His first experience of that kind having been erotically aversive, it seems unlikely that it led to either his homosexuality or his prostitution, and his sexual interest in boys seems to have developed quite independently of prostitution activity. His attraction to young boys, though highly eroticised, was paternalistic. Unlike the more predatory types of paedophile, he considered sex with boys a possibility only when they also wanted it. The distinction between young boys who consciously want sex and others who do not reflects a reality that has emerged from other surveys (West and Woodhouse, 1990, p. 118). He was revolted by the idea of men using boys for brief sex and then losing interest. If any moral can be drawn from the story it is that the over-simple notion that a boy's encounters with an elderly paedophile *cause* him to become a prostitute and adult molester needs to be challenged. Real life is far more complicated.

19

Legal Control

Private morals and public policy

In many countries outside Europe, including some half of the American States, sexual contact between males is a criminal offence. Although it has not been illegal in England since 1967, provided it is in private and between two persons who must both be over twenty-one, it is still disapproved of by large sections of the populace, regularly criticised in the tabloid press and resolutely condemned by the Jewish, Christian and Islamic religions. Prostitution by either males or females is also an offence in many countries, but again this is not so in Britain, although its practice is hedged about by ancillary laws. The offences of 'male importuning' (applied to homosexual propositioning in public places), 'procuring' (securing a sexual partner, paid or unpaid, for a third party) and 'living on immoral earnings' (applied to any material benefit derived from another person's prostitution) or allowing premises to be used by prostitutes are all punishable by imprisonment – although fines are more common nowadays. Where either one or both parties to a male homosexual transaction, paid or unpaid, are under twenty-one, or if the behaviour occurs in a place accessible to the public, they are liable to imprisonment for two years for 'indecency'. If a man over twenty-one commits buggery with a consenting young man over sixteen but under twenty-one he is liable to go to prison for five years. Should a homosexual transaction involve a willing boy under sixteen the offence counts as an 'assault' punishable by ten years imprisonment or by life imprisonment if buggery occurs (Howard League, 1985, p.182). Employers or managers at escort agencies and massage parlours lay themselves open to charges for brothel keeping, profiting from the earnings of prostitution and procuration, all imprisonable offences. Masseurs offering 'duos' (two sex workers plus the client) contravene a provision of the Sex Offences Act 1967 which makes homosexual acts in the presence of a third party an imprisonable crime. Section 31 of the Criminal Justice Act 1991 includes most imprisonable homosexual offences among those for which sentences may be passed (not exceeding the statutory maximum) commensurate with the seriousness of the offence, or the combination of the offence and other offences associated with it or, in the case of Crown Courts, for such longer term as in the opinion of the court is necessary to protect the public from serious harm from the offender. Many sex workers are prepared to oblige sado-masochists, but in English law one cannot give consent to sexually motivated physical assault. This law has been used recently against fifteen men who took part in consensual and unpaid S & M bondage, beatings and master/slave games. They included an international lawyer and others of considerable social status, and substantial prison sentences were imposed. The prosecution made use of videos of some of the activities, seized by the obscene publications unit of Scotland Yard, showing piercing and torture. The judge commented that 'courts must draw the line between what is acceptable in a civilised society and what is not' (*The Times*, 1990).

With severe penalties applicable to client, customer and organiser in many male prostitution transactions, the trade continues only because the forbidden acts take place in private and are relatively rarely detected and prosecuted and when they are they do not normally receive anywhere near the maximum sentence. This state of affairs is hardly satisfactory. The relatively low level of detection and enforcement suggests that the law is impractical and permits the minority who are prosecuted to feel unjustly persecuted. A substantial body of opinion regards consensual sexual transactions, for payment or otherwise, as 'not the law's business', unless they involve a minor who cannot give fully informed consent (a reasonable presumption, perhaps, in the case of a boy under sixteen, but not so in the case of young men of seventeen to twenty). In a pluralist society ideas of right and wrong vary and many would consider acts of prostitution a matter for the individual conscience that should not be made criminal in the absence of obvious harm or abuse. Criminalisation of those who use or provide services for which there is a substantial demand is not always an efficient method of regulation. It tends to operate unevenly, encourage ancillary offences and promote more serious problems than the abuses it is trying to suppress. This can be seen in the history of legislation in different countries on abortion, gambling, alcohol, contraception and female prostitution. Consideration of how the law operates at the present points to the direction law reform might take.

The process of law enforcement is often a struggle between the detective powers of the police and the concealment and avoidance techniques of the law breakers. In the context of policing morality the vigour with which the law is applied varies according to the police directives currently operating in the local force and the public visibilty of the behaviour in question. If activity occurs so discreetly that nobody is offended or complains the police may leave it alone. Where public opinion is divided on the value of moral laws police are liable to criticism both for enforcing and for failing to enforce. On the ground, the style of enforcement can be affected by the moral attitudes of individual officers.

Street workers and the police

The incidence of convictions for importuning and other prostitution related offences among the Streetwise sample, the reported circumstances of some of the charges and the resulting sentences have already been described (see pp. 124-7). Further information about street workers' interactions with police were obtained from eleven attenders at the Streetwise Day Centre, none of them part of the main research sample of 50, who were interviewed in a less structured way that allowed us to probe more deeply into this and certain other topics. Their attitudes displayed a pervasive hatred of police, sometimes based on contacts in connection with offences unrelated to prostitution. Their most vociferous complaints, however, arose from a perception of police as antagonistic and prejudiced and prepared to misuse their powers to harass gay men. Their accounts of the techniques they used, with varying degrees of success, for trying to avoid arrest while soliciting throws some light on the otherwise puzzling phenomenon of a substantial trade being pursued in public places without it being immediately obvious to the uninitiated.

Several men said they had never been caught for soliciting and put this down to caution in making contact with punters unobtrusively.

Case 55 let punters make the first move. 'In the West End I'll never approach anybody. I'd expect them to approach me, 'cos there's more people up there that aren't what you think they are . . . [but] if they've got the gall to approach me, then generally they are a punter. I let them ask a few questions and then you can usually tell what they are and who they are.'

Case 51 was another who succeeded in evading the police. 'Only once have they ever stopped me and that was in Birmingham years ago. I was just cruising, looking for a punter, and this policeman came up and said to me, "Do you know what this street's used for?" I turned round and said, "It's used for walking on." He couldn't do anything. I just walked off and that was it.' Although he had been operating in Piccadilly or Victoria Station three or four times a week for eight months he had never been stopped since. Around Piccadilly 'they stop in the car, but they don't come directly out to you, they just sort of cruise up and down past you, because if they get straight out of the car and come and chat to you and the police are watching they know what's going on.' At the station 'It goes on all the time. I work afternoons and nights. I just go round and stand there, opposite the public toilets, because that's where they all come out of and cruise round. You see these old guys walking past you and looking at you and they just give you the eye like, give you a signal to go with them. You talk to them outside, discuss money and what you are going to do, and that's it.' Hassles by the police occur 'Because people make it obvious what they are. The way you stand . . . the way thay act and everything, they walk round really camp. I just stand there acting straight . . . I just

stand there as though I was waiting for a bus or something, just smoking
. . . Some of them, if they see a policeman, they panic. If the policeman
sees them and he knows they're scared or whatever he's going to know
what they're up to. I just act normal. Or if I think they're looking at me
suspiciously I call round and ask them the time.' At the station 'You could
pick one up in half an hour, another time you could be standing three
hours . . . I stay in the same place and police have seen me sitting there or
standing there for hours and never suspected anything. It's because I'm
not known round there . . . I carry it off. It's probably the way I dress as
well, because I dress straight.'

Case 59 said he never been questioned about soliciting. 'The best time
to go down the station is the rush hour during the week, 'cos there's so
many people about and you get the business men who are punters coming
out of the office and they're looking for a bit of fun after a hard day's work.
You just stand about. After you've been doing punters for a while you can
just tell straight away if a guy's a punter or not by the way they're
loitering about and the way they're looking at you . . . Usually if you make
contact with a punter eye to eye a lot of them will walk out of the station
and if you follow about 30 or 40 yards behind them they'll usually go
round the corner and wait and you get them that way. As you walk past
you both say "Hello" and that way the police can't do anything. Because
you are out of the station they just think you've walked off. If they haven't
seen you make eye contact with the bloke, then they can't do anything.'
On the other hand he was a known heroin user and resented how he had
been repeatedly stopped in the street and rudely questioned and searched
in public view.

Case 52 also claimed to have a method of avoiding arrest. 'If a punter
comes towards me I'll look. If he looks I'll sort of smile and wink. Then I'll
wait till he walks ahead and then I'll follow him. Then I'll probably ask
him if he has a light or the time and then I'll always look at his feet . . .
'cos you can tell if they are the Old Bill by the feet. The police, no matter
what they are wearing they will always have shiny shoes. If they are
wearing jeans and tee shirts they will always wear trainers that look
brand new . . . If I don't think he is right I just won't do it. I'll just say I'm
not interested and walk off.'

It is doubtful if this man's behaviour was really so circumspect for he
reported having had five convictions for importuning, seventeen for
highway obstruction and one for gross indecency with a punter in a hotel
lavatory near Piccadilly. 'There was cameras in the hotel and the camera
just spotted us going down there, so they called the police and the police
came in with the plainclothes men . . . I was found there, he came in and
caught us doing it. You know, there was no way I could deny it because it
was on camera.' He had become very well known to the police and had
some unpleasant confrontations. Sometimes his behaviour was deliberately provocative. 'When there's no punters about what I normally do is I

walk along Piccadilly spotting plainclothes police.' He was doing this and pointing out the detectives to the lad with him when 'they got the hump because I had spotted them.' He was followed into a café, accused of importuning and given five minutes to get away. 'Because I've been arrested about five times for importuning the police, now, as soon as they see me know I'm an easy pick for them. They don't have to do the paper work. All the police do is say I'm a well known prostitute.' Once a policeman 'grabbed hold of me, didn't say anything, just got hold of me, so I turned round and went bang . . . The next minute two others jumped on me.' He was roughly handled, handcuffed and thrown into a van. On the way to the station 'they kept on saying "You've got AIDS" and all the rest of it. "Scum of the earth, you're just nothing but a homosexual who one of these days is going to get AIDS and die and we're going to laugh when you do." So they took me back to the police station.' Once there he threw another punch when a policeman snatched his cigarettes and received 21 days for assault. He had just got out of prison where 'you just keep your mouth shut about what you're in there for in case it gets about'. He had avoided any hassle by asking to share a cell with another rent boy he knew who was inside for burglary and wounding.

Instances when the police had behaved with consideration and propriety were recalled by some of the same informants who also alleged that on other occasions they had been the butt of bullying, insults and unjustified arrests. It was the latter experience that usually determined their attitude.

Case 53 remembered an early incident when he was inexperienced and promptly agreed and got into the car of a man who had come up to him and asked him if he was 'looking for business'. It proved to be a plainclothes policeman who questioned him politely about why he was prostituting and whether he was on drugs. He was kept in a cell overnight and released with a warning without being charged. On subsequent arrests, however, he was 'treated like shit'. Once 'this old policeman came into the cell and started calling me a pouf, a fucking whore. an AIDS carrier and all that. I thought he was going to lay into me.' His experiences made him nervous of policemen. Recently he had been on his way to a gay club one evening when he noticed an attractive man across the road eyeing him. He would have liked to make contact, though not for money. However, a policeman walking by noticed, came up behind and grabbed his shoulder. 'He had a grin on his face, I think he was a bit understanding, and he goes "You fucking pouf you should not do it out in the open, you will get fucking arrested. I will let you off this time." You know, when I looked around at him I actually pissed myself, 'cos I thought they would take me in again.'

Case 58 reported no bad treatment by police, but thought that was because they had found him carrying drugs and thought he was hanging around for that reason rather than renting. 'They hate rent boys, they hate the whole idea of it.' He had once been arrested for importuning, but had insisted at the police station that he had only asked for a light. On that occasion he was treated 'all right, because I'm one of the sort of people that when I'm nicked I'm quiet, I don't say nothing to them. I'm not one of these people that give them all mouth and start fighting with them. I just sit there and just say nothing. It's "No Sir, Three bags full Sir" – that sort of thing.'

Several men described violence and threats by police.

Case 57 was especially bitter. 'They've got photos of most of the rent boys. What they do is CID go along, under cover, and take photos and pretend to be tourists taking photos in Piccadilly, but they're taking photos of us rent boys really . . . The thing is I wasn't doing it that night, I was just walking along the street and they stopped me for it. But the police had been after me for ages. He was fabricating in the court, saying I was talking to men all along Shaftesbury Avenue. They get to know your face around Piccadilly and they're bastards. Once they know your face they'll come after you and pin you for any fucking reason . . . I got nicked for highway obstruction seven times.' He described how police had done 'a swoop job' around Piccaddilly in a van – 'Boys in the back, that's it!' He was thrown on the floor, his arms twisted behind him and called 'queer bastard, little fucking prostitute'. In the police cell 'They put a mattress against you, get the truncheons and go whack with the truncheons so it goes into your stomach and it bloody hurts . . . There was four of them and they were all going at me. I mean they fucked up my inside, but there's nothing I can do to prove it.' He thought some police had been decent. One fancied him and let him go after they had had sex in the cell.

Case 61 alleged both false arrest and threats. 'I was just walking through Piccadilly one day and I went into the hotel for some cigarettes and then a policeman came out and said I was importuning . . . He said he'd seen me talking to people and then he'd overheard me talking. I'd never spoken to anybody.' At the police station they told him they'd seen him around a lot and were going on past experience. 'They said they'd beat me up if I said I was not guilty . . . Who was I to argue, even though I didn't do it there was two to one.' He was convicted and fined £150.

This man also mentioned that it was not only the police that rent boys on railway stations had to fear. There were young small-time gangster types who follow rent boys and punters in order to beat up the punter and take his money or who threaten the rent boys to make them get information about punters for them.

It is apparent from these descriptions, as well as from the opinions of ordinary users of the stations, that the male soliciting activity which takes place there is sufficiently covert not to create an obvious nuisance. The law of importuning, however, has been held to apply without regard to whether anyone is affronted by or even notices the behaviour. The police are required to enforce that law. That some of them should do so in an unsympathetic manner would be unsurprising in view of the condemnatory moral stance taken by many authorities on matters of homosexuality and prostitution, especially where contacts between boys and older men are concerned. The opinions about the police voiced by these interviewees were similar to those given by rent boys contacted by the Streetwise Youth outreach workers. In addition to complaints of harassment by needless name calling in public, they were told of a practice of searching the boys and removing or making derisory comments about their condoms. It was said also that packs of literature and condoms that had been donated by outreach workers could be used in evidence at court that they had been engaged in prostitution. If this occurs it is surely against the public interest; the carrying of condoms by sexually active young men should not be discouraged, whoever their partners may be. Another complaint was about use of the catch-all 'highway obstruction' to clear the streets and make arbitrary arrests.

Action against massage parlours

Massage parlours that allow sex acts on the premises are definitely at risk of police intervention, especially if they break the law in other ways as well, for instance by using under-age workers or by use of drugs. Agency [F] was a case in point, its activities being revealed through the prosecution of the two young men who were running it. They were themselves drug users and former street prostitutes, who recruited others of similar inclinations to work for them. The police investigation was carried out mainly by under-cover officers following the two lads and witnessing alleged acts of pimping around the Piccadilly Circus area. The descriptions come from rent boy witnesses, some of whom worked through the agency. Their accounts must be treated with some reserve, but they convey a fair picture of the nature of this poorly organised and indiscreetly run enterprise, in which partying at weekends took priority over business needs and mounting debts, and boys not yet sixteen were recruited to service the clients.

One of the witnesses had attended the Streetwise Youth Day Centre, but he was not one of the sample interviewed. In his statement to the police he said that it was after a sexual assault by his stepfather that he began thinking he was bisexual. When released from care at the age of sixteen he came to London specifically to work on the rent scene in the West End to earn money to buy his own place. He got to know a lot of other rent boys through meeting them in the Piccadilly Circus area and in the nearby gay bars where most of the renting activity went on. He made the acquaintance of one B.S. who always had lots of money and who had a reputation for doing a lot of punters himself as well as arranging punters for others. He knew that B.S. and C.B. had set up an escort agency in a flat at ————. It was well known among rent boys that punters were being taken there, where they would choose one of the boys present, who would either perform for them at the flat or accompany them elsewhere. Clients could also phone the number of the flat to have boys visit them, bringing drugs if they wanted, cannabis or speed. B.S. and C.B. would take a cut of a third or a half of the boy's earnings. The lowest charge for the service was £50 or £60. Boys given accommodation at the flat would have to pay £10 to £15 per week rent and buy their own food. If they were lazy and not working C.B. would throw them out of the flat. C.B. had told him that they had 20 to 30 boys available for work at the flat at various times during the day and that they could easily make £500 a day through the boys, most of whom were sixteen to seventeen years of age. C.B. also would talk to him quite openly about the boys there and how much money was coming in. He went on to recall instances when C.B. had arranged meetings with punters on behalf of rent boys, one of whom was only fourteen years old.

Another rent boy witness told the police he had started working as a prostitute in the West End at fourteen years of age. When he was sixteen B.S. had begun to introduce him to punters. At the time he looked and claimed to be eighteen. B.S. would tell clients who liked young boys his true age, but for those wanting older boys would say he was eighteen. He went on to describe two meetings arranged by B.S. at which he and B.S. had threesomes with the customers. The first customer produced cannabis for smoking and the second, who was a doctor, furnished, at B.S.'s request, some ether to inhale. The first man gave him £40 and B.S. £100. Later in the year, when both he and B.S. were working for another male escort agency, B.S. showed him a book of matches that had a logo '———— Escorts' written on it, together with a telephone number. Because he now had his own agency B.S. was less often to be seen at the agency where the witness was working. The manager there would not let B.S. near the boys' telephone numbers or see the agency files for fear of competition. Sometime later the witness was with B.S. when the latter went out and bought, at a cost of £700, a mobile hand-held telephone with a range booster, saying it would increase the business of his agency.

A third witness, claiming to be no more than an acquaintance, described how C.B. had introduced him to gay bars and clubs and shown him how the rent boys worked at Piccadilly. Because he was being kicked out of his home he was allowed to come to stay at the flat where C.B. and B.S. were starting up the agency. He did not take part himself, but was party to their discussions, including a plan to advertise with match covers. At first it was just the two of them working, but soon B.S. started going out to get boys from Piccadilly, aged sixteen to eighteen, who stayed off and on at the flat. B.S. wanted him to work the phone, for which he could earn £100 a week, but he declined. He would have had to find out from punters who rang what they wanted and tell them what was on offer, like 'well endowed' or 'skinhead' or 'dirty greaser'. He would hear

B.S. on the phone describing the boys as 'very good looking', 'smooth skinned' or 'he's twenty, but looks much younger', always trying to emphasise that they looked young. As the business increased a lot more boys started staying over at the flat. When either B.S. or C.B. had accepted a phone booking he would ask the boys who wanted to do it, or if there wasn't anyone else B.S. would do it himself.

C.B. didn't go out on jobs but ran the agency and answered the phone and sometimes asked boys staying at the flat for money for their lodgings and keep. On returning from a job boys would give B.S. or C.B. about £20. B.S. was always interested to know what the punter had wanted or whether he wanted the boy again. If boys did not hand over money he would get upset and one boy who failed to hand over money for a week was kicked out of the flat. B.S. and C.B. both seemed always to be in the money and B.S. wore flash clothes, but there was a time when the phone was cut off because the bill was unpaid, though later they got in an answerphone and a cordless phone. Once a punter's cheque bounced and B.S. made a big fuss.

At weekends a man would visit the flat with an eighteen-year-old and bring along a big lump of cannabis. The agency would virtually close down, no one would answer the phone and they would all sit around smoking and watching videos. The witness said he was finally chucked out of the flat because he had told the landlady, when asked for his rent, that he had already paid it to C.B., who had kept it.

Another witness said that when he was sixteen he was sleeping with C.B. at the flat. Other boys living there were working independently as rent boys. Then B.S. moved in and organised them. The witness was taken back into care briefly, but ran away and returned to the flat. He knew the agency was now active there as some of the punters came to the flat. He had also seen adverts for the agency in shop windows and recognised the telephone number. B.S. arranged punters for him. He got £40 or £50 for each punter, but occasionally as much as £100, the sums being arranged by B.S. The work was mostly hand jobs and he used to do maybe two punters a week. He didn't need to do more as C.B. was still partly supporting him, though he paid for his own meals, drinks and fares. He heard of C.B. taking kids of thirteen or fourteen to a punter who would get them to defaecate on his head, for which B.S. would get £20 or £30.

Yet another young runaway who stayed at the flat claimed to have rebuffed B.S.'s attempts to seduce him and to recruit him to the rent boy business. He had heard C.B. arguing with B.S. about the agency being at a flat in his name which was liable to get him into trouble.

Another witness said he hesitated to tell all at first because he was afraid of C.B. and B.S. He had been recruited to work for them by C.B., who said they were fed up with getting arrested at Piccadilly and so had started an agency. B.S. boasted he had £100 punters and showed a book of some 20 or 30 pages of addresses and directions. They also had details of rent boys recorded separately, some of them with photos. The boys were made to sign to say they were over twenty-one. He did about 20 punters for the agency, paying 30 per cent of what he took to B.S. and C.B. The agency charged £35 for anal intercourse during the day and £45 at night. Some of the rent boys were as young as fifteen and B.S. charged more for them. There was a lot of dope smoked in the flat, and one visitor brought cocaine, which they all snorted. Another young rent boy said he had been invited back to the flat by C.B. B.S. tried to get him to hand out the advertising matches to punters and rent boys in the West End, but he thought it too dangerous. Rent boys used to visit or stay at the flat and if they agreed to work for the agency their details were put on cards with their photos. B.S. would sit in a café with his mobile telephone while C.B. ran the flat and got money for rent and drugs. They were never short of cash but were also claiming 'dole'.

A debt recovery official confirmed that large sums were owing for telephone services at the flat, and the owner of the premises confirmed that C.B., who always paid the rent in cash, was three or four months behind when they left.

Whatever might be thought of the merits of better-run sexual services, this agency was evidently one whose irresponsible management and blatant flouting of many laws invited prosecution.

In another case, one that occurred during this research, the owner of a massage parlour was prosecuted after police had kept observation of the comings and goings at the premises from a flat opposite. Approaches were made by under-cover officers posing as clients and finally the premises were raided and the workers there arrested. The investigation provided the court with proof of the basically sexual nature of the service. Early one morning the police took possession of rubbish bags collected from the premises by dustmen, searched through them and located '9 used condoms with what appeared to be faeces attached thereto' and '40 stained tissues some of which also appeared to have traces of faeces thereon and all of which appeared to have semen stains'.

Inspector A booked into a room at a luxury hotel nearby and phoned the number given in a magazine advert and asked the cost of a massage. He was told £40 if he called or £70 if he wanted a visit. He said he had a friend with him and could two men come. He was told that might not be possible, but they would ring back. They did so and said two boys could come at £70 each. He asked, 'What do I get for £70?' and was told, 'It's for a massage. I don't like to discuss anything else on the phone. You can speak to the boys when they come to you, but you won't be disappointed, everything is inclusive.' The Inspector and another officer were both in the room when the boys arrived. One said he was a student and the other said he was working as a chef. They asked for the £70 and said that they kept half and gave half to the agency. Asked what they would do for the

£70 one said, 'We give you a massage and if you want we suck you', and the other said, 'I can fuck you or you can fuck me, whatever you want.' The Inspector expressed concern about AIDS but was told there was no need to worry, they had condoms with them supplied by the agency. At that point a warrant card was produced and both boys were arrested for assisting in the management of a brothel.

Sergeant B, who had been involved for the previous two weeks in surveillance of the premises, called at the address saying a friend had told him where to come for a massage. He was invited in and told the price, £40. He said the lads at his office were paying it for him as a birthday treat, but he hadn't expected it to be so much. Smiling and winking, the manager said 'The cost is inclusive, you understand.' 'You mean hand relief and that?' 'I am not allowed to say, but what you do in there with your masseur you arrange with him.' 'That's fine, but I don't want to pay for hand relief on top of the £40.' 'You don't have to, that's inclusive.' When the sergeant was shown the boys waiting to perform massage he feigned surprise, said he had expected women masseurs and that the guys in the office must have played a joke on him and this was not his scene at all. He then left.

Constable C telephoned for an appointment and was told the price, £40 for a full body massage, and given the address. 'What about extras?' 'I can't talk over the phone about that, what is your name?' On arrival he was told to look through the glass panel into the masseurs' room where two men in their early twenties were sitting on cushions wearing only boxer shorts. He chose one, who duly came out and ushered him into a massage room with dull lighting and soft music and told him, 'Strip off please.' He left his underpants on but was told, 'You can take them off as well.' The masseur rubbed all over his chest and stomach with oil, asking if he liked it, and then went on to the genital area. While doing this the masseur slipped off the boxer shorts and stood naked with an erect penis rubbing against the constable's side while starting to masturbate him. 'I only came here for a massage, I don't want anything else.' 'I'm sorry, I didn't know you were straight. Everyone that comes here comes for the sex.' 'I don't know if I'm straight, I came to see if I was or not.' 'Well you came to the right place to find out.' The masseur then put back on the boxer shorts and continued with a regular massage, chatting casually meantime. The constable learned that the masseur was gay, enjoyed making the clients feel good, received 'a very good wage' and was allowed to keep what he got in tips. The owner did not mind the clients having sex because he got the money for it. When he was in the shower after the massage the curtain was pulled aside and the masseur, again naked, stood there and reached down to grab the constable's penis. 'What are you doing?' 'After the massage you might like to try again.' 'Look, I am not gay, I don't want anything else.' As he was dressing and polite conversation continued the constable agreed, 'I might come back if I want to turn and I will ask for you.' He paid the £40 to the man at reception desk and left, having been in the place an hour.

After the investigation had gone on for almost three weeks police raided the premises and arrested everyone there, on the same day as the two workers who were on an out call to a hotel were arrested by police decoys. Having been told that no action would be taken against them some of the agency employees made statements exonerating themselves but incriminating the owner. One man, aged twenty-three, said he had answered an advert in a gay newspaper, gone for interview at the agency, been shown some massage techniques, and started work a couple of days later, charging £40, giving the owner £20 and keeping £20 for himself, plus any tips. He had been asked for sex by some of the clients but had refused. Another man, who said he had worked there for just a week, gave similar details, but said that only one of the six clients he had serviced had asked for sex, and he had refused. Some of the clients had asked for 'poppers' which the owner had supplied.

When the case came to court the owner received a fine of a few hundred pounds, which was only a fraction of the amount the police investigation, involving many days of observation from a rented flat, must have cost. The business continued much as before.

These police findings confirm much of what has already been described regarding the running of sexual service businesses, some of which pay scant regard to any laws. Except for one or two of the best established businesses, most of the agencies appeared to be committing ancillary illegalities, such as tax evasion, employment of foreigners without permits, using unlicensed premises, committing acts of 'procuration' or involving boys under twenty-one. All were operating under threat of adverse publicity. While the research was still under way one of the places where several of our informants worked, which had operated under the guise of a health club and sauna, shut down following an attack by the *News of the World* (7 Oct. 1990). It was alleged that 'Club visitors could hire a young masseur in skimpy shorts for £24 an hour [and] a 20-year-old masseur offered our investigator full sex for a further £50 or milder forms of gay sex for £30 in the privacy of a massage cubicle'. The local authority began an investigation, but without waiting for the result the club surrendered its licence.

Advertisers' experiences of police intervention

Openly announcing a prostitution service would be illegal, but as has been seen advertisers themselves and editors of the magazines that print their material exercise caution in avoiding explicit sexual terms. Nevertheless, many adverts provide ample reason to suspect they are a cover for a sex trade that may be illegal. Certainly, massage parlours that advertise for callers and provide paid sex on the premises are effectively brothels, and 'keeping a brothel' is an imprisonable offence. Prostitution not being in itself an offence, one might imagine that what happens in the privacy of the masseur's home is of no concern to the law, but it is an imprisonable offence 'for the tenant or occupier of any premises knowingly to permit the whole or part of the premises to be used for the purposes of habitual prostitution.' Like the law on 'immoral earnings' this may render others besides the prostitute punishable. If a masseur should be so incautious as to make the first sexual move towards a new client who is a police plant he would be guilty of indecent assault. Those who advertise with euphemisms such as 'dominance' and 'well equipped leather room', indicating that they cater for sado-masochists and keep the necessary equipment in their homes, incur yet another risk, since the victim's consent is no defence to a charge of assault.

Some practitioners were unperturbed by legal considerations, having never had any problems. On *Visit 118* the masseur mentioned that he had never had any trouble with the police. They knew what he was doing and they had visited him when they were looking for someone. He knew that massage parlours got raided, but he thought that the police tolerated individual masseurs so long as the sex aspect was kept private. He doubted that his neighbours knew what sort of business he carried on. If he had been a woman receiving lots of male callers they would have realised. *Case 104* was of the same opinion. 'Twice I have been contacted by the police and asked to cooperate in murder enquiries. Once I went to the station and once they came here. Both times they indicated that they knew what I did and that they did not want to hassle me about it. I suppose the murdered persons had used masseurs or something. So I have never had any problems with the police and in fact I've never had any legal problems at all. I doubt whether my neighbours have any idea what I do and have certainly never made any comments,' *Case 108* had also been questioned in connection with a murder inquiry: 'Some guy had been hacked to death and he had a *Gay Times* with several masseurs' numbers circled and one of them was mine ... But they were around before that. It was this under-cover cop. As soon as I opened the door I knew he was a cop. He just came in, looked at everything, asked what I did and so on, just gave me £10 for my trouble and left ... It didn't worry me, as far as I was concerned I pay my taxes ... I know [another masseur] had a couple of people who have done the same thing, have come in and looked and asked a couple of questions, given him some money and left.'

Police intervention may be more likely if pornographic materials are being sold. Advertisements sometimes include mention of the availability of videos, but presumambly only to make the session more exciting, not for distribution. *Case 106*, a masseur who was otherwise rather scrupulously legitimate, mentioned having been caught in this way, much to his discomfiture. His attitude to the incident and his interactions with the police could hardly be in greater contrast to the descriptions of their confrontations given by some of the street workers. He had sold some porno tapes to customers and written a letter to one of them. Unknown to him this man was dealing in pornography in a big way and when the police raided his letter was discovered. 'Eight months later they raided me at seven in the morning and it was the most horrendous experience I have ever had in my life. It was awful.' He had a large collection of tapes but they found only seven that were pornographic. Others they did not find he got rid of. A week later he had to go to the police to recover his collection. 'They said they were going to give me a caution. This guy was very pleasant. He said, "Do I need to caution you?" I just said, "No, opening the door to seven of you at seven in the morning was enough." I am a very law abiding citizen and I just hated it . . . I offer a proper massage, I have a proper room as you have seen, not like most of them, so I don't see what they could raid me for.'

Most masseurs felt fairly safe from police intervention, but *Case 116* had the bitter experience of instant loss of his profitable business and lavish lifestyle following a police raid. On release he was in penury, finding himself sick with AIDS and unable to work. He had been unusually reckless, having been 'arrested a few times and pleaded guilty [to importuning] because I'd been caught in the act. If you are caught in the act you've got to go guilty – one of the pitfalls of the business . . . I'd been taken in, but I'd always got bail and turned up at court the next day and paid the fine.' That was before he acquired a luxury flat and a regular private clientele, but even then he continued cruising around Piccadilly because he enjoyed it, with the result that he was yet again arrested for importuning, although on this occasion he successfully challenged the charge.

'I was in the West End wandering around as per usual, just by myself. I noticed that two people were following me and I thought, "I'll get out of here quick!" I just sort of fled and headed down towards where my car was.' A policeman in plain clothes cut him off and he was taken to the station, detained overnight and charged with importuning. 'I hadn't spoken to a single person, but when they got me to the station they said they had been watching for half an hour and I had approached three people. I said that I hadn't approached anybody except girls and boys whom I knew on the streets, and that was the truth.' At court next day he was remanded in custody but on returning after three days 'all charges were dropped. They couldn't prove anything because I had a lawyer who was demanding they produce the people in court who'd been spoken to.'

Eight months later, 'They raided me at home, they busted my flat. I don't know how they got in the building, but the first thing I knew about it the door was flying down. I was in bed with a client . . . They said they had been watching me for about eight months, watching where I went, who I met. When I was being questioned at the station they were giving me dates and times and places where I had been . . . It was obvious I'd been caught and I was prepared to pay the price for it [but] . . . the police wanted me to go on three weeks remand while they accumulated all the evidence together. They wanted it to go to Crown Court and make a show case of it, because they were pissed off because I'd managed to go for so long and accumulate so much wealth and make a business out of doing what I did.' His 'minder', who had resisted the police during the raid, was charged with assault and 'I was charged with running an immoral house'. He gave permission for the police to return and search the flat because he knew there were no drugs there. They found and listed many suits with expensive labels and they costed the flat and its contents, evidence which they used to prove he had an income he could not account for. 'I said I was being given gifts, these were all gifts, but it didn't go down too well. The police asked for a three week remand and the court agreed.' He was kept in isolation because it emerged that during his previous remand he had been tested and found to be HIV positive. In view of this the court did not proceed with the charges. 'The one provision was that if I ever turned up at court again on an immoral charge, whether it be for running an immoral house or importuning or prostitution or anything like that then I'd be charged with attempted murder.' In any event 'when I found out I was HIV positive and spent three weeks in prison thinking about it I knew there was just no way I could carry on working'.

This story suggests readiness on the part of the police to intervene in a home-based 'massage' business when they see fit. The fact that this man was so well known to them as a street worker was probably one reason.

Escort workers out on visits to hotels may not incur much risk of arrest, but they are liable to ejection by security staff. *Case 515* explained, 'From working in advertising and things I had a lot of experience of going in and out of expensive hotels and I never got stopped, but nearly every escort I know gets stopped sometimes, either through not dressing right or not having the right air. To go into the Carlton or a place like that at 3 in the morning you need a certain air – you need to look fairly smart, not necessarily with a tie on, but not just jeans and that – you just walk indignantly straight past the counter or reception, suss out as quickly as possible where the lifts are and head straight for them. But don't stop at the reception and talk, because as soon as you do that most hotels think you are an escort or something and won't let you in. I was very good at just walking in.'

*

The likelihood of police intervention depends less upon the letter of the law than upon the circumstances of the offence. The most vulnerable are the street workers whose activities can be observed without entering private premises and against whom convictions are easily secured.

Self-employed masseurs break the law just as much and are readily traceable through their advertisements, but they are seemingly of little interest to the police. Their activities are less likely to lead to complaints from members of the public and their entrapment by police masquerading as clients for sex could provoke controversy.

20

Foreign Experience

Amsterdam

Numbers of British sex workers gravitate to Amsterdam because it is not far away and male prostitution services are more organised and officially tolerated. The situation there has to be seen in the context of Dutch society, which is noted for its tolerance of minorities and its pragmatic approach to social problems uninhibited by insistence on moral conformity. Both the voluntary and public sector social services in Holland are highly developed and well financed. The country manages to control its crime problems with much less use of imprisonment and much shorter sentences than are customary in the UK. In Amsterdam, the worst excesses of the heroin sub-culture are avoided by the use of a bus circulating at night providing methadone and a needle exchange service to addicts. The consumption of cannabis is tolerated as being relatively harmless, and it can be bought in any of scores of coffee bars displaying as a sign the characteristic leaf of the plant. Child sexual abuse within families is the province of a confidential doctor system whereby problems are resolved through treatment rather than resort to the public prosecutor. On 13 November 1990 the Dutch Lower House passed a law proposal that (except where the perpetrator was in authority over the child) all non-violent sexual contacts with children from twelve up to sixteen should not be prosecuted in the absence of a formal complaint from the young persons themselves or from their parents or guardians or from the Child Protection Committee concerned with sexual abuse within the family. The guides to safe sex produced to combat the spread of HIV infection were for a long time much more explicit and informative for the young than anything commonly available in the UK. Gay bars are numerous and undisguised and no attempt is made to hide the business of the district where female prostitutes sit openly in windows under red lights or to conceal the 'houses for boys' or the shops selling gay pornography. Businesses that sell sex are recognised and licensed under a City Planning Ordinance and workers are subject to health checks, including HIV testing. The 'boy' brothels do not need to pretend to offer massage, they advertise openly in gay guides. Here is one such advertisement:

Founded in 1973, this is Amsterdam's oldest gay male bordello, and upstairs is the other half of the business, the Blue Boy Club, which arranges liaisons with any of the young men present.

This is no seedy back street bar, however, where you must 'knock three times and give a password'! Prostitution is legal in the Netherlands and the Why Not is a public bar where anybody can feel welcome. It is comfortable and warm and you will usually find several young men at the bar. Although they may discreetly open a conversation with you, they will not pester you.

On Thursday, Friday and Saturday evenings there is a striptease show with a cover charge of HFl 25, but at other times you can enjoy a free porno video on the screen above the bar. Those who have already met a friend, or are still looking for a companion, those who would like to visit a cinema, or buy videotapes, will find these attractions upstairs in the Blue Boy Club.

There is a small and very comfortable bar upstairs from the Why Not. In the soft light the young men who are available entertain you, wait and chat. Usually, some of them are English-speaking although, alongside the Europeans there are also blacks and sometimes orientals. Screens in the corners of the bar show pornographic movies while you relax.

There are some youthful looking 18-year-olds here, as well as men in their 20s, and if you meet someone you like you can retire with him to one of the large, clean and attractively-decorated bedrooms, each of which is furnished with a double bed, shower and video. Lubricants and condoms are provided in each bedroom, and your chosen partner will usually expect you, the customer, to wear a condom. The charge for the complete service is usually about HFl 175. Tips are not expected but are naturally appreciated.

S/M partners can also be arranged, along with the use of the adjoining S/M room, or if you are unable to visit the club, a young man can be sent to your hotel (price HFl 200).

The Blue Boy also includes two cinemas, one showing films of teenagers and the other of older men. Entrance to the cinema costs HFl 10 per screen per day and you can return as many times as you like during the day. If you see a video that you paricularly enjoy, then it is probably one of the several hundred tapes that the Blue Boy offers for sale. These include a wide range of American imports, French films from the studios of Cadinot and Tony Dark, and a few films from the orient which are difficult to find elsewhere.

Note that all the tapes are for the European PAL tv system only, and cost about HFl 200-250 each.

The Best Guide Book Service (1990, p. 207) furnishes details of what is on offer at six male brothels which it describes as 'reputable' and 'very aware' of the threat of HIV infection. They 'generally provide special "safe sex" condoms free of charge'.

One of our informants had actually witnessed a striptease show at the establishment whose advert has just been quoted. It was a solo performance on a small stage in front of the cinema screen by a man in his late twenties. He began with the usual slow, ritualistic divesting of clothes, followed by sexual displays and contortions and the insertion of a dildo into the anus. Then he came down into the audience of some fifteen or twenty men, edged his way along each row of seats, presenting his large and still erect penis to each in turn to fondle or suck, before returning to the stage for further masturbation and final ejaculation.

The informant got to talk to the performer afterwards and invited him for a restaurant meal. He turned out to be from a middle-class Roman Catholic family and respectably employed in the post office. He said he was doing the striptease act regularly because it made money – he was buying a house on the proceeds – and because he enjoyed doing it.

As in London, S & M services are also available. One elderly man (*Case 302*, p. 273) gave an account (here summarised from notes) of an experience some six years ago. He had gone to an address listed in an Amsterdam gay guide as having 'S & M possibilities'. It was an ordinary looking coffee bar except for some gay adverts on the walls. A middle-aged lady behind the bar showed no surprise when he mentioned he had got the address from a gay guide, but told him to come back later to see Gunther. When he did so he found that a corner of the room, which he had noticed previously was fenced off with some bars like a prison cage, was now occupied by a naked young man in handcuffs. Customers, both men and women, were chatting together taking no notice, but any casual tourist entering might have got a shock.

He was joined at his table by a leather-jacketed man in his twenties. This was Gunther, a 'master', in the S & M sense, who explained the session would cost £45. He accepted and was escorted to a loft closed off behind him with a trap door. On hooks all round the black painted walls were various objects of restraint or torture – metal rings, clamps, chains, whips, canes, leather straps, spiked collars, handcuffs and so on. Hanging from a roof beam was a chain hoist. There were also a wooden structure with arm holes like the old public stocks in which criminals were immobilised, a hammock-like contraption of leather straps into which the occupant could be fastened, and a kind of stool with a large upright dildo fixed in a position to impale the sitter.

The experiences he underwent on this and subsequent occasions included being held naked in handcuffs dangling from the ceiling while being beaten with a riding switch, being blindfolded and tied up with clamps festooning nipples and genitals, being spreadeagled across a table while hot candle wax was dripped onto delicate parts of the body, being suspended upside down from the hoist, being wound round the body with heavy rope until he looked like a mummy with only the genitals sticking out, being required to fellate the 'master' and finally being masturbated to climax. He recalled that when not giving the brusque orders that were part of the ritual Gunther was polite, friendly and hospitable, offering a drink before and after each session and providing a telephone number for further contact. Gunther obviously took a pride in his work and spoke of the skills involved in assessing clients' needs and providing maximum pleasure. The idea of having a strict time limit, which the owner of the loft wanted to enforce, was most unwelcome. Gunther said he had accumulated a lot of equipment of his own and was planning to open his own establishment independently.

On a later visit he phoned Gunther and was told the loft was no longer available, following a dispute with the owner, but that they could go to a private club with similar equipment. The premises, on the ground floor, consisted of three rooms. The first was a comfortable lounge with a well stocked bar from which Gunther offered drinks. Photographs of women dressed in leather and boots hung on the walls, plainly intended to stimulate S & M fantasy. Gunther explained that the club was used by heterosexual men and women with S & M interests. The second room was essentially similar in arrangement to the loft previously used, but without the ceiling hoist. The third and smallest room looked like a doctor's surgery. It contained a dentist's chair and a couch covered in a white sheet and various tubes and syringes scattered around, presumably for people wanting to play with enemas and the like. The sexual encounter was much the same as before.

Dutch policies of tolerance might be thought to condone any and every excess, but the aim is to contain problems within reasonable limits. When disapproved activities attract harsh legal measures those involved are forced into hiding and become part of an underworld where unregulated abuses escalate. Should trouble occur in a male brothel that is legal there need be no hesitation in calling upon the police for help, which is a far cry from the hole-in-the-corner situations in Britain. Where a business carries on openly, public pressure can be brought to bear to see that it is conducted properly, that employees are not under age and that health checks are encouraged.

Case 52, one of those who had experience working in a male brothel in Amsterdam, explained the advantages as follows: 'The police don't bother you because you carry cards and they say you can go for tests, tests for AIDS and all the rest of it. Over here you have to work on the streets because the clubs get a bit heavy, they don't like too much renting. So I work on the street and it's more dangerous because you get psychopaths and you get the police. In Amsterdam the police know what goes on and they leave you alone as long as you carry this card along with you constantly and it gets stamped to say you've had your check and you haven't got AIDS.' There is safety in working in a brothel 'because you're in a building and there's other people there. If the geezer starts getting nasty there are like alarms in all the rooms and you press the alarm.'

On a visit to Amsterdam the author spent some time in the bar of the Blue Boy Club, bought drinks for one of the young men employed by the brothel and was able to talk with him about his work. He was twenty-one, said he came from the North of England and had done two years of nursing training but had given it up because the pay was so 'lousy'. He was gay himself and on a visit to Amsterdam with a friend he had called in at the Blue Boy where both of them had been offered work. He accepted, though he would never have done such a job in England as he would hate people knowing. He had heard about male escort agencies in England, but he did not like the idea. He had a horror of being caught by the British police. His parents thought he was working in some sort of clinic in Holland. He goes back home to them every three months. He was doing the work out of choice and thought he would continue for another year at the Blue Boy, but not after he got to twenty-three. He disliked the idea of 'older queens' trying to carry on longer and was shocked to be told that some gay masseurs in England were middle-aged. He was spending quite a bit of what he earned but also saving some for his return to England when he would look for different work, perhaps in insurance. He felt he was being treated well. He did only safe sex and had HIV tests every three months, all negative. Most of the boys would not be fucked, but there was an S & M loft and he thought that some things done up there involving drawing blood and fist fucking were unsafe. Financially he was doing well, he got half the fee charged clients, paid no tax on what he earned and could keep tips. He was good looking and said he had no trouble producing an erection and pleasing customers.

Neither this description, nor those of the London street workers who had experience of Amsterdam, suggested they were kept in brothels against their will. Boredom with the routine, homesickness and competition from newly recruited younger workers were the likely reasons for their returning to England. A much less favourable version, however, was given by some rent boys to a British television producer (Jenkins, 1990). They alleged bullying and coercion by owners of the brothels of boys unable to leave because they are on the run from the police.

The existence of organised brothels has not eliminated the street and bar prostitution trade in Amsterdam. The author visited a bar advertised in a *Gay Times* guide as 'basically a downmarket bar for rent boys'. He was immediately hailed by a group of young men sitting at a table outside with the question 'Are you American?' and 'Won't you come and sit with us?' Having sat down and got some drink, casual, exploratory conversation began as they introduced each other, one was said to be from Belgium and a very camp black youth was said to be American – 'Anyway his father is American.' Eventually one of them suggested going inside 'to talk' and went to an empty table in a far corner where, over some more drink, he explained that this was a bar for 'business boys'. He was told he would get his fee, but all that was needed was talk about the business. Notes of the conversation were written up immediately afterwards.

Case 227. 'Bert' was glad to talk and apologised for having to accept money. He came from a town in East Holland, had never been to England, but spoke English fluently. He said he was twenty, but he looked younger. His appearance betrayed his trade. Slim built, he wore black jeans, a nondescript T shirt, jewelled sleepers in his ears and incongruous leather cowboy boots with spurs. He wished his story were different, but he would 'tell it as it is'. His mother was a heroin addict who worked as a 'window prostitute' and he had been brought up in children's homes all his life. He thought the name on his birth certificate was not his true father. As a child he was effeminate, liked girls' toys and had felt from an early age that he was gay. A lot of sex went on between boys in the homes, which he enjoyed, and he also enjoyed sexual attentions from two adult members of staff.

In the small town where he lived as a boy he used to meet men for sex in a park frequented by homosexuals. By the time he was thirteen he realised he could get them to pay him. He ran away from the children's home and went to stay with one of them. This man had many well off friends who were invited round to have sex with him. Suspecting the man was being paid without sharing it with him he felt 'used' and so went off to stay with another, but that didn't last long and he was brought back to the children's home. By the time he was fifteen he was a 'problem' boy. He didn't want to attend school and the home did not want him any more. Although not yet quite sixteen he was allowed, by special arrangement, to live out and draw the state unemployment allowance. He moved to Amsterdam and stayed with a 'sugar daddy', a man in his fifties, with whom he had a lot of sex at first, but no longer, although the man is still good to him. While living with that man he also worked at one of the clubs for boys. The owner was taking a risk, because the workers are supposed to be over eighteen, but he was told to say, if the police called, that he was a younger brother of one of the workers and was just visiting.

At this time he was being required to service some five customers each day, on top of which the owner wanted him for sex and his sugar daddy also. He had always liked having sex with men, pleasing them and getting their affection, but the sex was getting too much. In addition, the boys at the Club were on drugs and gradually he got hooked on cocaine and intravenous heroin. The doses he took increased slowly, almost without him noticing, till he was spending an awful lot of money. He showed his arms marked with old injection tracks and said he had also had to use veins in his feet. He had also had trouble with his mouth from the cocaine. He used to take a mixture of the drugs; they made him feel he could do anything. He used to have to go shoplifting to get more money for drugs and was caught and put into detention for various periods, adding up to about one year out of the four he worked for the Club. His sugar daddy always took him back when he was released and gave him things. He thinks he really loves that old man.

The Club charged customers 150 guilders for an hour session, of which he got half. He does only oral sex. The owner would have liked him to agree to anal sex as he looked young and customers wanted him for that. He would have agreed when he was desperate for money for drugs, but he just found it impossibly painful. He was scared of AIDS of course, but that was not the reason for his refusal. He has always been able to get an erection with anyone. If they are ugly he just has to close his eyes. The heroin did not stop that, though it did prevent him ejaculating. He fellates customers without a condom, unless they want to come into his mouth. He has had many HIV tests, all negative. He thinks he would want to die if he got infected.

Four months ago the owner of the Club refused to take him back because he had got into so much trouble. Now he works independently from the gay bar. The drugs were making him ill and he was no longer pleasing the club customers. He has been taken on by a clinic, which he attends regularly. He gets oral methadone, but the doses are being steadily reduced. He follows their programme conscientiously because he has now found a boyfriend of his own age who is not a prostitute and they plan to settle down together. The clinic tests his urine and he is not supposed to take heroin, cannabis or even alcohol. He will not drink again before his next test in two days. If he cooperates with the clinic for some months and remains free of drugs they will help him to get a regular job. He would like to have some more schooling or training. The clinic do not approve of him renting. He will tell them about the interview, but not that he was paid for it.

The author also had the chance to converse with one of the regular patrons of this bar, an American in his sixties, who said he found the place 'very *gemütlich*', the boys were like a family, an impression that the author had already obtained. The American said he had been a client of these rent boys for many years and had got to know many of them quite well. The barman was a transvestite who liked the more masculine types of rent boy. The boys were very much individuals and it was hard to make generalisations, but many came from terrible homes. Of course they all wanted money, but it was more complicated than that. Some appreciated having a substitute father. Many were self-centred pleasure seekers. He would let them stay at his place for short periods, but he would not give them a key or trust them too far. He had learned from his own and others' experience that it was fatal to let them move in permanently, they were too unstable to sustain a relationship, having little concept of the needs of the other person. On his periodic visits to Holland he liked to renew friendly contact with those he had seen before, taking them out, giving them clothes, helping them clean up, but not giving them too much money. People had told him of dreadful experiences of being robbed and beaten up, but he had never had anything serious happen beyond petty pilfering. Some of the boys would deliberately keep an emotional distance and avoid a relationship, but on the whole hustlers in Holland were readier to make friends than those in California. The boys' sexual performance was very varied. He rather liked those who were bisexual; their experience with women seemed to teach them things about pleasing the sex partner.

This cursory glance at the Amsterdam scene (which has not included consideration of any home-based, self-employed sex workers) shows how official recognition of their existence permits male sex services to be developed in ways that provide more civilised and protected conditions for worker and customer alike. Regulations concerning, for example, the minimum age of employees, can be enforced and abusive employers driven out of business. The full potential for enlightened control has not been achieved, however, even in Amsterdam. Representatives of the Schorer Foundation (a state-funded gay counselling organisation) found a lamentable lack of knowledge about safer sex among workers in some boys' houses. Dispatching leaflets and condoms was not enough to get through to a multi-lingual group, some of whom were illiterate. They concluded that more active intervention was needed by the owners to support boys in resisting dangerous demands by some clients (*Pink Paper*, no. 105, 13 Jan. 1990, p. 14).

Decriminalisation is not a panacea. It would be unrealistic to expect brothels to eliminate street prostitution altogether. A residual street scene may appear more sordid than ever. *The Best Guide* (1990, p. 14) refers to the Amsterdam freelance rent scene as being at a 'low ebb' and warns against street workers at cruising spots near the station and elsewhere. 'Most are either junkies or thieves or both and are more interested in ripping you off than giving you a good time.' Street prostitution is a deceptively attractive solution to the immediate needs of the rootless young. In Amsterdam, as elsewhere, there are persons impelled to sell themselves long before eighteen, the age when they can do so within the law. There are always some who lack the motivation or the stability needed to function as regular employees or to avoid becoming casualties of the drug subculture. The chances of reclaiming to society some of these disaster-prone individuals, however, are better in Holland where there is more understanding of variant sexual practices and social services are well developed. The example of 'Bert', just cited, is a case in point. The unusually liberal arrangements in the Netherlands may not long survive the increasing integration of regulations and standards throughout the European Community. Even in Amsterdam controls are being tightened, for instance businesses may no longer recruit new sex workers by advertising.

San Francisco

Like Amsterdam, San Francisco has the reputation of a city that is particularly tolerant of gays. It has in fact a large gay community with many political activists who have spearheaded gay rights and demanded anti-discrimination laws. In November 1990 voters approved a 'domestic partners' law which would allow gay couples to register at city hall as being responsible for each other's basic economic needs. Several members of the Board of Supervisors (the local authority) are openly gay or lesbian. In December 1990 the Board voted unanimously in favour of a resolution calling upon the Californian state legislature to legalise same-sex marriage. Some years ago when a gay Supervisor was murdered and the killer received a reduced sentence on psychiatric grounds riots and protest processions ensued (Weiss, 1984). Before the AIDS epidemic changed everything, San Francisco gay bath houses and gay bars with dark back rooms were renowned the world over as centres for non-stop promiscuous and orgiastic male sex. The commercial sex industry still flourishes in the shape of gay sex shops, cinemas and adverts for so-called 'massage'.

Although still finding it necessary to employ massage and similar euphemisms for sexual services, American gay newspapers and magazines are able to advertise in more explicit terms. The *Bay Area Reporter* (7 June 1990) carries three pages of adverts for massage, escorts and models. Most include body and sometimes penis measurements and carry photographs of the advertisers, sometimes clad in jock straps doing nothing to conceal erect penises. Here are a few examples that can be compared with the British adverts previously cited (see p. 187).

Pretty man, hung 9'', 6', 195. B/builder, blond, blue, nice big hands . . .

Handsome, 6', 165# Man with a BEER CAN SIZE tool

A butt you can fit in the palm of your hand on an extremely handsome tan gymnast with ½'' nipples on massive pecs. 5'9'', 155#, 8''c, 24 yrs. $80 in/$100 out

Hairy trucker, 32 years old Stud want you to downshift with his thick, sweaty 8½''. $60

Pleasure torture. If you've been curious about bondage and sensual S & M go ahead and risk a call to a great teacher

My sling room is well stacked with mirrors, boots, restraints, leather and rubber gloves. Tell me what you want. Expect great time. 1st hour $100 in/$120 out

Another American publication, *The Advocate* (13 March 1990) avoids photographs from individual advertisers, but the text can be just as exotic:

Know the pain and pleasure of exquisite titwork, masterful ballwork & the hard excitement of spanking

This magazine has an international circulation and includes some adverts from Europe, including Britain. The following example, signifying great versatility and inserted by one of the masseurs who was interviewed for this research, is clearly intended for the cognoscenti:

London: Telephone xxxxxx: Expert : Top : F/F : Toys : W/S : Gr: F : Sling : Leather : 34 : 6' 2'' : 160# : MC : Visa [Christian name] Central.

More specialised magazines feature still more explicit notices. Here are two taken from *Drummer*, a publication directed at males interested in homosexual sadomasochism. They appeared under sections headed 'Models':

HOT HORNY PARTY ANIMAL

Fist fucking (top) versatile in toys, tit-cock-ball action. Reasonable rate for long, hard 3-ways, group sessions . . .

MASTER'S MASTER

Leather Master, very muscular, XXXhndsm. Tom of Finland looks, intelligent, tall, 36. S & M, Discipline, Punishment. Lt to Hvy C/B and nipple work, VA, Humil., Submission, Spanking, Riding Crops. Pain/Pleasure. Daddy & more. International model. $125 min . . .

San Francisco has an unusual concentration of such adverts and services, but other large American cities, New York especially, have their share. The adverts suggest individual enterprises rather than massage parlours – a point confirmed by one experienced informant, *Case 306* (see p. 226). It has not been possible to investigate the San Francisco masseurs directly, but the sex activities on offer appear much the same as in London. The distinctions noticed in London between the more expensive and sophisticated advertisers, who provide a relatively skilled service, and the cruder approaches of the rough street traders, have been reported also in San Francisco (Weisberg, 1985, p. 37).

As in Amsterdam, the existence of gay bars, organisations and social groups and the availability of advertised sex for money has not eliminated the San Francisco street boy trade, as was amply confirmed by a stroll down Polk Street and an interview with Rev. R.R. Rhuddy, an Anglican priest who works for the San Francisco night mission. The mission is essentially a crisis intervention service. Workers walk the streets where night people are to be found and offer to try to find them emergency shelter. For the under-eighteens, hostels are available where they receive help in obtaining more permanent accommodation, work and sometimes foster-homes. The usual condition is that workers may communicate with the juvenile's parents, so as to avoid legal complications. The hostels will not tolerate continuing drug use and continuing involvement in prostitution and many of the adolescent males are too rebellious to accept these conditions. One of the hostels goes further, detaining the juvenile if he is found to be 'wanted' or 'on the run', and calling in criminal justice agents to deal with him. For adult males accommodation is more difficult to find as most of the hostels are full up by the time of night when clients are located.

The mission work is not specifically focused on male prostitutes, but Rev. Rhuddy has encounters with many of them. His impressions are worth quoting because they echo so strongly what others have said about street workers in London and elsewhere. Some are heterosexual and tend to limit their sexual repertoire, though they have trained themselves to get erections to satisfy customers. Others are of ambiguous sexuality, but most are gay and some have been rejected from their parental homes on that account. Many have run away from really terrible homes, but some have left because they were attracted by the gay scene, the city life and the reputation of San Francisco. In the past, the street workers used to look cleaner and behave discreetly in attempting to interest potential clients. Recently, however, simultaneously with increased involvement with drugs, especially speed and crack, the street workers look more dishevelled, importune more recklessly and are often obliged to steal to get more money for drugs.

Most of the rent boys dream of finding a rich 'sugar daddy' who will provide for them and look after them while leaving them freedom to enjoy themselves. In fact older men do sometimes befriend youngsters over long periods, putting them through college and setting them on good careers. Rev. Rhuddy knows of one young concert pianist who 'owes everything' to the sugar daddy who rescued him from the streets. Others sadly lose out when the older man's interest wanes as he finds another younger and more attractive protégé.

Rev. Rhuddy thinks HIV infection is very prevalent among male street workers in San Francisco, but the city is well equipped to deal with AIDS casualties. Hospitals in the city are not only expert but also humane and concerned, hospices are available and charities help, even to the extent of providing accommodation for relatives visiting the dying. Unfortunately, the sick tend to gravitate to San Francisco because services elsewhere are less developed.

In San Francisco the author was able to interview one former street worker. This was arranged through an introduction to a wealthy, middle-aged gay man who was acting as an unusually beneficent sugar daddy. The account given at this recorded interview was supplemented by information which the sugar daddy had obtained through independent inquiry.

Case 206. Ken was aged thirty-four. He wore a leather jacket and was of superficially unremarkable appearance, save for large ear rings and rather camp mannerisms. He was, however, a transvestite who liked visiting bars dressed in outrageous drag, and he was taking oestrogens to develop feminine breasts. He could turn violent if his flamboyance attracted rude comment. At other times he sported chains and Nazi emblems. The hormones he was taking prevented him from obtaining erections, but he was nevertheless very preoccupied with sex and liked being the passive partner in sado-masochistic games. He was infected with HIV, had a lowered T cell count and was being given AZT, but appeared unaware of the serious nature of his medical state. He was still sleeping with men encountered in bars and he liked anal sex, but he accepted the need for condoms. He had been introduced to his sugar daddy by another gay man who had found him on the street where he had been sleeping rough in company with a friend of long standing, another gay street person. His sugar daddy had installed him and his friend, who was a chronic alcoholic, in a comfortable flat and had undertaken complicated negotiations with welfare authorities to provide them with financial support.

Ken was verbally fluent and provided spirited descriptions of his early life, but he was of limited mental capacity and could not read or count properly. In shops he relied on presenting a note and trusting the change was right. He was trying to learn to read the time on clocks. He was socially inept and disorganised to such an extent that his sugar daddy had given up trying to get him into any regular work and instead employed him to do odd jobs in the garden and the like.

Whatever his innate deficiencies, Ken's social development had been further retarded by gross abuse and neglect. His mother was very young when she married his father, who was already middle-aged and had a number of children. Ken remembers being a very effeminate child and says he used to go to school in a girl's dress and with very long hair. When he was about ten, the family met with financial disaster. His father took him out of school and he became a child dancer in a circus. His first sex experiences were with his father, starting when he was about six. His father used to have anal sex with him. He enjoyed it and had warm feelings towards his father and grew up thinking it was an old Italian tradition for men to have sex with boys. As a boy dancer he was hired out and used by men for sex and porn photos. His father 'didn't mind letting me do that as long as I got paid for it'.

While he was still in his teens his father died and his mother took up with another man. When he was fifteen he was deserted by his mother and stepfather and left to fend for himself on the streets. From the age of sixteen he became a street hustler dressed in drag and found the work congenial. 'I just adore dresses. I love them. I like to be a girl. I like men to go with me as a woman. I love it . . . I've mainly made money for being a drag queen out on the street, sometimes in bars. It all depends where they're at. I'd get big bucks for that you know.' In addition, 'I got into the higher brackets of like S & M. Stronger stuff, like leather, chains, stuff like that. It was not that necessarily serious or real bad or whatever. That kind of sex is very good for the stimulation of the body.' He insisted, 'I have never been forced into anything I didn't want to do. I was tied up because I wanted to be. I was gay because I wanted, I was fucked because I wanted it.' Some drag queens on the street were beaten up, but 'none of that stuff ever happened to me, because I knew the rules. I was a street person for one thing and I knew the rules of the city. As a matter of fact used to be the cock of the walk . . . It was our street. We used to go around that little S curve all the time, and when I say "we" I mean me and about 60 other drag queens.' He would make maybe $100 a time, $200 a night, 'practically every night, but not all the time. Sometimes you make it, sometimes you don't.' He made enough not to have to steal. He worked the streets in Houston for some years and it was there that he was jailed on various occasions for prostitution for periods of one to three months when police cleared the streets.

Ken had lived with a gay lover for some eleven years. He used to dress as and play the part of a wife. At this time he also had some legitimate but short-lived jobs. At the same time, 'I was still doing my [prostitution] thing.' The affair finally broke up because of his lover's domineering and hostile mother. He has a Platonic relationship with his present friend. They drifted to San Francisco together. 'He's a gay bisexual. I do not like straight people. All they do is cause you grief and worry.' Recently he has given up prostitution, except occasionally because he still enjoys it and sometimes needs to supplement his welfare payments. 'But actually it's not for the money part, that part is right down. It's like, once you get the gambling fever when you're young you just go on. You just get into it and you like it, you like getting paid for it. A lot of guys don't like it. They kind of feel they're cheating themselves, or they're being dirty or something like that. They don't realise that they're actually helping out the person. I believe in give and take, that whenever somebody has something to give it should be that way.'

Not much can be deduced from a sample of one, but it was noteworthy that he shared so many of the characteristics of British street workers, including deprived background, early sexual abuse, gay orientation, alienation from conventional work and ultimately welfare dependency. He was unusual in appearing both subjectively self-satisfied and objectively well provided for by his sugar daddy.

Morocco

Perhaps because they keep unmarried females carefully sequestered, Arab countries like Morocco have earned a reputation among Western observers for a high incidence of male homosexual behaviour, in spite of it being against both their religious and their civil laws. Low wages and massive unemployment among a burgeoning young population have encouraged dealings with tourists wanting drugs and sex and only too ready to pay for them. In the Sixties sexual services flourished, even though gay publications and advertisements were unknown. Some of Morocco's larger towns, notably Tangier, were favourite venues both for gay tourists and for gay European ex-patriots wanting easy sexual access to boys and young men. Gay bars owned by foreigners flourished, as did some notorious and crowded bar-restaurants on the beach where local boys paraded in bathing trunks waiting to be propositioned by the admiring groups of gay male tourists. Seedy steam baths hidden away in a maze of back alleys provided hot rooms where boys could be taken for sex sessions. One of these was actually a brothel where the proprietor provided the visitor with a selection of youths according to choice. Boys could be seen hanging about near the entrance hoping to be called when need arose. Boys sitting at the tables of pavement cafés would smile invitingly at passing tourists or hail those they had already successfully importuned. It was common practice for a gay tourist to take over a boy of his choice for the duration of his holiday, allowing him to act as guide and procurer of whatever else he wanted. The chance to get a work permit from a European country, without which they could not obtain a passport, was eagerly sought by Moroccan youths and as the date of departure approached they would plead with the tourist to try to find them a post abroad. Foreigners who had bought villas held court at gay parties and employed houseboys who happily obliged with sexual as well as domestic services. All of this is vividly described in the frank diaries of the playwright Joe Orton (Lahr, 1986) and in various novels, such as Robin Maughan's *The Wrong People* (1970).

Circumstances have changed and Islamic principles are increasingly enforced. Laws to prevent foreign ownership of businesses and property brought about the closure of many gay establishments. Tourists with the appearance of hippies on the look out for drugs were refused entry. Locals caught selling drugs were employed by police as decoys to trap others. The change has been documented in *Spartacus International Gay Guide* (1988). In Morocco 'homosexuality is reportedly illegal and is persecuted ... The rejection of affluent Western tourism and its occasional distressing results is noticeably increasing. The Islamic fundamentalists have also become noticeably more aggressive towards gays in recent years, no doubt also because of prostitution, which is rigorously combatted. In the meantime Morocco has become anything but a paradise for lovers of Arab boys. Raids on tourists are increasing ... most hotels have gone over to the system of not allowing local boys to be taken up to the rooms.'

Through a contact in England who had once employed him, an interview was secured with 'M', a Moroccan who had been an active prostitute in the Sixties but was now bemoaning the changes. He came from Tangier but travelled for interview to Casablanca. Shown the Spartacus listing of gay bars in Tangier he said he knew them all, but more than half were either closed or taken over by Moroccans who no longer catered to the gay trade.

Case 207. M was a middle-aged man of forty-seven dressed in worn but respectable looking clothes. He was swarthy, poorly shaven, pot-bellied and had few remaining teeth. In between interview sessions he was obliged to seek out a cheap dentist to have two further teeth extracted that were causing severe pain. It was difficult to imagine him as a youth attractive to homosexual tourists, but some old photographs he carried showed that he had once been handsome. He accepted all too eagerly any alcoholic drink on offer, and the fee and expenses provided were clearly of great importance to him.

He appeared motivated to tell the truth as he saw it, and in spite of some difficulty with language a coherent account emerged gradually. The story is reconstructed from notes made during or immediately after interviewing, but no attempt has been made to quote his remarks verbatim or to reproduce his style of speech.

Born in Tangier in 1941, M was sixth in a family of eight. When he was nineteen his father, who had served as a soldier in the Spanish army, died at the age of sixty, following a 'stroke' which had left him paralysed. His mother, to whom he had always been very close, died only four years ago. Both parents were loving and caring and he recalled them with affection. They had been prepared to deprive themselves to feed the family, and even when the children were quite big they worried about them and came looking for them if they stayed out late. It was a close knit family, but blighted by increasing poverty. When his father's term with the army came to an end work was hard to find and there were times he had to go out begging for bread.

At the age of seven M began at Koran school where he learned to recite the Koran and to read and write Arabic. At twelve he was sent to a French state day school for boys. Because of his family's poverty he was forced on occasion to go to school hungry and without shoes. In 1956, with the coming of independence from the French, his situation worsened as free school meals and the free supply of notebooks and other materials ceased. Having no money to buy books he was laughed at by other pupils and started to truant. He found he could do things outside to make money and so he spent more time out of school than in. When his father died he gave up education altogether, but by then he could write and speak French as well as Arabic.

M started on alcohol at fifteen and has been a heavy drinker ever since. When his father was alive he would be beaten if he came home drunk, but that did not deter him. In later years, after an evening of drinking, he would stay out all night rather than face his mother in that state.

From the age of ten, when he first became sexually active, his interests were directed to both boys and girls, although his earliest experiences were all with boys. They took the form of mutual anal intercourse, carried out in secret in school lavatories and similar places. He quickly found that he did not like being anally penetrated, although many other boys, in spite of an initial fear of being hurt, soon learned to enjoy it. He thought that the reason for this dislike might have been a frightening experience at the age of seven. He was walking in a somewhat isolated situation

tside the town when a man grabbed him round the throat with the
obvious intention of committing anal rape. Even at that age he knew
about the mechanics of intercourse. He screamed loudly and a farmer
came to the rescue in time. He remembers the assailant, now an old man
and still living in Tangier.

M thinks that many Moroccan males, when they are young and access
to women is difficult, have anal intercourse with each other. Active
fellatio and other acts are not generally practised by Moroccans. M's own
first experience of heterosexual intercourse was at sixteen, while still a
schoolboy, with a Spanish prostitute who charged only a few pesetas, but
for many years after that his contacts were nearly all with males. He had
many casual contacts as as well as some brief love affairs with boys.

He started obtaining money for sex when he was fourteen. Men would
follow him when he was walking on the beach. One day a Spanish man
invited him back for coffee and, after fellating him, which he much
enjoyed, unexpectedly presented him with a Spanish banknote, but it
turned out to be an item of almost valueless change. He soon got into the
way of meeting tourists, offering to show them around the town, and
agreeing to sex if they wanted it. For a time he had a pimp, about seven
years his senior, who 'sold' him to tourists, but he 'shook him off' as soon
as he learned how to make contacts himself.

M soon became familiar with the beach bars and bathing huts where
male tourists of all ages would chat up the local boys and make terms
with them, either for quick sex more or less on the spot or for visits to
their hotel rooms or holiday flats. There were also a number of hotels
patronised exclusively by gay men that permitted their residents to
entertain Moroccan visitors and also some hotels that let rooms by the
hour to male couples. Of an evening, after the beach trade was over, he
could meet tourists in the gay bars. M picked up a working knowledge of
Spanish and English and developed into something of a leader among the
rent boys through his literacy and his facility for getting acquainted with
foreigners. His standing was further increased through being taken up at
the age of seventeen by an American artist in his thirties who was
temporarily resident in Morocco, with whom he stayed for over six
months. They went touring all around the country in a jeep and procured
many boys with whom they both had sex, although on occasion the
American would show jealousy.

During tourist seasons M made a comfortable living and enjoyed a
more interesting life than if he had found routine work in a factory, as did
some of his acquaintances. As he grew into his twenties he was better
able to exploit his intelligence and good looks and he became more
selective about the men he would permit to have sex. He disliked sex with
men of fifty or older, but would procure other boys for them and help them
find drugs or bargain for souvenirs. His clients were all foreigners, never
Moroccans, and although he had dealings with women tourists none of

them ever asked him for sex. He would perform anal sex on clients and allow them to fellate him but was reluctant to manipulate their genitals. M was never forced into sex acts against his will. He was wary of powerful men and would soon complain and make a noise if a client tried something he did not like.

In his early days as a prostitute M would earn something like £12 a week, about £2 to £4 on each occasion. He did not ask for a specific sum in advance, hoping that by not doing so he would be given more. Nowadays, he says, boys in Tangier get much more, probably £50 a time, and he himself came to expect more as he became more experienced. In his thirties he was obtaining a minimum of £20 and, at least during the summer season, refusing anyone who could not afford him.

At the age of twenty-three he met a British tourist, then in his thirties, who took a great fancy to him and who eventually obtained a permit for him to work in England. He was pleased and excited at first, but he never settled down, moving from one job to another. Looking back, he thinks the trouble was that he had been used to too much freedom, never having been required to keep working hours or being told what he must do. One job he lost after cutting a man with a bottle in a drunken brawl, for which he was fined. Through introductions from another gay Englishman he had known in Tangier he obtained a job as houseboy to a wealthy Londoner who immediately departed on holiday leaving M in charge. This man's former houseboy, aggrieved at being replaced, tricked M into letting him and some of his friends into the house for a party. They set about robbing the place and M fled to neighbours. When the police came they found compromising photos of young boys in the house, with the result that on his return the owner was sent to prison.

After about eight placements M left England feeling fed up and saying he didn't want to leave for good. He soon regretted it, but could never get his permit and passport back and reverted to his previous mode of life. His British sugar daddy continued for several years to visit and helped him procure a small flat that had been used by Europeans. M lived there for some years, but admits that it became 'quite notorious' on account of the many young men he took back there. A woman neighbour threatened to denounce him.

At this period he was drinking heavily and smoking a lot of cannabis. Following a drunken fight he was imprisoned for a month. When conscription for all men from eighteen to thirty came into force he avoided it by falsifying his identity card to make himself appear just over the age limit. He was still attractive to gay men, but he spent money he got from them on drink and paying adolescent boys for his own sexual pleasures.

In his later thirties he began to change. He gave up smoking both cannabis and tobacco because he felt it was damaging his health. He began to feel guilty about his homosexual habits, which he had always striven to conceal from his relatives. He thought he should get himself a

wife and family. As he grew older acceptable tourists were less interested
in him sexually, so he tried to make his money by concentrating on his
other services, such as introductions to drug dealers, money changers,
safe places for sex and willing boys. Things were beginning to get
difficult, however, as the number of tourists was diminishing and the
authorities were becoming stricter. He was tired of having to 'rush
around' all the time and wanted to settle down. He was in love with a boy
of seventeen and formed a plan to marry this fellow's sister so as to be
able to enjoy both worlds. His old mother sensed something 'wrong' and
arranged instead a marriage to the young daughter of a local farming
family. M agreed, even though it meant a tearful parting from his young
male lover.

Wanting to set up a small bazaar stall to produce an income on which to
marry he tried to make money by joining a group smuggling untaxed
tobacco off ships in the harbour. One of their number proved to be a police
plant and M was arrested. He had to give up his flat to meet the payments
needed to avoid imprisonment and was reduced to walking the streets
with a basket of souvenirs to sell to tourists. His marriage started
unhappily in the home of his in-laws. This he found unbearable because
of their attempts to control his movements and stop him staying out late.
After the birth of his first child he was able to claim a place in subsidised
state accommodation reserved for those without jobs or money. He is still
there, with a wife and three children, living in two rooms, in a mud and
straw dwelling, with no electricity, no paved road, no postal service and a
charcoal burner for heating.

His marital sex life had been good. He had tried to ignore homosexual
temptations, but he had been a few times with young men and felt guilty
about it. Allah might forgive these things before marriage, but not after.
He was bitter about being unable to obtain regular work, feeling himself
better qualified than many of the younger and less educated men who
carry the badge of an official guide. Unfortunately, without a substantial
sum of bribe money, or some friend or relative in the bureaucracy, it is
impossible for him to acquire one, so he is subject to periodic harassment
by the police who arrest him and humiliate him at the station until he
hands over some money. They do not really care about what he does so
long as they get paid. With fewer tourists and the crackdown on
prostitution and the drug trade his opportunities for making money are
much reduced and his family is destitute. M now earns a little money as a
scribe, helping the less literate to answer letters or cope with the
innumerable forms required by the bureaucracy. He also coaches some
foreign residents wanting to learn Arabic and he goes down to the
harbour when ferries arrive offering to help tourists locate accommodation or find places of interest.

When the issue was put to him directly M agreed that many of his
former schoolfellows were now better placed than he, enjoying posts in

the police or in the vast army of clerks employed in government administration. Of his three brothers, one was sick, but the others were employed. He blames the system that provides jobs only for those able to pay bribes. He admitted, however, that the years spent in drinking and pleasure-seeking had reduced his chances of securing steady work.

M felt very embittered about his poverty and the lack of state support for his children. He complained also of sneers and sarcastic comments from younger Moroccans who were jealous of his associations with tourists. They knew of his past prostitution activities and insinuated that any contact he made must be for that purpose. In spite of disapproval from his wife and sister he could not stop drinking. If he tried he would become irritable and nasty with his children. He wished he could get his family out of the country to some place where they would have a better chance.

This history, played out in a vastly different culture, is interesting in having many parallels with those of street workers in Britain, even to the incident of attempted sexual assault as a boy. M began as a wilful rebel from a poverty-stricken background, a school truant who learned early to enjoy male sex and also to exploit it for money. At first he was materially successful, forgetting education and career and spending his gains on drink, drugs and sex. The effort to satisfy employers in Britain proved too demanding for him. He reverted to prostitution and drug dealing, but as he grew older and times became harder he became more reckless in law breaking and lost his accommodation. He consented to an arranged marriage, but could not support his family or control his drinking. He grows increasingly embittered, jealous of peers who have overtaken him in legitimate jobs, and blames the unfairness and corruption of the social system. In summary, social adversity coupled with a wilful temperament and urge for instant gratification led to prostitution. This proved to be no long-term solution and left him bereft of means to support himself properly once that career ended. His ultimate fate, like that of some of the former street workers in London, looks set to be one of progressive social dereliction which, as he sadly points out, the state does little to prevent.

Thailand

Information on the rent boy scene in Thailand, a country renowned for its facilities for sex tourism (Smith, 1990), was obtained from various sources: (i) a forensic psychiatrist who had spent a lot of time in that country; (ii) Barbara Gibson, one of the Streetwise Youth team leaders who, while on a visit there, made inquiries about male prostitution and the AIDS problem; (iii) one of our anonymous volunteers who has close connections with a distinguished Thai family and who spent part of his holidays making inquiries and visiting bars that provide boys for rent; (iv) a written account by a German tourist, kindly translated by David

DeMassey, JP; and (v) miscellaneous advertising leaflets. There was substantial agreement about the nature of the set-up in Bangkok and the popular seaside resort of Pattaya. The summary following is an amalgam of the details supplied by these informants. They do not mention self-employed masseurs.

Thai culture, based on Buddhist tradition, is largely devoid of the censorious Judaeo-Christian attitudes to variant sexuality. Although a lifestyle that flouts the tradition of family continuity through the generations is suspect, revulsion towards homoeroticism is muted and anti-gay pressure groups were unknown until controversies about AIDS surfaced. Unlike some Western views, Thai opinion does not condemn sexual relationships between men and sexually mature teenage boys with the severity it reserves for paedophile relationships with children. Initially Bangkok's gay bars and discos were mostly patronised by locals, but over the last two decades they have become popular with tourists and some of them either employ male prostitutes in conjunction with their male cabaret shows, or else allow male prostitutes to operate freelance among the customers. Male street prostitution has had a much longer history in Bangkok and has traditionally featured not only effeminate transvestites but 'young male toughs ... who worked at anything from pimping to robbery' in addition to their prostitution trade (Jackson, 1989, p. 242). The existence of organised bar-brothels has by no means killed the street boy trade in which many of the operatives are heterosexually identified and would not wish to become labelled by attachment to a gay bar.

As in Amsterdam, there is no proscription of advertisements for what are effectively venues for male prostitution. For example, a list under the heading 'Go-Go bars and massage: Men only' appearing in the September 1990 issue of an English language publication for tourists, *What's on in Pattaya This Week*, included the following:

MEMORY. New men bar with over 30 young, clean, charming boys. Cabaret show 12 p.m.

BOYS BOYS BOYS. Experience even more the oriental night life where your fantasies become reality.

Here are descriptions of how these venues operate:

The place is crowded, especially with young boys, some of them dressed, or partly dressed, or naked. The guest is taken to a sofa and the waiter takes his order. Every drink costs the same, whether whisky, beer or cola, namely 70 Baht (25 Baht = 1 US dollar). The drink is promptly served and when paid for the guest can watch everything at leisure.

The room is decorated and furnished in white. There is a bar on one side and comfortable chairs and sofa in the middle. At one end is a door that leads upstairs to some 'Relaxing Rooms' for prostitution. The customer must pay 150 Baht for the use of a room. If a customer leaves the premises with one of the boys he must pay the management 200 Baht for allowing the boy to leave during working hours. A lad who goes out with a customer is the envy of his comrades, since they are not paid anything for dancing or walking about practically naked in the bar. All that the management provides them is a place to sleep, rather than sleeping out in the park, and rice for their meals. They can stay in the building when it is not open to the public, from 2 a.m. until 9 p.m. Only those taking part in the cabaret show get wages, otherwise they rely on the generosity of the visitors. They are not allowed to pressurise the guests, however, nor do they. If a guest shows no response to an advance the boy leaves him alone. Each boy has a number on the side of his pants so a visitor can let a waiter know whom he desires.

There is a stage, the back of which is covered with mirrors, on which about eight boys dance. It is about 70 cm high so they can easily jump on or off. From 9 till 11 in the evening the boys take turns in dancing on the stage, naked, touching and manipulating their sexual parts. Some of them get erections and are clearly pleased to 'show off' in this way. Up to 50 boys take part in this naked dancing. At another bar as many as 100 boys take part, but each one stays on stage for only about three minutes.

The boys who go on the stage should not be under eighteen years of age, by police order. Most are between eighteen and twenty-three, but many Thai boys look young for their age and can appear to be only about fifteen.

The actual show begins at 11 o'clock. The first item is of lads dressed up as female singers. Then a muscular body-builder shows his strength. The third act is a lad doing a striptease, the climax being when he ejaculates a stream of 1 metre distance. The audience applauds and an attendant cleans the stage floor. Then follows a dance with two boys holding burning wax torches, the wax melting onto their bodies as they dance. Then two boys sensuously wash each other all over with soap and water. In the last act two boys, after first making great play with putting on a condom, have homosexual intercourse on the stage under subdued lighting. The show ends there and the stage is lit again for the boys to continue go-go dancing until 1 or 2 a.m.

[Another establishment, a bar and massage house,] is run by a transvestite who greets one at the reception area. Inside is a large stage area up front where about 80 boys sit. Around the room are raised platforms where go-go boys dance, moving around clockwise every so often. At given periods all the boys get up and dance en masse, fully clothed. Drinks are served, for which one pays at the end of one's stay. The boys wear numbers and I gave the number of one I liked and asked to talk to him. He was sent for and came and joined me and a drink was produced for him. We agreed that the following evening he would give me a massage. I arrived as arranged and he was sent for. I was taken to the massage rooms in another part of the building where he was preparing a water bed. There were AIDS stickers all over the place and condoms in the room. He kissed me and then took his clothes off and also helped me off with mine. He made a great noise whipping up soap suds in a bowl which he proceeded to throw over me and the bed. Then he got on top of me and made all sorts of movements with his body, finishing with his feet up under me, toes round my penis . . .

[At another bar] the go-go boys start dancing with their clothes on, but then strip down to see-through G strings. From 11 p.m. there is an artistically staged water ballet every half hour. Coloured lights illuminate the water, visible through large portholes, while music plays. A boy dives in with white shorts which light up in special effects. A second follows, wearing tight, long trousers. They move swim around gracefully and finally strip off and perform erotic movements and embraces in the water. I looked into the rear of the building where the massage rooms were. All was very clean and again posters about AIDS were on display.

Informants remarked upon the willingness, skilfulness, athleticism and apparent pleasure with which the boys cooperate in active or passive anal or oral sex, but they do not like sado-masochistic activity which seems alien to the gentle Thai temperament. The bar workers are not necessarily ashamed of their job. An informant who enlisted one of the boys as a holiday companion was struck by the lad's readiness to tell people about the place where he worked, it being a bar renowned for employing only the best. The workers are more likely to identify as bisexuals than as gay, bisexuality carrying less of a stigma in a culture relatively relaxed about sexual practices and leaving open the expectation that the young man will eventually marry and start a family. The boys do not take clients to their own rooms. If a client wants to see them away from the bar there are hotels that will let a room for the night or by the hour with no questions asked if a tourist turns up with a young man.

It is likely that tourists, many of them middle-aged and physically unattractive, form a too rosy impression of the sex workers' situation. Certainly some of the boys engage in the work out of choice, as in the case of students working temporarily or hotel waiters dabbling in the prostitution scene, but others come from poor homes in the countryside with little chance of earning as much any other way. As in most third world countries, the glimpses of luxury and sophistication afforded the male prostitute contrast sharply with his ordinary living standards. A lucky few become the regular protégés of wealthy tourists.

The AIDS epidemic is a serious problem in Thailand. One health worker interviewed by Barbara Gibson explained that bar owners are now required to register their prostitute employees who must have HIV testing every three months. He complained of indifferent cooperation in this regard on the part of bar owners who did not keep to their declared intentions. Some of them were charging their employees for condoms that had been given out free. That the sex tourist trade, both heterosexual and homosexual, flourishes in the era of AIDS is viewed by many as a regrettable reflection of economic circumstances. On the other hand, as one informant put it, 'The sex industry in Thailand, being tolerated and not driven underground, is thriving and keeps up a high standard. Services are delivered with a smile and do not seem sordid. The boys giving their services are proficient and honest and I heard of no instances of things being stolen from clients.'

*

The information about Thailand and the other places discussd in this chapter was limited by problems of access, but it was sufficient to show how the male prostitution trade is shaped by cultural and economic pressures. In Thailand and Morocco most of the prostitutes' earnings came from Western visitors, although there was no suggestion of any lack of native men wanting homosexual activity. In San Francisco, as in England, clients were predominantly fellow countrymen. The Amsterdam brothels catered largely to tourists from countries where there is less tolerance of male prostitution. In neighbouring Belgium, for example, after a series of trials, Professor Vincineau, a lawyer, was finally acquitted in 1987 of charges arising out of acts of 'debauchery' (a term used to cover paid sex) which were said to have occurred at the 'Macho' sauna which he owned. Also in Belgium, Luc Legrand, publisher of *Tels Quels*, was charged in connection with personal sex contact advertisements appearing in that magazine. The defendants were acquitted, possibly because of their declared policy of refusing any advertisement with the slightest suggestion of prostitution or paedophilia (*Tels Quels*, Sept. 1989). In Morocco gay sex tourism flourished only so long as the authorities refrained from vigorous application of repressive laws. In the United States prostitution is theoretically totally illegal, but in San Francisco, as in London, it is usually only the street prostitutes who are actively pursued.

Conclusion

The most important conclusion to come out of this survey is the danger of generalisation about male sex workers. There are enormous variations in lifestyle, in the organisation of the business, in the environment in which it is carried on, in the sexual activities involved, in the relationship between customer and client, in the amount of money that changes hands and in the degree of concealment from legal scrutiny. Equally, practitioners differ as individuals. The opposing stereotypes of young social outcast and smart young man operating a successful call boy service are exemplified in their contrasting modes of work. Although there was a certain amount of overlap, the street worker samples were different from the agency workers interviewed and even more unlike the group of privately advertising masseurs. These contrasts called for separate consideration of men operating by direct contact with clients in bars and other public places – the street workers – and the off street workers operating through personal or agency advertisements.

The divisions are not absolute, since some practitioners do change from one method of work to another or combine different methods. Many street workers, however, lack the personal or financial resources to break into other modes. They often find difficulty fitting into more organised methods of working. Employers can be choosy about age and physical appearance and if they have no base or telephone where they can be contacted agencies may be reluctant to take them, even for attendance on shifts at a massage parlour. Those who gravitate from the streets to successful work in the advertised sex industry are usually better situated to begin with than the typical street worker.

Street work practice involves particular risks. Only the street workers were exposed to risk of arrest for importuning. Others, with the exception of workers in agency massage parlours, who might at any time be raided by the police, were relatively secure from police intervention. Contrasts between the street workers and the others were not just related to their mode of work, there were marked differences in backgrounds, attitudes, motivations, lifestyles and social problems. Plenty of examples were found to fit the popular stereotype, backed by many previous surveys, of the homeless, runaway rent boy, most likely a school drop-out, coming from a broken or rejecting family, who has likely spent years in different children's homes and emerged untrained, indisciplined and unfit for regular employment, who lives by his wits, getting by on drugs, prostitution and petty crime. A majority of the street worker samples displayed these characteristics to a greater or lesser extent, but there were few such among workers in the advertised sexual services, some of whom were operating to all outward appearance as successful and ostensibly legitimate businessmen, accepting payment by credit card, paying tax, and making sufficient profit to live in comfort, finance mortgages and even subscribe to pension funds. Careers in male prostitution are not pursued only by rebels, misfits and social incompetents. The present findings strongly support the views of Tim Robinson (1990) who points to the presence on the London scene of substantial numbers of better established workers with good levels of education and social achievement. The present survey, by virtue of limited access and resources, has concentrated on the problems at the lower end of the sex industry more than on the characteristics and lifestyles of the more up-market workers. That does not mean that street workers are necessarily more numerous. The relative size of the different groups is a matter for speculation.

A majority of street workers described themselves as gay or bisexual, and this was undoubtedly a factor in steering some homeless youths, whose alternative means of survival would be begging or pilfering, towards the rent scene. Among workers in the advertised services self-identification, usually as gay, occasionally as bisexual, was virtually universal. Most of them had decided to take up the work because they were attracted to it rather than because they had no alternative means of livelihood. Many obtained satisfaction from pleasing customers and sometimes finding pleasure themselves. Some, particularly among private masseurs, combined the sex trade with other more conventional employment. Most of the men, including the street workers, were clear about their sexual orientation at the outset and remained unchanged by prostitution practice.

Street work provides a means of survival for the most deprived and alienated. Many came from broken or chaotic homes and had experienced rejection, violence, or plain neglect. Some were running away from unpaid fines or unsettled criminal charges and dared not apply for welfare benefits or seek registered employment. Not all street workers, however, were so desperate. A few in our samples had come from reasonable family backgrounds and had not been forced into homelessness. Rather than feeling they had no alternative some had felt attracted by the rent scene. For those happy with a gay lifestyle there was plenty of sex, gay company and regular visits to gay night clubs, easy access to ready cash and recreational drugs and hospitality available both from similarly minded peers living in squats, shared flats, etc. and from friendly punters only too pleased to entertain an attractive youth. They might seem to an outsider to be living in a fool's paradise, but the risks attached to street work and the insecurity of their arrangements in the long term did not weigh too heavily with young men who were for the moment enjoying themselves. The fantasy, highly unlikely of fulfilment, of a life of leisure supported by a wealthy sugar daddy was in some minds. A less implausible ambition was to find accommodation suitable to receive clients. Few were doing anything very realistic to achieve that aim, although one man interviewed in the supplementary sample, who had received help from the Streetwise Youth Project in the past, had done so and succeeded.

A career in advertised sexual services carries some disadvantages, mainly related to the intolerance of conventional society and the difficulty of combining it successfully with a private sex life, but it need not be destructive. For individuals who are able to manage their work and their finances efficiently and prudently, it can be on balance personally rewarding. Organised around advertisements and telephone contacts, the flourishing off-street sex industry provides semi-legitimate employment, but still agency workers and masseurs cannot declare the real sexual nature of their service. Some, including foreigners, were not declaring themselves employed at all and those who were, especially the self-employed workers, had much scope for tax evasion. This situation is not unique to the sex industry, but the necessity to operate sex services clandestinely probably encourages other forms of illegality. The men attracted to work in the advertised sex services were from a far wider range of backgrounds than were the street worker samples. There was nothing to suggest a high incidence of early deprivations or damaged personalities. They were remarkably articulate, as the quotations will have demonstrated, and many were well educated, accustomed to middle-class social expectations and standards of living and able to organise their lives, their business, their expenditure and their savings competently. Some of the more up-market and sophisticated escorts presented a smart, fashionable appearance and a cultivated line of small talk for the benefit of their clientele; accomplishments which few street boys had the necessary basic education or the opportunity to develop. These better placed workers tended to distance themselves from the label rent boy, if by that was meant a street worker forced by circumstance to parade in public and sell his body to all and sundry for dubious reward. Even the street workers were often reluctant to label themselves prostitutes, since the word has acquired unpleasant associations with female 'sluts' and 'whores' passively surrendering a vagina in a mechanical way to any man who wants to make use of it.

As might have been expected from their choice of occupation and generally uncloseted gay lifestyles, some of the workers in advertised sexual services were confirmed individualists and opposed to conservative social attitudes, such as blanket condemnation of recreational drugs, but relatively few had had serious problems with drink, drugs or the law. The self-employed masseurs in particular were generally better placed than street workers, by virtue of personality and circumstance, to exercise choice and self-determination, to guard against the diseases associated with unsafe sex and to escape the pressures that lead to addiction, crime and social disaster. Some of them had not gone into the trade until they were adults and capable of making informed and unforced choices, and some had skills or careers that they had not completely relinquished or might return to in the future. Although, like the street workers, they foresaw a time when age would oblige them to quit the sex industry, some masseurs were able to continue well into middle age, especially if they were prepared to cater to clients wanting dominance and sado-masochistic activity for whom youthful good looks were a less crucial requirement. This was less true of agency workers, since their employers needed people attractive to the majority of clients, but some of the older masseurs felt they had the edge on younger colleagues in their experience in finding ways to please customers and in willingness to take time to do so. Some were enjoying a certain amount of job satisfaction, conscious of being part of an expanding industry and proud to be performing a necessary service well.

We found no reason to believe that unwanted sexual molestation in childhood favours entry into prostitution. Such incidents were unduly frequent in the street worker samples, but usually in association with inadequate parenting, lack of supervision and institutional placements. Being aversive experiences, it is not so easy to see why they should favour either the development of a homosexual orientation or the choice of prostitution work requiring many male sexual contacts. Except for the link with a constellation of adverse circumstances they seemed irrelevant.

We found no evidence that boys learn to use sex for money through being bribed as children to submit to unwanted molestation.

Sexual contacts between young boys and older males that are found enjoyable and not regarded by the boy as molestation may have a different significance. Incidents of this kind were also reported, mostly by the masseurs and agency workers, who were more decided about their gay identities than street workers and readier to enlarge on such matters, and mostly by men aware from their early years of being attracted to other males, although they may not have understood and identified with homosexuality until later. The determinants of sexual orientation, whether heterosexual or homosexual, are as yet little understood, but it seems likely that boys who seek out or welcome sexual experiences with older males are already predisposed to a homosexual orientation, which may in turn facilitate entry to homosexual prostitution if, for whatever reasons, that decision is taken. Society's disavowal of childhood sexuality (especially homosexuality) can lead some frustrated boys, whose sexual feelings develop early, secretly to seek both physical release and understanding from adult strangers contacted in public places, notably men's lavatories. Because of the condemnatory stance of parents and other authorities, much youthful homosexual activity is necessarily clandestine and this encourages attitudes to sex that break the barriers common in heterosexual contexts, including the barrier of age. Being offered money after sex can introduce a boy to the idea of turning pleasure into profit, but this is hardly an important factor. At the age when most enter the prostitution trade that fact of life is very well known quite independently of events in childhood.

Many sexual assaults happening in later years were described during the interviews. Street workers in particular were conscious of the risk of assault and many gave accounts of incidents where they had been forced by clients and their accomplices to submit to unwanted, painful or damaging sexual acts. Interestingly, just as many men reported assaults in the course of sexual contacts unconnected with prostitution, which suggests that the risk is to an extent inherent in some gay male lifestyles, but the incidents that occurred during prostitution work were sometimes particularly frightening. Nevertheless, sexual assaults are very rare in comparison with the number of prostitution encounters that pass off smoothly. Reports of sexual assault in later years did not appear closely connected with whether or not incidents of early sexual molestation were recalled.

The main samples did not include men who, as children, had been regular prostitutes for paedophiles, and only one man was located who seemed to have been involved with a child sex ring. Since paedophiles wanting small boys are few in number compared with the population of male homosexuals, the paedophile trade must be much smaller, and certainly more hidden, than the rent boy scene which we were able to probe without much difficulty. On the other hand, the popularity of post-pubertal adolescents among punters was frequently mentioned, but that, of course, is a phenomenon common to the clients of both male and female prostitutes. What is sometimes referred to as hebephilia (*hebe* is Greek for puberty, and *ephebos* is a Greek term for a male who has reached puberty), love of the recently physically matured, is not the same as child molestation, and in many cultures would not be regarded as a problem, at least in heterosexual contexts.

The present survey adds little to what is already known from other surveys about the prevalence of HIV infection and the likely risks of its spread. Sex workers as a group have greater awareness of the dangers than most young heterosexuals, but they are undoubtedly exposed to high-risk sexual activity, especially those working from the streets whose practices are incautious or, on occasion, especially when intoxicated from alcohol or drugs, positively reckless. On the other hand, many have multiple sex contacts apart from their prostitution activity and in their private lives appear to take fewer precautions against infection than when working with clients. Prostitution practice may add little to a risk that is already present. Many sex workers are keener to observe safe sex practices than their clients. Being more numerous and more likely to have heterosexual contacts clients can become vehicles for the spread of HIV.

The survey was intended to be primarily descriptive, but of course the observations have implications for social policy. A radical re-thinking of attitudes towards the sex industry and a change in methods of social control is needed. The notion that male sexual services are totally evil and to be repressed at all costs should be challenged. The demand is such that it is unrealistic to think that the law could ever succeed in eradicating prostitution. Reasons for an especially great demand in the homosexual world for commercial sex are easy to comprehend. Social disapproval discourages many men from an openly gay lifestyle and creates a demand for impersonal and clandestine sexual outlets. Heterosexual society is changing, but still tradition and parental responsibilities encourage permanent partnerships. These pressures do not apply to gay relationships, which are often short-lived. This fact, coupled with the high valuation of youthful good looks in male homosexual circles, means that older gay men may find the search for a partner increasingly difficult and payment an obvious solution.

Severe repression may reduce the sex trade and drive it underground, but then it carries on in sordid fashion, exploited by criminal entrepreneurs, becoming linked with such social evils as blackmail, assault and robbery, and endangering both workers and clients. The advantages of official recognition of the existence of the male sex industry, as in Amsterdam or Thailand for example, are easy to see. The business can be regulated, a civilised environment provided, workers and clients protected from exploitation and abuse, the use of condoms and medical checks insisted upon, taxes collected, under-age youths excluded, etc. This in itself does not provide a solution to every problem. So long as society at large frowns heavily upon such arrangements, the entrepreneurs attracted to the trade may not be the most respectable and responsible of businessmen and regulations may be hard to enforce. The street trade can be reduced, but it will not automatically disappear. Rent boys too young, too unattractive, too rebellious or too delinquent to fit into a controlled setting will still try to operate outside the system. We had examples in the survey of street workers who had found employment in Amsterdam brothels, but on account of their irregular lifestyles and heavy use of intoxicants had not benefited from the more regular income they were getting and had quit after a short time. Nevertheless, a legitimate sexual service does provide a place for the more capable sex workers; it reduces their dependence on street work and gives their clients opportunities to enjoy a safer service.

The existence of laws (see p. 285) that make it almost impossible to provide a sexual service without committing a crime seems to encourage rather than prevent the nastier aspects of the trade. An 'age of consent' for homosexual contacts as high as twenty-one effectively criminalises young male prostitutes as well as their clients. Transactions can go wrong and serious abuses occur without the police being called in because victims are themselves defined as criminals. For the moment the police operate these laws with considerable discretion. Whereas street workers complain of unnecessary abuse and harassment, police do not normally intervene and charge with importuning men making contact with other men in gay bars, although as the law stands male 'importuning' for gay male sex is an offence even if money is not involved. Charges of 'gross indecency' in connection with behaviour that is consenting and in private are rare when the participants are eighteen or more, notwithstanding the fact that the criminal law includes men of nineteen and twenty. As some sex masseurs explained, police were well aware of their activities and made use of them when crimes involving homosexuality were under investigation, but made no attempt to interfere with their business. The fact that some masseurs can advertise so openly 'duos' (i.e. two persons plus the client) and S & M practices, both of which are technically crimes, shows that the authorities are, perhaps sensibly, not too concerned about these matters. On the other hand, some masseurs had been subject to interrogation and some massage parlour workers had been involved in raids and prosecutions for brothel keeping, so there was really no part of the sex industry where workers could feel confident that they might not at some time, through accident, malicious informers or an unexpected change in police policy, find themselves in the courts. It is not the best way to encourage good practice within the industry to connive with the pretence that the services do not exist while maintaining the threat of prosecution.

It would be difficult to argue that soliciting on the street for homosexual prostitution, even though it may occur more discreetly, should be any less of an offence than soliciting by women. That it should be punishable by imprisonment, when female soliciting is not, is less justifiable. Arrests are inevitable among those who persist in seeking custom on station concourses, around lavatories and on well known street corners, but there seem to be sustainable complaints concerning the way some police carry out the task and produce exaggerated evidence in court.

A relaxation of the law would be beneficial. Laws controlling heterosexual and homosexual behaviour should be the same, the age of consent should be the same and the bar on the presence of a third party when homosexual acts take place should be removed. The definition of and penalties for male importuning should be the same as for female soliciting. There should be reconsideration of the blanket prohibition of prostitution adverts and of erotic massage parlours and of the liability of organisers of sex services to prosecution for 'immoral earnings'.

Because of the antisocial tendencies of some street workers, in particular their involvement in generalised delinquency, their abuse of intoxicants and their unwillingness to fit into the requirements of ordinary employments, their very real needs are apt to be neglected by the helping services. It is important to realise that these features are not so much a consequence of involvement in prostitution as an expression of character and circumstances established prior to entry onto the rent scene. It could be argued that by obtaining money for sex they are damaging the community less than if they depended on begging, pilfering and robbing. Street work is a way of surviving that appeals to those who are not averse to homosexual contacts, can see the chance of easy money and have few scruples about how they make it, but, as we have shown, the long-term future of men who take this route is often very bleak, for themselves and for the community that has to bear with them. On the other hand the future for such individuals would probably be equally bleak had they never discovered the rent scene. Although research access to former sex workers in their later years was very limited it was enough to indicate that early adversity and early developing antisociality were the main determinants of social disasters later on. A period of engagement in prostitution did not destroy the future for those who began with social and personality attributes that enabled them to pull out when it suited them. This is not to suggest that because they have such severe problems the less fortunate street workers should be rejected as beyond help, but rather that they should have more intensive and prolonged help and much greater understanding than their unappealing characteristics usually attract. A young man found working on the street as a rent boy is likely to be in need of help for a multiplicity of personal and social problems. This is in fact the philosophy and the justification for much of the work done by the Streetwise Youth Project, work that needs effort on a much larger scale than is possible for one small voluntary organisation.

The fact that so many street workers had been in care and that some began prostitution while still in the charge of local authority social services must raise questions as to the quality of care, particularly at the point of transition into the community (Perks, 1986). Unhelpful restrictions prevent Streetwise Youth and other organisations from offering alternative help to young persons under sixteen because they are still theoretically in the legal care of parents or social services (Jervis, 1987).

Some street workers, who may not have been very long on the game, are less deeply enmeshed in street culture and its anti-authoritarian stance. They are potentially able young men who have resorted to prostitution after trying unsuccessfully to establish their independence by moving to London. To some extent current social policy is to be blamed for this. Recent welfare legislation has had the effect of decreasing teenagers' access to benefits and is authoritatively believed to have helped to swell the number of young single homeless and encouraged begging, shoplifting, drug dealing and prostitution. It has been estimated that around 50,000 young people in London experience homelessness each year (Thornton, 1990, p. 5). The increase in divorce and remarriage means that more and more children find themselves in care or overstaying their welcome in the parental home. Poor employment prospects for the untrained young in many provincial towns have encouraged migration to London where accommodation is expensive and in short supply. The Social Security Act, 1988, Section 4, abolished the entitlement of young people of sixteen or seventeen who are not mentally or physically handicapped to income support. If not in regular employment or continuing education they are expected to enlist in Youth Training Schemes, but as the pay is low and many complain that the tasks given them are menial, with little actual training or prospects of permanent work, motivation to enter or remain in the system is often lacking. Certain very limited categories of under-eighteens can get temporary income support, for instance if they can prove they have no available parental home or have recently left residential care, but this leaves out in the cold a large number who find it hard to amass objective evidence sufficient to convince reluctant local authorities to provide places for them away from their putative home base. Their homes may officially exist, but are often so unhappy, punitive, unfriendly, exploitative or intolerant of homosexuality that they prefer life on the streets. Where income support is applicable it is payable two weeks in arrears, which is no help to the destitute trying to get a foothold in privately rented rooms that almost always require a deposit of two weeks or more in advance. Thornton (op. cit., p. 31) also points out that benefits are fixed at lower levels for those under twenty-five, which means that it is more difficult for them to maintain independent accommodation.

Jobs are hard to get if the applicant has no fixed address and accommodation, other than short-term hostel places, is costly and hard to secure without the backing of recognised employment. Housing authorities have not been required by statute to provide for the young single homeless as they must for other categories. A safe and permanent place of their own to live, free from the irksome restrictions, absence of privacy and sometimes primitive conditions that prevail in some hostels, was the greatest ambition of many of our interviewed street workers. Admittedly, experience showed that some could not settle down or keep a regular job even when these opportunities were provided, but for others these basic requirements, which so many take for granted, could suffice to tip the balance from long-term alienation to successful integration into mainstream living. Those who cannot manage independently without getting into trouble, in addition to whatever else they need by way of counselling, supervision and training, still need a roof as a first necessity. From a social policy standpoint one might think the benefits of more generous provision for the resettlement of the single homeless would be cheap at the price.

*

In summary, the message which comes out of this survey is that some sex workers are real problem personalities, some would do other things if given proper access to jobs and housing, but others are pursuing a chosen vocation in a reasonably contented and effective manner. A knee-jerk reaction of total repression and condemnation of the providers of paid homosexual services and their clients is unnecesary and counter-productive. Years ago this author wrote (West, 1977, p. 228):

> For all its dangers and problems, homosexual prostitution, like any other institutionalised human relationship, is neither wholly white nor jet black, but a varying shade of grey, according to the circumstances and characteristics of the individual participants.

Nothing in the present survey has brought about a change in this opinion.

Bibliography

Agnew, J. (1986) Hazards associated with anal erotic activity. *Archives of Sexual Behavior, 15*, 307-314.

Allen, D. (1980) Young male prostitutes: a psychosocial study. *Archives of Sexual Behavior, 9*, 399-426.

Allesbrook, A. and Swift, A. (1989) *Broken Promise: the world of endangered children*. London: Hodder and Stoughton.

Altman, D. (1986) *AIDS and the New Puritanism*. London and Sydney: Pluto Press.

Bagley, C. and Young, L. (1987) Juvenile prostitution and child sex abuse: a controlled study. *Canadian Journal of Community Mental Health, 6*, 5-26.

Baker, A.W. and Duncan, S.P. (1985) Child sexual abuse: a study of prevalence in Great Britain. *Child Abuse and Neglect, 9*, 457-467.

Baker, C.D. (1980) Preying on backgrounds: the sexploitation of children in pornography and prostitution. In L.G. Schultz (ed.) *The Sexual Victimology of Youth*. Springfield, Ill.: C.C. Thomas, Ch. 21.

Barnard, M., McKeganey, N. and Bloor, M. (1990) Male prostitution: a risky business. *Community Care*, 5 July, No. 821, 26-27.

Barrington, J.S. (1981) *Sexual Alternatives for Men*. London: Alternative Publishing.

Beadle, J. (1990) *Doing Business*. London: GMP.

Bell, A.P. and Weinberg, M.S. (1978) *Homosexualities: a study of diversity among men and women*. New York: Simon and Schuster, pp. 73-78.

Bell, A.P., Weinberg, M.S. and Hammersmith, S.K. (1981) *Sexual Preference*. Bloomington: Indiana University Press.

Benjamin, H. and Masters, R.E.L. (1964) *Prostitution and Morality*: Ch. 10: Male Prostitution. New York: Julian Press.

Best Guide Book Service (1990) *Best Guide to Amsterdam and the Benelux*. Amsterdam: Eden Cross (ISBN 90-6971-024-2).

Bloor, M., McKeganey, N. and Barnard, M. (1990) An ethnographic study of HIV-related risk practices among Glasgow rent boys and their clients. Report of a pilot study. (Glasgow University Social, Paediatric and Obstetric Research Unit.) *AIDS Care, 2*, 17-24.

Bolton, F.G., Morris, L.A. and MacEachron, A.E. (1989) *Males at Risk: the other side of child sexual abuse*. Newbury Park, C.A.: Sage.

Boswell, J. (1980) *Christianity, Social Tolerance and Homosexuality*. Chicago: University of Chicago Press.

Boswell, J. (1988) *The Kindness of Strangers*. London: Penguin.

Boulin, B., Desjeunes, J.M. and Alfonsi, P. (1977) *La Charte des Enfants*. Paris: Stock.

Boyer, D. (1989) Male prostitution and homosexual identity. *Journal of Homosexuality, 17*, 151-184.

Briere, J., Evans, D., Runtz, M. and Wall, T. (1988) Symptomatology in men who were molested as children: a comparative study. *American Journal of Ortho-psychiatry, 58,* 457-461.

Brongersma, E. (1986) *Loving Boys.* Vol. 1, Elmhurst, N.Y.: Global Academic.

Brongersma, E. (1990) *Loving Boys.* Vol. 2, Elmhurst, N.Y.: Global Academic.

Bullough, V. (1976) *Sexual Variance in Society and History.* London and Chicago: Chicago University Press.

Bullough, V., Deacon, M., Elvcano, B. and Bullough, B. (1977) *A Bibliography of Prostitution.* New York: Garland.

Burgess, A.W. and Clark, M.L. (1984) *Child Pornography and Sex Rings.* Lexington, M.A.: Lexington Books.

Burn, S. (1989) Massaging the figures. *The Pink Paper,* No. 64, Mar. 18, p. 7.

Butts, W.M. (1947) Boy prostitutes of the Metropolis. *Journal of Clinical Psychopathology, 8,* 673-681.

Cahill, T. (1986) *Buried Dreams: inside the mind of a serial killer.* New York: Bantham Books.

Calhoun, T. and Pickerill, B. (1988) Young male prostitutes: their knowledge of selected sexually transmitted diseases. *Psychology, 25,* 1-8.

Campagna, D.S. and Poffenberger, D.L. (1988) *The Sexual Trafficking in Children.* Dover, Mass.: Auburn House, Ch. 3: Hustling.

Canada (1984) *Sexual Offences Against Children* (Badgley Committee Report). Ottawa: Canadian Government Publishing Centre.

Cates, J.A. (1989) Adolescent male prostitution by choice. *Child and Adolescent Social Work Journal, 6,* 151-156.

Caukins, S.E. and Coombs, M.A. (1976) The psychodynamics of male prostitution. *American Journal of Psychotherapy, 30,* 441-451.

Chester, L., Leitch, D. and Simpson, C. (1976) *The Cleveland Street Affair.* London: Weidenfeld & Nicolson.

Cockrell, J. and Hoffman, D. (1989) Identifying the needs of boys involved in prostitution. *Social Work Today, 20,* 20-21.

Coleman, E. (1989) The development of male prostitution activity among gay and bisexual adolescents. *Journal of Homosexuality, 17,* 131-149.

Coombs, N.R. (1974) Male prostitutes: a psychosocial view of behavior. *American Journal of Orthopsychiatry, 44,* 782-784.

Cory, D.W. (pseudonym for E. Sagarin) and LeRoy, J.P. (1963) *The Homosexual and his Society: a view from within.* New York: Citadel, pp. 92-104.

Coutinho, R.A., Van Andel, R.L.M. and Rysdyk, T.J. (1988) Role of male prostitutes in spread of sexually transmitted diseases and human immuno-deficiency virus. *Genitourinary medicine, 64,* 207-208.

Craft, M. (1966) Boy prostitutes and their fate. *British Journal of Psychiatry, 112,* 1111-1114.

Criminal Justice Act 1988, Section 160. Possession of indecent photograph of child.

Cusack, D. (1975) Male prostitution for both men and women. In J. Sandford (ed.) *Prostitutes: portraits of people in the sexploitation business.* London: Secker and Warburg, pp. 171-179.

Davidson, H.A. and Loken, G.A. (1987) *Child Pornography and Prostitution.* U.S. National Center for Missing and Exploited Children.

Davidson, M. (1970) *Some Boys.* London: David Bruce.

Davies, P.M. and Simpson, P.J. (1990) On male homosexual prostitution and HIV. In P. Aggleton, P. Davies and G. Hart (eds.) *AIDS: individual, cultural and policy dimensions.* London: Falmer.

Deischer, R.W., Eisner, C. and Sulzbacher, S. (1969) The young male prostitute. *Pediatrics, 43,* 936-941.

Deischer, R.W., Robinson, G. and Boyer, D. (1982) The adolescent female and male prostitute. *Pediatric Annals, 11*, 819-825.

Delph, E.W. (1978) *The Silent Community: public homosexual encounters.* Beverly Hills: Sage.

Dietz, P.E. (1978) Male homosexual prostitution. *Bulletin of the American Academy of Psychiatry and the Law, 6*, 468-471.

Dimock, P.T. (1988) Adult males sexually abused as children. *Journal of Interpersonal Violence, 3*, 203-221.

Doshay, L.J. (1943) *The Boy Sex Offender and his Later Criminal Career.* New York: Grune and Stratton.

Dover, K.J. (1978) *Greek Homosexuality.* London: Duckworth.

Drew, D. and Drake. J. (1969) *Boys for Sale.* New York: Brown.

Earls, C.M. and David, H. (1989) A psychosocial study of male prostitution. *Archives of Sexual Behavior, 18*, 401-419.

Eglinton, J.Z. (1964) *Greek Love.* New York: Oliver Layton.

Ellerstein, N. and Cameron, J. (1980) Sexual abuse of boys. *American Journal of Diseases of Children, 134*, 255-257.

Enablers. (1979) *Juvenile Prostitution in Minneapolis.* St. Paul, Minn.: Enablers.

Ennew, J. (1986) *The Sexual Exploitation of Children.* Cambridge: Polity Press.

Fechet, J. (1986) *Garçons pour Trottoir.* Paris: La Découverte.

Finkelhor, D., Meyer Williams, L. and Kalinowski, M. (1989) *Nursery Crimes: sexual abuse in day care.* London and Beverly Hills: Sage.

Fisher, B., Weisberg, D.K. and Marotta, T. (1982) *Report on Adolescent Male Prostitution.* San Francisco, CA.: Urban and Rural Systems Associates. Washington, DC.: US Dept of Health and Human Services, Youth Development Bureau (cited in Weisberg, 1984).

Forman, B.D. (1982) Reported male rape. *Victimology, 7*, 235-236.

Freyhan, F.A. (1947) Homosexual prostitution: a case report. *Delaware State Medical Journal, 19* (5), 92-94.

Friedrich, W.N., Beilke, R.L. and Urquiza, A.J. (1988) Behavior problems in sexually abused boys. *Journal of Interpersonal Violence, 3*, 21-28.

Galloway, D. and Sabisch, C. (eds.) (1982) *Calamus: male homosexuality in twentieth century literature* (J. Cocteau. The White Paper). New York: Quill.

Gandy, P. and Deischer, R.W. (1970) Young male prostitutes: the physician's role in social rehabilitation. *Journal of the American Medical Association, 212*, (10), 1661-1666.

Gauthier-Hamon, C. and Teboul, R. (1988) *Entre père et fils. Prostitution homosexuelle des garçons.* Paris: Presses Universitaires.

Gerassi, J. (1966) *The Boys of Boise.* New York: Macmillan.

Gibbens, T.C.N. and Silberman, M. (1960) Clients of prostitutes. *British Journal of Venereal Diseases, 36*, 113-117.

Ginsberg, K.N. (1967) The meat-rack: a study of the male homosexual prostitute. *American Journal of Psychotherapy, 21*, 170-185.

'Gold' (1978) A good rub down. Gold investigates the massage scene. *Gold. The International Magazine for International Men.* No. 4, April, 18-19.

Goldstein, P.J. (1979) *Prostitution and Drugs.* Lexington, Mass.: Lexington Books.

Goyer, P.F. and Eddleman, H.C. (1984) Same-sex rape of non-incarcerated men. *American Journal of Psychiatry, 141*, 576-579.

Greenberg, D.F. (1988) *The Construction of Homosexuality.* Chicago: Chicago University Press.

Groth, A.N. and Burgess, A.W. (1980) Male rape: offenders and victims. *American*

Journal of Psychiatry, 137, 806-810.

Gurwell, J.K. (1974) *Mass Murder in Houston*. Houston: Cordovan Press.

Halpern, D. (1990) *A Hundred Years of Homosexuality*. London: Routledge.

Hamilton, W. (1980) *Kevin*. New York: St Martin's Press.

Hardwick, N. (1990) Asleep on the streets. *Social Work Today, 21* (No. 43) 5 July, 19-20.

Harris, M. (1973) *The Dilly Boys: the game of male prostitution in Piccadilly*. Rockville, Md.: New Perspectives.

Hart, J. (1979) *Social Work and Sexual Conduct*. London: Routledge and Kegan Paul, pp. 128-139.

Hauser, R. (1962) Homosexual prostitutes. In R. Hauser, *The Homosexual Society*. London: Bodley Head.

Hennig, J.L. (1978) Les Garons de Passe. *Enquête sur la prostitution masculine*. Paris: Editions Libres Hallier.

Hervé, G. and Kerrest, T. (1980) *Les Enfants de Fez*. Paris: Hallier.

Hoffman, M. (1979) The male prostitute. In M.P. Levine (ed.) *The Sociology of Male Homosexuality*. New York: Harper and Row, pp. 275-284.

Hollinghurst, A. (1988) *The Swimming-Pool Library*. London: Chatto and Windus.

Holloway. (1813) *The Phoenix of Sodom or the Vere Street Coterie*. London: J. Cook.

Howard League (1985) *Unlawful Sex: offences, victims and offenders in the criminal justice system*. London: Waterlow.

Humphreys, L. (1970) *Tearoom Trade: impersonal sex in public places*. London: Duckworth.

Hunt, C. (1986) *Street Lavender*. London: Gay Men's Press.

Hunter, M. (1990) *Abused Boys*. Lexington, Mass.: D.C. Heath.

Jackson, P.A. (1989) *Male Homosexuality in Thailand*. Elmhurst, New York: Global Academic.

James, J. (1982) *Entrance into Juvenile Male Prostitution*. Washington, D.C.: National Institute of Mental Health.

James, J. and Myerding, J. (1978) Early sexual experience as a factor in prostitution. *Archives of Sexual Behavior, 7*, 31-42.

Janus, M.D., Scanlon, B. and Price, V. (1984) Youth prostitution. In A.W. Burgess (ed.) *Child Pornography Sex Rings*. Lexington, Mass.: Lexington Books.

Janus, M.D., McCormack, A., Burgess, A.W. and Hartman, C. (1987) *Adolescent Runaways*. Lexington, Mass.: Lexington Books.

Janus, S. (1981) *The Death of Innocence*. New York: Morrow.

Jenkins, T. (1990) The lost boys. *The Listener, 124* (No. 3193) 29 Nov., 4-5.

Jersild, J. (1956) *Boy Prostitution*. Copenhagen: G.E.C. Gad.

Jervis, M.J. (1987) In the twilight zone of the 'rent boys'. *Social Work Today, 18*, (No. 39) 1 June, 5.

Justice, B. and Justice, R. (1979) *The Broken Taboo: sex in the family*. New York: Human Sciences Press.

Kaufman, A., Divasto, P., Jackson, R., Voorhees, D. and Christy, J. (1980) Male rape victims: non-institutionalized sexual assault. *American Journal of Psychiatry, 137*, 221-223.

Kaufman, A. *et al.* (1980) Male rape victims: Non-institutionalized assault. *American Journal of Psychiatry, 137*, 806-810.

Kinnell, H. (1989) *Prostitutes, Their Clients and Risks of HIV*. Birmingham: University Dept. Public Health Medicine.

Kinsey, A.C., Pomeroy, W.B. and Martin, C.E. (1948) *Sexual Behavior in the*

Human Male. Philadelphia: Saunders.

Kjeldsen, M. (1991) *Outreach work with young men involved in the 'rent scene' of Central London 1988/1989*. London: Streetwise Youth and Barnardos.

Klein, A.M. (1989) Managing deviance: hustling, homophobia and the body-building subculture. *Deviant Behavior, 10*, 11-27.

Kleinberg, S. (1987) The new masculinity of gay men, and beyond. In M. Kaufman (ed.) *Beyond Patriarchy*. Oxford: Oxford University Press.

Klemens, K.U. (1967) *Die kriminelle Belastung der männlichen Prostituierten*. Berlin: Duncker and Humblot.

Kraemer, W. (ed.) (1976) *The Normal and Abnormal Love of Children*. Kansas City: Sheed, Andrews and McMeel.

Lahr, J. (ed.) (1986) *The Orton Diaries*. London: Methuen.

Leith, A. and Handforth, S. (1989) Group work with sexually abused boys. *Practice, 2*, 166-175.

Lew, M. (1988) *Victims No Longer: men recovering from incest and other sexual abuse*. New York: Harper and Row.

Linedecker, C.L. (1980) *The Man Who Killed Boys*. New York: St. Martin's Press.

Linedecker, C.L. (1981) *Children in Chains*. New York: Everest House.

Lloyd, R. (1976) *For Love or Money*. New York: Ballantine Books.

Logan, P. (1989) *A Life to be Lived: homelessness and pastoral care*. London: Darton, Longman and Todd.

Lowman, J. (1989) *Street Prostitution: assessing the impact of the law*. Vancouver: A Report prepared for the Dept. of Justice, Canada.

Lukenbill, D.F. (1985) Entering male prostitution. *Urban Life, 14*, 131-153.

Luckenbill, D.F. (1986) Deviant career mobility: the case of male prostitutes. *Social Problems*, 33, 284-296.

McCormack, A., Janus, M.D. and Burgess, A.W. (1986) Runaway youths and sexual victimisation. *Child Abuse and Neglect, 10*, 387-395.

MacKay, J.H. (1985) *The Hustler* (translation of *Der Puppenjunge*, 1926). Boston: Alyson.

McMullen, R.J. (1987) Youth prostitution: a balance of power. *Journal of Adolescence, 10*, 57-69.

McMullen, R.J. (1988) Boys involved in prostitution. *Youth and Policy* (No. 28) 35-42.

McMullen, R.J. (1989) *Enchanted Boy*. London: Gay Men's Press.

McMullen, R.J. (1990a) *Enchanted Youth*. London. Gay Men's Press.

McMullen, R.J. (1990b) *Male Rape: breaking the silence on the last taboo*. London: Gay Men's Press.

MacNamara, D.E.J. (1965) Male prostitution in American cities. *American Journal of Orthopsychiatry, 35*, 204.

Marlowe, K. (1964) The life of the homosexual prostitute. *Sexology, 31*, 24-27.

Marlowe, K. (1964) *Mr. Madam: confessions of a male madam*. Los Angeles, C.A.: Sherbourne Press.

Masters, B. (1985) *Killing for Company*. London: Jonathan Cape.

Matthews, F. (1987) *Familiar Strangers: a study of adolescent prostitution*. Toronto: Toronto Youth Services (27 Carlton Street).

Maughan, Robin (Lord). (1970) *The Wrong People*. London: Heinemann.

Maughan, Robin (Lord). (1982) *The Boy from Beirut*. San Francisco: Gay Sunshine Press.

Merewood, A. (1990) An evening with Mike Arlen. *Action* (No. 23, March) 18-19.

Mezey, G. and King, M. (1987) Male victims of sexual assault. *Medicine, Science and the Law, 27*, 122-124.

Mezey, G. and King, M. (1989) The effects of sexual assault on men: a survey of 22 victims. *Psychological Medicine, 19*, 205-209.

Morgan, T.R., Plant, M.A., Plant, M.L. and Sales, J.(1990) Risk of HIV infection among clients of the sex industry in Scotland. *British Medical Journal, 301*, 525

Morse, E.V., Simon, P.M., Osofsky, H.J., Balson, P.M. and Gaumier, R. (1991) The male street prostitute: a vector for transmission of HIV infection into the heterosexual world. *Social Science and Medicine* (at press).

Morse, E.V., Simon, P.M., Balson, P.M. and Osofsky, H.J. (1991) Sexual behavior patterns of customers of male prostitutes. *Archives of Sexual Behavior* (at press).

Muir, K. (1989) Streetwise and money poor. *The Independent*, 4 Jan.

Muser, H. (1933) *Homosexualität und Jugenfürsorge.* Paderborn: Ferdinand Schoning Verlag.

Myers, M.F. (1989) Men sexually assaulted as adults and sexually abused as boys. *Archives of Sexual Behavior, 18*, 203-215.

National Association of Citizen's Advice Bureaux (1990) *Hard Times for Social Fund Applicants.* London: 115 Pentonville Rd., N1 9LZ.

O'Carroll, T. (1980) *Paedophilia – The Radical Case.* London: Peter Owen.

Ollendorff, R.M.V. (1966) *The Juvenile Sexual Experience and its Effects on Adult Sexuality.* New York: Julian Press.

Olsen, J. (1974) *The Man with the Candy.* New York: Simon and Schuster.

O'Mahony, B. (1988) Young people and prostitution. In *A Capital Offence: the plight of the young single homeless in London.* London: Routledge and Barnardos.

Perks, B. (1986) Telling it like it is. *Social Work Today, 18*, (No. 6), 6 Oct., 12-13.

Philpot, T. (1990) Male prostitution: the boys' own story. *Community Care*, 28 June (No. 820) 19-22.

Pieper, R. (1979) Identity management in adolescent male prostitution in West Germany. *International Review of Modern Sociology* (2), 239-259.

Pittman, D.J. (1971) The male house of prostitution. *TransAction, 8,* 21-27.

Plant, M.A. (1989) AIDS-related risk and prostitution: a pilot study. MRC interim report.

Plant, M.A. (ed.) (1990) *AIDS, Drugs and Prostitution.* London: Tavistock/ Routledge.

Plant, M.L., Plant, M.A., Peck, D.F. and Setters, J. (1989) The sex industry, alcohol and illicit drugs: implications for the spread of HIV infection. *British Journal of Addiction, 84*, 53-59.

Plummer, K. (1975) Homosexual prostitution. In *Sexual Stigma: an interactionist account.* London: RKP.

Poel, S. van der (1987) Male prostitution: professionals, amateurs and pseudo whores. Paper delivered at the International Conference on Gay and Lesbian Studies. Dec. 15th-18th, Amsterdam: Free University.

Polsky, N. (1971) *Hustlers, Beats and Others.* Harmondsworth: Penguin.

Porter, K. and Weeks, J. (1991) *Between the Acts: lives of homosexual men 1885-1967.* London: Routledge.

Price, V., Scanlon, B. and Janus, M.D. (1984) Social characteristics of adolescent male prostitution. *Victimology, 9*, 211-221

Protection of Children Act (1978) Section 1. Indecent photographs of children.

Radford, J.L., King, A.J.C. and Warren, W.K. (1989) *Street Youth and AIDS.* Kingston, Ontario: Queen's University.

Randall, G. (1989) *Homeless and Hungry: a sign of the times.* London: Centrepoint, Soho.

Raven, S. (1963) Boys will be boys: the male prostitute in London. In H.M. Ruitenbeek (ed.) *The Problem of Homosexuality in Modern Society*. New York: Dutton, pp. 279-290.

Read, K. (1980) *Other Voices: the style of a male homosexual tavern*. Novato, CA: Chandler & Sharp.

Rechy, J. (1977) *The Sexual Outlaw: a documentary*. New York: Grove Press.

Redding, D. (1989) Reaching out to the rent scene. *Community Care* (No. 759) 20 April, 24-26.

Redding, D. (1989) Smashing a sub-culture. *Community Care* (No. 765) 1 June, 14-16.

Redhardt, R. (1968) Zur gleichgeschlechtlichen männlichen Prostitution. In Reng and Redhardt (eds.) *Prostitution bei weiblichen und männlichen Jugendlichen*. Stuttgart: Enke.

Redley, S. (1984) Horror of sex for sale boys. *Northamptonshire Post*, 25 Oct., p. 5.

Reiss, A.J. (1960) Sex offenses: the marginal status of the adolescent. *Law and Contemporary Problems, 25*, 309-333.

Reiss, A.J. (1961) The social integration of queers and peers. *Social Problems, 9*, 102-120.

Risin, L.I. and Koss, M.P. (1987) The sexual abuse of boys: prevalence and descriptive characteristics of childhood victimisations. *Journal of Interpersonal Violence, 2*, 309-323.

Robinson, T. (1989) *London's Homosexual Male Prostitutes: power, peer groups and HIV* (Project Sigma, Working Paper 12) London: Polytechnic of the South Bank.

Robinson, T. (1990) Boys' own stories. *New Statesman and Society*, 24 Aug., pp. 10-12.

Rogers, L. (1989) A summer in the city for rent boys. *London Evening Standard*, 26 Sept.

Ross, A.V. (1969) *Vice in Bombay*. London: Tallis Press.

Ross, H.L. (1959) The 'hustler' in Chicago. *Journal of Student Research, 1*, 13-19.

Royle, D. (1990) *Pleasing the Punters*. Exeter: Third House.

Ryan, G., Lane, S., Davis, J. and Isaac, C. (1987) Juvenile sex offenders: development and correction. *Child Abuse and Neglect, 11*, 385-395.

Ryan, J. (1986) A boy prostitute's perspective. *Gay Community News*, 20-26 July, 5-12.

Russell, D.H. (1971) From the Massachusetts Court Clinics: on the psychopathology of boy prostitutes. *International Journal of Offender Therapy, 15*, 49-52.

Salamon, E. (1989) The homosexual escort agency: deviance disavowal. *British Journal of Sociology, 40*, 1-21.

Sandfort, T. (1987) *Boys on their Contacts with Men*. Elmhurst, N.Y.: Global Academic.

Schofield, M. (1965) *Sociological Aspects of Homosexuality*. London: Longman.

Schetky, D.H. (1988) Child pornography and prostitution. In D.H. Schetky and A.H. Green (eds.) *Child Sexual Abuse*. New York: Brunner/Mazel.

Search, G. (1988) *The Last Taboo: sexual taboo of children*. Harmondsworth: Penguin.

Sereny, G. (1984) *The Invisible Children: child prostitution in America, Germany and Britain*. London: Deutsch.

Shaw, C.R. (1930) *The Jack-Roller*. Chicago: University of Chicago Press.

'Shelter' (1989) *Young Homeless People Write about their Lives*. London: Shelter.

Silbert, M.H. and Pines, M.A. (1981) Sexual child abuse as an antecedent to prostitution. *Child Abuse and Neglect, 5*, 407-411.

Smith, C. (1990) Sodom and Gomorrah by the sea. *Observer Magazine*, 19 Aug.

Smith, P. (1987) A place of safety. *New Society*, 21 Aug., 18-19.

Snodgrass, J.G., Geis, J.F., Short, Jr. and Kobrin, S. (1982) *The Jack-Roller at Seventy: a fifty-year follow-up*. Lexington, Mass.: Lexington Books.

Sonenschein, D. (1972) Hustlers viewed as dangerous. *Sexual Behavior, 2*, 20.

Sorensen, R.C. (1973) *Adolescent Sexuality in Contemporary America*. New York: World Publishing.

Spitzer, P.G. and Weiner, N.J. (1989) Transmission of HIV infection from a woman to a man by oral sex. *New England Journal of Medicine, 320*, 251.

Stephens, A. (1989) Working on the streets. *The Age* (Victoria, Australia) 9 Dec.

Steward, S. (1991) *Understanding the Male Hustler*. New York: Haworth Press.

Stiffman, A.R. (1989) Physical and sexual abuse in runaway youths. *Child Sexual Abuse, 13*, 417-426.

Streetwise Youth (1990) *Annual Report*. London, SW5.

Sutor, J. (1964) *The Erogenous Zones of the World*. New York: Book Awards.

Tate, I. (1990) *Child Pornography*. London: Methuen.

Taylor, A. (1991) *Prostitution: what's love got to do with it?* London: Macdonald Optima.

Taylor, G.R. (1953) *Sex in History*. London: Thames & Hudson.

Taylor, G.W. (1989) Sins of the flesh. *Maclean's* 17 July, 10-12.

Thomas, R.M., Plant, M.A., Plant, M.L. and Sales, D.I. (1989) Risk of AIDS among workers in the 'sex industry': some initial results from a Scottish study. *British Medical Journal, 299*, 148-149.

Thompson, N.D., West, D.J. and Woodhouse, T.P. (1985) Socio-legal problems of male homosexuals in Britain. In D.J. West (ed.) *Sexual Victimisation*. Aldershot: Gower.

Thornton, R. (1990) *The New Homeless*. London: SHAC (London Housing Aid Centre).

Tindall, R.H. (1978) The male adolescent involved with a pederast becomes an adult. *Journal of Homosexuality, 3*, 373-382.

Tirelli, U. *et al.* (1988) HIV-1 seroprevalence in male prostitutes in Northeastern Italy. *Journal of Acquired Immune Deficiency Syndromes, 1*, 414-415.

Troiden, R.R. (1974) Sexual encounters in a highway rest stop. In E. Goode and R.R. Troiden (eds.) *Sexual Deviance and Sexual Deviants*. New York: William Morrow, pp. 211-228.

Urban and Rural Systems Associates (1982) *Report on Adolescent Male Prostitution*. Washington: US Dept. of Health and Human Services; Youth Development Bureau (cited in Weisberg, 1984).

Van Wyk, P.H. and Geist, C.S. (1984) Psychosocial development of heterosexual, bisexual and homosexual behavior. *Archives of Sexual Behavior, 13*, 505-544.

Vander Mey, B.J. (1988) The sexual victimisation of male children: a review of previous research. *Child Abuse and Neglect, 12*, 61-72.

Visano, L.A. (1987) *The Idle Trade: the occupational patterns of male prostitution*. Concord Ontario: Vista Books.

Waldorf, D. and Murphy, S. (1990) Intravenous drug use and syringe-sharing practices of call men and hustlers. In M. Plant (ed.) *Aids, Drugs and Prostitution*. London: Tavistock/Routledge.

Walmsley, R. (1978) Indecency between males and the Sexual Offences Act 1967. *Criminal Law Review* (July), 400-407.

Walters, D.R. (1975) *Physical and Sexual Abuse of Children*. Bloomington, IN: Indiana University Press.

Weeks, J. (1980) Inverts, perverts and Mary-Annes: male prostitution and the regulation of homosexuality in England in the nineteenth and early twentieth centuries. *Journal of Homosexuality, 6*, 113-234.

Weisberg, D.K. (1984) Children of the night: the adequacy of statutory treatment of juvenile prostitution. *American Journal of Criminal Law, 12* (1), 1-67.

Weisberg, D.K. (1985) *Children of the Night*. Lexington, Mass.: Lexington Books, pp. 20-83, 153-188.

Weiss, M. (1984) *Double Play: the San Francisco City Hall killings*. Reading, Mass.: Addison-Wesley.

West, D.J. (1982) *Delinquency: its roots, careers and prospects*. London: Heinemann.

West, D.J. (1977) *Homosexuality Re-Examined*. London: Duckworth.

West, D.J. and Farrington, D.P. (1977) *The Delinquent Way of Life*. London: Heinemann.

West, D.J. and Woodhouse, T.P. (1990) Sexual encounters between boys and adults. In C.K. Li, D.J. West and T.P. Woodhouse (eds.) *Children's Sexual Encounters with Adults*. London: Duckworth.

Wilson, A. (1989) Paying the price of a rent boy's fun. *Sunday Times*, 25 May.

Wilson, P.R. (1981) *The Man They Called a Monster*. North Ryde, Australia: Cassell.

Winick, C. (1962) Prostitutes' clients' perceptions of the prostitutes and of themselves. *International Journal of Social Psychiatry, 8*, 289-297.

Winick, C. and Kinsie, P.M. (1971) Male homosexual prostitution. In Winick C. and Kinsie, P.M. (eds.) *The Lively Commerce: prostitution in the United States*. Chicago: Quadrangle Books.

Wisdom, C.P. (1989) The cycle of violence. *Science, 244*, 160-166.

Wyatt, G.E. and Johnson Powell, G. (1989) *Lasting Effects of Child Sexual Abuse*. London: Sage.

Glossary of Slang

AC-DC	Bisexual
Acid	Lysergic acid hallucinogen, LSD
Affair	Regular (homosexual) partner
Bandit	Fruit (gambling) machine
Black	Black cannabis
Blow job	Oral sex, sucking
Body positive	HIV positive antibody reaction
Brief	Solicitor, lawyer
Butch number	Masculine style homosexual, male or female
Camp	Using exaggerated homosexual mannerisms
Cards	Employment registration document
Cards, off the	Employment undeclared to tax authority
Chicken	Young boy
Come	Ejaculate (as noun or verb)
Come down	Stressful withdrawal from drugs
Cottage	Public convenience
Cottaging	Cruising public conveniences for sex contacts
Crack	Cocaine derivative
Dildo	Artificial or toy penis
Dope	Drug, usually cannabis
Dose	A sexual infection, commonly gonorrhoea
Downers	Sedative drugs: valium, etc.
Drag	Female dress on a male
Drag queen	Transvestite homosexual
Dyke	Masculine style (butch) lesbian
Ecstasy	A new stimulant drug
Fitted up	Victimised by police plant, framed
Fix	Intravenously given drug, usually heroin
Fuck	Act of anal penetration of male
Game, on the	Working as a prostitute
Gear	Illicit (hard) drugs; special clothing
Hand job	Act of masturbation
Hash	Cannabis
Hustler	Male prostitute. Also one who takes money without sex
Joint	Cannabis cigarette
Meat rack	Pick-up zone
Punter	Prostitute's client
Poppers	Amyl nitrite capsules
Queen	Effeminate homosexual
Rent	Sex for money
Rent boy	Male prostitute
Rimming	Licking anus

Rolling	Robbing (a punter)
S & M	Sado-masochistic activity
Scam	Fraud, rip off
Scat	Sexual play with faeces
Scene, the	The milieu of gay prostitution
Score, to	To find drugs or a buyer for sex
Skipping	Sleeping rough
Smack	Heroin
Smoke	Cannabis
Speed	Amphetamines
Stick, to get	To be anally penetrated
Straight	Heterosexual, conventional
Sugar daddy	Older homosexual patron who gives long-term financial support
Sulphate	Amphetamine sulphate
Toy boy	Young male sex partner for older female
Trick	Client, sex customer, punter
Water sports	Sex play with urine
Working men	Male prostitutes
Works	Equipment for injecting drugs

Appendix:
Sample Interview Schedule

Interview Guidelines

     This is a structured interview with many open ended questions.
The suggested form of words may need to be changed or amplifyed according
to circumstances. Where immediate pre-coding is possible this can be marked
on the sheet, by ringing appropriate answer.

NA = Not applicable   NK = not known   U = uncertain, unclear

---

1 Case number   ....

2 Date of interview   ....

3 When were you born ?   ....

4 Where were you born ?   London.   Provinces.   Abroad.

5 Ethnicity   White Caucasian   Other(specify) ....

6 How old were you when you came to London ? Always in London. Age ....

7 Do you have a regular place to stay at present?   Yes   No

8 (If No) Where did you spend last night ?

9 (If yes) What sort of place are you staying in ?   House, Flat, Bed sit,
                                              Squat, Hostel,
                                              Other ....

10   ... Is it your place, do you share it, or are you   NA., Tennant, Shared,
        just a sort of guest ? Do you have to pay ?   Paying lodger,
        Is the rent book in your name ?   'Guest'

11 How long have you been at this place ?   NA   ....months

12 Is it just a temporary arrangement ?   NA   Yes   No

13 How many different places have you stayed in the
    last six months ?   ....

14 (If sharing) Who do you share with ?   Other rent boys
                                        Male Friend(s)
                                        Male affair
                                        Female affair
                                        Other
                                        N.A.

Now about your early background -

15 Were you brought up by your own natural parents ?   Yes   No

16 (If yes) Were you separated from one or both
your parents at any time ? (If so) What was the   Father Died
reason and how old were you at the time ?   Mother Died
                                        Parents Split
                                        Sent away
                                        Ran away
                                        Other
                                        NA

17   At age ....

Your own father :-

18   About how old is he ?   ....

19   (If dead) How old was he when he died, and how long ago ?
                         NA   ....years   ....years ago

Father (cont.)

20 Are you in touch with him ? Yes Rarely) Never NA
                                      Hardly)

21 What is (was) his usual occupation, what
         did he do ? ....

22 Was he often unemployed ? Yes No NA NK

23 How do/did you get on with your father, do/did you
                                          like him very much
                                          Like him
                                          indifferent
                                          dislike him
                                          hate him
                                          N.A.

Your own mother

24 About how old would she be ? .... years

25 (If dead) How old when she died? How long ago ?
                    NA ......years   ....years ago

26 Are you in touch with her ? Yes Rarely) Never NA
                                      Hardly)

27 Did she have a job outside the home ? What was it ? No job
                                                       ....

28 How did/do you get on with your mother, do/did you
                                          like her very much
                                          like her
                                          indifferent
                                          dislike her
                                          hate her
                                          N.A.

29 How did your parents get on with each other ?
                                ? Well
                                ? Just OK
                                ? Many rows
                                ? Actual fights

30 Did your father have any special problems , like
                                ? Debts   Yes No NA
                                ? Drunkenness   Yes No NA
                                ? Illness   Yes No NA
                                ? Mental trouble Yes No NA

31 And did your mother have any special problems
    like that ?
                                ? Debts   Yes No NA
                                ? Drink   Yes No NA
                                ? Illness   Yes No NA
                                ? Mental trouble Yes No NA

32 When you were young, say around 10, were you looked after Ok,
         did you get ?
                                ? Regular food   Yes No
                                ? Clean clothes Yes No
                                ? Toys   Yes No

33 Were you often beaten ? Yes   No

34 Did you ever run away from home ? No   Yes   Often

35 (If yes) How old were you the first time ? ....years

36 (if ran away) What was the reason for running away that first time ? Where did you go ? What did you do ? How long did you stay away ?

37 At home, as a child (say under 10) were you

Very happy	1
Happy	2
Just OK	3
Unhappy	4
Very unhappy	5

38 Have you ever been in a children's home ?   Yes   No

39 Have you ever been with foster parents ?   Yes   No

(If family composition anomalous ask about the main substitute parents and what they were like?)

---

40 Do you have any (full) brothers **or sisters?**   **Only child**
How many altogether in the family ?   Youngest
Where do you come in the family, oldest, youngest, middle?   Middle position
                                                     Eldest
41   Total sibship ....

Now about your schooldays -

42 What kind of school did you go to ?   Boys only
                                               Mixed sex
43   State secondary, Comprehensive, Boarding
                Special School (ie. maladjusted, ESN)

44 Did you like school ?   Yes   No

45 How did you get on with lessons, were you   Above average 1
                                                About average 2
                                                Below average 3

46 Did you make friends at school, did you have   Many friends 1
                                                  Just average 2
                                                  Few friends 3

47 Did you play truant much ?   3 Often   2 Yes   1 No

48 What age did you leave school ?   ....years

49 Did you pass any exams at school ?   Yes   No

50 (If so) What ?   ....

51 Since leaving school have you attended any college or night school or done any courses or special training ?
                                               Yes   No

52 If so what ?

53 Have you been in a YTS scheme ?   Yes   No

54 If so what and at what age ?

Work History
55 Are you in full time paid employment at the moment, or   1 In full time employ
   part or doing any unofficial work without cards ?   2 In part time employ
                                                              3 Some unofficial work
                                                              4 Totally unemployed

56 Have you ever had a full time job ?
                                               Yes   5 No

57 What is the longest time you have kept a full time job   ....months
                                               NA

Work History (cont.)

58 Have you ever walked out on a job or been dismissed?   Never   Once or twice
How many times do you think ?   More often   NA (no job)

59 What is   the last paid job you did ? How long ago did   ....
it come to an end ?   ....
                                                NA (still working)   ....months

Now about sex -

60 How old were you, can you remember, when you first started taking a
sexual interest in anyone or anything ?   .... years

61 Were your first sexual interests mostly towards   Boys   4
                                                          Girls   2
                                                          Both   3
                                                          Unclear   8

62 Nowadays, are you turned **on by** -   Females only   1
                                       Mostly females, sometimes males   2
                                       Males and females equally   3
                                       Males mostly, but sometimes females 4
                                                Males only   5

63 As a boy, that is when you were under 14, did anyone ever involve
you in sex activities against your wishes ?   No   Yes
     (If yes ask for details of all such incidents and age when
     they happened and with whom)

64 Since then, since you turned 14, has anyone involved you in sex
acts against your will ?   No   Yes

     (If yes, get details of all such incidents. When, with whom,
     was it a 'punter' etc.)

Now about getting money for sex

65 How old were you the first time you got money for sex?   .... years
66 How did that come about ? (Get description.)
67 How old about was the person who paid you ?   ....
68   What sort of sex happened that first time   M PS AS   AF   PF   *
     Wanking ?   Other ....
     Sucking - He on you or you on he or both?
     Fucking - He did it to you or you to him?

69 Did you come yourself that first time ?   No   Yes

70 How did you feel about the sex you had that first time ? Enjoyed a lot   1
                                                          Quite enjoyed   2
                                                          Indifferent   3
                                                          Dislike it   4
                                                          Hated it   5

---

* NB M = mutual masturbation. PS = (passive) sucked AS= (active) sucking
     AF = (Active) anal fucking PF =(passive) being anally fucked.

71 How did you first get to know about being able to get money
for sex ?

Being propositioned	1
Talk among friends	2
Introduction to punter	3
Media Descriptions	4
Other	5

72 What was the reason for doing it that first time ?

Desperate for money	1
Short of money	2
Seemed easy money	3
Offer too good to say no	4
Other	5

73 That first time you took money were you on the run from
anything,(from home, in care, police, army, social   No   Yes
workers etc. ?)

Thinking about the times you have been most active on the game -

74 Did you make contact with punters - on the streets ?   Yes   No
                              in pubs ?   Yes   No
                              in clubs ?   Yes   No
                              in toilets ?   Yes   No
                              Through gay ads ?   Yes   No
                              Via escort agencies   Yes   No
             Being introduced by one punter to another ? Yes   No
                    Otherwise ....

75 How   would the amount paid be decided, would you

specify in advance	1
let client specify	2
negotiate in advance	3
take what is given after	4
other	5

76 In an average sort of week, how much would you get from punters ?

(Try to pin down a 'typical' week)   ....pounds

77 When you are getting that money from punters, are you also 'signing on',
getting money from welfare ?   No   Yes

78 Did you find you also had to get money in other ways as well,
like nicking things ?   No   Yes

    or drug dealing ?   No   Yes

79 What sort of age are most of the punters you've been with ?

    ....

80 When you go with a punter, who is in better control of the situation

The punter	1
The Rent Boy	2
Neither	3

        Why do you say that ?

                                    NA   Never   Happened
81   What happens if a punter does not pay up ?

        (Get examples if possible)   Leave

                                            Threaten

                                            Steal

                                            Beat up

                                            Other

82 What sort of sex do you have with punters ?

M	Yes	No
PS	Yes	No
AS	Yes	No
AF	Yes	No
PF	Yes	No
Tying up, spanking ?	Yes	No
Being tied up, spanked ?	Yes	No
Dressing up ?	Yes	No
Other things ?		
....	Yes	No

83 Are there some more kinky things you've had to do sometimes ?

(Details) e.g. water sports (pissing)	Yes	No
Other (e.g. shit) ....;	Yes	No

84 Are there some sex acts you refuse to do with punters ?

None	1
PS	2
AS	3
Swallowing semen	4
AF	5
PF	6
Other things	7

85 (If swallowing semen refused-
          How do you avoid that ?) ....

86 Do you use a condom with punters ?

Always	1
Usually	2
Never	3

87 What happens if a client doesn't want condom used ?

Never ask	1
Don't insist	2
Refuse unsafe sex	3
Leave	4
Other	5

88 Have you had a test for AIDS   No   Yes
89   (If yes) What was the result ?   Negative   Positive
      (If positive, ask about symptoms, illness etc.)

90 Have you had any other kind of sexual infection
                                Penile Gonorrhoea
                                Anal gonorrhoea
                                Syphilis
                                Scabies
                                Other
      (If answers positive ask about symptoms, to confirm diagnosis, and
        where and how treated)

91 When on the game have there been some times when you had no bed to
    go to for the night ?   No   Yes

Now some more about yourself

92 Apart from punters, do you have a regular sexual **friendship at the moment**

| | | | |
| with a female   ? | Yes | No |
93 (if yes)   How old would she be ? | ....Years |
with a male   ? | Yes | No |
94 (if yes)   How old would he be ?) | .... Years |

95 Have you ever had a 'sugar daddy' ?   Yes   No
      (If yes, get details)
96 (If no) Would you like to have one ?   Yes   No

97 What is your feeling about being on the rent scene, would you like
                        to continue as at present   1
                        to have better paying clients   2
                        to be less dependent on clients   3
                        to have a permanent sugar daddy   4
                        to give up altogether if you could   5
                    or have you already given it up altogether 6
                        Other ....

98 What would you say is your greatest worry in life at the moment ?
            (Details)

99 Do you have any problem with drinking ?   Yes   No

100 How much do you drink each day ?   ....

101 How much do you smoke in a day ?   None
                                        ....cigarettes
                              other ....

102 Have you used drugs ?   Yes   No

103 What drugs have you tried ?   Heroin (Smack)
                                        Methadone
                                        Cocaine
                                        Ecstasy
                                        Amphetamine (speed)
                                        Downers (e.g.valium)
                                        Cannabis (grass etc.)
                                        Other

104 Have you ever taken any of these regularly   Yes   No
      (If yes)   Which ones   Heroin
                                        Methadone
                                        Cocaine
                                        Ecstasy
                                        Speed
                                        Downers
                                        Cannabis
                                        Other

105 How much a week did you spend on drugs ?   ....pounds

106 What do you spend on rent at present   NA
                                        Welfare pays
                                        .... pounds a week

107 How much a week do you spend on food ?   .... pounds

Now about trouble. with the police

108 Have you ever had to go to court for anything connected with the rent
business, like importuning or obstruction or indecency ?   Yes   No

109 (If yes Ask how many times and for each occasion
     ask Age at time
          Court decision)

110 Have you ever been convicted for anything else such as   Drugs
                                                                     Theft
                                                                     Breaking
                                                                     Robbery
                                                                     Assault
                                                                     Damage
                                                                     Drunkenness
                                                                     Other

111 How many times have you been sentenced to prison or det. centre   0
                                                                               1
                                                                               2
                                                                               3
                                                                               4 or more

112 Have you been in prison on remand ?   Yes   No

113 How did you learn about Streetwise ?

114 What help have you had from Streetwise ?

115 What further help would you like from Streetwise ?

Index of Cases Cited

The Case numbers appear in **bold** type.

Index of Names

Subject Index